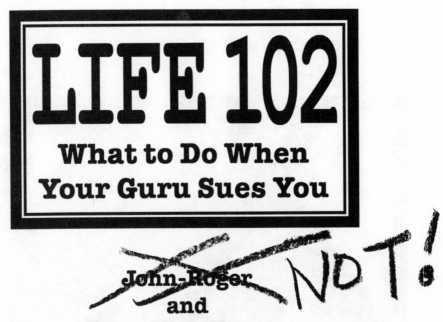

LIFE 102

What to Do When
Your Guru Sues You

~~John-Roger~~ NOT!
and
Peter McWilliams

Prelude Press
8159 Santa Monica Boulevard
Los Angeles, California 90046
1-800-LIFE-101

ISBN: 0-931580-34-X

Editors: Jean Sedillos, Charles Neighbors
Desktop publishing: Carol Taylor
Production: Paurvi Trivedi
Editorial assistance: Chris GeRue, Janet Stoakley,
Stephanie Horsley, Joyce Mills

John-Roger and Victor Toso, 1979.

This book is dedicated,
with appreciation,
to
Victor Toso

(Thanks for hanging in there.)

and to all those
who went from
sending the Light
to carrying a torch.

CONTENTS

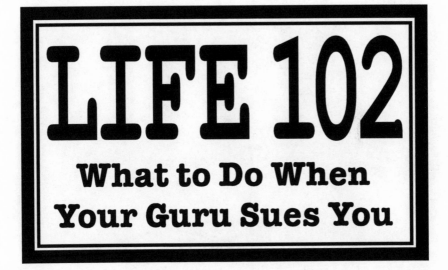

LIFE 102

What to Do When Your Guru Sues You

Lecturing on <u>DO</u> <u>IT!</u> in 1992. Notice that I had the intuitive presence of knee to cover John-Roger's name.

I Met the Buddha on the Road—
and He's Suing Me!

> The most costly of all follies
> is to believe passionately
> in the palpably not true.
> It is the chief
> occupation of mankind.
>
> H. L. MENCKEN

FOR FIFTEEN YEARS (1978–1994 R.I.P.) I was devoted to a self-styled guru named John-Roger. I put his name on books I wrote, including *LIFE 101, DO IT!,* and *You Can't Afford the Luxury of a Negative Thought*—the latter a book I should re-read *immediately*. I published and promoted the books myself, and two of them appeared on the *New York Times* bestseller list.

I gave John-Roger every spare penny the books generated—more than $1,000,000. In addition, the books rehabilitated his shabby public image, and brought heaven knows how many (it pains me to think about it) into his cult, the Church of the Movement of Spiritual Inner Awareness (pronounced *Messiah*).

I did all this not from love, but fear: I thought if I didn't, I would die. (I actually believed John-Roger's lies that he was keeping me alive. More on this soon.)

In 1994, after I was successfully treated for depression, the scales fell from my eyes, and I saw that the Great and Powerful Wizard was just a little man behind a curtain pushing buttons and charging admission to Oz.

I tried to leave quietly, but, to quote Norma Desmond from *Sunset Boulevard:* "No one walks out on a star!" She said that, of course, just before pulling the trigger six times. The bullets from John-Roger thus far have been (1) he's filed a lawsuit demanding

> He will lie even
> when it is inconvenient,
> the sign of the true artist.
>
> GORE VIDAL

everything I own; (2) my offices were broken into—twice—and the only thing of significance stolen was the first draft of this book; (3) I was physically attacked by three of John-Roger's highest honchos, including his heir-apparent; and (4) I've received hundreds of obscene calls and annoying hang-up calls—traced by the police back to a phone controlled by John-Roger.

I wrote this book to answer some of the questions that plagued me:

- How did I get here?

- How did a writer with a good track record get so far off track?

- How did I come to think this guy was God, or at least more directly connected to God than any other human life-form?

- How did I come to believe that this man *literally* had the power of life and death over me?

- How did I let him convince me that my only chance for life—not just "eternal life," but life right here on earth—required my writing, publishing, and promoting books with *his* name on them (and, of course, forking over the profits)?

- How could I be such a dope?

After much research and a lot more soul-searching, I think I have found the answers—or at least *my* answers. Like most answers, they explained a lot more about my life than the immediate questions demanded.

What I learned applied to *all* harmful relationships—relationships that often start out oh-so-good—be they with people, careers, habits, beliefs, or even with ourselves.

The answers also explained the methods used by those who want to control us, what they will do to get that control (whatever they can get away with), and what *we* must do if we want to keep our control where it belongs—with us.

I thought these answers might be valuable to others—that's why I published this book. It's not just the story of a wicked guru and his wayward disciple; it's a tale of personal freedom—lost and found; its risks and rewards.

> *Listen,*
> *everyone is entitled*
> *to my opinion.*
>
> MADONNA

I pray you find some answers of your own in these pages—and a few laughs, too. Thanks for reading.

INTRODUCTION

What Does a Rampaging Guru Have to Do with You?

> I do occasionally envy the person who
> is religious naturally,
> without being brainwashed into it or
> suckered into it
> by all the organized hustles.
> Just like having an ear for
> music or something.
> It would just never occur to
> such a person for a second
> that the world isn't about something.
>
> WOODY ALLEN

AS YOU BEGIN reading this book (or are deciding whether or not to read this book), the message I'd like to convey is best stated in the cliché: "Don't throw out the baby with the bathwater."

In exposing John-Roger and, yes, sometimes mocking the silliness of his "teachings" and the absurdity of my believing in them, please don't think I'm knocking God, spirit, religion, personal growth, the New Age, alternative medicine, belief, faith, seeking, or learning. I am not.

For example, all the information in the books I wrote for John-Roger (THE LIFE 101 SERIES) I still think is accurate, helpful, and useful. The part of the books I regret—and enthusiastically retract—is my endorsement of him and his cult. Oh, to be able to remove those two pages from the back of each of those books! (I figured it out: If it took me thirty seconds per book, and I worked at it eight hours a day, it would take me 5.7 *years* to remove those appalling pages. Yuck.*)

---

*Please help me: tear out the pages labeled "For Further Study: The Organizations Founded by John-Roger" in the back of any of THE LIFE 101 SERIES books and mail them to me. For each set of pages, I'll send you a $3 credit, which can be applied to anything we sell at Prelude Press, including the NEW CERTIFIED 100% JOHN-ROGER-FREE editions of the books. Please send the offending pages to me at 8159 Santa Monica Blvd., Los Angeles, California, 90046. Thank you!

> *Underneath this flabby exterior is an enormous lack of character.*
>
> OSCAR LEVANT

So tell your friends: call them up and say: "Peter McWilliams doesn't support John-Roger anymore!"

And they will say: "Who the hell cares?!"

Which begs the obvious question: "Why the hell should *you* care?"

Well, first, the reason you should care has nothing to do with *me*, and very little to do with John-Roger. We're just the main characters in a story that I think is kind of entertaining. (If it hadn't happened to me, I think Kurt Vonnegut—or Stephen King—would have had to invent it.) I've tried to make it amusing, but even *that's* not why I think you should read it.

I also don't think it's worth reading just to find out all the dirt on John-Roger I have been able to unearth (although some of it *is* fun). It's true I believe that John-Roger should be avoided like an infomercial, but it's not worth reading this book just to be warned about him: his circle of influence—while absolute—is too small.

But this book *does* explore an evil—or at least something that's being used in evil ways—I think would be helpful, perhaps even essential, for you to know about.

That something is *programming*. It's used to manipulate us when we don't even know it. Ignorance of its existence is no excuse. In fact, the less you know, the more the programmers of the world like it. The more we know about it and how it works, therefore, the more we can protect ourselves (and those we love) from unwanted programming, and free ourselves from it if we've already been "caught." (And, to one degree or another, we all are, we all are.)

As much as we like to think we are independent-minded, free-thinking, autonomous individuals, the fact remains that some part of us is still susceptible to programming.

Programming can happen to anyone. Intelligence, education, common sense, belief, or convictions offer little protection. All it takes is *repetition* (the slow route) or *vulnerability* (the fast route) and, eventually, we're hooked. Master programmers—from cult leaders to cigarette companies to government agencies—do both, as often as possible, whether you like it or not.

Ironically, *the more immune to programming you think you are, the more susceptible you become.*

If we *know* and *accept* that we are programmable, we can be, as Descartes probably never said, *en garde.* It is those who are *quite certain* they are safe, secure, and impregnable—such

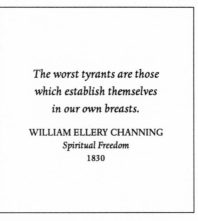

The worst tyrants are those which establish themselves in our own breasts.

WILLIAM ELLERY CHANNING
Spiritual Freedom
1830

as I felt I was in 1978 when the whole mess began—who are most easily preyed upon by the likes of David Koresh, Jim Jones, Philip Morris, and John-Roger. The "independent thinkers," once programmed, become among the most valuable assets a cult leader can own.

That's what I was for fifteen years: Owned.

My story is almost a textbook case of programming. I was looking for one thing and I was sold something else before I even knew it. Once I bought it, it became a part of *me:* my ground of being shifted; my inner compass was recalibrated. I did not become a walking zombie selling flowers at the airport—I used every bit of *my own* intelligence, creativity, education, and common sense to follow the *programmed* direction.

I thought I had made a free-will choice. I had not.

And it's not just cults we have to worry about: the number of people and organizations around us *quite consciously* trying to program us is astonishing. It's so all-pervasive, we seldom notice it: advertising, politicians, a good deal of the media, government, special interest groups, religions—the list seems endless.

Then there are those who try to program us but are not always aware that they're doing it (but if they knew how to do it better, they would!)—friends, relatives, employers, employees, enemies, lovers. (We ourselves, of course, are far from innocent on this score.)

Then there's our self-programming. Yes, someone else may have written the script, but we bought the performance rights and are staging our own production. If we tell ourselves "I'm not good enough," "I need [A PARTICULAR PERSON OR THING] to be happy," "I'm unworthy," or "I hate myself," we're programming ourselves

> *A man never reaches*
> *that dizzy height of wisdom*
> *that he can no longer*
> *be led by the nose.*
>
> MARK TWAIN

with lies that, with enough repetition, become true. (Call it the Cult of Mediocrity.)

When we know about programming, we can (a) use it constructively with ourselves; (b) use it with integrity with others; and (c) protect ourselves from programming we don't want.

That's what this book is about. It uses my fifteen years of in-cult-tation as the vehicle for discussing destructive programming. For me, I had with a cult leader a bad relationship I was programmed to think I *had* to have. For you, maybe it's a bad relationship with another person, or a job, or a family member, or a habit, or a project, or a belief. Please look for the *themes* in my saga: you may discover in yourself a familiar tune.

But what about this baby and bathwater stuff?

The evil is *programming,* not *what* is being programmed. People often confuse these two and throw out the baby (the message, some of which may be good) with the bathwater (the fact that programming was used to convey the message).

For example, John-Roger is not typical of spiritual teachers, religious leaders, or gurus in general. Some people may read this book and say, "I'm going to avoid *all* spiritual teachers, religious leaders, and gurus." That would be throwing out the baby with the bathwater.

Not only would those readers be keeping themselves from the possible benefits offered by spiritual teachers, religious leaders, or gurus who actually *have* something to offer, they would also be creating a false sense of security: keeping away from spiritual teachers, religious leaders, or gurus is *not* going to keep them safe from programming. They would, in fact, be overly susceptible to the programming that went something like: "Spiritual teachers, religious leaders, and gurus are *bad.* Come, believe in *this.* We don't *have* any spiritual teachers, religious leaders, or gurus!"

John-Roger *is* typical of a person with little integrity who attempts to program others without their consent for his own selfish purposes. Because he uses uninvited programming to control others in the name of God, he is a typical cult leader: "Believe in me, do what I say, give me your money, and everything will be fine—if not here, then in the hereafter."

Whatever it takes to get a person to become a believer is fair game, including (no, *especially*) deception and intimidation. A cult leader's justification: "This is a war with the Evil One, so it's not *you* who's being tricked and terrorized; it's the One who has imprisoned you! You *want* to love God! You *want* to love the guru! *All people* in their heart of hearts want to love the guru! Whatever wicked deeds it takes to wake you up and shake you away from the Evil One are a blessing." And on and on. (Usually what cult leaders *really* want is money, power, and sex.)

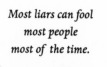

Most liars can fool most people most of the time.

DR. PAUL EKMAN,
On research showing people to be surprisingly inept at detecting lies,
New York Times
February 12, 1985

Note that this is the pattern in *all* destructive relationships: someone or something gets you to believe that *he or she* is essential to *you* and *you* had better do what *this person* says or *you* are in deep horse doo.

The solution? Counter-programming and reprogramming. If you're aware you're being programmed, you can program in what *you* want even while the programmer is making the attempt. "Smoking will give you pleasure!" the billboard programs. "Being able to breathe freely is more pleasurable," you counter.

If you already are programmed, you can *re*program yourself. "I'm unworthy" falls to the repetition of "I am worthy," "I can't" can be replaced with "I can," "I hate myself" is drowned in the sea of "I love myself." (More about counter-programming and reprogramming in a later chapter of this book.*)

The solution, part two: learn to trust *yourself.* Rely on yourself, think for yourself, love yourself, honor yourself, enjoy yourself. People who genuinely do this are *very* difficult to program. To the degree you're *not* doing that, I'd be willing to bet it's programming that's keeping you from it. So, we're back to reprogramming.

Sure it's a lot of work. Freedom generally is.

The price of freedom, after all, is external, internal, and eternal vigilance.

*Yes, that was a hook—a type of programming.

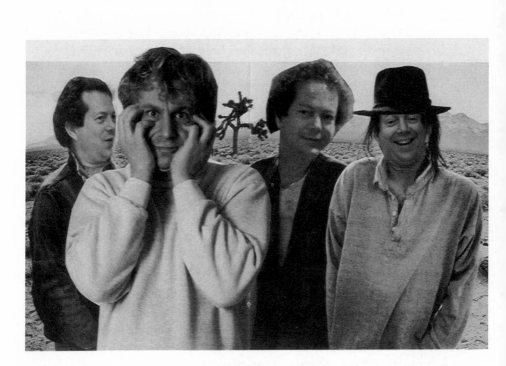

CHAPTER ONE

Where the Streets Have No Names

> I want to run.
> I want to hide.
> I want to tear down the walls
> That hold me inside.
> I want to reach out
> And touch the flame,
> Where the streets have no name.
>
> U2
> *Joshua Tree*

LATE 1988. California. I only had nine months to live. Maximum. And they were apt to be rather unpleasant months at that.

I discovered this distressing news while driving through the Joshua Tree National Monument with John-Roger. I kept looking for a monument. Was Joshua Tree the name of a battle site, like Little Big Horn? Should I, then, be looking for a military monument? Or maybe Joshua Tree was the name of a great Native American Chief (or, more likely, a U.S. Cavalry Commander) and I should search for a statue memorializing him.

Wrong again.

As it turns out, we were *in* the monument. The whole place—all 559,955 acres of it—*is* a national monument. A national monument, I learned, is a hunk of federally owned and protected land with some historic or geological significance that has not yet been elevated to national park status.

Also, I kept looking for *trees*. Everything there was spectacular: smooth, rounded, sand-colored rock formations and millions and millions of incredible cacti, each with tens of thousands of amazingly thin, amazingly sharp protective needles. That was all I saw: rocks, sand, cacti, and the endless blue sky.

But where were the trees . . . the Joshua trees?

> *There are scores of thousands of human insects who are ready at a moment's notice to reveal the Will of God on every possible subject.*
>
> GEORGE BERNARD SHAW

Yet another discovery: the cacti *were* the Joshua trees—the Joshua tree cactus. Oh.

That explained why this tree-shaped cactus was all over the cover and liner notes of the U2 *Joshua Tree* CD. I had purchased a copy of *Joshua Tree* from the Yucca Valley K-Mart about a mile from the entrance to the monument. I thought it might be fun—even significant—to play it as we drove through Joshua Tree. That didn't go over too well: John-Roger's musical appreciation, it seems, did not extend to anything with electric guitars. Well, *Hawaiian* electric guitars, maybe.

♓ ♓ ♓

Earlier in 1988, I had been asked by the director of public relations for Insight Seminars to teach ("facilitate," Insight calls it) a basic five-day Insight seminar for the people at AIDS Project Los Angeles—be they staff, clients (that is, people with AIDS or ARC), friends and relatives of clients, or caregivers.

I said I would be glad to do it, but I wanted to design a seminar especially for people with life-threatening illnesses. I was told this was fine, as long as it didn't cost anything and as long as it didn't take too much time.

You see, in early 1988 there was this *Los Angeles Times* article looming on the Insight/MSIA horizon. The article was going to be damaging. John-Roger said it would be "negative." Negative, in this case, was another word for "truthful." The *Los Angeles Times* was going to tell the *truth* about John-Roger and his "family" of nonprofit tax-exempt organizations! That *was* negative.

Prior to the article's imminent publication, John-Roger and his organizations—especially Insight—were doing as much preemptive positive PR as possible. This was not easy because, frankly, John-Roger and his organizations, including Insight, hadn't done much to be worthy of positive press. There was no history of social consciousness—no feeding the poor, comforting the sick, housing the homeless; that sort of thing.

To the world at large, John-Roger and his organizations were about as useful as a man who inherits large sums of money, avoids paying taxes, lives in a mansion, and comments occasionally that the poor are poor only because they refuse to work.

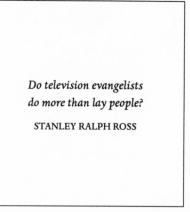

Do television evangelists do more than lay people?

STANLEY RALPH ROSS

So, a quick social-consciousness campaign was underway. What better way to show the world that John-Roger and his organizations *really cared* about the less fortunate than to do a free Insight seminar to help people with AIDS? It was approved by John-Roger and added to the list of events that J-R and everyone surrounding J-R hoped would be *newsworthy;* newsworthy enough to get news crews out; newsworthy enough to "balance" the truth that was on its way.

I was happy to help out. John-Roger was my closest—in fact, only—link to God. After all, any good priest would drop everything to defend the Pope from attack if asked politely by the Vatican, no? (I was, after all, one of John-Roger's ministers, one of his *ordained* ministers. I could, legally, perform marriages in California, if I ever found any two who wanted me to make them one by law, which I never did.)

In early 1988, equally as important as supporting J-R in his hour (year? lifetime?) of need, I found compelling the idea of doing a seminar especially for people with life-threatening illnesses.

Personally.

Life, death, and health were foremost in my mind. My best friend in all the world, Maurice, had died only a few months before. I had watched a kind, loving, gentle man become a bitter, complaining, obnoxious mess in the month between Thanksgiving and Christmas, 1987. Tuberculosis carried him off, a strain that none of the doctors had seen in decades—and in *New York City*. He was eighty-seven.

Maurice was an artist. He was part of Gertrude Stein's salon in Paris during the 1920s and early '30s. There he knew everyone from Picasso (liked him) to Hemingway (couldn't stand him). Maurice was old enough to have died in either world war, but didn't. He was sexually active for forty-five years before a cure was

> *Maurice Grosser*
> *comes from Alabama.*
> *He wakes early,*
> *and is ready to work*
> *as soon as the light is steady.*
> *In painting, he is assiduous,*
> *indefatigable, literal, systematic,*
> *exhaustive.*
>
> VIRGIL THOMSON

discovered for syphilis which, for 400 years, had been as frightening a sexually transmitted disease as AIDS. When he was a child, a cholera epidemic swept through his town. It got worse and worse. Eventually it was discovered that the main water supply to the city ran underneath the cemetery: the more cholera victims buried there, the more contaminated the water supply became. Maurice vividly remembered the flu epidemic of 1918, which killed twice as many Americans as World War I. He told me they would stack empty wooden coffins on street corners. You could either take a coffin, put a body in it, and return it to the street, or take the body to the street and put it in a coffin. Trucks came around regularly to pick up full coffins and drop off empty ones.

Maurice had survived all of this, but he did not survive an illness that was common in his youth ("consumption" it was called, because it literally *consumed* the person) and was almost unheard of in 1987.

I missed Maurice every day—not just from the day he died, but from the day he drifted into dementia. He was no longer the same person. It was as though some other *being*—not just a traveling death-show of microorganisms—had infected his body. This new being was astonishingly unpleasant to be around. If I had still been a practicing Catholic, I probably would have called a priest to perform an exorcism.

What *was* this rare strain of tuberculosis? The doctors knew nothing about it. Like most forms of tuberculosis, it was probably contagious, but the doctors couldn't say *how* contagious or what the gestation period was or whether one would die a romantic death like Greta Garbo in *Camille* (in which she became more and more ephemeral until she just *transluced*), or a horrible, miserable death, like Maurice's.

I was with Maurice until the end, when his room was on the contagion-floor of the hospital, where I agreed to wear a disposable, blue-paper "gown," but refused to wear the disposable mask. (If Maurice woke up, I didn't want him thinking he was in a high school production of *Planet of the Apes.*) I absolutely refused to

follow the nurse's strict instructions not to touch
Maurice. Toward the end,
touch was the only way to
reach him, to communicate
love and comfort and caring.

> *Maurice makes friends*
> *(and keeps them),*
> *reads books*
> *(and remembers them),*
> *takes exercise*
> *(by doing things and going places)*
> *and cooks.*
> *He has lots of company.*
> *People like his warmth*
> *and his laughter.*
>
> VIRGIL THOMSON

And now, in early 1988,
Maurice was gone, and I
missed him, and I was scared:
What if it happened to me?
Could I have been caught by
the same disease-devil that
consumed Maurice?

I was also a thirty-seven-year-old gay male who had lived in
both Los Angeles and New York during the Golden Age of Sex—
which also, as it turns out, was the Golden Age of Transmission.

The Golden Age of Sex was the decade from about 1968 to
1978. Syphilis—the great medical death-threat that underpinned
religious anti-sex teachings—had been conquered by 1945. By
1968, the first generation since Columbus discovered America
(and, some historians say, syphilis) to grow up without a "you can
die from sex" upbringing was coming of age. I was among them.
People were experimenting and breaking free of guilt. The pill
made casual heterosexual sex possible, gay lib made casual homosexual sex inevitable.

By 1978, for any practical person, the Golden Age was over.
Another life-threatening sexually transmitted illness had surfaced—not AIDS, yet: herpes. Although we certainly don't think
so today, in 1978 doctors were telling us that herpes—which you
can get from *kissing*, for heaven's sake—would eventually attack
your spinal cord and you would die a terrible death.

By 1980, the panic about herpes was subsiding, but the rumors
about AIDS were increasing. The rumors sparked a wildfire of
fear, dread, and panic that continues to this day. In 1988, they were
raging. I wanted to do something to control them within myself.

When I was asked to do the seminar, I used it as an "excuse" to
do the work I had been avoiding. I threw myself with a passion
into the study of death and dying, healing and health. I realized for
the first time my mortality; I felt a fraction of the loss one must feel
to lose *everything* and *everyone* in this world.

Death.

> *Death is a very dull,*
> *dreary affair,*
> *and my advice to you*
> *is to have nothing*
> *whatever to do with it.*
>
> W. SOMERSET MAUGHAM

One of the few things we are all going to experience, and yet among the least discussed, the least prepared for. By experiencing my own death, I believed, I could be reborn into the moment, the here-and-now, the present. So, I allowed myself to mourn, for both Maurice and myself.

I also began designing processes. In the seminar I was creating, I wanted to use video in the way Insight seminars used songs. The video of Bernadette Peters singing *Move On* from Stephen Sondheim and James Lapine's sublime Broadway production of *Sunday in the Park with George* became the theme of my seminar:

> *Move on.*
> *Stop worrying where you're going.*
> *Move on.*
> *If you could know where you're going,*
> *you've gone.*
> *Just keep moving on.*
>
> *I chose and my world was shaken.*
> *So what?*
> *The choice may have been mistaken,*
> *The choosing was not.*
>
> *You have to move on.*

I began writing things down, things I wanted the seminar participants to have copies of. Mourn the loss of your own life; learn to enjoy each moment. How to mourn? How to accept? How to enjoy? I drew on my then-thirty-seven years of experience and from that wellspring of wisdom common to us all I had tapped into during rare periods of transcendent creativity. I wrote and wrote and wrote.

I also found quote after quote after quote. I had nothing new to say. It had all been said before, written far better than I could ever hope to. Maybe I should just give the participants a collection of quotes. But, buoyed by Stephen Sondheim's lines from *Move On,*

> *Stop worrying if your vision is new.*
> *Let others make that decision,*
> *They usually do.*
> *Just keep moving on.*

And, especially, the last lines of the song:

Anything you do,
Let it come from you,
Then it will be new.

Give us more to see.

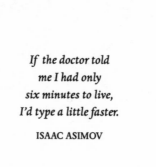

If the doctor told
me I had only
six minutes to live,
I'd type a little faster.

ISAAC ASIMOV

So, book-writer that I had been since 1967, I decided on putting it together in a book: *You Can't Afford the Luxury of a Negative Thought*, a phrase I knit together from sound advice from the past. (Sound advice I soundly ignored.) The subtitle was even more important: *A Book for People with Any Life-Threatening Illness—Including Life*. That was the angle I would take: since life is a sexually transmitted terminal illness, there need not be a *struggle* between Life and Death—we are all going to die; there's no point denying *that* reality. So it's not the struggle between Life and Death, but what to do about the *wiggle* between birth and death.*

I had found *so* many quotes that some of the pages of my book had more quotation marks on them than words. I decided to use a variation of the format I had used twelve years before in writing *How to Survive the Loss of a Love*. (Melba Colgrove, Ph.D., and Harold H. Bloomfield, M.D., provided the medical information; I provided my own experiences, and wrote it all into a book.) Advice and poetry alternated, giving the reader intellectual information (the advice) on one page and emotional identification (the poetry) on the facing page.

I wrote *You Can't Afford the Luxury of a Negative Thought* as though John-Roger and I had written it together. His previous

---

*See what I mean? George Santayana already had the idea in 1922 and said it far better than I could when he wrote: "There is no cure for birth and death save to enjoy the interval." He, of course, borrowed the idea from a thousand others, including Pindar (518–438 B.C.): "Seek not, my soul, the life of the immortals; but enjoy to the full the resources that are within thy reach." Thousands would copy the idea from Santayana, including first-rate copyists such as Thornton Wilder, who wrote in his 1942 play *The Skin of Our Teeth*: "My advice to you is not to inquire why or whither, but just enjoy your ice cream while it's on your plate—that's my philosophy." Speaking of playwrights, Eugene O'Neill (who survived tuberculosis in 1913, only to die forty years later of another illness altogether) called the time between birth and death a "strange interlude." The best I could create was "a wiggle," and even *that* I borrowed from Alan Watts.

> I haven't read
> any of the
> autobiographies
> about me.
>
> ELIZABETH TAYLOR

books (which he didn't write, either) had been mostly spiritual. This, as far as Insight was concerned, would not do. They were desperately trying to debunk the myth (read: truth) that Insight was a recruitment arm for John-Roger's Church of the Movement of Spiritual Inner Awareness. Insight was sold as "practical personal growth for everyday life," and this it delivered as well as any popular "training seminar" on the market. But that was just the sale, the bait. Beneath it, Insight was there to get people into MSIA. Bait and switch.

Every executive and leadership position in Insight, including facilitator, was held by MSIA ministers and John-Roger's personal initiates, myself included. The *one* exception to this rule was a delightful, generous man from Philadelphia who loved Insight but wanted nothing whatsoever to do with John-Roger's spiritual teachings and, especially, not with his *church.*

Prior to The Great *Los Angeles Times* Scare, this man was considered something of an embarrassment to the Insight hierarchy: he was, after all, not a minister and not an initiate; he wasn't even reading John-Roger's Discourses on his way to *becoming* a minister and initiate. Pressure was put on him, from subtle to Insight-ful. (At one meeting attended by all the Insight big-wigs, including John-Roger, the pressure was so strong I had the feeling that if the dear man had simply said, "Okay, I give up!" John-Roger would have initiated *and* ordained him on the spot.) But despite years of "enrollment" from the best enrollers Insight had to offer, he remained, joyfully, what he always had been: Jewish.

Now, however, with the doom of the *Times* looming above Insight, he was a godsend. (He always *was* a godsend, but John-Roger and the Big Kahunas at Insight were finally realizing it.) Insight presented him as the *typical* Insight administrator: self-made, financially successful, adorable, and, by the way, *not a member of MSIA, an initiate, a minister, or in any way a follower of Sri John-Roger, guru.*

Insight had existed for the ten years preceding 1988 simply because it seemed to make John-Roger happy (and money). Making John-Roger happy (and money) was the overriding goal of everyone who ran Insight. The CEO, Candy Semigran, had followed John-Roger faithfully since the 1960s, when she was thirteen and he was her high school English teacher. As far as I know, she still follows him. The second-in-command in 1988 and the director of train-

> *They all sit around feeling very spiritual, with their mental hands on each other's knees, discussing sex as if it were the Art of Fugue.*
>
> JOHN OSBORNE

ings was the man who basically stole the Insight training from Lifespring (he was a Lifespring trainer at the time) and laid it as a gift at John-Roger's feet. He was (and still is) a man deeply in need of approval from an all-knowing, all-powerful father figure. In the drama of Russell Bishop's life, John-Roger plays the role of *paterfamilias* to perfection.

All of us at Insight asked: "What do I want?" We answered: "To please John-Roger. What does John-Roger want?" The unquestioned adoration he received from his devotees in MSIA. (But J-R also wanted "his space," which meant, roughly, "Worship me in person on my schedule, not yours.") Hence, the three primary Insight seminars (Insight I, Insight II, and Insight III) took the unwary personal-growth seeker along a carefully calculated course which led, by the end of Insight III, to MSIA.

That so few of the 50,000 people who had taken Insight by 1988 went on to study seriously with MSIA—less than five percent—was a testament to the innate intelligence of the Insight participants. MSIA was (and is) a jumble of whatever happened to catch John-Roger's fancy from the time he was born in Rains, Utah, in 1934, to the time he incorporated MSIA in 1971. The cosmology of MSIA was, and is, an ungodly mess. It didn't take long for even a brain-damaged garden slug to realize there was no divine order—or energy—in MSIA.

Alas, I lacked such intelligence. More accurately, whatever intelligence I had was short-circuited by the Insight process. Instead of tearing me down to build a better me—a more me-in-control-of-me me—they tore me down, and built a John-Roger devotee in my place. In 1988, I was grateful for Insight's having tricked me. (That, too, was part of the programming.)

I was an initiate and a minister, and saw no reason why *everyone*

> *I know not, sir,*
> *whether Bacon wrote*
> *the works of Shakespeare,*
> *but if he did not*
> *it seems to me that he missed*
> *the opportunity of his life.*
>
> J. M. BARRIE

shouldn't be an initiate and a minister. (Deception was a small price to pay for saving a soul, no?) So, I gladly joined the 1988-let's-keep-the-world-from-discovering-the-truth-about-Insight-and-John-Roger campaign.

Part of the campaign was making John-Roger a "co-author" of a book, even though his only contribution had been to suggest that I listen to a cliché-encrusted forty-five-minute "Light Study" he had done with one of his initiates and ministers who had (and subsequently died of—in my arms, as it turns out) AIDS. That, skimming the final manuscript, and writing "OK J-R" on every page, was all John-Roger did.

When finished, *You Can't Afford the Luxury of a Negative Thought* weighed in at 622 pages, a gargantuan length for a self-help book. But I couldn't find one word or one quote I didn't want the people attending the seminar to have, so 622 pages it was.

As much as Insight wanted the favorable PR, they did not want to pay for printing the book. ("No extra expenses, remember?") Besides, Insight had done just fine, thank you very much, without a book of any kind. John-Roger—who controlled Insight's purse strings as totally as he controlled the purse strings of MSIA—didn't think Insight should spring for it, either. Unnecessary expense. But, hey, Peter, why don't *you* pay for the printing?

As I seemed to be the only person who believed in the book enough to put money on the line for it, I did. My mind was set on giving the two hundred participants the best seminar I could give them—even if I had to pay for it myself.

Supported by a group of phenomenal volunteers ("assistants" in Insightese), we presented the You Can't Afford the Luxury of a Negative Thought Workshop at the Insight building in Santa Monica, California, over two consecutive weekends in early August 1988, starting the day after my thirty-eighth birthday. It was one of the best presents I have ever given myself. Such love. Such fear. Such joy. Such depth of pain. Such laughter.

When it was all over, I returned to *my own* healing (my illness, as always, turned out to be fear) and to my own career: writing books, selling books, and being the occasional on-air consumer electronics correspondent for the *Today* show.

Then a strange thing started happening. People began writing me for copies of *You Can't Afford the Luxury of a Negative Thought*. At first, they were seminar participants asking for extra copies. Then mail arrived from people who

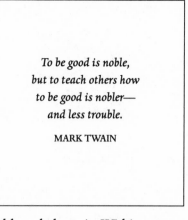

To be good is noble, but to teach others how to be good is nobler— and less trouble.

MARK TWAIN

had not taken the seminar but had heard about it. Within two or three weeks, I got letters from people across the country who didn't even know there *had been* a workshop. In addition, Insight sold the book at its regular seminars. It was an instant sell-out. Something in it was touching a nerve.

I thought seriously about having the book published by a New York house. My publishing company, Prelude Press, was, shall we say, in hiatus. Permanent hiatus, I thought. I hoped. I had self-published since 1967, when I was seventeen, and I was tired of it all. Exhausted, in fact. The writing *and* publishing of (and being cheated out of all my profits for) *The Personal Computer Book* and its friends *(Personal Computers and the Disabled* being the one I'm most proud of) during the first half of the 1980s left me determined to be an *author,* and to get my books published through genuine *publishers* just like every other *author.*

Most of the books I had written and self-published had a good enough track record for some New York publishers to at least *listen* to what I might propose. Random House, for example, turned down in 1986 my proposal for an ongoing set of books called THE LIFE 101 SERIES—but at least they *considered* it. In 1987 I had published a book through Prentice Hall called (ever-modestly) *The Peter McWilliams Personal Electronics Book.* Perhaps there was a market for a book with the quirky title *You Can't Afford the Luxury of a Negative Thought.*

I sent the book to twenty publishers. I got twenty rejections.

So, there I was, driving around the Joshua Tree National Monument (I bet you thought we'd *never* get back there), with John-Roger, the first time we had spent together truly alone, without the ubiquitous members of his personal staff in tow.

> *God is love,*
> *but get it*
> *in writing.*
>
> GYPSY ROSE LEE

I was walking a careful line. On one hand, I was trying to "hang out" with him, although simply hanging out with God's most important earth-emissary in 25,000 years was not easily within my range of behavior. On the other hand, I wanted to tap his source of Divine Wisdom—not just Divine Wisdom about Joshua trees and ground squirrels, and not merely generic Divine Wisdom like Moses from the Mountain and Dr. Joyce Brothers from the talk show dispensed—I wanted Divine Wisdom as it applied to *my life, personally, here and now.*

Between small talk that was remarkably boring—the sort of banter that goes on between Super Bowl innings or half-times or whatever the time is when the players are not playing—I would ask a personal question or make a personal request. I asked that he send the Light to Maurice (whereas anyone could send the Light, only John-Roger could *send the Light*). He did. I knew at last that Maurice's eternal future was assured. The mere fact that Maurice's name had passed through John-Roger's consciousness was enough; more than anybody deserved, in fact: it was an act of grace.

I told John-Roger how nice it was to spend time with Maurice and his best friend, Virgil. They were both in their late eighties and devoted to each other. When they were in a room together, the bond between them was as perceptible as sunlight and as ancient as the pyramids. They maintained separate apartments and led separate but intertwining lives; they were not lovers in the sexual sense. They had been, though. Around 1925.

The most important thing I learned from Maurice and Virgil (who was a composer) was that, for a creative person, there is no such thing as retirement: each of them did three to four hours of creative work a day, every day. (There were no weekends for creative people, either.) Although Maurice's hands were gnarled with rheumatism, and although he had plenty of money to live on, each morning he was up and painting: from nature in the summer; still-lifes and personal sittings in the winter. (He never accepted a commission to paint a portrait: he painted those he chose to paint, and then gave the sitter the canvas—worth thousands—as his way of saying, "Thank you for spending this time with me.")

I told John-Roger of Maurice's frighteningly swift disintegration, his dementia, how quickly he was consumed. Although he had died almost a year ago, I still missed him. (After Maurice's death, Virgil began a gradual, downward descent which continued, without reprieve, until his death from nothing special at ninety-three.*)

> *It is easy—terribly easy—to shake a man's faith in himself. To take advantage of that to break a man's spirit is devil's work.*
>
> GEORGE BERNARD SHAW

John-Roger and I discussed *You Can't Afford the Luxury of a Negative Thought*. While the best minds in American publishing were saying there was no market for the book, letters kept coming in: "The book saved my life," "I can't thank you enough," "*Please* send a copy to my mother (but don't tell her I sent it)."

I was in a quandary. I still believed in the book enough to publish it myself—with all that would entail. John-Roger and I discussed the financial details: whatever the profit was, we'd split it. Our plans were very casual, very friendly. Profit was not important, we agreed: getting the book to people who wanted it, was.

But what about my health?

Ever since Maurice's death, the great cloud of consumption and whether I had contracted it cast its shadow. I told John-Roger I was afraid I might not be alive to complete the publishing of the book. It was also my oblique way of asking him to consult his crystal ball as I had seen him do with so many others and give me the answer medical science lacked: I asked him, "Do I have tuberculosis?"

"Yes," J-R said casually, looking out the passenger window. It was as though I had asked him, "Do you like root beer?"

Panic. Dread. The part of me that had grown so masterful at hating myself proclaimed its victory: "See? I *told* you your life wasn't worth anything." (I later learned that this attitude is just a symptom of depression, but I certainly didn't know it at the time.

*In Virgil's family, centenarians were the rule, not the exception. If somebody died before ninety-five, people would lament, without a hint of sarcasm, "He died so young."

John-Roger, who has a degree in psychology, must have.)

U2 characterized the Joshua Tree Monument as a place "where the streets have no names." At that point it was a good thing the streets had no other cars, either: My driving was erratic enough to have wiped out more vehicles than your average demolition derby.

> *We're beaten and blown*
> *by the wind*
> *Trampled in dust.*
> *I'll show you a place,*
> *High on a desert plain,*
> *Where the streets have no name.*
>
> U2
> *Joshua Tree*

But the best was yet to come.

After a silence as pregnant as Mother Earth, John-Roger added, almost as an afterthought: "You got AIDS from him, too."

AIDS!?

AIDS!?

How could I have gotten *AIDS* from Maurice? We shared neither a bed nor needles. I expressed my incredulity to John-Roger in the most diplomatic way possible. How could *that* have happened?

"Any number of ways," J-R said, watching the passing cacti. "If one of his tears got in your mouth, that would do it." Everything I knew about AIDS transmission went right out the window.

"But I'm perfectly healthy," I protested.

It was a reflexive response. Had I my wits about me, I would have said something else, *anything* else. John-Roger's response to any questioning of his powers usually was to say, "Fine. You win. Have it your way. Good luck." And that closed the subject. Period.

Instead, John-Roger turned and looked at me for the first time since his Hiroshima and Nagasaki blasts.

"AIDS is in your aura," he said, looking at the space around my body. "It hasn't physically manifested yet, but it will soon. You'll be dead in six months; nine months if you do everything you can to fight it." It was spoken with as much concern as if he were telling me I had a spot of leftover lunch on my chin. No big deal.

Well, maybe not to *him*, Grand Imperial Poo-bah, God's drinking buddy, and all that. *I*, however, had a slightly different, entirely more worldly reaction.

I'm glad I can look back on this now with a sense of humor. I had no such sense then, under the relentless sun, where the streets had no names, and the disease I was to die from in nine months had only been given a name a few years before.

I was in shock. Numb (the title of a later U2 song which I wish I had had to distract me for an instant from my own stunning numbness). I began making lists of whom to contact, how I would contact them, who would get what from my feeble estate (whoever got my house also got the mortgage), and what I would like done with my ashes.

> *When you don't have any money, the problem is food. When you have money, it's sex. When you have both, it's health. If everything is simply jake, then you're frightened of death.*
>
> J. P. DONLEAVY

Like most of my relatives, I rose magnificently to a crisis. It was the day-to-day crap I couldn't cope with.

Looking through the windshield at nature's glory, I remembered the opening lines from the film *Missouri Breaks*.

"Sure is beautiful country," a young cowboy observes.

"I guess you appreciate it all the more now," an older, wiser cowboy remarks.

"Yes, sir," the young one says. We then find out the young cowboy was caught rustling and is about to be hanged: they were only riding around until they found the nearest tree.

There were plenty of trees out there, Joshua trees, and I felt as though one had been shoved inside me, ten thousand prickly needles and all. Death was inevitable: all I had to do was wait for internal bleeding and nature to take its course. But what about all the *pain* while I'm waiting? The physical pain of the illness. The emotional pain watching those close to me struggle to show me a courageous face. The mental pain of the dementia some AIDS patients had.

That I should unquestioningly believe John-Roger and his "spiritual diagnosis" of my health was standard operating procedure around MSIA. John-Roger, after all, knew everything. He was "consciously aware of all levels of existence simultaneously." The 1979 edition of the MSIA *Handbook for Ministers of Light* takes John-Roger's omnipotence for granted, then tells his ministers how to keep such mastery from becoming a problem when trying to "describe John-Roger":

> I want to feel sunlight on my face,
> See that cloud of dust disappear
> without a trace.
> I want to take shelter from
> the poison rain
> Where the streets have no name.
>
> U2
> *Joshua Tree*

John-Roger Can See All. Remember, however, you might frighten a person in the beginning if you tell him John-Roger has the ability to know everything we're thinking and doing at all times. Though the person may not believe this at first, once he does start realizing it might be true, he's apt to feel frightened.

Also carefully programmed into all John-Roger's students is the idea that bold and dramatic leaps of faith are not just recommended, but *necessary* for spiritual growth. In the Soul Awareness Discourse to be read in the eighth month after becoming his student (Discourses are one of John-Roger's primary forms of teaching), John-Roger tells this story:

> A long time ago a mystic was approached by a young seeker who wanted to know God, and the mystic asked, "How much do you love me?" The young seeker said, "Oh, tremendously." The mystic said, "Then throw yourself over the cliff." The seeker replied, "I'm not going to do that." The mystic said, "Then you don't love me, and if you don't love me, how can you give yourself to me?"

Eventually the seeker—disappointed by the world—returns to the mystic:

> So the seeker again came to the mystic and was asked again, "How much do you love me?" She said, "With all my heart, with all my mind, with all my Soul." The mystic said, "Then throw yourself over the cliff." Without hesitation, the seeker ran and threw her body over the cliff, but before she hit the ground, the mystic reached out and stopped her and said, "Now, let's travel into the God realms." The seeker was ready now.

I was ready.

Maybe I should just end it now, I thought.

That day.

Drop J-R off at the Desert Oasis Motel, drive back to L.A., compose a will, a few personal notes, a multipurpose farewell letter, and end it. Cleaner that way. Neater. More efficient. Let the handful of people who would mourn mourn, and let them get on with their lives. And I'd get on with whatever it was I would be getting on with.

I had already written my epitaph:

> When I'm gone, let me go.
> Don't pull me back to this earth
> that I've loved and hated so.
>
> Wish me well on my journey,
> as I do on yours,
> and if we meet again,
> let's leave that in the hands of God.

> MEPHISTOPHELES: *In this mood*
> *you can dare to go my ways.*
> *Commit yourself; you shall*
> *in these next days*
> *Behold my arts and with*
> *great pleasure too.*
> *What no man yet has seen,*
> *I'll give to you.*
>
> GOETHE
> FAUST

My next question to J-R was going to be, "Is it clear for me to commit suicide?" John-Roger taught that *all* death, including suicide, could not happen unless the High Self of the individual okays it. If one attempts suicide and the High Self *doesn't* okay it—if the "window" to "pass into Spirit" is not open—it's coma time. I had no way of knowing about windows into spirit; but for John-Roger, seeing if my window was open was easy.

But J-R spoke first.

"If you keep writing and publishing the books," he said, never straying from the offhand, casual tone he assumed at the first prognosis, "I'll handle the health issue for you."

What? What? I was looking for permission to die, and now I had a chance to *live*? All I had to do was what I was doing anyway, writing books, only add J-R's name to the cover, say "we" instead of "I," and give him half the profits? (Talk about "publish or perish!")

Hey! What a deal!

I was torn between the New Age maxim "Nothing's too good to be true" and the Old Age common sense "If something's too good to be true, it is." I had him state the terms again.

Yes, the terms were as I had first heard them: life and health for co-authorship credit and half the profits. J-R then squinted and unfocused his eyes the way he has of squinting and unfocusing his eyes, as though he were looking at something not-quite-there.

"This company will be successful," he said. He knew my previous two companies had not been. "I'll handle that, too." Wow! In business with God! How could I lose?

> FAUST: *I shall get well,*
> *you promise me . . .*
> MEPHISTOPHELES: *By natural means*
> *you can*
> *acquire a youthful look,*
> *But it is in another book . . . Done!*
> FAUST: *Another hand clasp! There!*
> MEPHISTOPHELES:. *. . write away*
> *as unabated*
> *As if the Holy Ghost dictated!*
>
> GOETHE
> *Faust*

"And when you sell the publishing company," he said, as though he were reading far-off writing, "you'll get more than a million dollars for it."

Life, health, guaranteed success, and a million dollars, too. Hubba hubba!

I signed on, and signed away my soul: my common sense, my inner wisdom, my knowledge, my experience.

But then, John-Roger and Company had spent ten years programming me for this day.

CHAPTER TWO

I Shall Please

> Because these wings are
> no longer wings to fly
> But merely fans
> to beat the air
> The air which is now
> thoroughly small and dry
> Smaller and dryer than the will
> Teach us to care and not to care
> Teach us to sit still.
>
> T. S. ELIOT

SPIRITUAL teachers often offer to intercede when bad things are happening to good people (good people being defined as their followers). This intercession can be prayer, laying on of hands, puja, incantation, meditation, treatment, faith-healing, rituals, ceremonies, and many others. To the degree that these work, great. (And, quite often, to the degree the believer believes they work, they work. At least that's what the healers say when the healing *doesn't* take: it's the *lack of faith* on the part of the unhealed, not the lack of ability of the healer, that causes healings to fail.)

All this is well and good, as I see it, because *as long as one gets proper medical treatment* it's good to believe that God's on your side, slugging it out with old devil illness.

Even proper medical treatment includes placebos: "Here, take four of these pills (which are nothing but sugar but cost $50 anyway) a day, and you'll be better by the end of the week," the Medical Authority intones* and, lo, by the end of the week, some people are (praise medical science!) healed. As Voltaire noted: "The art of medicine consists of amusing the patient while nature cures the disease." It's the modern equivalent of "sacrifice a chicken and the evil spirit will leave you." Sometimes it works.

*"We have not lost faith," as George Bernard Shaw observed, "but we have transferred it from God to the medical profession."

> When something good happens
> it's a miracle and
> you should wonder
> what God is saving up
> for you later.
>
> MARSHALL BRICKMAN

The word *placebo* itself is Latin, meaning "I shall please." It comes directly from the Service for the Dead, which is known in Catholic circles as the *Placebo*. The priest makes an opening statement in Latin, and the first word of response from the congregants' lips is "*Placebo*...." Some say this Service for the Dead is not so much for the dead as it is for the living—to comfort them, to console them, to *please* them. Hence, placebo: I shall please.

Doing pleasing things and making pleasing promises to promote healing has a long history. Hippocrates acknowledged it four hundred years before there *were* any dead Catholics: "For some patients, though conscious that their condition is perilous, recover their health simply through their contentment with the goodness of the physician." Placebos also have a reputable present, one of successfully proven results for which even charging a professional fee—be it from a priest or physician—is in order.

John-Roger, however, added one minor stipulation that hasn't been seen in reputable circles since the Reformation—or at least since Rasputin: In exchange for my health, I had to keep putting John-Roger's name on books I was writing, plus fork over half the profits.*

It was a safe bet for John-Roger: if I lived, he got his name put on books and a tidy income; if I did not live, who would be left to challenge his co-author status? It was, as they say in the New Age, a "win-win" situation: whether I lived or died, John-Roger won.

John-Roger, of course, has no power over life and death. It's hard to believe I didn't see that then. (It's hard for me to believe *a lot* of things in this story—*and I lived through them.*) He talked movingly about his mother and father succumbing to cancer—*after* he had "inherited the mantle of the Mystical Traveler con-

---

*This arrangement was later changed to John-Roger's receiving a certain amount of money for every book sold *regardless* of profits. I tended to use the profits on things such as giving away free books. Silly me: I thought the goal of writing books was to get helpful information to people who wanted it—regardless of ability to pay. John-Roger later informed me that the reason he got involved with the books was *money*.

sciousness." Followers of John-Roger died on a regular basis: Ruben—if anyone deserved an extension on this earth due to saintly behavior, it was Ruben. Ken, a man younger than I with lung cancer, a devout follower of J-R's for more than twenty years, died the rapid, painful death dictated by the course of his illness. Paul, who at every

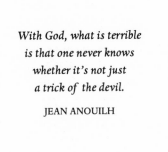

With God, what is terrible is that one never knows whether it's not just a trick of the devil.

JEAN ANOUILH

available opportunity asked for—and thought he had received—John-Roger's help. Becky, whom John-Roger went to and sent others to for healing. Kathy, who went about as gently into that good night as Axl Rose on PCP. The list goes on and on.

As to health, John-Roger was so frequently, nay, *continuously* ill that announcements for all of his public appearances contained the disclaimer: "John-Roger's health and schedule permitting."* Being part of an "inner circle" (but not one of the inner-most circles), I was privy to reports on J-R's failing health and hospital stays that did not make the run-of-the-mill Movement rumor mill. During the years in which he was supposed to be keeping me alive and healthy, I know of at least three times when John-Roger nearly died.

And then there were those people, "beloved of the Traveler," who had chronic illnesses and were in pain most of the time.

If he couldn't save those who died or heal those who lived—even himself—how could I believe he would keep *me* alive and healthy? Well, just as those who believe that for every drop of rain that falls, a flower grows—*a biological impossibility*—I believed that John-Roger would keep me alive and healthy as long as I wrote books, put his name on them, published them, and gave him half the money. (More on *why* I believed this lunacy later.)

Let's assume for a moment, however, that it *were* true; that John-Roger had the ability to maintain life and health and distribute it at his pleasure. Is it, shall we say, *appropriate* to dispense life and health on the condition of fame and fortune? Is it *ever* ethical to perform a spiritual act or act of healing in exchange for a *perma-*

*This became something of a joke around John-Roger's organizations: people would often tag onto agreements—especially important ones—". . . my health and schedule permitting." One couple even considered incorporating it in their marriage vows.

nent percentage of the recipient's livelihood? I think not.

Besides, if a person had such considerable spiritual gifts, wouldn't it be just as easy to, say, turn sulfur and quicksilver into gold and bypass the bestseller lists altogether?

> *He did not stand shivering*
> *upon the brink,*
> *he was a thorough-paced liar,*
> *and plunged at once into*
> *the depths of your credulity.*
>
> CHARLES LAMB
> 1775–1834

CHAPTER THREE

Programming

My land,
the power of training!
of influence! of education!
It can bring a body up
to believe anything.

MARK TWAIN

A T THIS POINT you might be saying of me, "This seems to be a reasonably clever, overly cynical, excessively curmudgeonly man," and you may be wondering, "How did he fall for all this [EXPLETIVE OF YOUR CHOICE]?"

As you can imagine, I've wondered this myself. In fact, if it had not *happened* to me, I would find it difficult to believe. A psychiatrist treating one of the people who left the Movement simply could not comprehend how an intelligent, sophisticated, street-smart woman such as his patient (she was even a *lawyer,* for heaven's sake) could ever swallow such nonsense. Try as she might, she could never quite get him to understand. This chapter is my attempt to understand it myself.

The reason John-Roger got me to believe that he and God were roommates in college is simply *programming.*

Programming works despite intelligence, education, age, economic status, or even *belief* in that which is being programmed in. All programming requires is repetition; enough repetition and the person being programmed suddenly discovers a new truth within: the message that's been programmed.

Like most techniques, it can be used for good or evil. It's a form of subconscious learning by rote, like repeating multiplication tables over and over until one day you just "know" them. We were programmed to speak our native language and to walk. Now

> *What is it men cannot
> be made to believe!*
>
> THOMAS JEFFERSON
> 1786

we do both without "thinking about it." That's what programming does: the message being programmed becomes a seemingly natural, integral part of your psyche: the message springs automatically and effortlessly to the mind as easily as "Two times two is . . ." or "There's no business like . . ." or "To be or not . . . ."

One positive application of programming is *affirmation:* people choose a life-enhancing attitude they want to have about themselves ("I am worthy," for example), repeat it constantly (whether they believe they really are worthy or not), and, eventually, they "discover" one day, "Hey, I *am* worthy."

Affirmations applied in an evil way have been called mind control, thought control, propaganda, or brainwashing. If something—even something you don't agree with intellectually, morally, or emotionally—is repeated often enough, eventually you believe it.

The amount of time it takes to successfully program someone is reduced significantly if the person is emotionally vulnerable. Depression, loss, illness, fear, sleep deprivation, improper diet, stress, fatigue, or being removed from familiar surroundings or people all tend to make a person more susceptible to programming. Emotional vulnerability tills the soil and programming plants the seeds. The more the soil is tilled, the more the seeds grow and flourish, the richer the harvest.

The effectiveness of unwanted programming (programming not wanted or chosen by those being programmed) was observed most markedly when American prisoners of war were captured by the North Koreans and subjected to anti-American, pro-Communist diatribes. To break down their resistance (create vulnerability), the prisoners were deprived of sleep, food, and physical comforts (locked in cold cells without blankets, and intentionally infected with illness). They were also kept completely isolated.

After they "broke" (that is, after the programming "clicked" inside them) they were well fed, well clothed, given lots of time to sleep, and allowed to enjoy the company of other brainwashed Americans. Once returned to full physical strength and health, these men made films that were sent back to the United States. In these films, they denounced all that the United States stood for and praised communism to the hilt. It was not unusual for prisoners of war—under torture or threat of torture—to make such statements. The difference here was that these men *genuinely believed* what they said.

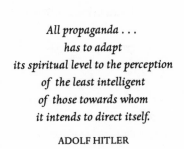

*All propaganda . . .
has to adapt
its spiritual level to the perception
of the least intelligent
of those towards whom
it intends to direct itself.*

ADOLF HITLER

They didn't just parrot what they were told to say, but—fully accepting the fundamental premise that the United States was bad and communism was good—added *their own* thoughts, ideas, and examples to the argument.

The people who take fullest advantage of this phenomenon are American advertisers. They've learned that if you repeat a simple message often enough, people tend to believe it. It even works, they've discovered, with messages that *irritate* you. In fact, with programming, they found that *any* emotional reaction—positive or negative—was better than no reaction at all. Hence, when you see a commercial and ask yourself, "Are they *trying* to irritate me?" the most likely answer is "Yes."

Financed by the advertising industry, the study of programming has become a science. Studies have shown that people do not even need to be conscious that they are receiving information. An image can be flashed on a screen ("Drink Coca-Cola") so quickly the viewer's mind doesn't have time to consciously process it, or a message relayed so softly that the brain doesn't consciously "hear" it; you could even be sound asleep and the message will still make its impression. Some studies show that the message makes a *more* profound impression then, because the conscious mind is unable to use such *anti*-programming tools as logic, reason, or common sense. These methods are known as *subliminal programming.*

Another form of programming is *implanting.* Non-message information ("filler") is presented in the same style and level of intensity until you grow accustomed to it. Then there is a sudden shift of tone and intensity, THE MESSAGE IS DELIVERED; and the tone and intensity returns to its previous level. You've probably seen commercials of a noisy, rat-race world, interspersed with brief passages of total silence in which the sponsor's product is

> *My old friend William Wyler*
> *used to say,*
> *"If you're going to give*
> *the audience a shock,*
> *just before it,*
> *almost reduce them to boredom*
> *so that bang, they sit up."*
> *He's quite right, of course.*
>
> DAVID LEAN

slowly and sumptuously consumed. The reverse can also be true: a lawyer once used implanting against me. (Can you imagine!) She would rattle on quietly, not looking at the jury, and begin a sentence: "If I successfully prove my case, and you decide Mr. McWilliams does not deserve the money he is asking for . . ." at which point she would look directly at the jury, raise the volume, add to her voice a tone of authority, and complete the sentence: ". . . *the law says you must send Mr. McWilliams home from this courtroom without a penny!*" She immediately looked away and continued in her softer, nonauthoritative style.

Another form of implanting includes touching the person while delivering the intended message. Lovers intuitively use this technique. It's also used by salespeople, doctors, ministers, and prostitutes. People are far more open to being implanted when touched. The same is true of other physical, sensual delights: eating, drinking, listening to music, taking drugs, and so forth.

When programming begins, we often feel *wonderful* about whatever is being programmed in—or at least wonderful about those doing the programming. That's how the programmers *want* us to feel—they'll do whatever it takes to get us to feel good so they can get what they want. In relationships, that's called seduction. In business, it's known as salesmanship. In psychology, manipulation.

The programmers provide us with whatever feels good (based on our *own* tastes and preferences, which they carefully research). Once we start to feel good, the programming begins: "You feel good because of _____." And *they* fill in the blank: you feel good because of this product I want to sell you; you feel good because of this idea I want you to believe; you feel good because of *me*.

The programmer's goal is to make you *other-directed*—to affirm the lie that most of us are already preprogrammed to believe: "It's the things and people outside us that make us happy." While it's certainly true that things and people *contribute* to our happiness, the *experience* of the happiness is primarily our own.

First, we have to *like* what it is that's "making us happy." This means *our* preferences, tastes, propensities, and predilections come into play. If *you* don't like country music, Clint Black is not going to make *you* happy (musically, at any rate). If *you* don't like Van Gogh, "Starry Night" will only darken your walls. If *you* don't like caviar, the finest Beluga is just salty black stuff.

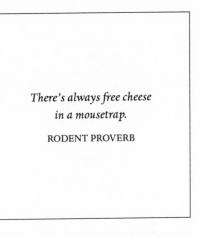

There's always free cheese in a mousetrap.

RODENT PROVERB

Second, the portions of our body that perceive and feel happiness are entirely our own. Our eyes, ears, nose, taste buds, and sense of touch are *ours* alone. Whatever the inner processing mechanism—the whole astonishing physico-bio-electrical communication network inside us—is all ours. Whatever the sense of "I" that puts it all together and says, "Ahhhhh," that's ours, too.

Others may provide us with exquisite food, but the taste that lets us appreciate it is in us. Others may do adorable things for us, but our ability to adore is ours. Others may provide us with a sexual Magic Mountain, but the sensual delights and orgasmic reactions occur within us.

To be other-directed (believing that people and things outside us are more important than what we think and feel) is deeply ingrained—without it, how would Madison Avenue sell us everything they do? Their basic line: "Buy this *product* (an external thing) and you will be happy, satisfied, and loved!"

Without that other-directed belief "Without someone to love, I'm nothing," how would songwriters, screenwriters, and, yes, self-help writers make a living?

Without the other-directed belief "You need *this job* in order to survive," would workers put up with so much crap, or without the belief "I'm essential to this company," would so many employers tolerate so much incompetence?

The other-directed belief "You need us to protect you from every conceivable risk in life," allows government to grow uncontrolled, take more and more of our money, and butt its authoritarian nose into more and more areas of our private lives.

So a lot of people have a vested interest in keeping us other-

> *The great enemy of the truth*
> *is very often not the lie—*
> *deliberate, contrived,*
> *and dishonest—*
> *but the myth—*
> *persistent, persuasive,*
> *and unrealistic.*
>
> JOHN F. KENNEDY

directed. The programming that we *do* need specific things in order to be satisfied surrounds us. To some degree, most of us have bought at least a portion of that scheme. Such a fundamental misconception lays the foundation upon which individual groups or people can construct in us Dependence City.

By the time the "good" relationship (and it *was* good) goes bad, too often we are hooked. We "bought the program." We believe. We are convinced that "any day now" things will be "just like they were." We stay in the bad relationship—with a person, organization, relative, employer, employee, career, medical treatment, therapist, ideal, goal, religion, spiritual path, drug (including cigarettes and alcohol), diet, belief, or anything else—because we feel we *have* to, we *need* to, that our life won't be complete without it.

One of the most fascinating things about programming is that we *genuinely believe* that *we* believe it. The programmed message doesn't seem foreign or unusual or controlling us in any way. We are firmly convinced it is *our choice* (and heaven help anyone who tries to talk us out of our choice). Only it is not *our* choice. But we are *programmed* to think it is.

For example, the first of Alcoholics Anonymous's Twelve Steps to overcoming addiction (and that's precisely what the programmed message becomes: an addiction) is to admit that "I have become powerless over alcohol." For an alcoholic, the idea that drinking is a *free choice* is eliminated immediately. For alcoholics to refuse a drink even when the programming says "Drink!" does not, then, seem to be denying themselves.

But that's just what breaking away from programming is like: it feels as though you are not being true to yourself. This is because of the way programming hooks us—and why it's so utterly diabolical when used against us.

As the programmers repeat their message over and over, we begin to ignore it. This happens whether or not we believe in the message. After enough repetitions, we don't even notice it. (Have you read what's on the bottom of the pages of this book recently?

LIFE 103: Send Peter McWilliams lots of money.

Probably not.) We become unaware of repetitive things fairly quickly. Even though we're unaware of them, they go into our subconscious anyway.

*One should always be wary
of someone who promises
that their love will last
longer than a weekend.*

QUENTIN CRISP

Experienced programmers know that the secret to successful programming is to keep the message *simple* and *the same.* In advertising they're called slogans ("Coke Is It!" "They Satisfy!" "We Do It All For You!"), in politics they're keynotes ("Nixon's the One!" "All the way with LBJ!" "Never Fail: Vote For Quayle!"), in romance they're gushes ("I love you!" "I love you a lot!" "I love you more than I've ever loved anyone before!").

The messages dig into the subconscious, one after another, day after day, until—suddenly, without warning—they all *come together.* A revelation! "Coke *IS* It!" "Nixon *IS* the One!" "They *DO* Love Me!" The realization seems to *come from inside yourself* precisely because it is *inside yourself* where the oft-repeated message was stored. All those impressions abruptly crystallize into an awareness—an awareness that seems to be entirely your own.

At this point, your ground of being shifts. Your fundamental benchmark is altered. The standard by which you judge all other standards changes. It's as though your inner compass has been recalibrated: you *firmly believe* that True North lies in a direction other than North.*

When this shift takes place, you do *not* become a zombie. You are still a rational, intelligent, capable, educated human being *heading in the wrong direction in a rational, intelligent, capable, and educated way.*

When I tell people I was programmed to believe John-Roger was God's surfing buddy, they sometimes say: "You didn't *look* programmed." *Programming doesn't have a "look."* We are, well, *programmed* to believe that anyone whose mind is controlled becomes a robot-like creature who looks at you with Valium eyes and

---

*This is known as the *North effect,* named after one of its most famous contemporary victims, Oliver North. No, no. Just kidding. Just trying to brighten up the bottom of the page (which I bet you are reading now—for a while).

> *The devil is easy to identify.*
> *He appears when you're terribly*
> *tired and makes a very reasonable*
> *request which you know*
> *you shouldn't grant.*
>
> FIORELLO LA GUARDIA

monotones: "My Master wants you to come with me."

It's not like that at all. While under John-Roger's spell I wrote books, I just put his name on them; I made money, I just gave him most of it; I appeared on talk shows, I just made sure I gave him lots of credit; I had relationships, I just dragged them into John-Roger's cult.

More on programming and how you can protect yourself from it, as well as how to get out of the programming once you've already received it in the chapter, "Counter-programming and Re-programming." For now, let me tell you how I got programmed, and how it affected me.

⚖ ⚖ ⚖

[Note: in APPENDIX A, entitled "A Brief History of Me," I describe my pre–John-Roger involvement with personal growth, spirituality, writing, and publishing. Feel free to read it at any time—or never. It's not essential to the story at hand but provides background some may find interesting.]

CHAPTER FOUR

Insight I: Introduction to Indoctrination

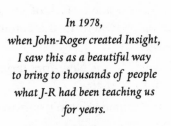

In 1978,
when John-Roger created Insight,
I saw this as a beautiful way
to bring to thousands of people
what J-R had been teaching us
for years.

CANDY SEMIGRAN
CEO of Insight Seminars
1987

FALL 1978. I was depressed. *Very* depressed. By early 1977, my profits from two books I had written and published, *The TM Book* and *How to Survive the Loss of a Love,* amounted to $250,000. It was burning a hole in my bank account. What to do? I had two obvious choices: buy the Greenwich Village townhouse I was living in, or start a greeting card company.

I started a greeting card company. Wrong. Not only did I lose my $250,000 (fast), but I found myself an additional $250,000 in debt. Then it got worse. There was a paper strike, and no paper could be found to reprint additional cards. This meant the card racks—given free to a store with its first order—were getting empty, and when they became too empty (with no replacement cards in sight), the racks were tossed into the alley, and the remaining cards returned to us. Furthermore, these stores never wanted to see our cards again. Oh, the sad story goes on and on.*

I wasn't just heading toward bankruptcy or sliding toward bankruptcy, I was *bungee-jumping* toward bankruptcy. For me to say, "I'm on the edge of bankruptcy," was about the same as saying, "My canoe is on the edge of Niagara Falls."

*Meanwhile, the value of the townhouse went up and up. By the late 1980s, I am told, at the height of the New York real estate market, it had reached a value of $4 million.

> *Purpose of these seminars is to introduce concepts and techniques for gaining physical, emotional and mental balance, and for finding inner peace. It is to learn how to assume responsibility and create in a positive, constructive manner.*
>
> HANDBOOK FOR MINISTERS OF LIGHT
> on how to present MSIA
> to public institutions

I sought solace in self help.

Each weekend I would do something related to personal growth. One day while browsing through a New Age magazine, I saw a full-page ad for a training called Insight. It promised personal growth and practical techniques for life. I could use some of those. Something inside me said, "I'll do this."

I called the number at the bottom of the ad and was told that the New York trainings had been canceled due to lack of enrollment. I asked when the next training anywhere in the country would be.

"Well, one starts tonight in Philadelphia," the New York Insight person answered, "but you don't want to go there."

"Why not?" I asked. "It's noon; the training doesn't start until 6:00, and Philadelphia's only two hours away."

"Are you sure you really want to?"

I could see why the New York trainings lacked enrollment.

I got the details from the excessively cautious enroller, packed a few things, and headed for Philadelphia.

Although the training was scheduled to start at 6:00 p.m., by 7:30 p.m. there wasn't even a *hint* that the doors to the training room were going to open any time in the next decade. This didn't seem to faze the soon-to-be participants. They sat around in the halls of the conference center, milled about, chatted, shared food; a young man played guitar. As I was to write later (for the Insight newsletter): "It seemed as though these people were trucked in from some point further along in the New Age."

Unbeknownst to me (I have been waiting twenty years to use the word *unbeknownst* in a book), almost every Insight participant other than myself was a member of John-Roger's Church of the Movement of Spiritual Inner Awareness. Most, in fact, were ministers of the Church.

I later discovered that Insight was the brainchild of Russell Bishop, who was a trainer for Lifespring. In early 1978, Russell did essentially the Lifespring Basic Training for a group of MSIA people in Los Angeles. There was skepticism among the MSIA community about the new training. John-Roger took care of that—and took a trip to Hawaii as well. To quote the *Los Angeles Times*:

> *There is a sort of transcendental ventriloquy through which men can be made to believe that something which was said on earth came from heaven.*
>
> GEORG CHRISTOPH LICHTENBERG
> 1764–1799

> Just before the first Insight training, John-Roger held a meeting to introduce the new program to his ministers. He began his talk by announcing that he had just returned from Hawaii, where he attended a "four-day meeting up on a high mountain peak . . . called through the Traveler Consciousness . . ." and attended by "the spiritual hierarchy of the planet," including Jesus, Krishna and other "ascended masters."

> He then assured his ministers that the new program they were being asked to take would give them a chance "to look at the teachings of the Traveler . . . in a different perspective."

Well, after this kind of cosmic sales pitch, the training was full—and it was a hit. Soon, all the MSIA communities around the country wanted to take the training. One problem: what sort of royalty should Lifespring be paid? Solution: screw Lifespring. Change the name to Insight and claim John-Roger created it. That's just what they did. Russell quit his job with Lifespring and spent his time leading Insight trainings around the country. (To add insult to injury, Russell hired away one Lifespring trainer after another to work for Insight.)

Did I say a hit? The John-Roger–founded organization that presented Insight, Golden Age Education, had revenues in 1977 of $90. In 1978, thanks to Insight, the Golden Age revenues were $1,094,679—all tax-free.

The Insight I attended in the fall of 1978 was, I believe, the second Insight seminar to be done in Philadelphia. *Finally* the doors opened, and we filed in. There were about two hundred of us, and we sat in neat little rows facing a stage. There was music playing.

Two impeccably groomed, well-dressed men took the stage. One was the aforementioned Russell, the other a handsome member of John-Roger's personal staff, Victor Toso. They chatted casu-

> A hypocrite despises
> those whom he deceives,
> but has no respect for himself.
> He would make
> a dupe of himself too,
> if he could.
>
> WILLIAM HAZLITT
> 1823

ally with the group. I liked both of them immediately. Someone in the audience asked a question:

"Is J-R going to give a seminar after the training?" There was a general murmur indicating that a J-R seminar—whatever *that* was—would be a welcome event.*

"Well, I'd certainly like that," said Russell, becoming suddenly and inexplicably coquettish, "but you'll have to ask John-Roger."

Almost everyone shifted in their seats to look toward the back of the room. All eyes seemed to focus on an unkempt, slightly pudgy man, wearing a loose-fitting Hawaiian shirt. Was this John-Roger? If so, I wondered, why didn't Russell just ask him directly instead of telling the questioner that he would have to ask John-Roger? John-Roger walked up the middle aisle, handed something to Russell, headed again toward the back of the room and, almost as an afterthought, said in the general direction of the person asking the question, "No, I'm not going to be doing a seminar." His attitude seemed one of near-contempt.

There was a chorus of disappointed groans. I remember thinking, "Who the hell cares if this guy gives a seminar?" The two men on the stage were much better role models for what I wanted to learn than this scruffy guy who couldn't politely answer a simple question. Without so much as acknowledging the group's disappointment, John-Roger left the room. Following in his wake

---

*A John-Roger Soul Awareness Seminar is John-Roger speaking for about an hour on just about anything that comes into his head. It is not what John-Roger *says*, however, during the seminar, but the *energy* he spiritually transmits that makes his seminars worthwhile. Any negative feelings felt during a seminar are "a release of karma." If you fall asleep, that's "soul transcendence," or "traveling with the Traveler." The audio or video tapes of these seminars absorb the bad karma and negativity released by the individual listening to or watching them. Anyone else who listens to or watches the same tape picks up the original owner's stored negativity. It is therefore, according to John-Roger, very important to purchase your own tapes and not listen to anyone else's. This form of spiritual copyright protection John-Roger instigated when he heard people weren't *buying* tapes at $10 each, but *copying* them or *loaning* them to others. Not "spiritually" acceptable.

were several handsome young men. (He had lousy taste in shirts, but great taste in men.) It was the last we were to see of him that weekend.

I liked the Insight training: it was gentler than est, and had more activity than Actualizations.

How can I believe in God when just last week I got my tongue caught in the roller of an electric typewriter?

WOODY ALLEN

Allow me here a brief aside to explain how seminar trainings work. Roughly the first half of the seminar is spent looking at an individual's darker side: guilts, fears, angers, disappointments, hurts, inadequacies, unworthinesses, and all the other aspects we consider negative about ourselves. Focusing on all this negativity for two or three days tends to make one feel, well, negative. Depression sets in. Self-esteem begins to deteriorate, both within the individual and within the group. (Some exercises—called *processes*—are intentionally designed to make each participant feel alien to and separate from the group.) In time, the shining example of sanity, hope, and enlightenment is the trainer. People do more and more of what the trainer asks, with less and less resistance.

At a certain calculated point halfway through the training, the trainer magically *switches it all around*. The group and all its members are encouraged to focus on good things, positive things, uplifting things. Process after process builds esteem, cohesion, and eventually love within the individual and within the group.

Then, toward the end of the seminar, there's one more great leap of faith into the negativity pool—except the pool has been drained, and it's been replaced by a trampoline. Down, down, down, negative, negative, negative ("Where's the water!?") and BOING! U-u-u-u-p you go. From then on, it's all positivity and the participants are flying high. This is when enrollment in future seminars—or MSIA—takes place. (This high lasts from a few days to a few weeks, depending on the gravity of one's life.)

It's pressure and release: it feels *so good* when the pressure stops—the greater the pressure, the better the release feels. The technique is not new, of course. The evangelicals, for example, have been using it since the early 1800s. Preachers go on and on about hellfire, damnation, bubbling sulfur, no chance, it's already

> *A casual stroll through the lunatic asylum shows that faith does not prove anything.*
>
> NIETZSCHE

too late, that's where you're going, let me tell you how terrible eternity is going to be, you miserable sinner. The *only* *hope* for salvation is to accept Jesus Christ, right now, as your Lord and Savior. If you do this, you'll be filled with grace, the light of the Holy Spirit will descend, and you'll be saved. If one takes the leap of faith, the pressure is released, and one is saved.

Pressure/release is used in advertising all the time: Your love-life's a mess? Nobody will date you? People who date you never call again? If they ever call again, it's because they called the wrong number? Is that what's troubling you, booby? Well, suck a Certs, drink a Coke, smoke a Salem, shampoo with Prell, conceal with Clearasil, brush with Pepsodent, dye with Lady Clairol, cover with Max Factor, lose weight with Jenny Craig, exercise with Jane Fonda, dress with Calvin Klein, smell like Elizabeth Taylor, and True Love will be yours.

Police use it to get confessions: it's called good cop/bad cop. The bad cop grills the suspect mercilessly, painting a picture of eternity in prison, sometimes backing up the verbal threats with physical assaults. Another cop comes in, protects the prisoner, sends the bad cop out of the room, offers the suspect a cigarette, and in the psychological release the prisoner confesses.

It's seen in relationships: "If I say yes on the first date, you'll think I'm a tramp," may be the excuse, but the underlying reason—the one seldom discussed but nonetheless well known—is that "Hello, I love you, lie down, thank you" simply does not allow enough *frustration* to build up so that, when finally released, love is a many-splendored thing.

Most plays and movies build up tension for about an hour and a half, then release it in what's called the climax. Comedies release the tension in laughs, tragedies in tears, thrillers in screams, and action/adventure in gasps. Laughter, tears, screams, or gasps, it's a manipulated release—and it feels great.

Once you know the pattern—pressure/release—you see it everywhere. There's nothing intrinsically wrong or bad or evil in the technique's being used in seminar trainings. The only question is: what are they selling? If they're selling self-esteem to the individual, then it can be good, productive therapy. If they're selling something else—something the person may not even remotely be in the market for—that's something else again.

> But make our fundamental
> convictions your own,
> join our brotherhood,
> give yourself up to us,
> let yourself be guided,
> and you will at once feel yourself,
> as I have felt myself,
> a part of that vast invisible chain
> the beginning of which
> is hidden in heaven.
>
> LEO TOLSTOY
> War and Peace

Insight trainings are something else again.

On the morning of the last day of the seminar following a particularly emotional series of processes about our parents, we were lovingly held in the arms of our surrogate parents and asked to listen to a song.

> Oh, awaken little heart
> To the one who you've been
> searching for
> From the start.
> You know that he's within you, little heart,
> You know that he's in you.

Most of the people seemed to know it and gently sang along while stroking, nurturing, and caressing their "children." It was a tender, vulnerable moment. That song ended, and another began:

> Star light, star wise,
> How nice to be like a child.

Almost everyone but me seemed to know that one, too. Had I missed some pop revolution? Had my abandonment of record stores in protest of the Bee Gees caused me to miss some hot, new group? The answer came in the next song:

> Everlasting, everlasting, everlasting
> Messiah.
> Everlasting, everlasting, everlasting
> Messiah.

Messiah? Was this a fundamental Jesus group? No, not if the next song was any indication:

> Sri John-Roger,
> Light and Sound,

> *Music is harmony,*
> *harmony is perfection,*
> *perfection is our dream,*
> *and our dream is heaven.*
>
> AMIEL

> *With your loving*
> *Peace surround me.*
> *I am open to receive*
> *With every breath I breathe.*

Although I didn't know it at the time, this was an in-house collection of MSIA songs. (And quite good songs they were, too.) As I drifted in the comfort of parental arms, I remembered that similar-sounding music had been played throughout the week: during breaks, as a song to introduce a process, as a song to conclude a process, as a meditation to be listened to at the end of an evening with eyes closed—in fact, this rather distinctive sound (now that I was paying a bit of attention to it) of two young men singing with acoustic guitars and electric bass, had permeated the entire training.

The song was done, and there was no further time to think about past musical interludes: we now were to focus on an exercise about the future called, appropriately, "What do you want?"

The "what do you want?" process started slowly, grew gradually, and built to a crescendo of jumping, screaming, near-whirling dervishes yelling what they wanted. For some reason, I fixed on freedom, and was jumping about, making eye contact with a partner, shrieking, "I want freedom!" "I want freedom!" "I want freedom!" The partner's job is to goad you on by saying things such as "Louder!" "How much do you want it?" "I can't hear you!" and other taunts used to great effect by drill sergeants and the Dallas Cowboys cheerleaders. I was going after freedom. I was going after freedom. Nothing would stop me from getting freedom. I yelled louder, jumped higher, and promptly blacked out.

I awoke on the floor, surrounded by assistants. I couldn't have been out for very long, as everyone was still jumping up and down and shrieking for what they wanted. Even my partner was still jumping up and down and shrieking—he seemed oblivious to the fact that I was no longer there. I was stroked and coddled by the assistants. I was poured into my chair just in time for everyone to close their eyes and quietly listen to another song "as though it were being sung from within your own heart." It told the story of a perfectly reasonable coyote, who couldn't understand why the animals crowd around "the Traveler."

Why do they show no fear?
He's drawing very near.
Why do they gather 'round him
When they all should run away?

The coyote, however, has a transformational moment:

His eye caught the Traveler's
And forever after he knew.
He's always in the hearts
of the flowers and the trees.
He's always in the hearts
of the rabbits and the bees.

When you jump for joy,
beware that no one
moves the ground
from beneath your feet.

STANISLAW LEC

From the babies in the forest
To the coyote that's in me.

The song was over, and the trainer said: "Is the coyote in you keeping you from the One you love the best? The One who loves you the best? Focus on what you *really* want and let go of all those coyote-like limitations, as you listen to the next song." It was sung by the same voice that had just sung about the coyote:

In the silence of my room . . .
Again you're there to comfort me
And the love in your eyes
When you smile on me
Moves me to the depths of my soul.

The song was nice, most of the people in the room were crying uncontrollably, but all I could think of was that I wanted a hamburger. Just then the trainer's voice chimed in: "We're going to take a meal break now . . ." Hey! This what-do-you-want stuff seems to work.

I hadn't given my blacking out a second thought—it felt very much like the times I would stand up too quickly after taking a hot bath. I always seemed to have the presence of mind to get down on the floor before consciousness slipped away entirely, so I would wake up unharmed on the bathroom floor none the worse for wear. (It was kind of enjoyable, in fact.)

Visions of double cheeseburgers, extra rare, danced in my head as we were finally released for our meal break. (The "morning" had gone on nonstop for about five hours.) I was immediately surrounded by assistants.

"I have never seen the Spirit hit anyone so powerfully in my life!" one said.

"It was like a lightning bolt came down from the highest heavens!" another said.

Yet another added, with slightly more awe and reverence than the previous two: "The Traveler must love you an awful lot to give you a gift like that!" That's it: play upon my ego—one of my twenty-two or twenty-three weakest points.

> Vanity
> is the quicksand
> of reason.
>
> GEORGE SAND

"I can just *feel* the energy radiating off of you now," still another said, his arms at his sides but his palms faced in my direction. "It's just such a blessing just standing near you."

To hell with the cheeseburger: feed me more praise.

They did.

They spoke about my joining the Movement, not so much that I needed the Movement, but that the Movement needed *me*. Hell, I didn't know which Movement they meant, but any Movement that needed me *that* much, well, a godly being such as I could only comply. By the time this love-in ended, I had just enough time to grab a bag of Doritos from the vending machine down the hall. But I didn't care: I had been fed adoration; the food of the gods. The assistants had devotion so refined it seemed to be one of the fine arts. Recruitment, too.

The training started again, and we did a process some refer to as the Love Bomb, also known as the hug line. The technical term is "moving meditation." Here you stand in a long, snaking line and directly face someone from another long, snaking line. We had a chance to "silently interact" with every other participant in the training, and most of the assistants. This was probably about two hundred fifty people. You would interact with the person in front of you and, at the trainer's instruction, sidestep to the right. This would put you in front of a new face, a new opportunity for interaction, and then you'd sidestep one to the right again where there would be another "Loving Heart."

It soon fell into a predictable pattern: meaningful eye contact, a full-body hug (none of this keep-your-pelvises-away-from-each-other-and-pat-each-other-on-the-back-to-show-you-don't-really-mean-it hug), a little more meaningful eye contact and, as the trainers would say, "Time for a new universe."

This went on for hours. *And guess what they played in the background?* I think only Mahalia Jackson recorded more spiritual songs than these two, soothing, male MSIA voices. When they ran out of songs, as eventually they did, they just started them over again. It was as

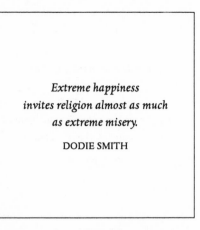

though we had tuned in the all-MSIA station: "Top-fifty MSIA hits! Twenty-four hours a day! 'Round the clock! You give us thirty minutes, we'll give you enlightenment."

All that hugging and goo-goo-eyed gazing and *love* made for a powerful experience.

Then it came time to sign everyone up for the Advanced Insight Training. From what I could tell, nearly everyone did. People who didn't have the money ($650, as I recall), were told to go around the room asking other people for money. While I was paying for my own seminar, three people approached and asked me for money to help pay for theirs. I think they were expecting maybe $5 or $10. I said I'd be glad to pay for the whole thing. Hell, I was so high I was glad to do *anything*. Besides, considering my financial condition, giving three people $650 each to do the Advanced Insight was not unlike the captain of the Titanic handing out complimentary deck chairs. ("Is there room on your lifeboat? Take some home for the kids!") One man wasn't sure if he could accept such a large gift. He closed his eyes and "went inside." When he came out, he could accept.

There was nothing left but the candle-lighting ceremony, in which everyone is given an unlit candle and, in a completely darkened room, the trainer ("Keeper of the Flame") starts by lighting his candle. Then, candle-by-candle, all the candles in the room are lit. As you pass the flame from one person to another, you are instructed to look the person in the eye and see the candle-lighting as a symbolic "passing of the Holy Spirit" from one person to the next.

Soon the room was alight with candles, held high and casting a romantic glow. The song they played was Debby Boone's "You Light Up My Life." I knew Insight had worked for me when I

> When sexual indulgence has
> reduced a man to
> the shape of Lord Hailsham,
> sexual continence involves no more
> than a sense of the ridiculous.
>
> LORD PAGET

stood there *enjoying* Debby Boone.

By the end of that first Insight, I admired Russell, but I adored Victor. No matter how much my self-esteem had been bolstered during the last round of positivity, however, I still couldn't find it in my imagination to be worthy of Victor.

John-Roger, it seems, had no such unworthiness. I was to learn, much to my surprise, that he was having sex with Victor on a regular basis—much to Victor's disgust. A few years later, Victor discovered, much to his surprise, that this "unique spiritual gift" was not something that John-Roger shared with him exclusively; the gift was more widely distributed than Victor, in 1978, could have imagined.

CHAPTER FIVE
a.k.a. Roger Delano Hinkins

MEPHISTOPHELES *steps forth from behind the stove while the vapour is vanishing. He is dressed as a traveling scholar.*

GOETHE
Stage direction,
FAUST

JOHN-ROGER is a fictitious name—not unlike the "Mystical Traveler Consciousness"—Roger Delano Hinkins bestowed upon himself. The "Delano" should not imply that he was an heir—or even an offspring—of any of that Delano money back East. No. When Roger Hinkins was born into a poor coal-mining family on September 24, 1934, his mother gave him the middle name of Delano because it was the depth of the Depression and she was an admirer of the new president, Franklin Delano Roosevelt.

Nineteen-thirty-four also saw the birth of L'il Abner, Flash Gordon, Mary Poppins, Laundromats ("Washaterias"), Alcatraz, MSG, and polyethylene.

The Utah coal-mining town in which John-Roger, his brother, and three sisters were born and raised is no longer there. It's not that it's a ghost town like so many others that dot the mining regions of Utah and Colorado—the town *is simply not there at all.* Just land, lots of land. One wonders: who would go to all the trouble to *de*-construct a town? Hitler did it with Lidice as a warning to other presumptuous towns that defied his authority.* But who would *un*-build Rains, Utah?

*On the day Hitler proclaimed to the world, "Lidicé is no more!" the artist Barton Lidicé Beneš was born. In so naming him, his father proclaimed, "Lidicé lives!"

> *The representative*
> *of the highest spiritual*
> *authority of the earth is glad,*
> *indeed boasts,*
> *of being the son of*
> *a humble but robust*
> *and honest laborer.*
>
> POPE JOHN XXIII

The town that was so much a part of Roger Hinkins's life is no more. That's true of a lot of Roger Hinkins's life history—it is simply not there. Most of what is known about him comes from John-Roger himself, and is mostly anecdotes. These reports are, of course, not entirely reliable (note my gift for understatement), coming from a man who is not only known to embellish anecdotes, but also to invent anecdotes and *then* embellish them.

For example: he tells the story that, as an early adolescent, his best friend committed suicide by hanging himself. Roger Hinkins, private eye, got to work on the case and proved that although the young man did put the noose around his neck, he had, in fact, slipped on some water conveniently discovered by young Roger. The hanged boy's family was eternally grateful to Roger for removing the "stigma" of a son who committed suicide. It did, however, bring up the question of yet another stigma: what was he doing with a noose around his neck in the first place?

Here, a plausible story becomes unlikely. Young Roger said—and the older John-Roger maintains—that some of his friends would practice hanging themselves, so that they could use it to frighten people. Not a typical skill boys want to develop. More likely, the friends had discovered the autoerotic qualities of a noose and partial strangulation not unknown to pubescent boys.

Alas, it's unlikely that we will ever know. John-Roger used the boy's death to emphasize young Roger's extraordinary sleuthing capabilities, nothing more.

He clearly idolizes his parents, romanticizing their memory far beyond an average person's. In his stories, his parents are hard-working, ordinary people who were both citadels of integrity, decency, and, most of all, *wisdom*. To hear John-Roger tell it, it was like being raised by Confucius, Judge Hardy, and Ward Cleaver all rolled into one—and that was just his mother. His father was part Jed Clampett, part Henry Kissinger, and part Brigham Young.

Those observing his life from the outside describe a father who didn't much like his son and a mother who was too forgiving, too attentive, too adoring. While the father liked Roger's rugged, outdoorsman brother better, the mother did what she could to protect her more sensitive son from the harsh realities of a Depression-then-wartime Utah coal mining town.

A man who has been the indisputable favorite of his mother keeps for life the feeling of a conqueror.

SIGMUND FREUD

Roger's youth, according to Roger, was a wondrous MGM-backlot childhood with an occasional round of fisticuffs (which young Roger won but then immediately remonstrated himself for); the pressures of the sprint and the loneliness of the long-distance runner in his chosen sport, track; and the heartbreak of an unrequited love.

In the latter, young Roger gave his high school letter sweater (his prized possession) to the girl he adored, only to discover that she had used it as a rag mop for cleaning the kitchen floor. Dad's sage advice to the brokenhearted Roger: "Son, the best cure for a woman is another woman." This bit of fatherly advice—popular, but psychologically unsound—would set the stage for all of John-Roger's future relationships. He sees all people (not just people we lust after, but people we love) as interchangeable. Lose one, pick up another, like a pack of matches. This also meant people were not just interchangeable, but *disposable*.

Combining his mother's unquestioning adoration and his father's people-we-love-are-interchangeable-parts philosophy may account for the adult John-Roger's inability to handle loss. Rather than mourn and move on, John-Roger fluctuates between "I'll get you!" and "Who the hell wants you anyway?" This unstable oscillation between revenge and denial is the cause of a great deal of misery in John-Roger's life, and of untold torment for those around him—especially, for those close to him who have left.

Is it little wonder, then, that his stock advice to those threatened with the loss of employment is: "Tell your boss: 'I was looking for a job when I found this one!' and walk out," or that his favorite song is "Got Along Without Ya Before I Met Ya, Gonna Get Along Without Ya Now."

⚖ ⚖ ⚖

> *It is when the gods hate a man with uncommon abhorrence that they drive him into the profession of a schoolmaster.*
>
> SENECA
> (c. 5–65)

At some point in the early 1950s, Roger moved from Rains to Salt Lake City. In later years, he would talk about his experiences as a police officer. In fact, he was, briefly, a part-time switchboard operator for the Salt Lake City police department. His "extensive work with patients in a psychiatric hospital" was as an orderly on the night shift: by the time Roger arrived for work each evening, the patients were sleeping their heavily sedated sleeps, and Roger's main function was to clean up the mess made during the day. He also claimed to be so revered by the hierarchy of the Mormon church that they once offered him the leadership of the entire organization. Not likely, as the leader of the Mormon church is the Prophet, and the Prophet is the oldest surviving member of the twelve Apostles of the Church. Roger, around twenty-five, was about half-a-century too young for Prophet.

In 1958, he received a degree in psychology from the University of Utah, packed his car and headed for San Francisco. He told me he worked there as an insurance adjustor. According to John-Roger, Roger Hinkins was no ordinary claims adjustor. He was the Columbo of insurance claims.

San Francisco in the late 1950s was a hotbed of Eastern religions, cultural experimentation, and unconventional spiritual practices. Sometimes all three combined. Roger made the rounds. He called himself a "metaphizzle."

In late 1963, while the world was mourning the death of John F. Kennedy, Roger Hinkins had a gall bladder operation. By this time, he had landed a job as a high school English teacher (just what every psychology major dreams of) in Rosemead, California. Rosemead—even in 1963—was one of the less-fashionable suburbs of Los Angeles.

Due to what was probably a sedative overdose, Roger Hinkins went into a nine-day coma. When he awoke, he was either enlightened or brain damaged—take your pick. He claimed to be both Roger Hinkins and another "being" who sometimes called itself "The Beloved" and sometimes called itself "John." Roger Hinkins put the two names together and pronounced himself possessed by John the Beloved. Although he probably would have been diagnosed as a schizophrenic at the Salt Lake City mental institution where he once worked, Roger Hinkins instead felt blessed by the presence of John the Beloved, the favored disciple of Jesus.*

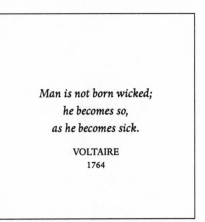

*Man is not born wicked;
he becomes so,
as he becomes sick.*

VOLTAIRE
1764

Whatever this awakening or brain damage was, it was apparently not enough to warrant his abandoning his post at Rosemead High. He continued there until 1970, when the principal, acting on complaints from the students that entire periods were spent by Mr. Hinkins teaching self-hypnosis and not American literature, visited Mr. Hinkins's third period class. Opening the door, the principal discovered, "It was just as dark as pitch. Usually I'm a very calm person, but I blew up right there. I turned the lights on. I jarred the kids right out of their reverie," he told the *Los Angeles Times.* "Right in front of the whole class, I said, 'Mr. Hinkins . . . I never want this sort of nonsense to happen again!'"

It never did. Mr. Hinkins got the sack. Or, in the more delicate vernacular of teaching, it was mutually decided by the principal and Mr. Hinkins that what Mr. Hinkins wanted to teach, Rosemead High didn't want taught, and vice versa.

From the mid-to-late 1960s—even after supposedly receiving the Mystical Traveler Consciousness in 1963—John-Roger's primary study was with Eckankar, a successful, worldwide spiritual group founded by Paul Twitchell. According to David Lane, Ph.D., who investigated both Eckankar and John-Roger extensively, John-Roger was a second-level Eckankar initiate and held Eckankar seminars—known as *satsang*—in his Rosemead, California, home while still a high school teacher.

Even then, however, John-Roger hardly presented traditional Eckankar satsang: he would "channel" the "spirit of Brother Paul" (Paul Twitchell). This allowed Sri John-Roger Hinkins to appear more spiritual and more connected than your average run-of-the-

*Interestingly, John is only referred to as "the Beloved" of Jesus in the Gospel written by John. Thus, we only know that John was "the Beloved" of Jesus because *John* said so. This is an absolute hallmark of John-Roger's claim to divinity: John-Roger is divine because John-Roger *says* John-Roger is divine.

mill satsang slinger. It also allowed Dr. John-Roger Hinkins (the Sri and Dr. seemed interchangeable, but whoever or whatever bestowed him with such honors is a mystery) to modify Eckankar teachings to his personal point of view.

> The vanity of teaching
> often tempts a man to forget
> he is a blockhead.
>
> LORD HALIFAX

The major problem was that Paul Twitchell was still very much alive and didn't really *need* any channeling, thank you very much.*

When Paul Twitchell died in 1971, the Eckankar organization needed a new leader. The leader of Eckankar is known as the Spiritual Traveler. The selection was to be made in Las Vegas,** so John-Roger Hinkins traveled to the gambling center of the United States and applied for the job. He no doubt claimed to have channeled any number of messages from "Brother Paul" (especially now that Brother Paul was no longer around to contradict such messages) stating that the next leader of Eckankar should be someone "with the initials J-R.H." The Eckankar hierarchy was not impressed, and J-R.H. did not get the job.

Like so many other hopeful Las Vegas visitors, John-Roger went bust. In a style that would soon become his personal trademark, "poor me" almost immediately became "the hell with you," and John-Roger simply stole the Eckankar teachings, claiming they were his own.*** When the Eckankar organization threatened to sue, Sri John-Roger Hinkins made one minor alteration: he changed the name of his special consciousness from Spiritual Traveler to Mys-

---

*One can only imagine with what fury John-Roger would respond if he heard that one of *his* seminar leaders—who are under strict instructions to call in the Light, chant *ani-hu* for a few minutes, put on a John-Roger audio or video tape, collect some money, forward it to MSIA, and that's it—began "channeling the spirit of brother John-Roger." Such an errant seminar leader would get a stern letter from MSIA faster than you could say, "Knock it off, you presumptuous insect."

**According to Dr. Lane, Eckankar started in San Diego in 1965, but soon moved to Las Vegas for tax reasons.

***Ironically, unknown to John-Roger, Paul Twitchell had stolen the Eckankar teachings from the Radhasoami tradition of Northern India. (Twitchell's pilferage is detailed in David Lane's book, *Making of a Spiritual Movement,* Del Mar Press, Del Mar, California.)

tical Traveler. And, to trump Paul Twitchell permanently, *Dr. John-Roger Hinkins* also gave himself the Preceptor Consciousness, which is superior to *all* Travelers—Mystical, Spiritual, or Arkansas.

> *The true teacher defends his pupils*
> *against his own personal influence.*
> *He inspires self-trust.*
> *He guides their eyes from himself*
> *to the spirit that quickens him.*
> *He will have no disciple.*
>
> AMOS BRONSON ALCOTT
> 1840

With a less-than-stellar departure from a less-than-stellar high school, Mr. Hinkins was not likely to get another teaching job anytime soon. So, he went into the guru business. Living room lectures were set up by his former high-school students and people he met on the "metaphizzle circuit," as he put it. These were held in private homes, and reached from Santa Barbara to San Diego. The "love offering" was $3.00 per person, and with twenty to forty people per living room per evening, Sri John-Roger, guru, was making $60 to $120 per night—not bad for the early 1970s. The die was fully cast in 1971 when the son of a prominent financier turned over a large segment of his fortune to John-Roger, and a brother and sister turned over $80,000 each—their entire inheritance—so that John-Roger could more fully do his "spiritual work."*

Good-bye Mr. Hinkins, hello John-Roger.

Large sums of money meant the tax people might come sniffing around, so John-Roger set up a tax-exempt, nonprofit organization called the Church of the Movement of Spiritual Inner Awareness.

Following the example set by the pigs in George Orwell's *Animal Farm*, who continuously revised their principles to keep themselves always in control, quite a number of John-Roger's early teachings are no longer taught. For example, John-Roger said that the "office" of the Mystical Traveler Consciousness was held by a single individual for only a few years at most. After John-Roger held the office (and the houses, and the cars, and the staff, and the

---

*Although the brother and sister who donated their entire inheritances to John-Roger have left the Movement—and both proclaim John-Roger a charlatan—the son of the financier is still with John-Roger. John-Roger has convinced this man that he (John-Roger), through spiritual intervention, saved the man's life. This man has turned over all of his money to John-Roger, continues to turn over any family inheritance he receives, and currently works for no pay at John-Roger's ranch shoveling horse manure. Literally.

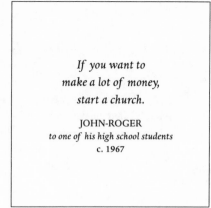

If you want to
make a lot of money,
start a church.

JOHN-ROGER
to one of his high school students
c. 1967

adoration) of the Traveler for significantly longer than a few years, that teaching fell by the wayside. John-Roger also taught that there was one and only one Mystical Traveler at a time. This was no longer mentioned when John Donnelley-Morton became a Mystical Traveler, too. A letter from the "Movement of Spiritual Inner Awareness, Inc." dated July 5, 1988, announced the "passing of the keys":

> We have joyful news that we want to share with you. At the Initiates Meeting on June 19, 1988, John-Roger passed the keys to the Mystical Traveler Consciousness to John Morton. J-R also said that he still holds the Mystical Traveler and Preceptor Consciousnesses.

And then there's Sai Baba. Sai Baba has an enormous following in India. One of the secrets of his success is that his followers believe he can materialize things. From trinkets to diamonds, the gifts Sai Baba gives his devotees are said to come (literally) from his hands. There is also said to be a special box in which the necessary funds to pay all Sai Baba's bills can perpetually be found. Thus, Sai Baba's followers receive, but they never have to give. In this country, he'd be elected president.

John-Roger took his closest devotees (that is, the ones he liked plus whoever could afford it) to India to meet Sai Baba. John-Roger was taken by Sai Baba—*and* by the tens of thousands of worshipers who hung on Sai Baba's every word. Sai Baba offered to perform a special ceremony on specially selected male John-Roger followers. (John-Roger was not selected.) The five-minute private ceremony involved "anointing" the genitalia of said male followers with "bachelor oil." The anointing with bachelor oil assured that the celibacy desired by the spiritually seeking male would be easy.

Although John-Roger ridiculed Sai Baba for such practices, John-Roger himself was, by that time, using similar spiritual promises to get far more elaborate sexual favors from handsome male members of his own staff—and handsome non-staff devotees as well.

Upon returning to America, John-Roger declared Sai Baba "the physical leader of the Movement of Spiritual Inner Awareness." When Sai Baba made it clear that he had no desire for John-Roger to lead his American contingent, the divinity of Sai Baba in John-Roger's eyes diminished. Then it turned nasty. John-Roger wondered aloud why a piece of gift jewelry materialized by Sai Baba turned his skin green. "A *real* avatar could manifest gold as easily as copper," he said, implying that Sai Baba did it all through sleight-of-hand.

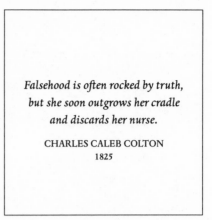

Falsehood is often rocked by truth,
but she soon outgrows her cradle
and discards her nurse.

CHARLES CALEB COLTON
1825

Those who knew John-Roger in the early 1970s say he was a different man than he is now. One, who later became a psychologist, claims that John-Roger went through a "personality disintegration" during the later 1970s. The John-Roger of the early 1970s was a warmer, kinder, more loving man—a man who, to a great many, lived what he taught.

By the early 1980s, this was no longer true.

The disintegration must have been well on the way by 1977. In that year, a minister drove his pickup truck to John-Roger's Mandeville Canyon home to help one of John-Roger's live-in staff move to an apartment closer to the university where the young man wanted to complete his education. His meager possessions were all he had after years of working full-time for John-Roger as a live-in volunteer.

Earlier, during a seminar, John-Roger had praised this young man for taking such good care of John-Roger's father as he slowly died of cancer. His appreciation was heartfelt and tearful. Today, however, John-Roger saw the young man's return to school as an abandonment of John-Roger.

John-Roger ran from the house, yelling, "Are you trying to *steal* Church property? *God's* property?"

He began grabbing possessions from the trailer and throwing them on the dirt driveway. "You're not taking *this* Church property!" he would scream with each item he threw to the ground.

Mostly it was books the young man had collected. He had marked pages and highlighted text. They were the young man's most prized possessions. John-Roger threw them, one by one, into the dust.

> There is a lot
> of spiritual deceit that goes on.
> The word level
> can be very deceitful,
> but give people time
> and most of them
> will demonstrate by action
> where they are spiritually.
>
> JOHN-ROGER
> 1977

As he destroyed the young man's books, John-Roger yelled that the young man was cut off from Spirit through all eternity; that his "turning from the Light [John-Roger]" was an unforgivable "spiritual crime"; that he was hopelessly lost to the "Kal [negative] power."

The young man was crying uncontrollably.

"Please, J-R, please . . ." he kept saying, begging for his books; begging for his immortal soul.

The minister looked on in horror. Then John-Roger started on the cardboard box containing the young man's few meager clothes. These too he cast in the dirt.

"God paid for these clothes," John-Roger screamed, "and no minister of the Kal power is going to get them!"

"John-Roger, I need my *clothes!*" the young man begged between sobs, "Please let me have my clothes. Let me *buy* them."

John-Roger stopped. "Bring me one hundred dollars, cash, and you can have the clothes." At this he turned and walked in the house, stepping on as many articles of clothing and books as possible.

The young man, having lived under a John-Roger–required vow of poverty for eight years, had no money. The minister didn't have one hundred dollars, either, but drove the young man—still crying—to someone who did and would loan it to him.

They returned and, as they drove into the compound, John-Roger walked out the front door. He was just behind the door, watching all the time.

"Do you have the money?" John-Roger asked in the tone of a kidnaper asking for the ransom in a B-movie. The young man handed over one hundred dollars. John-Roger *counted it.*

"All right," John-Roger said, and watched carefully as the young man packed his dusty clothes. They filled one cardboard box. He was not permitted to take "God's" books.

The psychologist who noticed the personality disintegration lived and worked with John-Roger for thirteen years. In that time John-Roger developed, according to this psychologist what is known as a Narcissistic Personality Disorder. This diagnosis was confirmed by two psychiatrists who knew John-Roger well.

According to the *Diagnostic Statistical Manual,* which is the standard diagnostic reference tool for psychiatrists and most psychologists:

> *Men first feel necessity,*
> *then look for utility,*
> *next attend to comfort,*
> *still later amuse themselves*
> *with pleasure, thence grow*
> *dissolute in luxury,*
> *and finally go mad*
> *and waste their substance.*
>
> GIAMBATTISTA VICO
> 1744

Diagnostic criteria for 301.81 Narcissistic Personality Disorder

A pervasive pattern of grandiosity (in fantasy or behavior), lack of empathy, and hypersensitivity to the evaluation of others, beginning by early adulthood and present in a variety of contexts, as indicated by at least *five* of the following:

(1) reacts to criticism with feelings of rage, shame, or humiliation (even if not expressed)

(2) is interpersonally exploitative: takes advantage of others to achieve his or her own ends

(3) has grandiose sense of self-importance, e.g., exaggerates achievements and talents, expects to be noticed as "special" without appropriate achievement

(4) believes that his or her problems are unique and can be understood only by other special people

(5) is preoccupied with fantasies of unlimited success, power, brilliance, beauty, or ideal love

(6) has a sense of entitlement: unreasonable expectation of especially favorable treatment, e.g., assumes that he or she does not have to wait in line when others must do so

(7) requires constant attention and admiration, e.g., keeps fishing for compliments

(8) lack of empathy: inability to recognize and experience how others feel, e.g., annoyance and surprise when a friend who is seriously ill cancels a date

(9) is preoccupied with feelings of envy

Sure sounds like John-Roger to me. I read these characteristics to several other members of his staff who left from 1983 through 1988. They *all* give John-Roger a perfect "9 out of 9."

One psychiatrist who knew John-Roger well explained to me that John-Roger is psychotic; specifically, a sociopath. This means John-

> No man,
> for any considerable period,
> can wear one face to himself,
> and another to the multitude,
> without finally getting bewildered
> as to which may be the true.
>
> NATHANIEL HAWTHORNE
> 1850

Roger thinks nothing of hurting or even destroying anyone in order to get what he wants. This allows him to lie, cheat, steal, deceive, embarrass, humiliate, threaten, harass, use physical force or violence without even a twinge of guilt, shame, or fear of retribution. John-Roger is quite proud of his total lack of remorse, claiming this lack of "negativity" is just another sign of his evolved spiritual state.

Like a spoiled child, John-Roger wants what John-Roger wants when John-Roger wants it. Whatever it takes for John-Roger to get what he wants is, as far as John-Roger is concerned, perfectly acceptable behavior.

Those who believe John-Roger is the most God-connected human on earth in 25,000 years become—where John-Roger is concerned—sociopaths, too. His loyal followers will do *anything* to make John-Roger happy. All the laws of society and human decency are subservient to the Law of God, and John-Roger's desires are the closest thing we have on earth to God's Pure Law.

Some of John-Roger's followers, who wouldn't *dream* of hurting anyone in any other circumstances, would hurt any person or break any law if they thought it was necessary to get J-R (God) what he (God) wanted. Perhaps psychiatry should add a new subcategory to sociopaths: the *spiritual* sociopath. These are truly upright, moral, and do-no-harm people *except* when they think God's Will is involved. John-Roger is a *pure* sociopath; he *creates* spiritual sociopaths.

I should know. I was one of them.

Different people have given different reasons as to the cause of John-Roger's Narcissistic Personality Disorder and his sociopathic behavior.

Some say as John-Roger became increasingly surrounded by sycophants—he started to actually *believe* that he was God. Others say it's an ongoing mental degeneration caused by the nine-day coma and its after-effects. Others say it's simply his unhealthy lifestyle and drug abuse.

By the 1970s, John-Roger had left his track-star days far behind.

He'd become entirely seden-
tary. He read books or
watched TV. His diet was red
meat and sugar. While he surrounded himself with healthy
eaters who seemed to enjoy
carrot juice, raw vegetables,
and yogurt, John-Roger would
have none of it. Eggs and
bacon for breakfast, meat for
lunch, meat for dinner, and
desserts all around. (I once

> *Power intoxicates men.*
> *When a man is intoxicated*
> *by alcohol*
> *he can recover,*
> *but when intoxicated*
> *by power*
> *he seldom recovers.*
>
> JAMES F. BYRNES

saw him finish off three—count 'em three—chocolate milkshakes
at Denny's while discussing how much weight he had lost on his
current diet. This was after a cheeseburger deluxe with a double
order of fries. The coleslaw went untouched.)

While there's little evidence to support the idea that John-
Roger dabbled in illegal drugs, his abuse of prescriptive medication is well-documented. According to one of his former staff
members, John-Roger's bathroom shelf was lined with hundreds
of bottles of over-the-counter and prescription medications. In his
early Movement years, he was addicted to a nasal decongestant
that also had a "kick" to it. He sprayed and sniffed continuously—
even during seminars.

Soon, Percodan became his favorite. Any health-care professional in the Movement capable of writing a prescription would
find him- or herself spiritually flattered by John-Roger, followed by
a phrase they became accustomed to, "How about a 'script
for . . . ." The drug game John-Roger played: as long as it was obtained through a prescription, it was okay. He was, however, excessively self-righteous about recreational chemicals obtained in *non*-
prescriptive ways. People were warned that if they took any
"illegal" drugs in the two years they were waiting for their first
initiation, they were not likely to get it. The annual ministerial
renewal form included a question, "In the past year, have you taken
any non-prescription, illegal drugs?" If the answer was yes, the
chances were very high that the ministerial credentials would be
revoked. In J-R's Drug Policy, if you purchased, say, Dexedrine on the
street, that was wicked. If you could flatter or deceive a physician
into prescribing Dexedrine, that was just fine.

In addition to Percodan, John-Roger's ongoing drug of choice
seemed to be alcohol. He claimed that when alcohol touched his lips,

> ... thus by his fraud,
> and by the assistance of
> his cunning servants,
> he obtained the kingdom;
>
> BOOK OF MORMON
> Alma 47:35

it became water. This allowed him to drink heavily and appear to remain a teetotaler at the same time. Why, if alcohol became water, he didn't drink water—far less expensive than alcohol—was never explained. To say John-Roger drank like a fish does an injustice to fish.

Whatever the reason, there seems to have been a degeneration from the early 1970s to the early 1980s. Many of the people who still follow John-Roger from "the old days" remember his kinder times, and chalk up almost two decades of cruelty, ill-temper, and extreme moodiness to "he's just not feeling well." Considering his hypochondria, that's true: he *never* feels well.

⚖️ ⚖️ ⚖️

By the time Russell Bishop brought Lifespring and laid it on John-Roger's altar, saying, "Let's carve it up and call it Insight," the pattern had been set. John-Roger was it.

No.

John-Roger was *IT!*

Never again would he be subservient to anyone else's thought, opinion, or philosophy. Never again would he try to join forces with another spiritual or temporal teacher. Those who were not willing to accept John-Roger as IT could seek their ITness elsewhere. All the new faces flowing in through Insight proved to him that his IT was as irresistible as gravity; destined to draw innumerable lesser ITs to him.

From 1985 on, John-Roger increasingly isolated himself, which made him more and more testy, which made him isolate himself even more. He preached love and openness and sharing while practicing just the opposite.

John-Roger explained that, like Job, pain is what you get when you are God's favorite.

CHAPTER SIX

My First John-Roger Seminars

> Whatever deceives
> seems to produce a
> magical enchantment.
>
> PLATO

SEPTEMBER 1978. Before leaving that first Insight in Philadelphia, I was given—several times—the address of the taped John-Roger seminars in New York, which just happened to be the New York Insight office. I was asked to commit to attending at least three seminars before making up my mind about John-Roger.

I agreed.

The John-Roger taped seminars were held on Monday nights in a pleasant loft on Canal Street in lower Manhattan. It was good to see some of the Insight people again. Prior to watching the video tape, everyone sat in a circle on the floor, the Light was called in, John-Roger was asked to (by remote) heal everyone and remove any karma or negativity that might be released, and each person in the circle was given an opportunity to "make a contribution."

A candle was passed around. The person holding the candle could contribute anything he or she wanted. Sometimes it was a story from the previous week, sometimes a problem, sometimes a "win"; sometimes it was placing something or someone in the Light for the highest good.

Contributions done, everyone lay down on the carpeted floor (pillows were everywhere) and got comfortable. The lights went out and they showed the video seminar. There was John-Roger, in his Hawaiian shirt, explaining how essential he was to the functioning of the planet earth, how cozy he was with God (none cozier), and how those who reject his teachings *might* get another chance after 25,000 years—or was it 25,000 incarnations?

I was appalled. What arrogance. What megalomania. What a lousy shirt.

> *Always make the audience suffer as much as possible.*
>
> ALFRED HITCHCOCK

It reminded me of a Gilbert and Sullivan song:

> *You must lie upon the daisies*
> *and discourse in novel phrases*
> *of your complicated state of mind,*
> *The meaning doesn't matter*
> *if it's only idle chatter*
> *of a transcendental kind.*
> *And everyone will say,*
> *As you walk your mystic way,*
> *'If this young man expresses himself*
> *in terms too deep for me,*
> *Why, what a very singularly deep young man*
> *this deep young man must be!'*

One grueling hour later, the video was over. The Light was called in again (had it left?), and the formal part of the evening was over. Cookies, apple juice, and milk were served. There was general milling and chatting. Some asked me what I thought of the seminar. I smiled my best Henry Kissinger smile and said that it certainly had made an impression on me. When people heard that this was my first John-Roger seminar, they became excited:

"John-Roger will come to you in your sleep tonight and give you your astral initiation!"

Oh, joy. Would I get a Hawaiian shirt, too? But out loud I asked, batting my eyelids ever so slightly, "Astral initiation? What's that?"

"The astral initiation," I was told, "is when John-Roger comes to you in your dreams and initiates you to the astral level of consciousness."

"Oh," I said. I knew no more than I did before I asked the question, but for some reason I no longer wanted to know the answer. The information, nevertheless, continued:

"John-Roger comes to you while you're sleeping and shows you all your past lifetimes and how terrible they were, and all your future lifetimes and how terrible they will be if you don't accept the gift of the Traveler Consciousness."

It is piteously doleful, nodding every now and then towards dulness; well stored with pious frauds, and like most discourses of the sort, much better calculated for the private advantage of the preacher than the edification of the hearers.

EDMUND BURKE
1770

"The gift of the Traveler Consciousness?" I heard myself asking, a reporter's reflex.

"Yes. The gift of the Traveler Consciousness comes directly from God and it allows you to bypass all the psychic-material levels and go directly home to the heart of God *in this lifetime!*"

"Hmmm," I hmmmed.

"Then if you want the gift of the Traveler Consciousness, John-Roger initiates you into the astral realm, right there in your dreams!"

A little explanation at this point seems more than in order. According to John-Roger's cosmology,* the "psychic-material worlds" are made up of five levels: the *physical, astral, causal, mental,* and *etheric,* all of which terminate in *Soul.* Climbing "the golden staircase to Soul" is our purpose on this earth. John-Roger gives each of his followers a leg-up on each rung of the ladder by *initiating* the follower's movement into the next higher realm. Thus, there are physical, astral, causal, mental, etheric, and Soul initiations.

The physical initiation happens when we are born: we initiate our physical journey on this planet. John-Roger, through the Mystical Traveler Consciousness, takes care of the physical initiation at birth (don't tell Mom). He then sort of hangs around until such time as (a) one hears about John-Roger, (b) one sees a photograph of John-Roger, or (c) one hears John-Roger's voice. That night, when one is in the "dream state," John-Roger visits and reviews all

*And there will not be a test on *any* of this.

the terrible past lifetimes, etc.

Those perceptive, fortunate, and clever enough to accept the gift of the Traveler then find themselves at some event sponsored by one of the organizations founded by John-Roger. There they hear about seminars, eventually get on Discourses, and everlasting joy follows shortly thereafter. (According to John-Roger's teachings, one certainly need not die for the joy to begin.)

> Only among people
> who think no evil
> can Evil monstrously flourish.
>
> LOGAN PEARSALL SMITH

If, on the other hand, you are wretched, wicked, and ungrateful enough to turn down the astral initiation in your dreams, you will get another chance, if you are good, in roughly 25,000 years (give or take a tape-seminar Monday).

After two years of studying with John-Roger, one is entitled to request the causal initiation. Requesting it doesn't mean you'll get it, but almost everyone does. This sets up the pattern—which becomes increasingly ingrained with future initiations—that one's relationship with John-Roger in the *physical* world is directly connected to how well you do in the *spiritual* world. In fact, there are no further guidelines as to when one might receive the mental, etheric, and much-sought-after-but-hard-to-get Soul initiations— it's all based on John-Roger's whim. To get them, one makes a written request, and John-Roger eventually responds yea or nay.

But those initiations for me were *years* away, and here I was, in 1978, standing opposite someone after my first John-Roger seminar, being encouraged to accept the gift of the Traveler Consciousness when John-Roger crept into my sleep that night, because I wouldn't get another chance until 26,978 A.D.

She was so hopeful that I would say, "Yes! I promise to accept!" that I hated to tell her the disappointing news: I had heard of John-Roger *and* seen his picture (seen his whole body, in fact) and heard the sound of his voice at Insight the week before. The news, however, was far from disappointing to this devotee: she became ecstatic. If I had been with John-Roger's "physical form" last week, then I *certainly* was visited by John-Roger in the dream state *that night,* and since I was attending a John-Roger seminar, that meant I *had* chosen to accept the gift of the Traveler's Consciousness—I was, after all, attending the seminar that night.

This circular (or was it centripetal?) logic was sufficient unto her, and she gathered others around her who heard the Good News of my recent astral initiation and my choice to follow John-Roger back to the heart of God. I was congratulated enthusiastically, and I was hugged and wel-

> *The avaricious man is like*
> *the barren sandy*
> *ground of the desert*
> *which sucks in all the rain and dew*
> *with greediness,*
> *but yields no fruitful*
> *herbs or plants for*
> *the benefit of others.*
>
> ZENO

comed and it felt like Insight all over again. Together again for the first time: the devotees of John-Roger.

There was only one problem: I couldn't stand the guy.

⚖️ ⚖️ ⚖️

A week later, I returned for my second seminar. I said I'd do three, and a commitment, after all, is a commitment. Besides, I was curious to see how much worse it could get. Also, I missed the Insight people.

The video seminar was full of more "look-at-me-I'm-God" prattlings from John-Roger, but this week I didn't mind it as much. After, it was *chocolate cake* and milk. Ummm. And the people were so nice.

I was lovingly encouraged to "get on Discourses." Discourses are John-Roger's primary form of spiritual teaching. Pay $100 for twelve Discourses, read one Discourse a month, and enlightenment (or, in MSIA parlance, *soul transcendence*) was guaranteed.* There are twelve years' worth of Discourses—144 in all. The Discourses are numbered, not surprisingly, 1 through 144. There's a certain social strata at MSIA vaguely related to Discourse number. "Which Discourse are you on?" is a common question. But that's not as significant as the answer to the question: "What level *initiation* do you have?" But more on that later.

---

*I was later to learn that John-Roger did not write the Discourses; in fact, John-Roger wrote almost nothing that had John-Roger's name on it—certainly very little published material. The very concept and name "Discourses" was pilfered from Eckankar.

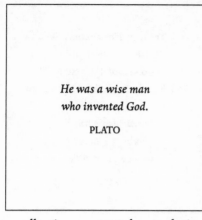

He was a wise man who invented God.

PLATO

By the third week of taped seminars, I felt part of the group. I decided the best way to get through the video portions of the evening was to ignore the my-good-friend-God stuff and listen to whatever practical suggestions John-Roger might have to offer. In his scatter-shot speaking style of homilies, anecdotes, "good advice," bad jokes, childhood recollections, personal growth tips, spiritual explanations, and, of course, the ubiquitous message, "J-R is God," there was at least one thought worth considering—and it was fine to go to sleep during the rest of it. John-Roger said so; encouraged it, in fact. And then there was the soft, carpeted floor, and the pillows. After all, if you fell asleep during a seminar, it wasn't sleep at all: it was Soul Travel.

Soul Travel or subliminal programming?

Funny, I didn't even consider that as I nodded off.

CHAPTER SEVEN

The Mystical Traveler and Preceptor Consciousness

> *Trying to put into words*
> *what J-R does is difficult at best.*
> *And in speaking with new people,*
> *terms like Mystical Traveler*
> *or Preceptor*
> *are even more difficult to explain.*
>
> MSIA
> *Handbook for Ministers of Light*

A LLOW ME to give you a summary of who John-Roger claims to be spiritually and a short summary of his teachings in a format that—I hope—won't put you to sleep.

John-Roger claims to be the "physical embodiment" of the Mystical Traveler Consciousness and the Preceptor Consciousness.

Let's get the Preceptor Consciousness out of the way first: no one knows what the hell the Preceptor Consciousness is.

If you look up *preceptor* in the dictionary, you'll find it's just a fancy word for *teacher*. All that we know about the Preceptor Consciousness, as "physically embodied by John-Roger," is that it only comes around once every 25,000 years, and John-Roger is it. When he goes, it goes. No matter what level of consciousness one may achieve in this lifetime, this once-in-two-hundred-fifty-millennia Preceptor Consciousness permanently keeps John-Roger superior—at least in John-Roger's cosmology—for the *past* 25,000 years and the *next* 25,000 years. The ultimate spiritual trump card. That's it on the Preceptor Consciousness.

On the other hand, John-Roger has given a great deal more information—entirely too much, some might say—about the Mystical Traveler Consciousness. In fact, the term *Mystical Traveler* is simply one coined by John-Roger. Hence, he can define it any which way he chooses, depending on what he wants from a situ-

> Faith, *n. Belief without evidence in what is told by one who speaks without knowledge.*
>
> AMBROSE BIERCE

ation. By coining his own essentially meaningless phrase (he could have chosen Cosmic Rider, Universal Mover, Transcendental Journeyer, or any other*), John-Roger becomes at once the foremost authority on the Mystical Traveler, the ultimate arbitrator in any disputes concerning it, and its physical embodiment.

The Mystical Traveler is a direct link to God. According to John-Roger's teachings, a mystical traveler is in each of us; we just aren't aware of it as fully as we might be. *The* Mystical Traveler *is* John-Roger. According to John-Roger, he is fully aware of the Mystical Traveler Consciousness within him, and also maintains complete *conscious* awareness of *all levels,* inner and outer, known and unknown, here and hereafter, throughout the universe. (No wonder the guy has so much trouble sleeping.) Because John-Roger has this ability, the "mantle" of the Mystical Traveler Consciousness was given to him. (Or was he given the mantle and then these abilities erupted? I forget.)

Some ask: "What is the connection between John-Roger and Jesus?" This quote from John-Roger should explain that:

> The line of authority starts with Melchizedek. Melchizedek was the High Priest . . . He was a direct radiation or emanation of the man who later came as Jesus Christ. At that time the Priesthood of Melchizedek was established on the planet.
>
> The step above that is the office of the Christ. The office of the Christ would be like the presidency of some country. Many people can occupy that job. . . . When Jesus came on the planet he occupied the office of the Christ.
>
> Above that is the Mystical Traveler Consciousness. Now, Melchizedek instituted the law of tithing. Christ instituted the Light of the world. Jesus said, "While I am in the world I am the Light of the world." When he left the world there were Travelers present. The Travelers are the Light of the

---

*Actually, John-Roger only coined *half* of it: Paul Twitchell, founder of Eckankar, which John-Roger studied in the mid-1960s, called himself the Spiritual Traveler. By the late 1960s, John-Roger was calling himself the Spiritual Traveler, too. (Spiritual Traveler II?) The Eckankar organization did not like this one little bit, and threatened to sue. John-Roger went from Spiritual to Mystical.

universe. So they don't deal specifically with just the earth. That comes under what we call the messiah or the Christ. The Traveler's job goes through many universes and planets. The Preceptor Consciousness is one that goes clear outside of creation. It goes beyond your imagination. But that is the direct line of authority into God.

> *And Jesus answered*
> *and said unto them,*
> *Take heed that*
> *no man deceive you.*
> *For many shall come in my name,*
> *saying, I am Christ;*
> *and shall deceive many.*
>
> MATTHEW 24: 4–5

In other words, John-Roger is far greater than Jesus.

According to John-Roger, there has always been—and will always need to be—someone "in the physical body" on this planet "anchoring" the Mystical Traveler Consciousness. That is, throughout history, there has been one person on the planet earth who *consciously knew* he or she (although they seem to be disproportionately he's) was the Mystical Traveler. The person anchoring this energy need not *do* anything with it. (As John-Roger once told me, he could be running a video store and still successfully anchor the Mystical Traveler Consciousness.)

The idea is that the energy from God—*all* the energy from God this planet gets *in any form*, in fact—comes through the physical anchor point of the Mystical Traveler, like a giant switching station, which then dispenses this essential spirit of life to the earth. (All this and running a video store, too. Amazing.)

Historian John-Roger informs us the Mystical Travelers "throughout the ages" include nearly every famous male personage since—and including—Adam.

Please keep in mind that this is not a listing of those who have had the *generic* mystical traveler consciousness we *all* have. This is a list ("Revised 3/17/92" according to MSIA) of those who were *consciously aware* that they were "holding" the Mystical Traveler Consciousness while they lived. As MSIA literature states:

> John-Roger told us that throughout the history of this planet, a Mystical Traveler has been present, as an anchor, to allow dispensation of the gifts that the Traveler energy brings. There has never been a time when a Traveler did not walk this planet, although some did so with a very low profile, and others much more publicly.

> Nothing shocks me more
> in the men of religion
> and their flocks than
> their . . . pretensions
> to be the only religious people.
>
> JEAN GUÉHENNO

This, obviously, is a list of those who did it "much more publicly."

John-Roger's listing of the Mystical Travelers begins with Adam, the first man. Contrary to all known archaeology and most accepted theology, John-Roger gives the dates of the first man as "4485 B.C.–3555 B.C." The Mystical Traveler Consciousness then went to Seth, "third son of Adam and Eve"; Hermes Trismigestis; Enos, "son of Seth"; Mahalalel, "grandson of Enos"; and Jared, "son of Mahalalel."

We haven't even gotten to Noah yet (who, of course, was a Traveler), and already we find an inconsistency. John-Roger was quite clear that there was one and only one Traveler on the planet at any one time. Now we have a problem that repeats itself several times during John-Roger's listing of historical Travelers: a lot of these people had overlapping lives.

For example, according to John-Roger, in the year 3500 B.C., the Travelers Adam, Seth, Hermes Trismigestis, Enos, Mahalalel, Jared, Enoch, Methuselah, and Noah were all alive. Was the Traveler Consciousness like a time-share condo? Was it handled like a child-custody case? Or did they pass it from person to person like the Harlem Globetrotters warming up? Alas, we are not likely to get the answers to these burning questions: John-Roger has stated that he's not going to answer any more questions about the history of the Travelers. No wonder.

Fortunately, so much of the rich history of the Travelers is already written down. Continuing after the Flood, we have Shem, "third son of Noah"; Eber; and Imhotep, "the first Egyptian to build in stone." Apparently it's okay for Travelers to keep slaves and bisexual harems, as Imhotep had plenty of both. Then there's Ragau, famous for his spaghetti sauce; Terah, Abraham's dad; Melchizedek, whom we will discuss in the chapter, "God's Money—Tax Free"; and Abraham himself. Naturally, Abraham's three most famous direct descendants—Isaac, Jacob, and Joseph—were all Travelers, too.

Then we return to the fine tradition of warring, whoring, slave-keeping Travelers with Hammurabi, King of Babylonia. The

fun ends soon enough, however: we immediately move
on to the "father-in-law of
Moses," Jethro, and directly to
Moses himself.

Moses, of course, asked
Ramses II, a descendant of fel-
low-Traveler Imhotep, to free
the slaves Imhotep started
gathering a thousand years before. Moses was successful
and passed the ball to Joshua,

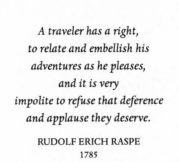

*A traveler has a right,
to relate and embellish his
adventures as he pleases,
and it is very
impolite to refuse that deference
and applause they deserve.*

RUDOLF ERICH RASPE
1785

but the Hebrews must have fumbled, because the ball went back
to Egypt and Pharaoh Akhenaton, husband of Nefertiti. Akhenaton must have committed too many fouls, because an Egyptian
never got to captain the Traveler's team again.

Next follows a succession of Old Testament powerhouses:
Elihu, Jesse, Samuel, Hosea, Elijah, Elisha, Amos, Isaiah, and then
we suddenly go Greek with Homer. Back to the Holy Land with
Jeremiah, over to Persia with Zoroaster, and back to the Bible with
Ezekiel and Daniel.

And now for something completely different: China, where
Lao-tzu and Confucius (who, according to John-Roger,* also had
overlapping lives) played ping-pong with the Traveler Consciousness until it bounced back to Pythagoras in Greece. The *Encyclope-
dia Britannica* says of Pythagoras: "None of his writings has survived, and Pythagoreans invariably supported their doctrines by
indiscriminately citing their master's authority." This tradition is
certainly kept alive by John-Roger's devotees: John-Roger is cited
around MSIA as often as Baptists quote the Bible.

Naturally, Socrates, Plato, Hippocrates, and Aristotle were all
Travelers. How could Arianna Stassinopoulos Huffington follow
any spiritual path that didn't contain Homer and these four?

We take a quick trip to India to visit Ram (or Rama), "the
incarnation of the god Vishnu," and then off to sunny Italy with

---

*I say "according to John-Roger" because he often fails to do his homework
when it comes to historical dates. Whereas John-Roger lists Lao-tzu's life as "604
B.C.–404 B.C.," which would make him an ancient Chinese sage, indeed, the
American Heritage Dictionary lists his lifespan as 604?–531? B.C. The question
mark, of course, means that there's some doubt as to whether 531 B.C. was the
date of his death—but it's unlikely that there is *so* much doubt that any historian
would accept that his life extended until 404 B.C.

> Christian, n. *One who believes*
> *that the New Testament is*
> *a divinely inspired book*
> *admirably suited to the spiritual*
> *needs of his neighbor.*
> *One who follows the teachings*
> *of Christ in so far as they are not*
> *inconsistent with a life of sin.*
>
> AMBROSE BIERCE

Cicero, the Roman Empire's greatest orator, and Virgil, ancient Rome's greatest poet.

But no sooner than we arrive we must say, *"Arrivederci, Roma,"* and march to Galilee with Pontius Pilate's centurions, where we discover one of the most famous Travelers of all, "Jesus the Christ—also called Jesus of Nazareth, Founder of Christianity . . . ."

According to John-Roger, when Jesus was finished being Traveler, he handed it over to John and James, both sons of Zebedee. It seems as though the mother of John and James may have had something to do with this. According to Matthew, chapter 20, verses 20 and 21:

> Then the mother of Zebedee's sons came to Jesus with her sons and, kneeling down, asked a favor of him.
>
> "What is it you want?" he asked.
>
> She said, "Grant that one of these two sons of mine may sit at your right and the other at your left in your kingdom."

This did not sit well with the other apostles: "When the ten heard about this," wrote Matthew (who was one of the ten) "they were indignant with the two brothers" (chapter 20, verse 24).

According to John-Roger, none of the other apostles received the Traveler Consciousness, nor did Paul, Luke, Mark, James (Jesus' brother, who apparently ran the early Church), or any other person in the New Testament.

Instead, it went to Claudius Ptolemaeus (Ptolemy), who concluded before his death around 150 A.D., that there were precisely 1,022 stars, all of which revolved around the earth, which was the center of the universe. This latter notion almost got future-Traveler Galileo burned at the stake by the Catholic church for supporting Copernicus's (not a Traveler) idea that the earth revolved around the sun. This from John-Roger's teachings:

> One important feature of the Travelers is that they came to bring to each period in history, and to the people they served, a special balancing, to assist in their upliftment.
>
> In surveying the greatest historical movements in recorded history, we see that a Mystical Traveler invariably stood in

the thick of each epoch, dispensing a great wisdom, accomplishing a wonderful balancing, or establishing a new era.

How Ptolemy's earth-centered universe—which hobbled astronomy for the next fourteen hundred years—could be considered "a wonderful balancing," "a great wisdom," or "uplifting" is beyond me.

> STUDENT: . . . *I'm now almost inclined to try Theology.*
> MEPHISTOPHELES: *I would not wish to lead you so astray. In what this science teaches. 'Tis best here too that only one be heard and that you swear then by the master's word.*
>
> GOETHE
> *FAUST*

But, let us not tarry on Ptolemy. It's time to move on to St. Patrick, Merlin, King Arthur *(I am not making this up)*, Mohammed, Quetzalcóatl (a Mexican "vegetarian god," according to John-Roger—I suppose worshipers sacrificed their first-born avocado to it), Omar Khayyám, St. Francis of Assisi, Joan of Arc (A woman! At last!—and the last woman, too), Leonardo da Vinci, Erasmus, Sir Thomas More, Paracelsus, Michelangelo, Francis Bacon, the aforementioned Galileo, Descartes, Rembrandt, Sir Isaac Newton, Voltaire, and Benjamin Franklin.*

In that last list you may have noticed, conspicuous by his absence, Shakespeare. This is because, according to John-Roger, although Shakespeare certainly *was* a Traveler, he is tired of being "called upon all the time," and asked not to be included on this list. In our respect for the old masters, let's not call on him, okay? Let's call on Bacon instead.

Amidst the metaphysical and transcendental writers William Blake, William Wordsworth, Ralph Waldo Emerson, Henry David Thoreau, Walt Whitman, and Kahlil Gibran, John-Roger inexplicably throws Abraham Lincoln.

As John-Roger explains: "Abraham Lincoln assisted to transmute the negativity of racial bigotry that threatened to destroy the most extensive form of democracy yet seen in recorded history." Oh.

All these great men (and woman) are here to help *you*, if *only* you follow John-Roger. As an MSIA publication gushes:

> John-Roger has also said that the physical embodiment of the Traveler enjoys the full support of all Travelers who have

---

*Voltaire and Franklin were both Deists and would have abhorred the notion of a single individual representing God's teachings.

> Sophia wished that Florence would not talk about the Almighty as if his real name was Godfrey, and God was just Florence's nickname for him.
>
> NANCY MITFORD

come before him, and that those past Travelers, present in a very real sense, line up behind the physical Traveler, as he does his work in the world. Those who study with the Traveler as his initiates share in the benefits of that radiant consciousness. It is humbling to realize that we, as students, studying with John-Roger, also share in this great ministry.

Humbling, indeed; and *humiliating* to think that I once believed all this stuff.

As to the lack of women among the Travelers, this is simply John-Roger's sexism. Obviously, the list is a fabrication, so why not include some of the influential women in history as well? As usual, John-Roger attempts to cover his personal prejudices with some spiritual shinola:

> J-R has indicated that women have generally not held the Traveler Consciousness because the energy polarities of the female body are such that women have difficulty "holding" the Consciousness and have "given it away" or allowed the Consciousness to pass through them and dissipate instead of grounding and channeling it.

"The energy polarities of the female body . . . ." Well, that explains everything. His sexism is, perhaps, a reflection of his Mormon background, in which only men are permitted to be High Priests, or perhaps it just reflects the general stupidity in our society that only men would be seen as capable of "grounding and channeling Consciousness."

Alas, being the physical embodiment of the Mystical Traveler Consciousness is a thankless task. In fact, the vast, vast majority of humans don't even know there *is* a Mystical Traveler. Golly, without the Mystical Traveler, the earth would be as barren as the moon. (Please do not confuse the ozone layer with the Mystical Traveler.) And humans are an ungrateful lot—they use electricity without stopping to give thanks to those working for the electric company, and they don't continually thank the Traveler for bringing God's energy to earth.

To make matters worse, the Mystical Traveler himself is not

allowed to *personally* feel any of this mystical energy flowing through him. So, just as the rain falling gently on a garden does not get to experience the benefits of being rained upon—that water simply becoming *a part* of every living thing in the garden—so, too, the Mystical Traveler, reigning over the dissemination of divine power, doesn't

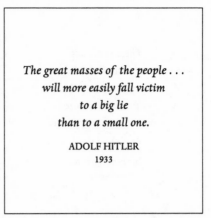

*The great masses of the people . . .
will more easily fall victim
to a big lie
than to a small one.*

ADOLF HITLER
1933

get to appreciate it, but only has the satisfaction of knowing he has *become* everything.

But, surely, God cannot allow the one who is doing so much work—the most essential work on the planet, after all—to go around without even a *taste* of this cosmic ambrosia which every other living thing gets to enjoy. This is why God created *devotees*. According to John-Roger, devotees "reflect back" to the Traveler a small portion of that which the Traveler gives so magnificently.

And what can devotees do or give the Traveler to make his life of endless giving, giving, giving more enjoyable?

Well, what have you got? To all devotees, apprentice devotees, would-be devotees, and those just thinking about it, John-Roger is very clear about what he wants: money. To John-Roger, it is clearly more blessed to give than to receive—as long as you're giving to John-Roger. But more on John-Roger's financial shenanigans in the chapter, "God's Money—Tax Free."

Closer to home are those who fulfill John-Roger's personal needs.

John-Roger's basic personality is one of not only "I want what I want when I want it in the way that want it," but also "and I don't want one damned bit more." This, and John-Roger's notorious moodiness, account for the few ceremonial devotional practices— such as surrounded Maharishi*—surrounding John-Roger. Instead,

---

*Maharishi, by contrast, surrounded himself with honorific rituals. The most well-known, in addition to being the most popular, was to give Maharishi a flower at every conceivable opportunity. People would stand in long lines, open palms pressed together, a flower held between the palms. Maharishi would walk along and receive the tribute by gathering armfuls of flowers—whether he wanted to or not. By the time I knew him well, he had become captive to his own ritual. The ritualized giving was acknowledged with ritualized receiving, which, as any member of the Royal Family will tell you, can be a real bore.

an ad-hoc network of compartmentalized John-Roger desire-fulfillment machines (a.k.a. devotees) has been established.

> There is no step,
> no crime or petty fraud he commits,
> which in the mouths of
> those around him
> is not at once represented
> as a great deed.
>
> LEO TOLSTOY
> *War and Peace*

To his Inner Circle, which numbers between one and two hundred, John-Roger is known affectionately as "the Chief." Whereas everyday devotees feel "in" by referring to John-Roger as J-R, so, too, this Inner Circle (of which I was a member for many years) communicates their special status to each other by referring to him not as J-R, but the Chief. "How is the Chief feeling today?" "Is the Chief busy?" and the oft-asked, "What kind of mood is the Chief in?" Ironically, the *innermost* circle refers to him most often as "John-Roger." I guess after you go far enough in, you find yourself back out again.

The Inner Circle includes administrators of the many John-Roger nonprofit organizations, cooks, housekeepers, horsekeepers, massage therapists, business advisors, legal advisors, gardeners, wranglers, high-tech experts, drivers, mechanics, maintenance people, writers, and healthcare professionals from acupuncturists to Zulu witchdoctors. (All right: I made up the Zulu witchdoctor part—but John-Roger *has* studied Haitian voodoo.)

And then there's sex—but let's not get *too* far ahead of our story.

What he wants—what he absolutely *insists* upon—from his Inner Circle is complete subservience. John-Roger has full power, authority, and control at all times.

Period. No questioning. No equivocation.

Once I was on my way to the airport to catch a plane, and Maharishi sent for me. I was told it wouldn't take long. I picked up the now-obligatory flower, went to his room, outside of which were the ever-present dozen-or-so people waiting to see Maharishi. I was told to have a seat; Maharishi would be with me momentarily. Three hours passed. My plane had long since departed, along with any hopes I had of fulfilling whatever the obligation was on the other end of the air corridor. I sat there, seething (it was so typical of Maharishi) (but then, seething is so typical of me), holding my flower. When Maharishi *finally* appeared, I offered my flower and he said, with noticeable contempt, which was entirely out of character, "Keep it!" At the time, of course, I was crushed. In retrospect, however, it's my guess that he had been waiting to say that to someone for *years*.

Being a spiritual sycophant (and a pretty good one at that) is an essential requirement for earning a place in the Inner Circle. In addition to this, in order to be part of the Inner Circle, you must have something specific to offer—something John-Roger wants enough to put up with having you around. (John-Roger fundamentally does not like people.)

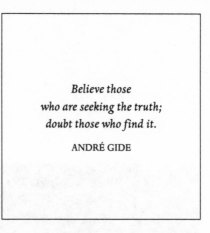

Believe those
who are seeking the truth;
doubt those who find it.

ANDRÉ GIDE

People with talents greater than John-Roger's from almost every calling belittle themselves so that John-Roger might feel big. He is so frequently moody, ill-tempered, and abusive to those close to him that when he's patronizing, condescending, or didactic, it almost seems like *love*. He is obsessed with constantly being reminded that he is special, the One, the Traveler—and if you fail to, even for a moment, you will be reminded.

Take, for example, the opening of "A Blessing From John-Roger":

Lord God,
as you've always heard me,
as you've always talked to me,
see if you can see it clear
to talk to the hearts
of these who are your people
that are choosing you.

The Lord God "always" talks to John-Roger, but apparently, never to his followers unless, of course, John-Roger specifically asks God to.

"He ain't heavy, Father, he's my brother," becomes "He ain't enlightened, Father, he's my initiate."

The New! Improved! reprogrammed me. Graduation Day, Advanced Insight,
November 1978. Wanna buy a flower?

CHAPTER EIGHT
Advanced Insights

> More than any time in history
> mankind faces a crossroads.
> One path leads to despair and
> utter hopelessness,
> the other to total extinction.
> Let us pray that we have the
> wisdom to choose correctly.
>
> WOODY ALLEN

NOVEMBER 1978. The Sunday before Thanksgiving I flew to Miami for my Advanced Insight (later called Insight II) which began at 9:00 a.m. sharp the following day. Whereas the Basic Insight Training was three evenings and two full days, the Advanced Insight was five full days—five *very* full days. It was limited to forty participants.

As with the Basic Training, both participants and assistants were made up of John-Roger's followers, most of them ministers of MSIA. A notable exception to this rule was John Thompson, who was co–leading the training with Victor. (Victor weaves in and out of my story like a golden thread.) John was recruited from outside the MSIA community because he had extensive experience as a trainer (in Lifespring, I think). This was part of Russell's ongoing program to teach spiritual people to be trainers, and teach trainers to be spiritual (spiritual being defined as "a follower of the Mystical Traveler"). Although John Thompson was poking about in J-R's teachings at the time he led my Advanced Insight, he was far from a devotee. He left Insight a few months later because, I was told, he was displeased with the way the Advanced Insight Workshops were becoming Mystical Traveler Trainings.

In hindsight, these conflicts between accepting John-Roger as the only conduit to God versus each individual's finding God in his or her own way were evident during my advanced training.

> *A good man giving bad advice*
> *is more dangerous*
> *than a nasty man*
> *giving bad advice.*
>
> CONOR CRUISE O'BRIEN

Whereas John would offer logical, practical explanations of things, Victor and the assistants would make spiritual interpretations. For example, people would occasionally hyperventilate, fall on the floor, and wiggle around for a while. When this happened to me, I asked John Thompson what happened. He said, rather casually, "You just lost control for a moment." The assistants and other participants, however, referred to it as "Spirit moving through."

At one point, one of the assistants told me I had "a dirty aura." She suggested I ask Victor for an aura balance. I did, and during one of the meal breaks, we went to Victor's room in the hotel where the training was being held and, for $60, he balanced my aura. (This was and is an official MSIA "Service.") Throughout the hour-long aura balance we talked. His love of God and his devotion to John-Roger were seductive. His personal warmth and charm, consciously channeled into service for others, was strangely restful. I think that hour spent with Victor discussing his love of Spirit did more than anything else to seal my decision to study with John-Roger.*

The Advanced Insight followed the standard pressure/release seminar training format, except this time the pressure was far more intense, so the release was far more spectacular.

The first two and a half days were not just a dip in the negativity pool; they were scuba diving—without a mask.

For example, one of the first processes had all forty participants seated in an arc, assistants and facilitators standing behind them. One by one each participant took center stage and said, "My name is _____, and I'd like some feedback from my universe."

---

*Years later, when Victor saw through the sham of John-Roger and I told him that he, personally, was a major reason for my deciding to study with MSIA, he howled in pain. "You were so sweet and persuasive," I said. "No, no!" he would yell. "Your kindness was so convincing," I purred. "Stop! I can't take any more," he'd scream. "Yes, Victor, if it wasn't for you, I never would have written best-sellers and put John-Roger's name on them, I never would have given him a million dollars, and I probably would have donated all that money to the poor." I was rubbing it in with a Roto-Rooter. "I can't stand it! I can't stand it!" Victor moaned.

All the participants stood, and delivered a barrage of negative comments. After delivering the "feedback," the participants sat down. The participant to whom all of this was directed then said, "What I heard was . . ." and then repeated as many of the negative epithets as he or she could remember.

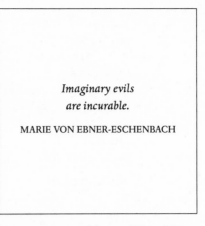

Imaginary evils are incurable.

MARIE VON EBNER-ESCHENBACH

Why negative? Because that's how the trainers set it up. "If we're here to grow," the trainer would say, "should we focus on the things that work in our life, or focus on the things that don't work?" We were convinced that we should focus on the things that *didn't* work. (There's another perfectly legitimate theory, never mentioned, that perhaps we should look at what *is* working and enhance it from the very beginning. This is, however, *not* the pattern used by Insight.)*

When I stood before the group to receive my negative feedback, and as the negative comments came rolling in, dozens at a time, like waves of polluted water on an already oil-soaked beach, I gradually reverted to kindergarten. I remembered playing Farmer In The Dell. In this *delightful* game, the one child not chosen by at least one of the other students becomes "the cheese." The cheese must stand in the middle of the circle, while all the other students sing, in that tauntingly cruel way children do so well: "The cheese stands alone, the cheese stands alone . . . ." Receiving all this "loving" negative feedback during Insight, I felt like a particularly smelly bit of cheese. It seemed to go on forever. After repeating the negative feedback I remembered, I said what we all were instructed to say, "Thank you for caring enough to share that with me." At which point the group responded in unison, "We care, Peter." Thus, delivering negative feedback became associated with *caring*—the more devastating the feedback, the more you cared. If you could bring someone to tears with your feedback, you might get the Nobel Peace Prize.

---

*Although one could leave a focus-on-the-positive seminar with more tools and a plan for greater productivity, Insight doesn't hold these seminars because they seldom have the emotional high of the pressure/release trainings. It's that temporary emotional high that makes it easier to sell whatever it is that needs to be sold: usually the next seminar, or, in the case of Insight, Discourses.

> Power is strength
> and the ability to see yourself
> through your own eyes and
> not through the eyes of another.
> It is being able to place
> a circle of power at your own feet
> and not take power from
> someone else's circle.
>
> LYNN V. ANDREWS

We had plenty of time to qualify for the Nobel. In the next process we milled about, made one-on-one eye contact with each other, did not touch, and delivered all the negative feedback we had for the other person. The only response the other person could make was the obligatory, "Thank you for caring enough to share that with me." Roles switched, and the dumpee became the dumper. Such caring!

This went on for several hours and segued directly into Lifeboat (later, Spaceship). Here the forty participants were the only passengers on a boat that was sinking. The one lifeboat would only hold five passengers. Which five of the forty were to be saved? For a couple of hours, we were allowed to thrash it out amongst ourselves, and decided to draw lots.

Then we did it the trainers' way. This involved having five "live" votes. Each participant went around a circle consisting of all the other participants, looked each participant in the eyes, and saying either, "You live" or "You die." Nothing else. This meant you had to look at least thirty-five people in the eye and say, "You die." It also meant that a significant number of the forty were likely to look you in the eye and say, "You die." A favorite trainer question: "Did you save a 'live' vote for yourself?" Those who failed to were "processed" by a trainer until they wished the boat would hurry up and sink so they could drown and get it all over with. When done with this "You die" voting process, the five people who were chosen to live sit in five chairs set up as the lifeboat, and the rest of the people, seated on the floor, go through a long, grisly guided meditation in which they drown. As they die, they lie back, and are dead.

And that was just a portion of the first day's fun, which began at 9:00 a.m. and continued until well after midnight. We were told to keep silence, were given a series of depressing questions to answer as homework, and told to meet the following morning at 9:00 a.m. sharp. The next day was lots more nastiness, culminating in The Cocktail Party.

For The Cocktail Party, an arena was made by placing chairs in a circle, backs facing inward. *Arena* is not the right word; it was more a corral. No, more a snake pit. The purpose of The Cocktail Party was to take all of these negative things you learned about yourself during the past day and a half of "caring" and "run them" (a trainer term) on everyone else, while everyone else was running their negativity on everyone else, including you. You were encouraged to be

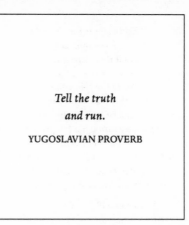

Tell the truth and run.

YUGOSLAVIAN PROVERB

very loud, very physical; no one could leave the circle, no one could sit down. If someone had an issue of, say, dependency, they were encouraged to physically lean on other people. If they had an issue of being emotionally attached, they were encouraged to physically attach themselves to people. Outright violence was not condoned, but leaning and clutching was.

The Cocktail Party began. It was mayhem. Yelling, screaming, leaning, clutching. Over-dramatized mental institutions from Bedlam to Charenton would have come to mind, except with all that pandemonium, I wasn't sure I had a mind at all.

It continued for hours.

Eventually, Insight limited The Cocktail Party to two hours. In these early days, it went on and on. As it continued, the circle was made smaller. If anyone stopped behaving like a mad person, the assistants ridiculed the party-pooper beyond belief. After a few hours, I was in something of a fetal position on the floor, crying. Four or five assistants gathered around me, pointed at me, and yelled: "Oh, look: there's the crying game!" "Look! There's the quitting game!" "There's the withdrawal game!" "There's the broken commitment game!" (By lying down I was not following the facilitator's instructions, which I had agreed to do.) "There's the resistance game!" "There's the non-participation game!" All the while I was poked and prodded and yelled at until I finally got back on my feet and started screaming at other people with the voice I no longer had.

After everyone was too hoarse to utter another intimidating sound (my guess is that it lasted somewhere between four and five hours), we were told to lie on the floor in the fetal position. (I was doing the right thing, I suppose, but too soon.) In a guided meditation, we were led back into the womb and reborn.

> *Skepticism is the chastity*
> *of the intellect,*
> *and it is shameful to*
> *surrender it too soon*
> *or to the first comer;*
> *there is nobility in*
> *preserving it coolly and*
> *proudly through a long youth,*
> *until at last,*
> *in the ripeness of instinct and discretion,*
> *it can be safely exchanged*
> *for fidelity and happiness.*
>
> GEORGE SANTAYANA

That was something of a release, but after The Cocktail Party, being questioned by the Inquisition would have been a release.

One process designed to "shift the energy" was casually referred to as "I've got a secret." It was no game show. People were asked to share their deepest, darkest secrets—the ones they felt particularly ashamed of and guilty about. *No matter what* people revealed, the trainers "forgave them" with God-like omnipotence. And I do mean *no matter what*. I once heard a woman confess that she had killed her mother in self-defense. She had gotten away with it. The facilitators forgave her, and moved on to the next person's secret, which was probably something like, "I pick my nose." I was studying to be an Insight II trainer at the time. Nothing further was done about the incident.

"Shouldn't we get this woman some psychological help?"

"No, no, no," I was told, "it will all be handled in the training."

On another occasion, I saw John-Roger *personally* forgive someone for not taking any action whatsoever to save his best friend who drowned within inches of the small boat the secret-teller was on. John-Roger's statement on the matter: "I didn't save him either, and I don't feel guilty about it. Why should you?"

The secret process had three important functions: (a) it supplied another round of pressure and release (the pressure of telling your biggest secret, followed by the release of being told "your secret is no big deal") and is expunged from your moral record; (b) it stripped away any remaining shreds of privacy and individuality; and (c) it gave the facilitators even more God-like power.

Then followed the Really Big Pressure and the Really Big Release. It was called "Getting Your Affirmation."

The goal was this: Find an affirmation that sums up all of your positive qualities in as few words as possible. But this is not just a literary effort: you must demonstrate to the entire group that, as you say your affirmation, it *unconditionally* brings to life all the positive attributes stated in the affirmation. And guess who was the absolute, final authority on whether or not you had "gotten your affirmation?" The trainer, of course.

That evening was spent trying out one affirmation after another waiting for one to "click." You were essentially told to find the Rosetta Stone that would open the combination lock of your heart, and be back in the room by 9:00 a.m., ready to demonstrate its effectiveness to the entire group and, more important, to the trainers.

> Well, I thought over
> the matter all day,
> and by evening
> I was in low spirits again;
> for I had quite persuaded myself
> that the whole affair must be some
> great hoax or fraud,
> though what its object might be
> I could not imagine.
>
> SIR ARTHUR CONAN DOYLE

All day on the third day, one participant after another got up in front of the room and desperately attempted to be joyful if their affirmation mentioned joy, loving if their affirmation mentioned love, and God-like if their affirmation mentioned divine. One by one, they were shot down by the trainers: not joyful enough, not loving enough, not God-like enough. Each was told to "sit down and work on it some more." (However *that* might be done.)

Here was almost the perfect process for the destruction of whatever self-esteem any of us may have had left: given an impossible task (acting positively enough to meet the trainers' standards of positivity—whatever they were) and given no specific method of getting there. Pressure was further increased when we were told that there "wasn't much time left for this process" and that those who didn't have an affirmation wouldn't be able to continue with the training—an affirmation being essential from this point on.

Throughout the day, whenever anyone had a particularly traumatic experience (roughly every half hour) the lights would go down, Neil Diamond music would come up ("Lonely looking sky, looking sky, lonely looking sky/Lonely looking day, looking day, lonely looking day"), and we would all take part in what is known as cradling. Cradling is when six or so people—three on each side—pick up another horizontal participant and rock him or her ("He ain't heavy/He's my brother . . ."). This would all go on for about an hour, and all the while off to one side of the training room people were performing like dancing bears for the trainers, who—like state lotteries—allowed just enough people to win (that is, get their affirmation approved) to keep the rest of us on the hook with the notion that yes, indeed, it *is* possible to get an affirmation.

> I have seen the Bird of Paradise,
> she has spread herself before me,
> and I shall never be the same again.
>
> R. D. LAING

For me, the torture was particularly excruciating: out of the forty participants, I was the thirty-ninth to have my affirmation approved. This happened after fifteen nonstop hours of attempts, rejections, and contradictory feedback—all negative. ("You're trying too hard." "You're not trying hard enough.")

When my affirmation finally was approved—in other words when *I* was finally approved—the release from all that pressure was ecstatic. Not since some of my early drug experiences a decade before had I felt so good. Little did I realize, however, that I *was* having a drug experience.

Whenever the body is under severe psychological pressure and that pressure is suddenly released, the body releases endorphins, nature's own internal whoopee! chemical. If, for example, you were told that there had been a terrible car accident and the person you loved most in the world was involved, that would be severe emotional stress. When told your loved one was perfectly fine, *endorphins ho!* The more intense the stress and the longer the stress continues, the greater the release of endorphins.

I had had three days of unending psychological duress or stress. Around midnight of the third day, when the pressure was released, I became an endorphin mainliner. It felt like a tranquilizer I once took, purchased on the underground market for a dollar. It reminded me of a cartoon I saw from the 1960s in which an obviously upper middle class couple are floating down a stream in a gondola surrounded by flowers, birds, and butterflies. The husband asks the wife: "What's the name of that tranquilizer we took?" I never did find out the name of the underground tranquilizer I took, but I did find out the name of the tranquilizer used by Insight: endorphins. When they say: "It was inside you all the time," they're not kidding.

The last two days were processes designed to make us feel better and better about ourselves and about Insight. Naturally, MSIA music played almost nonstop in the background, foreground, and, eventually, midbrain. We were encouraged to "enroll" everyone we knew in Insight, and there was quite a lot of talk about the best way of doing it. We were encouraged to volunteer for Insight.

We were also encouraged to maintain the "spiritual focus" we had found in the past five days, and, to this group, the words "spiritual focus" and "John-Roger" and "endorphin rush" and "MSIA" and "Discourses" were all synonymous.

Never eat in a restaurant where there's a photo of the chef with Sammy Davis, Jr.

ALF

I decided to accept John-Roger as my spiritual teacher.

I mean, what else could I do?

John-Roger circa 1977, before he got a shave and a perm. The MSIA-provided caption reads: "The aura that is seen around him suggests the spiritual Light with which he works and the spiritual power that is inherent within his consciousness." What I see is rim lighting and optical refraction, but if they want to believe it's an "aura," hey, that's okay with me. Similarly, the degree of "spiritual power that is inherent within his consciousness" is just as much a matter of fact versus faith.

CHAPTER NINE
The Valentine's Day Blizzard

WYMI—
the all-philosophy
radio station.

MIKE DUGAN

FEBRUARY 1979. I was traveling around the country in a last-ditch effort to salvage my dying company. As the product of the company was primarily love poetry, and as Valentine's Day was upon us yet again, I hired PR people to book me onto TV and radio shows that didn't know what the hell else to do for Valentine's Day. For those who wanted a counter–Valentine's Day theme, I was prepared to discuss How to Survive the Loss of a Love. The entire effort was useless: I might as well have been the commander of the Hindenburg as it crumbled in flames, crawling around in the metal framework with a fire extinguisher in one hand and bottle of rubber cement in the other. But, there I was, first stop Los Angeles, giving it the old college try. (Why didn't someone remind me I dropped out of college in my sophomore year?)

I arrived at LAX and went to Budget Rent-A-Car, where I had reserved the cheapest vehicle that still had four wheels and a windshield. In 1979, this was roughly three classes below a Pinto. They had the reservation, but they didn't have my car. In fact, they didn't have any cars. All right, I exaggerate: they had one car left. It was offered to me at the sub-Pinto rate, but with a profusion of apologies because, as the woman behind the counter explained, "It's a stick shift." It had been a decade since my last Volkswagen, hence my last stick shift but, hey, it's like riding a bicycle, right? I

> The old neighborhood
> has changed.
> Hurley Brothers Funeral Home
> is now called Death 'n' Things
>
> ELMORE LEONARD

was shuttle-bussed to the empty Budget parking lot where a brand new, burnt-orange Toyota Supra was waiting *just for me.* It was love at first sight. Although my next car would be a Prelude (hence, Prelude Press), the moment I became flush enough, I bought a Supra. It was only replaced years later by—another Supra.

I spent hours and hours just *driving,* acquainting myself with the joys of the Supra and reacquainting myself with the pleasures of Los Angeles, the city I moved to in 1972 when I finally got out of Detroit.* I had moved to New York in 1976 and, three years later, it was good to be back in L.A. (especially after leaving New York in mid-February).

I eventually arrived at the Chateau Marmont Hotel, where I had reserved the least expensive room. Unfortunately, that room was being used by a film crew (location work for *Debby Does It in the Dungeon,* I believe), but would I mind a fifth-floor room overlooking the Hollywood Hills—at the sub-humus rate, of course? Oh, if I must. The room and the Supra were such exquisite pain: I could hardly bear to leave either one. The two were, alas, like the Menendez brothers and love of mother: mutually exclusive.

By 1979, John-Roger had long ago abandoned his unemployed-school-teacher practice of delivering seminars door-to-door. By 1973, in fact, John-Roger had become tired of visiting other people's living rooms, so he bought one of his own: a 6,000-square-foot house on seven acres of secluded property in fashionable Mandeville Canyon. (Mandeville Canyon is about halfway between Beverly Hills and the Pacific Ocean if one follows the twisting path of Sunset Boulevard.)

But people wanted seminars, and John-Roger wasn't about to invite all those people into *his* living room (he used God's money to buy it, but God said it was okay for John-Roger to do what he wanted with it and he did *not* want initiates cluttering up the place.) What he *did* want was a place to house the collection of

---

*Lily Tomlin is a fellow native Detroiter. She was once asked, "When did you leave Detroit?" She responded, "When I found out where I was."

handsome young men he was gathering; what he *did* want was a large television in a large bedroom so he could stay up all night and channel surf using the newly installed cable system, which John-Roger was convinced was a personal gift from God; what h e *did* want was to shoot anything that moved—from coyote to ground squirrel— out any window with one of his hunting rifles.

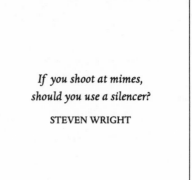

If you shoot at mimes, should you use a silencer?

STEVEN WRIGHT

So, the following year John-Roger purchased, with the increasing flow of money from well-heeled, well-flattered followers, a turn-of-the-century mansion built on an acre or two of property on the then-fashionable Adams Boulevard. In the 1930s, after Busby Berkeley made a fortune with his surrealistic choreography at Warner Bros., he bought the mansion for his mother, and promptly moved in with her. (The custom-made carpeting in the solarium, there even today, has an ornate "B" woven into the pile.) By 1974, however, the house, property, and neighborhood had fallen on hard times.

John-Roger dubbed the mansion the Purple Rose Ashram of the New Age, or PRANA—which means "breath of life." It was deemed "the home of the Traveler," as distinct from "John-Roger's house," to give visitors the *appearance* of being invited into the Traveler's living room for seminars. Seminars were now held (J-R's health and schedule permitting) twice a week, every Wednesday and Thursday evening. They attracted from two hundred to two hundred fifty people each night (generally the same people each night). With a "suggested donation" of four dollars per person, John-Roger would gather, tax-free, $1,600 to $2,000 per week.

By February of 1979, however, Insight had turned into such a money maker that $1,000 per night to John-Roger was really No Big Deal. As the Insight money increased, the seminars decreased, until they became Special Events that took place monthly, then every other month, then hardly at all. (In the past several years, the few live seminars John-Roger gives are generally "fund raisers" in which from $100 to $5,000 per person is charged. There are, perhaps, only two or three seminars per year in all of Southern California which charge the now-regular rate of $10.)

> *Some guy hit my fender,*
> *and I said to him,*
> *"Be fruitful and multiply,"*
> *but not in those words.*
>
> WOODY ALLEN

But this was 1979, and there were two seminars a week, and they took place on Wednesdays and Thursdays, and they cost only four dollars. It was the Golden Age of MSIA. New recruits (such as myself) were coming in through Insight, Insight was teaching the old-time MSIAers that life *on earth* could be beautiful, and people were moving to L.A. every day to be near the action.

While many of the old-timers missed the twenty-person living-room intimate contact they once had with John-Roger, they understood they could not keep the only earthly link to God all to themselves, so they did what they could to make the newcomers happy.

They also wanted to make John-Roger happy, and what *clearly* made John-Roger happy was an ever-expanding MSIA empire. There was already talk of a People Center, in which MSIA and Insight could have "a place of our own" to hold seminars, trainings, and workshops. There was talk of a retreat center, in which one could get back to nature—but not as far back to nature as the retreats at Lake Arrowhead, where one had to pitch *tents* and sleep in *sleeping bags.*

All these plans took more people to pay for them, and more people to keep the programs consistently filled. So, if J-R wanted more people, more people is what the faithful would deliver— even if it meant sitting in the dining hall and watching John-Roger on a TV screen rather than sitting in the living room and watching him "in person."

As an ashram (read: commune) PRANA was never more successful than in 1979. There were about a hundred people living in PRANA itself. MSIA leased a large chunk of the apartment building next door, called it PRANA West, and filled it with the PRANA-resident overflow. (Naturally, MSIA made money on this, too.) The remainder of the apartments were, for the most part, rented by MSIA people who were not PRANA residents. (I would later become one of the latter.)

PRANA and its adjacent apartments were paradise to the serious MSIA seeker: it was a *community.* And it was nice. There was only one problem: it was in the ghetto. It was near *Watts,* for heaven's sake—home of the famous Watts Riots. No expenses were spared—in both location and amenities—when it came to John-Roger's home, but when it came to everyone else's home, the ghetto would do. Of course, everyone believed they had the "protection of the Trav-

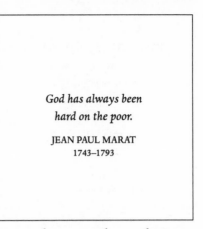

God has always been hard on the poor.

JEAN PAUL MARAT
1743–1793

eler"—even the two people who were shot, even those who were robbed, even those whose apartments were broken into, and even those who had their cars broken into, including myself.*

If John-Roger had been content with a suite of rooms within the commune, and had pooled his Mandeville Canyon money to purchase a "living center," PRANA could have been located, say, in the valley, which ain't Mandeville Canyon, but it ain't Watts, either. But John-Roger needed his seclusion, and we were happy to sacrifice our safety for his happiness.**

No one, however, was thinking about how J-R used God's money that 1979 mid-February evening I first visited PRANA for my first live MSIA seminar. John-Roger arrived in his chauffeured limousine. (On nights he felt like roughing it, he drove himself in one of his Lincolns.)

The rules were clear: "Give J-R his space." Specifically, this meant it was okay to say hello to J-R, and it was fine to hug him *if he moved to hug you first,* but other than that, leave him alone. If one had a question for John-Roger, one was to write it on a three-by-five card and "leave it on his chair." His chair was the over-

---

*I remember my primary concern was that the thieves stole John-Roger tapes and, according to MSIA teachings, if anyone listened to your tapes, *you* were responsible for the karma *they* released. What if I got the criminals' karma? Eeeek! I was relieved to learn that, although *my* karma might get on *them, their* karma would not get on *me.* Whew.

**John-Roger has added a house in Santa Barbara to his collection of domiciles, but still maintains the house in Mandeville Canyon. PRANA has become MSIA headquarters and something of a spiritual boardinghouse. It still is where it is; the neighborhood has gotten no better; the most recent riots understandably frightened the bejesus out of the PRANA residents. If John-Roger sold PRANA and his Mandeville Canyon property, he could still buy a big house in a better part of town, but no.

stuffed rocker-recliner placed on a podium in the living room. From this chair he would deliver his seminar. Prior to his seminar, while the "entertainment" (lots of guitars; lots of poetry; off-key singers; more guitars) was being inflicted upon the group, John-Roger would sit in his chair and write brief notes on the cards. Often these notes were simply "10%," which meant, as John-Roger explained, "You're bugging me." The "10% level" was everything material. The remaining 90% was spiritual. John-Roger agreed to take care of the spiritual; it was up to the initiate to take care of the rest. If the question had to do with anything material, John-Roger felt free to write 10% and go to the next card. At one point he even got a rubber stamp that printed 10%.

All this, of course, was for John-Roger's convenience. The vast, *vast* majority of questions that he did answer—both in writing and in public question-and-answer forums—were about personal issues: health, romance, money, the usual. There were very few questions about the "Soul realm," other than, "What can I do to get there?" which, of course, is a 10% question.

It became obvious over the years that John-Roger simply didn't *like* the people who worshiped him. In fact, there seemed to be an inverse ratio: the more devoted people were, the more contempt he had. His various "spiritual" explanations were simply high-sounding excuses for not saying the truth, the truth being: "I'll perform for you people, twice a week, but I don't want to hang out with you."

There's no reason, of course, why performers *should* hang out with their audience—few performers do—but John-Roger billed himself as a spiritual teacher, not spiritual performer. If John-Roger had been more honest, he probably would have had a much greater following—and had a lot more fun along the way. (Alan Watts, for example, called himself a "philosophical entertainer.")

His contempt for individual followers was obvious in the way John-Roger left at the end of seminars. It was explained that he would gather in his aura whatever karma was released from the group during the seminar. If anyone physically touched him after the seminar, he would have to process this negativity through his own physical body. Horrors! If untouched, John-Roger was able to "process the negativity in the auric state," so he would not have to take it into his physical body. Hence, it was essential that no one approach him after a seminar. John-Roger, then, got to make a swift entrance (give John-Roger his space) and a swift exit (don't touch John-Roger).

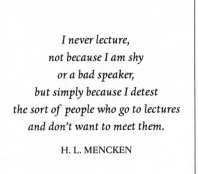

*I never lecture,
not because I am shy
or a bad speaker,
but simply because I detest
the sort of people who go to lectures
and don't want to meet them.*

H. L. MENCKEN

What more could we ask?

In that February, 1979, there was a sense of celebration at the John-Roger seminars. This little band of followers seemed to be truly fulfilling the prophecy made by their leader only a few years before: MSIA would encompass the world. Thanks to Insight, it seemed to be happening. And although the old-timers missed the intimacy of the old days, the excitement of being part of a worldwide spiritual movement, on its way home to the heart of God, superseded any loss of intimacy with the leader.

I mentioned entertainment, didn't I? Entertainment preceded every John-Roger seminar like the dusk precedeth the night. It was as intolerable as it was interminable. John-Roger explained it wasn't *meant* to be entertaining; it was meant to "burn off the karma" of those who were performing. (In John-Roger's cosmology, whenever you are inflicted with a more-than-normal dose of pain from John-Roger or any of his organizations, your evolution is accelerated.) I might add, it also burned off the karma of those who were forced to listen. There was one man, however, who was actually quite good. He had that dry-ridiculous British humor reminiscent of *Beyond the Fringe.** Some of the humor was directed at people in MSIA; some of the humor was directed at MSIA itself.

The next night during Talent Time, I got up (anything was better than sitting and listening to another rendition of "Amazing Grace," retitled "Amazing Traveler"; or someone announcing, "You won't believe I only started piano lessons two weeks ago,"

*He is one of the sad cases in MSIA: he's a brilliant wit and could have spent the last twenty years entertaining people—really making a contribution to the whole of humanity. Instead, what does he do? He counts beans for MSIA at slave wages. Ah, the waste, the waste.

> *When a thing is funny,*
> *search it carefully*
> *for a hidden truth.*
>
> GEORGE BERNARD SHAW

which was true: when he started to play, it seemed inconceivable that he had ever seen a piano before in his life). I told the group that I was the Mystical Tickler and Presumptive Consciousness, the founder of MESSIAH, which stood for Movement of Essentially the Same Stuff as Interpreted by yet-Another Hotshot. I told them my ashram was called PRA-NA-NA, home of the New Age Golden Oldies. At the end of every seminar, John-Roger always said, *"Barush Bashan,"* which meant, "The blessings already are." I told them I always ended my seminars with, *"Barush Bruce,"* which meant, "The blessings are in the mail." I also told them I was building some low-income housing next door to PRANA West and calling it Barush Ba Shanti Town.

The puns went on forever, and it was great fun. Then the real fun began. Most people, I think, found my presentation amusing, but a certain number found it appalling. After the seminar, they came up to me and looked me straight in the eyes (a technique learned at Insight) and said, "Don't you know who J-R *is?"* or "Don't you know what MSIA *is?"*

I had little to say. The questions were not really questions: they sailed beyond rhetorical, sped past retaliatory, and were intended to be bulls-eye retribution.

Some came up and "acknowledged" me for my *courage.* How could I *do* something like that? I got the distinct feeling it had seldom if ever been done before. Jokes about the Movement, occasionally; jokes about John-Roger: never. Certainly no one ever *burlesqued* John-Roger himself.

Some said it was funny but in bad taste. Philosophically, I found this criticism the most difficult to accept. I believe that if something is *truly* offensive, it's not funny. People who think something is funny, but then criticize the comic later for bad taste, are only trying to assuage their own guilt for having thought it funny in the first place.

In all, they were an enjoyable two nights, but there was work to be done: on with my publicity tour!

My PR person called me with incredible bookings for the next leg of my tour, Chicago. I was booked on all the top shows. (Back then there were a lot more local shows.) I congratulated my PR person for doing a remarkable job. There was, however, one teeny, tiny problem: snow. Chicago had been hit by the worst blizzard since Mr. O'Leary's cow

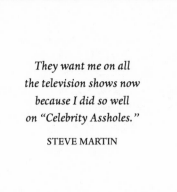

They want me on all the television shows now because I did so well on "Celebrity Assholes."

STEVE MARTIN

had kicked over a bucket of ICE-9 (or something like that). The *reason* I was booked on all those shows was because all the other guests for those shows couldn't get into town, and those who *were* in town, couldn't get around town. All I had to do was *get to the studios*, and I would be the Valentine's Day wonder of every show in town—Chicago's own cupid. What a distinction. What a challenge. I got busy.

First, there were absolutely no planes into Chicago: O'Hare was closed. Second, taking a plane into a nearby city (I think Milwaukee was open) and taking a train from there was out: Amtrak was closed. Third, taking a plane into a nearby airport and renting a car with snow chains and driving to Chicago was out: the roads around Chicago were reserved for emergency vehicles only.

After several frustrating hours (even phone calls weren't getting into Chicago very well), I looked out the open window of my hotel room, a portrait of despair. "What if I can't get to Chicago?" I bemoaned. "What will I *do* for the next week?"

It was sunny and 72° in L.A. (It's *always* sunny and 72° in L.A.) I looked down at the brick-red Toyota parked on the street. I thought of the nifty MSIA people I had met and the fun I could have with them. Back East was snow, creditors, failure, and misery. Out here was sun, Spirit, Supra, and fun.

I realized, once again, I was crazy.

The first time I realized I was crazy was when I was fifteen. I was brushing my teeth in the shower and spit out the gook. It landed on my foot. I instinctively jerked my foot away, and said, "E-e-e-e-u-u-u-u!" Immediately I rinsed my foot off, soaped it up, and rinsed it again. At that instant, I realized I was crazy. The gook was *in my mouth* only a second before, and I was now upset because it was *on my foot*. This, as far as I can tell, is the definition of crazy.

> *The major concerns of Emily Litella:*
> 1. *Conservation of*
>   *national race horses*
> 2. *Violins on television*
> 3. *Soviet jewelry*
> 4. *Endangered feces.*
>
> GILDA RADNER

Here I was in Paradise (and a remarkably inexpensive Paradise, at that) in which I could take a well-deserved break from eighteen months of relentless business pressures, and I was upset because I couldn't get to blizzard-bound Chicago. Crazy. I took a deep breath, and surrendered.

I decided to move back to California.

Master of the Universe? No.
Master of Programming? Yes.

> I am always at a loss
> to know how much to believe
> of my own stories.
>
> WASHINGTON IRVING
> Tales of a Traveler
> 1824

WHATEVER FORM of programming you care to name, John-Roger uses it.

John-Roger studied every form of thought and mind control, from the religious to the ridiculous.* It started with his Mormon upbringing, continued with his study of psychology at the University of Utah, his fascination with the behavioral modification work of Skinner, up through and including $5,000 machines claiming to beam invisible messages to people anywhere in the world—without their knowing it. For a while, his favorite book was *Influencing with Integrity*. Everyone on John-Roger's staff was told to read it; *Influencing with Integrity* was even required reading for an Insight program I took.

John-Roger certainly learned the techniques of influencing; alas, the integrity part didn't quite sink in.

The fundamental message John-Roger delivers in one way or another, over and over, is simple: John-Roger is *IT*. He is fully, consciously aware of all levels simultaneously, *and* all these levels will gladly do his bidding. The spiritual force within him hasn't paid a visit to this planet for 25,000 years (which places him above Jesus, Moses, Mohammed, Buddha, Confucius, or any other spiri-

*The religious and the ridiculous came together in 1994 when John Donnelley-Morton—in front of a thousand shrieking, crying devotees—kissed John-Roger's feet. More on this later.

Master of the Universe? No.
Master of Programming? Yes.

105

> Sin has many tools,
> but a lie is the handle
> which fits them all.
>
> OLIVER WENDELL HOLMES

tual teacher because, after all, the only ones we know about were written about, and writing didn't begin until the last "Preceptor Consciousness" had been gone about 20,000 years). To make sure his place in the future is secure, John-Roger proclaims that this Preceptor Consciousness will not come around for *another* 25,000 years. John-Roger is higher than any god worshiped by any religion on earth, East or West. Thus, he has no rivals; he is only trumped by God—but, since they're such good friends, this hardly matters. I mean, the entire universe is simply one of those Paul Newman–Robert Redford buddy movies starring John-Roger and God.

This message is conveyed over and over and over and over again—but always in bite-size chunks. The message is surrounded by flattery, good advice, bad advice, common sense, and whatever bits of trivia John-Roger has gathered from reading or channel-surfing.

As I have mentioned, one is encouraged to fall asleep while listening to John-Roger's seminars. One is also encouraged to play a seminar tape at bedtime while going to sleep. All of this allows for more successful "soul travel"—and, of course, more successful subliminal programming.

John-Roger is well aware of this: "While your conscious mind is at rest, during the sleep state;" he writes in the MSIA *Handbook for Ministers of Light,* "it will not question or block the spiritual action." The conscious mind "will not question or block" John-Roger's programming, either.

When one is consciously listening to his seminar, one is encouraged to "ignore" all the things that "don't apply to you" and look only for the "minute or two" during an hour-long seminar that is the message "the Traveler specifically has for you." All the other information was "for somebody else," and should be disregarded. Disregarded, perhaps—but the information enters the subconscious nonetheless.

And then there are spiritual exercises. Everyone is encouraged—strongly—to do two hours each day of spiritual exercises (or "s.e.'s"). For two hours, with your eyes closed, you think about guess what? Yes: John-Roger. He suggests that you "mock up" his image in your mind. He suggests that you visualize purple light: the color of the Traveler. The only time it's okay to open your eyes is to gaze lovingly at a photograph or painting of him. You can also "chant the sacred names of God"— names given to you by John-Roger and gods who are, you

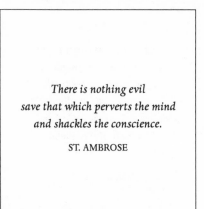

There is nothing evil save that which perverts the mind and shackles the conscience.

ST. AMBROSE

are continually reminded, far inferior to John-Roger. You can also play meditation tapes, which feature John-Roger's voice telling you, essentially, that you should feel absolutely terrific because, after all, you were clever enough and fortunate enough to discover John-Roger. And Innerphasings—a self-hypnosis audiotape made especially for you containing information you want to program into yourself, plus, of course, a few "words from our sponsor."

Seminars, combined with Discourses, the worshipful way in which John-Roger is treated by believers, the rumors of miracle healings (the far longer list of failed healings is never mentioned), John-Roger's demonstrations of his psychic powers (usually information he gathered surreptitiously combined with a crystal-ball-gazer's knack of throwing out generalities until the person being "read" awe-fully supplies specific information)—all goes in, seminar after seminar, Discourse after Discourse, retreat after retreat, year after year. (Workshops such as Insight or MSIA retreats increase vulnerability, thus shortening considerably the time needed for programming.)

At a certain instant, it all comes together. It does not gel or harden; it crystallizes—one moment it's not together, the next moment it is. One moment John-Roger is an occasionally interesting guy. The next minute he's God. Because it's been planted in your subconscious, the realization: "John-Roger is *IT!*" *seems* to come from *within you*. It is *your* realization. *You* had this breakthrough. "Nobody put me up to this; I discovered it *on my own.*"

Eureka! All problems are solved! From maternity to senility to eternity, *J-R is there* and will help you—*personally*—every step of the way.* "The Mystical Traveler will play all the roles in your life,"

*One of his favorite stories is the classic *Footsteps in the Sand*, in which the disciple looks back on his life and notices that when times were easy, there were two

Master of the Universe? No.
Master of Programming? Yes.

107

> Sometimes it is easier to see clearly into a liar than into a person telling the truth. Truth, like light, is blinding. Falsehood, on the other hand, is a beautiful twilight that enhances every object.
>
> ALBERT CAMUS

John-Roger proclaims on a meditation tape. John-Roger was there at our conception, and our birth when he "pushed us into the body." He never leaves us (it is our lack of *perception*, not his lack of *presence* that causes us to be unaware of him), and will be there to "take you from the body" at the moment of your death. Conception to cremation.

And that's how it works. From that point on, you're hooked. It would take a great deal of reprogramming to unhook you. But that's not likely to happen. Now that you *know* that John-Roger is God, and you *know* you came to this conclusion *on your own*, you then willingly take part in—even *seek*—more intense, more extreme, and more devotional programming.

Just to make sure that no reprogramming accidentally sneaks in, one is encouraged to leave behind non-believing friends, husbands, wives, children, parents, bosses, employees, and anyone else. You are encouraged to "chant the names of God"—or chant the name "J-R" or "John-Roger"—no matter where you are or what else you're doing. The exploration of other groups or practices is severely frowned upon.

Recreational activities such as reading books or watching television are considered frivolous. "Don't turn on the TVs until you've done your two hours of s.e.'s" is a common message. As one Devoted to the Light, one should be doing *significant* things: listening to seminar tapes, reading Discourses, s.e.'s, and *service*. And whom does one serve? The Traveler, of course. How does one serve the Traveler? Either volunteer for one of John-Roger's organizations, or go out and make some money and *donate it* to one of John-Roger's organizations.

All achievements, successes, and personal gains in a devotee's life are to be attributed to John-Roger. People who take credit for anything *personally* are accused of egocentricity, materialism, and

pair of footsteps in the sand and when times were difficult, there was only one pair of footsteps in the sand. "Why, during the hard parts of my life, did you desert me?" the seeker asks his master. "I did not desert you," the master answers, "Those were the times I carried you." With stories such as this, John-Roger moves from programming to *seduction*.

pride. The teachings of the Movement are clear: the bad in your life is your fault, the good in your life is John-Roger's gift.

Over time, most of your friends are Movement friends; your romantic relationships are with Movement people (or people who show a strong leaning toward the Movement); much of your business is done with people in the Movement; and, beyond your basic needs, all your money is spent on Movement activities.

> *I couldn't claim that*
> *I have never felt*
> *the urge to explore evil,*
> *but when you descend into hell*
> *you have to be very careful.*
>
> KATHLEEN RAINE

Given all this, perhaps it's easier to understand how John-Roger is able to get rich people to turn over all their money; get heterosexual (sometimes married) men to join him in sexual liaisons; and how he got a curmudgeonly, independent-minded writer to author books for him, give him piles of money, and thank him for the privilege.

Master of the Universe? No.
Master of Programming? Yes.

109

Face
concealed
to protect
the
innocent.

CHAPTER ELEVEN
Sex and the Single Preceptor

If you're going to have conjugal relationships with someone, do yourself a favor and have them with the most enlightened person you can find.

JOHN-ROGER

JOHN-ROGER has a Mormon background, conservative politics, and New-Age leanings. Naturally, he would choose a sex life that reflects these influences. I think it's fair to categorize John-Roger's sex life as closeted homosexual serial polygamy.

That John-Roger is gay is not an issue: it makes absolutely no difference to me, would probably make no difference to the vast majority of his followers, and is not even a complaint of the several men I talked to who John-Roger coerced into having sex with him. The only person who seems to think it's unacceptable for John-Roger to be gay is John-Roger.

The fundamental problem is that John-Roger uses spiritual promises, psychic intimidation, and severe breaches of the minister-congregant relationship to fulfill his sexual desires. It is this gross and invasive manipulation which those involved find objectionable. If he had used the techniques on women, it would be just as appalling.

Although John-Roger would vary his coercive approach based upon the individual, an overall pattern (at least in the cases where he was successful) is observable.

First, as with all John-Roger's manipulations, it's important that the victim (it's a harsh term, but that's what they are) believes that John-Roger has special spiritual connections that give him super-

> *If you enter
> into a sexual reltionship
> in deceit and dishonesty,
> you will create a karmic
> indebtedness that may be
> difficult to handle.*
>
> *I hope you understand this:
> it's important.*
>
> JOHN-ROGER

natural powers. (This explains why John-Roger has had far more success with the young men who already *believe* he is God than with those who must be convinced and *then* seduced.)

Second, John-Roger finds out what the person wants. You want to move to a higher level of consciousness? Transcend the pattern of reincarnation forever? Overcome the life-threatening illness (conveniently diagnosed by John-Roger)? Get rich? Get famous? It doesn't matter: if you believe John-Roger has it within his gift, he'll promise it to you.

Third, John-Roger doesn't simply *trade* the promise for sex, nor does he ask for sex as a token of *gratitude*—he wants sex with him to be seen as an *honor*. John-Roger gets no personal pleasure from sex, you understand: he *tolerates* it because he wants to give you the *spiritual* gift that goes with it. Here the deceptions have been many, and are as creative as they are appalling. They have included:

(A) If you have the "seed of the Traveler" in you, you cannot be lost to the Traveler throughout all time and space.

(B) Sex is an initiation into the highest spiritual brotherhood. If you begin to "slip" from the sanctity of this brotherhood, additional sexual activities (booster initiations, I suppose) will get you back in tune with God.

(C) John-Roger and his victim are already having sex on the "astral plane," which indicates it's a karmic situation strongly desired by the young man. The only thing keeping the young man from fulfilling the young man's *secret* (astral) desires is that the young man is "a chickenshit."

(D) Whatever physical pain, emotional disgust, or mental confusion the young man may experience as a result of sex with J-R is, in fact, "working off karma" in the fastest, highest way possible. If John-Roger loves you enough, he'll inflict discomfort because he wants to spare you countless lifetimes as, oh, a Biafran refugee.

(E) Sex is necessary to drive out an "evil spirit" or to protect one from a "psychic attack." Only the most intimate contact with the Traveler's physical body can save the young man in question from demon possession.

(F) For a young man with a Christian background, John-Roger explained that Jesus had sex with all twelve disciples, and that John was "the beloved" because he was the *sexual* favorite of Jesus—his *lover.*

(G) A young man with a general belief in the Bible is told by John-Roger that the rod and staff mentioned in the 23rd Psalm, verse 4, ". . . thy rod and thy staff they comfort me," refers specifically to John-Roger's erect penis. *(I am not making this up!)* What John-Roger failed to note was that the same verse begins: "Yea, though I walk through the valley of the shadow of death . . . ."

> *The idea here is honesty—*
> *if you're expressing lust,*
> *call it lust.*
> *If you simply feel sexy, call it that.*
> *Be honest.*
> *If you say it's spiritual*
> *and it's not,*
> *you may be committing a*
> *"spiritual crime."*
>
> JOHN-ROGER

(H) Sex with John-Roger would cure any illness. As John-Roger said, quite sincerely, to one of his male staff: "If you give me a blow-job, that will get rid of your cold." The staff member chose vitamin C instead.

Fourth, John-Roger wanted each of his sexual prey to believe that he was the *only* person with whom John-Roger was having sex. The connection was *unique.* He and he alone was so honored by the "Traveler's gift." For a period of several years, John-Roger was having regular sex with at least five members of his live-in staff and none of them knew about the others.

To accomplish this feat—which should assure John-Roger an honorary position in the Juggler's Hall of Fame—he concocted the following story: Since the Traveler is consciously aware of all levels of consciousness simultaneously, the Traveler, naturally, cannot sleep. The Traveler did, however, "lay his physical body down" so that the Traveler Consciousness can go bopping about other universes tidying up this and straightening out that. It was essential, however, when the body was down that someone "watched the physical body." When the Traveler Consciousness was out of the body, it seems, the body was susceptible to being "taken over" by "negative spirits."

Whoever had to watch the body, naturally, had to spend the night in J-R's bedroom. Before or after his "night travels" to save the universe, J-R would have sex with the young man, and the others did not know about it. J-R's foreplay was simply to say at some point in the evening to one of his staff, "You'll be watching the body tonight."*

To arrange privacy for a sexual liaison with non-live-in staff devotees was not difficult: Before disappearing behind looked doors, John-Roger announced that he would be doing a "counseling," "Light reading," "Innerphasing," "polarity balance," or "aura balance." As aura balances involve lying down, and polarity balances involved lying down and removing one's shirt, if John-Roger and guest emerged from the "spiritual service" with rumpled clothes, no one gave it a second thought.

When these excuses ran out, John-Roger said he required someone to do some "body work" on him. Indeed. Specific staff members knew specific techniques—one could crack his neck using a towel, another could put his "rib back in place" by pressing a point in his back—and when he needed that portion of his body "worked on," the appropriate staff member was summoned. Once that work was done, well, to quote the romance magazines of John-Roger's adolescence: ". . ."

In terms of sexual activity, John-Roger was, as they say, versatile. The young men on staff, however, seemed to specialize. The specialties were not chosen by the young men, but were assigned by John-Roger. His choice of partner for any given interlude, then, may have had more to do with the sexual *activity* he desired rather than the *person* he wanted to be with.

John-Roger collected his men in the same way a historical Mormon would gather his wives. He would have an attraction, pursue the young man with a dazzling courtship (God provided lots of money for this), and make whatever spiritual or physical promises (or threats) necessary. The young man would move in ("join staff"), receive a gold HU ring from John-Roger ("HU" means God—the

---

*What was it like to watch J-R's body? According to every former staff member I talked to, it looked a great deal like an overweight man sleeping. He would snore, toss and turn, and snore some more. John-Roger explained he was fully aware during all of these activities—he was simply *pretending* to be asleep to trick the negative forces into attacking his body so that he might "catch" them.

gift of the ring was synonymous with the marriage ceremony), and become John-
Roger's favorite until another
man stirred John-Roger's
fancy. Those who were no
longer the favorites would by
now have assumed more
practical duties—such as doing Insight trainings, spiritual
services, making sure John-
Roger had every material

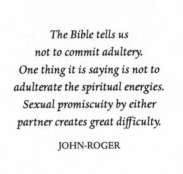

*The Bible tells us
not to commit adultery.
One thing it is saying is not to
adulterate the spiritual energies.
Sexual promiscuity by either
partner creates great difficulty.*

JOHN-ROGER

thing he desired, and so forth. They would still, however, be called
upon for sexual favors.

Also in true Mormon (as well as macho) tradition, although
John-Roger was allowed his pick of the harem—plus any outsiders
who succumbed to his spiritual seduction line or, in one report,
financial compensation—his staff was not permitted to have sex
with anyone else, inside or outside the Movement. (That the men
didn't have sex with each other was a given in that—other than
their interactions with John-Roger, which they believed to be spiritually necessary—the men were all heterosexual.)

John-Roger also traded spiritual favors with those he didn't
want sex from in order to get sex from those he did. Here, for
example, is how he "recruited" one young man to join his staff:

The man was tall, dark, and handsome (or, as Mae West might
describe him, "tall, dark, and then-some"). His girlfriend brought
him into the Movement. One of John-Roger's sexier post-ingénues
(John-Roger once announced to a group of about 400 that this
woman "had the best tits in the Movement") immediately glom-
med onto this hunk, who dumped his girlfriend (bad karma) and
was soon seen driving his new woman's Mercedes sports car up to
PRANA.

The new Movement couple went to Mexico for a vacation. The
woman's husband had just left her, and she was in need of, um,
intensive grief counseling. She could be heard throughout the hotel, at all hours of the day or night, screaming and moaning—over
the loss of her husband. The poor dear.

Knock, knock, knock. John-Roger had followed them. The
hunk was sent from the room while his future was decided by
those older and more, uh, spiritually experienced.

> The misuse or abuse of sexual
> energies can certainly lead you into
> areas of karma that may be
> difficult for you to resolve,
> and we certainly do not condone
> any activities of this type.
>
> JOHN-ROGER

"I want him," John-Roger told his negligeed disciple.

"I want him, too," she said.

"I'm the Traveler," he said.

"Can't we share him?" she asked.

"No," he said. The idea made John-Roger indignant. How *dare* she suggest such a sordid arrangement? Did she not realize that he is a man with moral standards?

By the time the meeting was over, John-Roger had a new staff member (break out the gold HU-rings), John-Roger called the woman's departed husband and told him it was his "karma" to return to her (which he did), and the woman got her Soul Initiation.

To his followers and the members of his staff with whom he was not sexually involved, John-Roger claimed to be celibate. But, he told his followers, he was not celibate from choice: all the "negative karma" he removed from his disciples and "transmuted" through his "physical body" required him to keep his physical energy intact. In other words, he was celibate as a service to and sacrifice for his disciples. In another instance, he said his enemy was "just too powerful" for congress with another human.

Not all of John-Roger's sexual conquests have been successful. Alas, there are some spiritually unaware handsome young men who refuse to face the fact that sex with John-Roger is not sex but a sacrament.

While traveling in Chile in 1980, John-Roger met a beautiful twenty-year-old. John-Roger, captivated, began his slow dance of seduction. (John-Roger is the most impatient of men in all but two areas: indoctrinating new members and sexual seduction.) John-Roger dazzled the young man with gifts and promises of God. He offered the young man a position on his staff and a green card, which he would obtain by giving him a "critical" job in one of his nonprofit organizations. John-Roger returned to Los Angeles, and the young man was to follow as soon as he could obtain a visa.

The United States embassy in Chile, alerted to John-Roger's true intentions by one of the young man's friends, denied the visa.

John-Roger sent the young man money, and suggested he go to Ecuador, establish residence, and get a visa from there. The Ecuadoran embassy, alerted by the Chilean embassy, refused. John-Roger recommended he go to Colombia. Same story. John-Roger flew to South America to handle the situation personally.

> To sexually seduce someone
> in the name of spirituality
> is considered a "spiritual crime"
> by the Lords of Karma.
>
> JOHN-ROGER

When he arrived, he found the young man had not abandoned his girlfriend—which John-Roger had insisted upon; she had traveled with him the entire time. "Didn't I tell you that women were a trap for men who wanted to walk the spiritual high country?" John-Roger asked. Why, John-Roger was *so* devoted to God that he hadn't even *looked* at a women sexually in *years*. The young man broke down, saying that finding God was the most important thing in his life, and he would leave his girlfriend behind.

John-Roger then performed a "spiritual aura balance" on the young man, and during the course of it fondled the young man's genitals. The young man was deeply confused. He sought help from a psychiatrist. The psychiatrist advised him, essentially, to go home to Chile with his girlfriend and do what he could to forget the whole thing.

The young man left home, left college (he was studying physics), nearly left his girlfriend, and spent almost two years wandering around South America on what John-Roger convinced him was a spiritual quest. The young man was but one more in a long list of individuals deeply harmed by John-Roger's use of spiritual promises to fulfill sexual desires.

I personally witnessed a miniature version of this saga around 1991. I was traveling with John-Roger and staff on his whistle-stop tour of the Eastern seaboard cities. The format was the same, city by city: A John-Roger seminar was announced, people paid money to get in, but before J-R spoke there was a long, laborious begging for money led by one or more staff members. An hour and a half later, J-R finally spoke. The next day, the traveling staff did "spiritual services" at seventy-five bucks a pop (each traveling staff member had to earn his or her expenses on the road by doing

> *Spiritual people can become well known as "bedroom athletes," but this is in no way a compliment. This is a misdirection and misappropriation of spiritual energy.*
>
> JOHN-ROGER

enough spiritual services each day to pay his or her own way), and then it was off to another city. The John-Roger seminars were video- and audiotaped, and later sold.

At one of these evening seminars, the brother of one of John-Roger's followers from Los Angeles attended. He was attractive, intelligent, young, and straight—John Roger's dream man *(du jour)*. Alas, the young man was not *quite* as devoted as John-Roger would have liked—but, what the hell, it was all part of the challenge, right?

John-Roger scooped up the young man, and he traveled from city to city with the rest of us. It was clear that we were all to be friendly to the young man, but not *too* friendly. This was especially true of me, the only gay person on the tour other than John-Roger. John-Roger used God's money to buy him first class tickets, meals, and hotel rooms. It was clear to all that John-Roger had found a new "guy."

John-Roger openly used his nightly seminars to flatter the young man. John-Roger, who has absolutely no trouble taking anything from anyone and never giving credit, gave the young man credit for *everything*. "I was talking to a really good friend of mine who said . . ." "One of the people with the most spiritual potential I've met in a long time was telling me . . ." and "Someone sent by Spirit for me to give special instruction to taught *me* something when he said . . ." The themes of the seminars were the importance of personal instruction, how much a more experienced person can teach a less experienced person, how there are shortcuts to Spirit when a master takes a liking to you, and so on. It was embarrassing.

This went on for about two weeks. At four o'clock one morning I was sound asleep in my hotel room when the phone rang.

"Where is he?" the voice demanded.

"Who?" I asked.

"Andrew [not his real name]," the voice sputtered.

"I have no idea," I said.

There was a pause. I heard muffled conversations—the staff

member obviously had his hand over the phone and was talking with someone else, almost certainly John-Roger. "When did you see him last?" I was asked. The tone was short, demanding, direct.

"When he was having dinner at the hotel restaurant with John-Roger," I said.

More muffled conversation. "Are you *sure* he's not there with you?"

> *So if you enter into these actions of spiritual deceit, you're going to harvest what you sow.*
>
> JOHN-ROGER

"Yes," I said.

"Okay. Let me know if you hear anything." Click. He hung up the phone.

Now that I was fully awake, I heard noises in the hall. It was common for J-R and staff to take all the rooms at the end of a hallway. This was one of those times and, based on the phone call I had just received, I knew the noise had something to do with the missing young man. I put on a bathrobe and went into the hall.

Staff members in assorted sleeping apparel were walking around the hallway or gathered in small groups talking quietly. They seemed to be gathered around one room, which I supposed to be that of the young man. I walked down the hallway and looked in. The door to the room was open, but it was empty. The bed had not been slept in or even unmade. "He is gone," somebody said over my shoulder as I peered into the room.

The whole scene reminded me of the resurrection of Jesus. There was the door to the tomb, open; the tomb, empty. In the New Testament, an angel explains "He is risen." Here, the explanation was, "He is gone." (Although I felt very sad for John-Roger at the time, I must admit now that thinking back on it and the fate in store for the young man if he had fallen for John-Roger's line, the Hallelujah chorus is playing in my brain.)

John-Roger was nowhere to be seen, nor was the staff member who called my room. The best anyone could figure is that the young man bolted in the night, leaving no note or explanation. Everyone eventually drifted back to bed. Our scheduled departure for the airport was 10:00 that morning. John-Roger arrived late and looked terrible. He didn't talk to anyone. He wore dark glasses

> *[If you misuse sexual energy]*
> *you may find yourself*
> *experiencing such a tremendous*
> *loneliness that*
> *no matter where you turn,*
> *nothing happens*
> *except that loneliness.*
>
> JOHN-ROGER

much of the time. For the remainder of the tour, he was a walking zombie. There was no doubt in anyone's mind that he had fallen heavily for the young man and was devastated by his departure. The seminars took on themes such as sadness, loneliness, betrayal, and desolation. A new tone of existentialism entered the Traveler's teachings.

John-Roger's attempts to reach the young man proved futile. The mother told John-Roger that her son was emotionally very upset, did not want to talk to John-Roger ever again, and John-Roger was not to call the house again. Period. Attempts were made to discover which of the traveling group was closest to the young man. Calls to him from these people proved fruitless as well.

But John-Roger refused to give up. In California a few weeks later at a retreat, John-Roger—who always has more than enough hands waving at him to be called upon to ask questions—said instead that the Light was over the head of the young man's brother. This, John-Roger explained, meant the young man's brother was supposed to go to the microphone and interact with John-Roger. What followed was a solid hour of John-Roger shamelessly flattering the young man's brother. The young man's brother knew exactly what was going on. So did the rest of us. It was clear that John-Roger was trying to get his devotee to betray his brother and call him on behalf of John-Roger. This the devotee, knowing the chaotic state of his brother's emotions since his intense encounter with John-Roger, refused to do. I am told he left the Movement shortly thereafter.

⚖ ⚖ ⚖

There's not a single account, story, anecdote, or shred of evidence to indicate that John-Roger *ever* had an ordinary, romantic relationship with either man or women. His loneliness must be unbearable, but it does not excuse him for the lives he has ruined—even for a time—in the process of fulfilling his sexual desires by promising God to those who place their trust in him.

Arianna Huffington just after being baptized in the river Jordan during a month-long PRANA Theological Seminar training in Egypt and the Holy Land, personally supervised by John-Roger. According to John-Roger: "Baptism is a way of symbolically dying and being reborn again. It's a way of dying to the 'sin' in our life and being reborn to the Spirit in our life."

CHAPTER TWELVE

Isn't It *Wonderful* How *Huffington*
Rhymes with *Washington?*

> *He said to himself: I shall see*
> *whether this wise Socrates*
> *will discover my*
> *ingenious contradiction,*
> *or whether I shall be able*
> *to deceive him and the rest of them.*
>
> PLATO

WHEN people (reporters in particular) say, "You seem *fairly* bright; how did you ever come to believe that John-Roger had a direct connection to God?," my best answer is to point to Arianna Huffington: she's far brighter than I, thought that John-Roger had a direct connection to God long before I did, and she *still* believes he does.

Reporters love that answer because (a) it's a quotable analogy, and (b) they know the conversation is about to turn to "hot news." If you read this book in October or November of 1994, you will probably know who Arianna Huffington is. If you read this book in 1995 or early 1996, you might say either, "You mean Senator Huffington's wife?" or "Who?" If you read this book sometime after 1996, you could either say, "You mean the First Lady?" or "Who?" As of this writing (August 1994), Arianna is hot.

Her husband, Michael Huffington, after a week or so in the United States Congress, began running for senator from the state of California. He has a good chance of winning: he's the only member of Congress with an unblemished record. That he has no record *at all* is beside the point: his record *is* unblemished. His only political drawbacks are that he's too liberal for Republicans, too conservative for Democrats, too rich for people in general, and a tad on the dull side.*

*I use the word *tad* here as in "Michael Jackson is a *tad* on the eccentric side."

> Ninety-eight percent of the adults in this country are decent, hard-working, honest Americans. It's the other lousy two percent that get all the publicity. But then—we elected them.
>
> LILY TOMLIN

The only skeleton he *may* have in his closet is himself: if the MSIA rumor-mill is true (and I'm not saying I have any first-hand information on this—nor do I want any—I'm merely reporting rumors), Michael is gay. That's no big deal, of course, but the *fun* rumor around MSIA is that his boyfriend when he met Arianna was named *John Rogers*.*

Other than this handful of probable, possible, and unlikely trifles, Michael Huffington is squeaky clean.

And then there's Arianna.

Arianna. Intelligent, charming, gifted, witty, attractive—what can anyone do but complain that such virtues, in excess, occasionally become vices? One can complain that Michael has too much money, or that Arianna has too much charm, but these are arguments that die in the ears of all but the too-petty.

And then there's John-Roger.

John-Roger. Arianna's Achilles heel. (That nod to Greek mythology is in honor of Arianna's maiden name, Stassinopoulos; to her first major book, *The Gods of Greece;* and to her accent.) That cultured, sophisticated, well-connected Arianna would choose John-Roger for *anything*—much less as spiritual teacher for the past twenty years—is beyond comprehension. That is, of course, until you understand programming; then it all makes sense.

Arianna believes John-Roger to be the closest thing to heaven on earth, and that all the mystical mumbo-jumbo taught by John-Roger is considered by Arianna gospel truth.

She admitted to a reporter as late as August 1994 that she was an ordained minister in MSIA. (This reporter was *good:* he asked the right questions at the right time.)

In the mid-1980s, Arianna was baptized in the river Jordan in a

---

*Again, that's just a rumor: neither John-Roger nor Arianna—nor any of Arianna's close friends—can keep a secret. But then, neither John-Roger nor Arianna—nor any of Arianna's close friends—has ever been known to let the truth get in the way of either an anecdote or an opportunity; hence, the rumor *might* not be true at all. On the other hand, where there's smoke there's friction—or so they say in politics.

ceremony officiated by John-Roger.

According to John-Roger in his book, *Baptism Through the Holy Spirit:*

> Baptism, through the Movement of Spiritual Inner Awareness, and in accordance with the teachings of the Mystical Traveler and Preceptor Consciousness, is a ceremony of full immersion.

One of the most astounding cases of clairvoyance is that of the noted Greek psychic Achilles Loudos. Loudos realized that he had unusual powers by the age of ten, when he could lie in bed and, by concentrating, make his father's false teeth jump out of his mouth.

WOODY ALLEN

At the point when you come up out of the water, a guardian angel will be placed with you by the Lord Jesus Christ who oversees this blessing and baptism directly.

You could call the angel "Jesus" or "Archangel Michael" or "Herman" or "Susie" or "Mary" or anything else. Understand very clearly that you can call your guardian angel anything you want.

If you were baptised in the true sense of the word, then you do have a guardian angel. A lot of people who have had a ritual performed and have been sprinkled with some water do not have a guardian angel, nor have they been baptised. It doesn't matter who says they were baptised, where they had the ritual performed, or anything else.

After you are immersed in the water, all of your "sins," all of the dumb things that you've done in your life, are erased and forgiven—you may come up out of the water feeling confused, disoriented, or dizzy for a few seconds. That means that you have wiped out your sins and negativity.

When the person receiving baptism says in his heart, "I'm sorry for all these things that I've done," that forgiveness goes back to and includes existences and lives prior to this one. It goes way back and lines up through all the karmic fields of all your existences. You get a shot at clearing and forgiving yourself for the totality of your existence, not just this lifetime. Most other groups and churches baptise for this lifetime and hope that's going to do it. The baptisms that are done and authorized through the Movement of Spiritual Inner Awareness are set up through Spirit before the physical ritual ever takes place. I line up the energies from Spirit so that when the person comes in to receive baptism, their karmic fields are lined up and everything is set up so they can receive maximum benefit from the baptism.

> *Delusions, error, and lies*
> *are like huge, gaudy vessels,*
> *the rafters of which are*
> *rotten and worm-eaten,*
> *and those who embark in them*
> *are fated to be shipwrecked.*
>
> BUDDHA

Let's look at what Arianna's belief that J-R is (nearly) God has meant over the past twenty years—to Arianna and to John-Roger. Then we can predict what Arianna's belief could mean for us all— if her political ambitions for Michael are fulfilled.

I first met Arianna in 1979 when we co–team-captained* an Insight training at Findhorn, Scotland. Big mistake. It was as though Rush Limbaugh's and Howard Stern's radio shows were suddenly combined, and they had to battle it out for airtime.

By making us co–team captains, Insight had violated one of the fundamental laws of physics: two prima donnas cannot occupy the same space at the same time.

But, oh, we tried, we tried. Arianna was the star of Insight and MSIA in London. She knew every assistant *personally*. Arianna, it is said (by Arianna), single-handedly brought Insight to London. She carried it across the Atlantic on her back like Mother Courage. Her role as co–team captain was an honorific one. Whereas I didn't know any of the assistants, Arianna didn't know anything about being team captain. That was no problem: I was happy to take care of the team-captaining stuff and free Arianna for more important matters—such as schmoozing. (Arianna is the best Gentile schmoozer since Cleopatra.)

The trouble was, Arianna wanted to *be* a team captain—that she didn't know how was a mere detail. To Arianna, being a team captain consisted of (a) feeding the assistants a full meal every hour (with "nourishing snacks" on the half hour), and (b) saying

---

*The team captain at Insight is responsible for managing the assistants and making sure that all the work that has absolutely no glamour attached to it gets done. All the glamour jobs are reserved for the facilitators. Speaking in front of the room, facilitator job; sitting in the back of the room, assistant job. Announcing that there will be a twenty-minute break, facilitator job; cleaning up the room during the twenty-minute break, assistant job. Telling people that if they feel nauseous, all they have to do is raise their hand and an assistant will bring them a "barf bag," facilitator job; holding the barf bag for the unhappy participants, assistant job. It was the team captains' job to somehow make cleaning, straightening, and bag-holding (for no pay) a *privilege*. Team captaining was not an easy job.

fo-coos a great deal. *(Fo-coos* was Arianna's pronunciation of *focus* which, to Arianna, meant, "Let's all *fo-coos* on Spirit for a while, then Spirit will do the work for us and we can all have some more food.") Alas, it takes a tad more than that (there's that *tad* word again) to get a seminar off the ground; trifles such as letting the assistants know what time

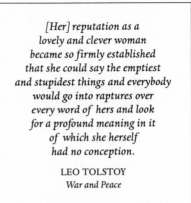

[Her] reputation as a lovely and clever woman became so firmly established that she could say the emptiest and stupidest things and everybody would go into raptures over every word of hers and look for a profound meaning in it of which she herself had no conception.

LEO TOLSTOY
War and Peace

they should be there and what they should be doing.

Arianna, however, taught me an invaluable lesson about politics: strike first, strike fast, strike hard.

Before I could get to the facilitator, who was about two minutes away, and let him know that, although we had been at it for five hours, the seminar room was not a seminar room but more closely resembled a Greek deli, Arianna had already called the Insight International headquarters in Los Angeles and told them —in detail—how *unloving* I was.

Well, *unloving* was simply the *worst* thing you could call anyone around Insight. Wicked, lewd, licentious, wasteful, inefficient, even late—all these were "opportunities for growth" to Insight and "challenges of acceptance and forgiveness" to MSIA. But *unloving?* Oh! By accusing me of that, Arianna cast me down among the Unforgiven.

As I was flayed and filleted (lovingly, of course) over international phone lines by the Powers That Be at Insight, I reflected on how much smarter Arianna was than I had given her credit for: she knew that after my official chastisement, any complaints I might have about her incompetence would sound merely defensive. To Arianna I was an interference—*she* had arranged this training, and *I* was not letting *her* be the *Queen*. (The role she has had, undisputed, since birth.) The impertinence of me! I was expendable, so, I was expended. The description she would later give Picasso fit Arianna perfectly: creator and destroyer.

The next week, to London where I team-captained an Insight I and Arianna team-captained an Insight II. They were taking place simultaneously in the same building, but in separate rooms. Here I saw an example of Arianna's extraordinary ability to create. She

> Whom the mad would destroy,
> first they make Gods.
>
> BERNARD LEVIN

was at the time having an affair with Bernard Levin, who was (and still is) one of the most respected, learned, and *feared* of all British critics. For a certain process in Insight II, which he was taking, Arianna got him to dress up as a ballerina—ballet slippers, white leotards, and all. Hell, if Insight could get Bernard Levin in a tutu, why should I marvel that Insight made me think John-Roger was God? And if in 1979 Arianna Stassinopoulos could make Bernard Levin look like Margot Fonteyn, is there any doubt that in 1996 Arianna Huffington can make Michael Huffington look like Ronald Reagan?

Over the years, I saw Arianna at numerous MSIA events. Her warmth was directly proportional to my material success: when I went bankrupt and was living next door to PRANA in an $85-per-month apartment, pure oxygen seemed more perceptible to Arianna than I; when my introductory computer books became successful in the early 1980s, Arianna seemed perfectly comfortable making me her uncompensated computer consultant. When Arianna abandoned hunt-and-peck to hunt for a husband, I became a blithe spirit again. And so it went. It was no insult—it was just Arianna.

In 1982, having conquered London's intellectual and cultural community, Arianna set her sights on New York. Greece, Britain, Manhattan—all islands were home to Arianna.

Her New York goal was not so much the intelligentsia or the creative, but the *social.* London society was so, well, *rigid:* to get in you pretty much had to be *born* in. One of the few things Arianna couldn't influence was her birth. But she *could* move to where charm, thoughtful little gifts, and a certain curiosity value meant more than bloodline.

Like any good salesperson, all Arianna needed was an introduction; she'd take it from there. She did. Arianna has the most uncanny radar: she walks into a room and instinctively knows who the most important person in the room is, the second most, the third most, and precisely the amount of time she must allocate to each.

Then she goes to work.

It's a joy to behold. It's also a joy to be held in Arianna's adoring, attentive gaze. She actually *listens*. She touches you, *so*. For your allotted season, the Grecian sun is warm indeed. She is with you fully in your moment, and when your moment passes, she passes on to another's moment.

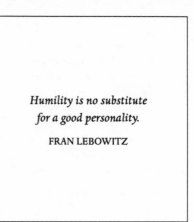

Humility is no substitute for a good personality.

FRAN LEBOWITZ

Arianna is also one of the great flatterers of the Western world. She studies for a party as she would prepare for a debate at the Cambridge Union (a British institution of which she was the first woman president). She learns whatever she can about each guest, then makes a point of mentioning it—always in the most positive light possible, always with just the right amount of enthusiasm: to a tender flower she sprinkles; to a mighty oak she gushes.

On the way to a social gathering she may stop by a bookstore, read a few paragraphs from the center of a book, then on meeting the author say, "I was reading your *magnificent* book today—I am *especially* fascinated by the part in which you said . . ." and then quote several sentences from the book, almost verbatim. Being an author herself, she knows that all she has to do is look at the now-enchanted writer with her wide-eyed adoring gaze, and the next several minutes will be consumed by the author's monologue. Arianna moves on, and the author proclaims that she is a *brilliant* conversationalist.

With these skills, it didn't take her long to be the toast-point of Manhattan, covered in Beluga. The only problem: she had no money. She was broke. All those thoughtful little presents cost thoughtless big dollars. She turned to her Source, her Abundant Supply: God—that is, John-Roger. John-Roger paid the bills (with God's money, of course), and Arianna threw the parties. The goal was to make John-Roger a social butterfly.

The difficulty is that John-Roger is a social aardvark. To say he's a liability at a cultured function is being complimentary. At her soirees, Arianna would seat John-Roger between the two most important people there. The VIPs would come away saying, "Who *is* that boorish little man?"

> [He] may have wished I had
> presented him as a combination
> of Charles de Gaulle and Disraeli,
> but I didn't . . . out of respect
> for de Gaulle and Disraeli.
> I described him as a cowboy
> because that is how
> he described himself.
> If I were a cowboy I would be offended.
>
> ORIANNA FALLACI

When you've been pro-grammed to love John-Roger, his lack of manners is seen as honesty, his ignorance as in-nocence, his condescension as divine forbearance, his caustic comments as loving feed-back (or, as he likes to say, "feed-forward").

Alas, the in-cult-uration process that allows (indeed, *insists* upon) loving John-Roger takes a little more time than the average dinner party. When guests not in the Movement questioned Arianna's wisdom at championing such a person ("My dear, have you lost your *mind?*"), Arianna remained faithful: "He's adorable once you get to know him; all it takes is a little time." Apparently, no one—even in New York society—had *that* much time.

Fortunately, J-R tired of the social whirl: these New York types just didn't worship him enough, poor things. Lack of perception, no doubt. Oh, well, back to L.A.—where Arianna was soon to follow.

California, here she comes!

Arianna had a book to write. She needed a retreat; a sanctuary. She needed to get away from culture, intelligence, and society. Los Angeles was the perfect place. She rented a house (a mansion, actually), called me to see if I could get a computer for her whole-sale, and got to work.

At the center of Arianna's Los Angeles cultural vacuum was, naturally, John-Roger. She would knock off a few chapters by the pool (which she often did in the you-know-what), then prepared for an evening with her *beau du jour.*

Shall we talk about the Hunt for the Husband?

It's doubtful that John-Roger fulfills his spiritual promise to "work closely with you at every step of the way into the heart of God," but there's no doubt that he'll work *very* closely with you if you're a qualified disciple in search of a rich and powerful mate. John-Roger and Arianna went to work. First she tried powerful, but not too rich (Bernard Levin); then she sampled both rich and powerful (David Murdock); finally, she settled on not much power, but very rich (Michael Huffington): with his money and her brains, power was inevitable—and the power would be *hers.*

Arianna's relationship with David Murdock probably influenced John-Roger more than it did Arianna. First, there was David Murdock's ranch, with the finest collection of Polish Arabian horses in North America. John-Roger wanted a ranch where Arabian horses ran free and he could ride among them. Within a few years, God's money provided him with just such a ranch.

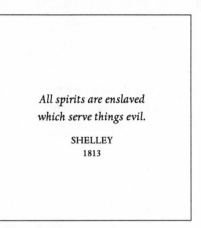

All spirits are enslaved
which serve things evil.

SHELLEY
1813

Then there was the stock market. Murdock would give Arianna investment recommendations (read: stock tips), but Arianna had no money to fully exploit these nuggets of wisdom. John-Roger, however, did. These tips allowed John-Roger to use God's money to make John-Roger money. Arianna's consulting fees, of course, continued. John-Roger liked the stock market: it was easier than traveling to Las Vegas, more profitable than a "fundraiser seminar," and didn't require his sending someone to the 7–Eleven to purchase lottery tickets.

Yes, John-Roger liked this David Murdock character very much. The trouble was, Murdock did not exactly want to be either married *or* president, two requirements high on Arianna's wish-list.

You see, Arianna wanted nothing less than the most powerful position in the world: the presidency of the United States. Alas, there is this picky little provision in the U.S. Constitution stating that the president must be native-born. Arianna would, of course, work on a constitutional amendment, but first she would become first lady. It was easier to get *to* the White House from *within* the White House, she figured. Surely in eight years, her president-husband could get just *one little amendment* passed:

> The constitutional provision that the president of the United States must be a native-born citizen shall not apply to persons named Arianna who have written bestselling books on Maria Callas and Pablo Picasso.

Simple, direct, humane—what legislator could resist?

When in the heat of marital negotiations (neither John-Roger nor Arianna understood the concept of courtship, but they *did* understand negotiations), Arianna would be on the phone to John-Roger every night, after every date, with a blow-by-blow description. Machiavelli would instruct his eager princess.

Prince Charming finally arrived—thanks to Fairy Godmother Ann Getty (who loathes John-Roger, and now, it seems Arianna, too)—in the form of Michael Huffington.

> *It is of great consequence to disguise your inclination, and to play the hypocrite well.*
>
> MACHIAVELLI

The low estimates of the Huffington family wealth begin at $600 million. Papa Huffington thought Michael's ambition to be president was just fine (a boy has to do *something* to fill his days), but Papa also knew that Michael needed a wife and family. Jerry Brown proved that those gay rumors don't just go away if you claim to be "spiritual" and date Linda Ronstadt. The public can accept, perhaps, *one* abnormality—and being outrageously rich is abnormal enough. Every other aspect of Michael's life would have to be mainline America.

Once Michael and Arianna met and Michael gave his tacit approval, the nuptial negotiations continued, between Arianna (backed by John-Machiavelli) and the Huffington family attorneys. It is said Arianna asked for and received a $1,000,000 prenuptial payment.

The merger—I mean the *marriage*—took place amidst the splendor usually reserved for the Queen's funeral. In the United States, traditionally, the father of the bride pays for the wedding. Arianna's father still lived in Greece where, traditionally, the father of the bride only provides two fertile goats, one of each gender. Arianna wanted something a *little* classier than that, so Ann Getty came to the rescue again and offered to pay for the wedding.

Ms. Getty had an intimate wedding and a small reception in mind—something that might fit comfortably into the living room of her townhouse. Arianna wanted to rent Madison Square Garden—with Yankee Stadium for the overflow—and pay-per-view cable worldwide. The compromise was still large enough to make Arianna's wedding the butt of conspicuous-consumption jokes for the next two years.* It cost Getty a rumored $114,000. Under-

---

*About six months after the wedding, I was having lunch high over San Fran-

standably, Getty refused to pay for the $35,000 wedding dress Arianna bought off the rack at Macy's or someplace. The wedding-dress bill went unpaid for a year. When it was paid, the check was from the Huffington accountants.

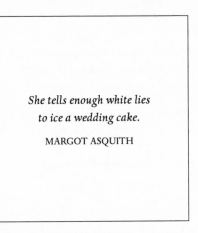

She tells enough white lies to ice a wedding cake.

MARGOT ASQUITH

When Hamlet expressed his displeasure that his mother married his uncle too soon after his father's death, he explained to his friend that it was due to thrift: the baked meats from the funeral provided cold cuts for the wedding. In the case of the Huffingtons, the baked meats from the wedding provided cold cuts for the announcement of Michael's political plans.

Oh, sure, first there were a couple of children to bear and a couple of mansions to buy and renovate, but that was all set decoration. The *play* was the thing in which Michael Huffington would capture the office of the king. Arianna got to work on the script: *Mr. Huffington Goes to Washington.*

Careful (i.e. expensive) political analysis showed that the congressional seat most likely to be won in the next election by a Republican with liberal leanings was the congressional district surrounding Santa Barbara, California. Michael Huffington, a life-long Texan, and Arianna, a dual citizen of both Greece and the United States, moved into a $4,000,000 shack on five acres in the most fashionable section of Santa Barbara County. "The climate is so Mediterranean," Arianna explained. "It reminds me of Greece—of home!" Right. (Isn't it *wonderful* how *Arianna* rhymes with *Santa Barbara?*)

After an unfortunate miscarriage ("The soul was not yet ready to come through," John-Roger explained, casually dismissing the potentially traumatic event), a healthy child was born and christened Christina. The infant personally received a formal Baby Blessing from John-Roger. Most Movement babies get blessed by

cisco with Werner Erhard and William F. Buckley, Jr. In the distance, tens of thousands of multicolored balloons were released. Buckley looked out the window and casually commented, "What? Is Arianna Stassinopoulos getting married again?" I didn't know until later that one of the pre-Huffington husband-targets was Werner. Oh, how I wish I'd known it then! I'm sure there was a much better show on Werner's face after Buckley's totally innocent remark than there was in the skies over San Francisco.

> Know what is evil,
> no matter how worshipped it may be.
> Let the man of sense not mistake it,
> even when clothed in brocade,
> or at times crowned on gold,
> because it cannot thereby
> hide its hypocrisy,
> for slavery does not lose its infamy,
> however noble the master.
>
> BALTASAR GRACIÁN
> 1653

lesser Movement personages. A truly important baby—that is, a baby whose parents have wealth and power—gets the spiritual jump-start in life only John-Roger can provide. There was never any doubt that the fruit of Arianna's womb would be blessed by John-Roger himself, John-Roger having personally seen to its conception and having blessed the fetus informally on any number of occasions.

A Baby Blessing is the MSIA equivalent of a baptism. (Baptisms in MSIA take place when one is eight or older.) "Physical imbalances" in the child are corrected (none of these has "manifested physically," of course—and, thanks to the Baby Blessing, never will), the level of Spirit from whence the baby comes is announced, and the child's purpose in this lifetime is delineated.

As there were few parents in MSIA who were more devoted, richer, or potentially more powerful than Arianna, it's little wonder that Queen Christina came from a higher level, endowed with greater gifts, and charged with a higher purpose, than any female child born since the advent of birthing.* (Female children must have a category of their own, of course: I'm sure you'll recall John-Roger's teaching that females "can't hold the spiritual energy" the way males can.) (Oh, to know what the "free-will donation" was for *that* blessing.)

To give you an idea of how intimate the private conversations between John-Roger and Arianna are, and how completely Arianna relies on John-Roger for both spiritual and temporal guidance, allow me to convey an incident that happened at an MSIA retreat. For approximately two hours each day during these retreats, John-Roger "takes sharing." This means you stand in front of a microphone and "share" with John-Roger anything you want. Then John-Roger "works" with you. John-Roger's work may or may not have anything to do with what you shared (usually it doesn't), but the longer one is worked with, the more Beloved of the Traveler you are assumed to be. Even being *called on* to interact with John-Roger is considered a divine gift.

*Christina held the title for almost three years, until John and Laura Donnelly-Morton's daughter, Claire, "came forth." Ah, fleeting spiritual fame!

At every John-Roger event I attended in which sharing was taken, Arianna was always chosen; John-Roger's working with her went on for a minimum of half an hour. In all, I've probably seen Arianna share with John-Roger a dozen times in as many years.

> Theology is an attempt
> to explain a subject by men who
> do not understand it.
> The intent is not to tell the truth
> but to satisfy the questioner.
>
> ELBERT HUBBARD

The representative sharing I am about to describe took place in late 1990 or early 1991. Arianna approached the microphone with characteristic calm. She explained to John-Roger and the group (which numbered around 400) that she, her husband, and Christina all slept nude together in the same bed: she insisted there be a strong "bonding" in the family.* Christina slept between Michael and Arianna. In addition to bonding, Arianna explained, she wanted Christina to be able to wake up at any time during the night and have immediate access to mother's milk. If there is anything Arianna believes in almost as much as John-Roger, it's breast feeding. Theoretically, it is her view that children should be nursed until they qualify for Social Security. It is equally essential, according to Arianna, that a child not have to *cry* to get fed: It should only have to reach up, and nourishment is instantly at hand—just like God.

This background given, Arianna asked John-Roger her burning question: "John-Roger, how can I have another child?"

John-Roger explained that Michael was a "man's man," but he was also a man. This meant, John-Roger explained, that Michael responded *mechanically* to sexual stimulation. He also examined Arianna's aura to see if there was "a soul hanging around waiting to come in." Apparently there was. But this was not a soul that "had to come in," it was "optional." Some effort on Arianna's part would be required. This is the summation of an answer that went on for probably twenty-five minutes. Arianna's next question concerned the difficulties she was having with her interior decorator, which I'm sure we would all be better off not hearing another word about.

Later during that retreat, during entertainment time, I stood

---

*The bonding phase has clearly passed: In both Santa Barbara and Washington, D.C., all three Huffingtons have separate bedrooms. Christina shares hers with her younger sister, Isabella, whose conception we are about to get to if I would just tell the story and stop adding footnotes.

up and read a mock letter to my mother:

Dear Mom,

Hello. How are you? I am fine. Here I am at Camp Hinkins. Today Arianna Stassinopoulos Huffington stood up and shared with John-Roger. Arianna Stassinopoulos Huffington is very much like Jacqueline Kennedy Onassis. The only difference between them is that Jackie was born rich and eventually married a Greek, whereas Ari was born Greek and eventually married rich.

> *I would live*
> *in a communist country*
> *providing I was the Queen.*
>
> STELLA ADLER

During the sharing, Arianna explained that her child slept between her and her husband in case the child wanted to be nursed during the night. Then she asked John-Roger her big question: "John-Roger, how do I get pregnant again?" Now here is Arianna, the first woman to be president of the Cambridge Union, bestselling author, intelligent, worldly; and here's John-Roger, Mystical Traveler, Preceptor, fully conscious of all levels of existence simultaneously, able to answer any question on any subject in the universe. And what does Arianna want to know? "How do I get pregnant again?"

To me it's fairly obvious: She's waking up and sticking her tits in the wrong face.

The weather continues fine.

Your loving son,

Peter.

Whether it was John-Roger's spiritual intervention, Arianna's abandonment of romance for reflex, or (who knows?) the advice in my letter to Mother, less than a year later a child was born unto the Huffingtons, a female child named Isabella. The Huffingtons now had the minimum number of offspring to allow Michael to drop the phrase "my children" in interviews and political speeches.* A little

---

*Michael, who appears to be emotionally removed from practically everything, seems particularly removed from his daughters. While staying in one of the guest rooms at the Santa Barbara property, which is directly adjacent to the children's open-air playroom and near the swimming pool, I was able to observe, unnoticed, Michael's interaction with his children. There was none. He arrived from the main house in a bathing suit and robe for his morning swim, put the robe in the playroom, took his swim, put his robe back on, gave an instruction to the children's nanny (he was paying a weekly fee to a swimming instructor

bonding and little nursing later (Michael was *far* less involved in this baby's bonding), they were ready for their manifest destiny: the presidency.

Once the campaign began, it was politics as usual—but with a far bigger bankroll than Santa Barbara elections had ever imagined. One night about 10:30 I received a call

> You can fool all the people
> all the time
> if the advertising is right
> and the budget is big enough.
>
> JOSEPH E. LEVINE

from Arianna. A Huffington investigator had dug up some dirt on one of Michael's opponents in the congressional primary. Would I please call—*right now*—the radio show on which his opponent was the guest and ask about the allegations? I couldn't mention that I was a friend of the wife of Michael Huffington—I was supposed to be an ordinary concerned citizen of Santa Barbara, although I'm neither ordinary, concerned, nor a citizen of Santa Barbara. Arianna wanted to throw dirt into the campaign, but didn't want anyone to know that it came from the Huffington camp. (Arianna—whose accent sounds like Zsa Zsa Gabor on Quaaludes—is, alas, permanently disqualified from stealth activities involving anonymous phone voices.) I called the radio station, asked the embarrassing question (which, as I recall, had something to with a minor financial discrepancy in the opponent's personal finances). After the show, Arianna called me back and proclaimed me the Huffington Hero of the Hour. Although I was asked *repeatedly* to come down and lick stamps at Camp Huffington, I demurred, and that phone call was my total contribution to the Michael Huffington campaigns.*

As the fall 1994 senatorial election approaches, Arianna understands that she must distance herself from John-Roger. The closer the election is, the more distant from John-Roger Arianna be-

whether the instructor was used or not, and he would like the nanny to see to it that the instructor was used more often in teaching his daughters to swim—it was hard to tell whether he was concerned with his daughters' aquatic abilities or about getting his money's worth), and went back to the main house. In all, he had to walk past his daughters four times, and there was no interaction *at all*.

*They haven't stopped asking: As late as July 1994, I received a letter, personally signed by Michael, asking *me* for money. *Me?* Michael Huffington asking *me* for money! I guess I shouldn't be surprised: It's about as backward as any other request in politics.

comes. As of this writing, August 1994, Arianna is telling the press that her relationship with John-Roger was brief and superficial, and her motive was to gather research for her book, *The Fourth Instinct*.

> *For it came to pass that they did deceive many with their flattering words.*
>
> BOOK OF MORMON
> *Mosiah 26:6*

This excerpt from her July 14, 1994, interview on *The Diane Rhem Show* in Washington, D.C., is fairly typical:

> John-Roger is still a friend of mine. I got value from the seminars I did with him. I got value from a thousand different things, though—books, seminars. I have really taken most of the things that were available on the spiritual marketplace partly as research for my book and for understanding the fourth instinct.

What a pro, Arianna! She starts with the truth, throws in some subterfuge, moves into direct deception, and ends with a plug for her book. Brilliant! All this in only fifty-five words—and the whole thing done extemporaneously. As it was with Reagan, you may not appreciate everything he did, but you have to admire how well he got away with it.

Let's take another look at the Arianna two-step (which she perfected at the John-Roger School of Dance and Dramatic Arts). After *brilliantly* dodging a direct question from a caller, the host of the show had the audacity to ask Arianna the same question *again!* No wonder the great leaders of our time are so mistrustful of the media. Let's pick up Arianna's answer in mid-avoidance:

> ARIANNA: . . . our whole response to everyday decisions changes when we realize that when we choose loving over hatred and forgiveness over vindictiveness, we are closer to our fourth instinct [YET ANOTHER PLUG! EXCEPTIONAL!], and this could be in very trivial small ways...
>
> DIANE RHEM: But now more directly to [THE CALLER'S] question: Do you still consider yourself a minister in John-Roger's organization?
>
> ARIANNA: There isn't anything like an organization to belong to.

Give me a moment. I'm all *verklemt*. Talk amongst yourselves. I'll give you a topic: "The only reason Arianna Huffington doesn't follow in the tradition of her mentor, J-R, and call herself A.H., is because the left-leaning liberal press is likely to make snide comments about what else those initials might stand for while smoking pot and ridiculing the exceptional record of one of our four greatest living ex-presidents, George Bush."

All right. I'm better now. Thank you. What a *sensational* demonstration of one of

> *I wouldn't want to mislead you by doing other than saying however easy it would be for me to answer the question you have asked,* it is not fair for me to go further than I have. And I would not read too much into that.
>
> IAN MCDONALD
> British Ministry of Defence spokesman

John-Roger favorite defenses: the semantic slip-slide. Note that Arianna answers a question that was not asked: "Do you belong to John-Roger's organization?" The question *was:* "Do you still consider yourself a minister in John-Roger's organization?"

Is Arianna an ordained minister in John-Roger's MSIA? *Absolutely.* But because the caller referred to MSIA as an "organization," Arianna saw those two big O's in the word *organization*, picked her loophole, and slipped right through. Like *butter.* It's like the woman is covered in *butter.*

But even if the question *were* "Do you belong to John-Roger's organization?," Arianna's answer is *still* patently false. If it wasn't, how could John-Roger write to two recalcitrant ministers:

YOUR MINISTERIAL CREDENTIALS ARE REVOKED . . .
YOU ARE NO LONGER INITIATES OF THE MYSTICAL
TRAVELER . . . YOU HAVE BEEN DROPPED FROM THE
ROLLS OF THE MOVEMENT OF SPIRITUAL INNER
AWARENESS, INC. . . . . EVEN THOUGH YOU ARE STILL
RECEIVING DISCOURSES THEY WILL ALSO BE DIS-
CONTINUED . . .

It seems there's *something* organized there to belong to—or at least some indication of what membership in MSIA consists of. The answer to all four of these requirements, with respect to Arianna, is a resounding *yes.* The only exception is Discourses, because she's already read all twelve years' worth, and now subscribes to the Soul Awareness Tape Series—a monthly John-Roger tape especially for devotees who are ready for more "advanced" (read: weird) teachings.

But enough talk about John-Roger. Let's return to Arianna's far more interesting *denial* of John-Roger.

Now we'll see one of the most dramatic defensive moves taught at The John-Roger School of Martial Arts and Dirty Fighting: DIRECT ATTACK. A caller asks a perfectly reasonable question about a very real concern:

> It is impossible
> that a man who is false
> to his friends and neighbours
> should be true to the public.
>
> BISHOP BERKELEY
> (1685–1753)

CALLER: I'm very depressed when I think that the wife of a member of a cult has a husband running for the United States Senate. I'm concerned about her influence, which seems to be considerable, on her husband for the people he is going to—if he wins the election—the people he is going to put into office with him . . .

ALERT! ALERT! The caller is asking a question that is *highly* embarrassing—the very point on which Michael Huffington may lose the election. No time for an ordinary semantic slip-slide—it's time to *interrupt* and *strike!*

> **ARIANNA:** What is this cult you are talking about? There seem to be a lot of calls coming from the same source.

Like the *truth*, Arianna? That *can* be an intimidating source.

> I do not belong in any cult, unless you consider the Greek Orthodox Church a cult.

Denials swiftly done, she moves *directly* to her first blow:

> Anything else is just scurrilous, and unless you can provide some evidence, I think it's best not to talk in those terms.

Oooo, *scurrilous*—I have to look this one up. I know it's bad; I just don't know *how* bad. Talk amongst yourselves. Let me give you a topic. "As the election nears, Arianna is going to do fewer and fewer talk shows where rude and obnoxious listeners can join the impolite and pushy talk show hosts in ganging up on our poor dear and make her resort to serious defensive measures."

Here it is. *Scur•ri•lous*. It's worse than I thought. "1. Given to the use of vulgar or low abusive language; foul-mouthed. 2. Expressed in coarse and abusive language."

I don't remember the caller's being foul-mouthed, vulgar, coarse, or abusive. But then, *cult* is not the four-letter word that might cost me the White House.

But Tiger Huffington is not finished with the scurrilous caller:

ARIANNA: *So, I would encourage you to get some more current information.*

CALLER: *I would be happy to get some more. I would be very happy to get some more information, because I vote in California and if you could tell me where to get it, I would be more than happy to read it.*

> *Every violation of truth is not only a sort of suicide in the liar, but is a stab at the health of human society.*
>
> EMERSON
> 1841

Scurrilous, scurrilous, scurrilous! How *dare* the caller take Arianna up on her challenge in such an open, friendly, willing-to-learn way? This caller is a low, dirty street fighter; that's all there is to it. Since there is nothing anyone can read that will get Arianna off the cult-hook, naturally she has no choice but to revert to John-Roger's *primary* teaching: "I am the final authority; *you* are a jerk. Listen up: I'll say this only one more time."

> **ARIANNA:** You can get it right now. I am a member of the Greek Orthodox Church. I do not belong in any cult.

Good, good. But now, suddenly, Arianna pulls out a samurai sword she had concealed somewhere on her person, and without warning—*whoosh!*—the caller is decapitated and disemboweled with one lightning sweep:

> And I believe that if you are a Christian, or if you consider yourself a religious person, bearing false witness is a spiritual sin.

Indeed it is, Arianna. Indeed it is.

By the way, do you notice that Arianna (whose command of English is impeccable) says, twice: "I do not belong *in* a cult." Yes, Arianna, you do *not* belong in a cult. But do you belong *to* a cult? And if you think that little slip was unintentional, you are underestimating the John-Roger minister who may be our next first lady.

Let's take a moment here and say a brief prayer for the Greek Orthodox Church. Poor Greek Orthodox Church. Arianna claims to be one of them. Worse, she claims its teachings are *John-Roger's* teachings. In her book (which I don't have to mention here as Arianna is doing such a superlative job of it), Arianna gives John-Roger's interpretation of the Bible—inaccuracies and all—and claims it's part of her Greek Orthodox belief. It is nothing of the kind. It's John-Roger multi-pilfered teachings, picked over by Arianna—a bone here; a mealworm there.

To give one example of Reverend Huffington's religious illiteracy (as learned in the John-Roger School for Bible Study and Choir Boy Training):

My book is really about Christ's teachings, which also happen to be the teachings of every major religion . . .

This is a perfect example of John-Roger's ersatz ecumenicalism: it reveals not even a superficial knowledge of the world's religions *and* a basic ignorance of Jesus's teachings. To say that the major world religions have certain beliefs in common is fine; to say that "Christ's teachings . . . [are] the teaching of every major religion" is absurd.

To prove her errant point, Reverend Huffington doesn't quote Jesus. She quotes John:

. . . because it's the teaching that's summed up in the first line of the St. John's Gospel, that God is love. That is a very simple statement, an incredibly profound statement.

Well, it may be simple and it may be profound, but it has nothing to do with "the first line of St. John's Gospel." In fact, it does not even appear in the Gospel of John *at all.* (The Gospels, of course, are the first four books of the New Testament: Matthew, Mark, Luke, and John) "God is love" *does* appear in the first of John's three epistles, or letters, and isn't even in the first line of *that.* John doesn't get around to it until the fourth chapter (1 John 4:8,16). (Those, by the way, are the only two times that "God is love" appears in the entire Bible. Jesus said quite a lot about love— even *commanding* his disciples to love one another—but he never defined God as love.)

Why would Arianna quote a portion of John's epistles as gospel? Because John—John the beloved—is the *same* John that inhabits the body of Roger Hinkins, transforming him into John-Roger. Or so Arianna (like all other MSIA ministers) believes.

When Arianna says "Christ," she doesn't mean Jesus the Christ—as she knows most of us will assume—she means *John* the

Christ (who inherited the Mystical Traveler Consciousness from Jesus on the cross), and, most specifically, *John-Roger* the Christ.

As we have seen, John-Roger claims not only to occupy "the office of the Christ" and, of course, the Mystical Traveler Consciousness (which he now shares with *his* John the Beloved), but clearly

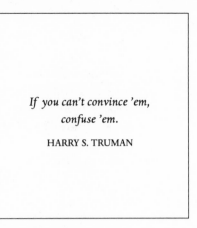

If you can't convince 'em, confuse 'em.

HARRY S. TRUMAN

puts himself one significant level above Jesus the Christ. To quote John-Roger:

> When Jesus came on the planet he occupied the office of the Christ . . . . Above that is the Mystical Traveler Consciousness [which Jesus had, too] . . . . The Traveler's job goes through many universes and planets. The Preceptor Consciousness [which Jesus did *not* hold] is one that goes clear outside of creation. It goes beyond your imagination. But that is the direct line of authority into God.

When a caller asked Arianna:

> Do you still believe that John-Roger still outranks Jesus Christ?

Arianna tries to laugh it off (oh, *silly* caller with your *silly* question):

> This is a little bit like 'Are you still beating your wife?' I never believed that, and he doesn't believe that, either.

You don't, Arianna? And John-Roger doesn't, either? Then why did the above quote appear in both the 1978 and revised 1986 editions of the *Handbook for Ministers of Light?* Haven't you read your own ministerial handbook in the past fifteen years? And how do you *know* what John-Roger does and does not "believe"?

If you'd like the Rosetta stone for interpreting Arianna's book, it is this:

FOURTH INSTINCT = MYSTICAL TRAVELER

That's it. Arianna took a kindly sounding chunk of John-Roger's Mystical Traveler teachings and found a more intellectually acceptable, pseudo-scientific term for it (the Fourth Instinct). But don't take *my* word for it: next time Arianna's on a talk show, call her and ask.

> It is inaccurate to say
> I hate everything.
> I am strongly in favor of
> common sense,
> common honesty,
> and common decency.
> This makes me forever
> ineligible for any public office.
>
> H. L. MENCKEN

⚖ ⚖ ⚖

The American public doesn't seem to mind if you did something foolish in your past. What Americans hate are *cover-ups*. Foolishness they can forgive; cover-ups they cannot. It wasn't the Watergate break-in that brought Nixon down; it was his cover-up.

Arianna has grown complacent since her debating days as the president of the Cambridge Union. Two decades of PR tours, society gatherings, and discoursing with John-Roger do little to sharpen the mind. In fact, one learns that most people—including reporters—believe what you tell them: they simply don't have the time to fact-check every statement made in an interview. Once a dishonesty gets in print, it's likely to be printed again, and that's how legends are made. (And Arianna knows legend-making well: she wrote biographies of two of the best self-legendizers of the twentieth century—Maria Callas and Pablo Picasso.) Even when Michael ran for the United States Congress, it was a local race and never would have reached national prominence had he not spent more of his personal money to be elected than any other congressional candidate in history.

Now Michael wants to be among the most powerful one hundred elected officials in America: the United States Senate. The results will be decided by California voters statewide, but the election is of national prominence. From this point on (August 1994), the limelight becomes the spotlight, and journalists *will* take the time to discover that Arianna is, quite simply, lying.

Nevertheless, she continues to defend John-Roger (as one would defend any semi-close distant acquaintance, you understand). When given a brief listing of the charges against John-Roger, Arianna asks, "If all these were true, why doesn't someone call the police?" Oh, I know that sort of answer well. I defensively used it for many years when questioned about John-Roger by the press. Rather than deny things I knew or suspected to be true, I would ask a *logical* question. The implication being: "I'm a sane, sound, reasonable, logical human being, and your very *question* is utterly absurd."

Alas, when under the spell of a cult—although one may *appear* logical—logic has nothing to do with it. The truth is what the leader *says* is true. Period. It's a matter of *faith*, not reason. But, because those heathens out there simply won't understand, one must *pretend* to be "one of them"— one of the logical, reasonable, ordinary people—when, in fact, one is not.

> *"Sincerity" is considered the international credit card of acceptance. . . .*
> *No matter how deeply in debt the user may be or how the card is misused, "sincerity" will erase all suspicion and validate all actions.*
>
> CHARLES SWINDOLL

In August of 1988, the *Los Angeles Times* story broke. When asked by *People* magazine to comment on the many allegations against John-Roger, Arianna flatly stated:

> These rumors have no validity. I have known John-Roger for 15 years, and there is nothing in my experience of the man to support any of these allegations. I have never once seen any evidence of him wanting to control people.

It was precisely the statement a well-controlled devotee of John-Roger was expected to make. It was particularly disturbing, however, that *Arianna* made such a statement. Prior to striking it rich in Texas, Arianna made her living as an investigative journalist. Her most successful books involved extensive research and interviews. Did Arianna interview all available witnesses concerning the allegations against John-Roger before coming to the conclusion "These rumors have no validity"? No. Although she certainly had complete access to the people who had left John-Roger, and was friendly with all of them before they left, she never interviewed them, never looked at the evidence, never did even the most superficial investigation.

She, as most of us in MSIA did, remained *intentionally* ignorant. Note her modifier, "in my experience." This is a fairly transparent cop-out—outrageously popular in MSIA—which essentially means: "If it didn't personally happen to me, it's not true." It's among the most *anti*-intellectual statements imaginable.

The last sentence of her defense ("I've never once seen any evidence of him wanting to control people."), Arianna knows to be completely untrue. The only thing that might make it *marginally* true is if she added: ". . . any more than I do." There's an old saying: "When a pickpocket looks at an angel, he sees pockets." To explain why Arianna might not see much control in John-Roger can be found in the paraphrase: "When a pickpocket looks at a pickpocket, she sees an ordinary, decent guy."

> *To ignore evil is to become an accomplice to it.*
>
> MARTIN LUTHER KING, JR.

Is Arianna any more guilty of defending the indefensible than I? Oh, my, no. I'm sure I'm even *more* guilty. The major differences, however, between us *now* are (a) She still believes his nonsense, and (b) I'm not heading for the White House—even for a tour.

This is the only reason I even *mentioned* Arianna in this book, much less devoted an entire chapter to her. You'll note that I have not mentioned the name of anyone studying with John-Roger except an occasional staff member in a key position. I respect "civilian privacy." I even left out the seemingly obligatory list of MSIA celebrity members. Had Arianna remained a writer who married rich, her name never would have crossed these pages.

When, however, your husband is running for a major national public office and you're not just running alongside but clearing the way, giving interviews, and arranging for the post-election victory dinner, your spiritual convictions and the behavior of the man you think has the most intimate relationship with God extant *are* issues.

When she pretends her spiritual relationship with John-Roger not only isn't happening now, but that it never really happened at all, that tells a great deal about how the wife of an elected official treats the truth. When Arianna drew the ring and Michael threw his hat into it, Arianna became fair game.

⚖ ⚖ ⚖

NEWS FLASH! THIS JUST IN: August 19, 1994. Dateline San Diego. Michael Huffington just revealed the "central theme" of his campaign for the Senate: welfare "must end"; the "spiritual revival" America is in the midst of will inspire "the basic goodness of people" to "begin taking responsibility for each other again."

Let's set aside for a moment the value of the idea itself (that's another book in itself). Concerning the "central theme" of *this* book, Michael Huffington's speech and his subsequent questioning by the press revealed that Huffington's "central theme"— and, more important, the *way* he elaborates it—is *entirely* John-Roger's. It duplicates— almost word-for-word—John-Roger's intellectual mushiness, hazy history,* and astonishingly impractical implementation.

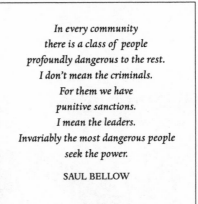

In every community there is a class of people profoundly dangerous to the rest. I don't mean the criminals. For them we have punitive sanctions. I mean the leaders. Invariably the most dangerous people seek the power.

SAUL BELLOW

I should know. The book *We Give To Love: Giving Is Such a Selfish Thing* I wrote in 1993 was the only book bearing both our names to which John-Roger gave input. He actually seemed to *care* about the subject ("selfless service"). He demanded *two* rewrites. (He had never before demanded rewriting of so much as a *paragraph.*) The book (monstrously unsuccessful) reads like a 1994 Huffington campaign speech.

A reporter recently asked me if Arianna was dangerous. The question caught me off guard. I'd never associated Arianna with danger. Determined, sure; self-centered, oh yes; manipulative, none better. But *dangerous?* No, I told the reporter, Arianna may be deceptive, but she's not dangerous.

But the question stuck in my mind. So I'm going to call the reporter and give a better, more thought-through answer: "Arianna will do whatever John-Roger directly asks her to do if it's within her power to do it—and John-Roger *is* dangerous."

---

*For example, when candidate Huffington was asked how his end-welfare plan might be implemented, he didn't really know—he could only cite historical inevitability: "We are going to see major changes as we get to the millennium, the year 2000. They have said, in past histories, as you get to events like that, there are major changes." Who is the "they" who "have said" these things? Certainly not historians. In the east, the Islamic empire was comfortably enjoying its golden age. In the west—such as it was—the last millennium was a dud: nothing much happened from 985, when the Vikings unsuccessfully settled Newfoundland, until 1050, when the Viking empire in Europe was destroyed. John-Roger, however, has borrowed the New Age concept that slipping from 1999 to 2001 will mean far more than 20th Century Fox becoming 21st Century Fox. Michael Huffington has accepted this inaccuracy from Arianna, who learned it from John-Roger. The "they" Michael quotes, then, can only be Arianna and John-Roger.

CHAPTER THIRTEEN

The Most Disgusting Chapter in This Book

About the worst advice
you can give
to some people is,
"Be yourself."

TOM MASSON

U P UNTIL NOW, I've only told you disturbing facts *about* John-Roger. Now I present the man himself. The majority of this chapter was written by John-Roger.*

Although John-Roger preaches "forgive and forget," the concept is about as far from his personal practice as is possible. Like most truly committed hypocrites, John-Roger wants you to forget and forgive all the evils *he's* done, but he's allowed to retain all his judgments against you.

"Retain" is an inaccurate description of what John-Roger does with his personal judgments. He collects them, categorizes them, nurtures them, and squirrels them away in the dark corners of his mind where they breed uncontrollably. In addition, John-Roger adds not just what you *did,* but what he *thinks* you did, which is always worse than what you actually did.

He does not, however, play the victim for long; almost instantly he becomes vindictive. He does not just seek revenge; he demands destruction. As I said earlier, psychiatrists who knew him

*That, in itself, makes this chapter unique. Although John-Roger's *name* appears on many books, articles, and 144 Discourses, he has written none of them: I was just one in a series of ghost writers. After reading this chapter, I think you'll see why—in addition to his being a lousy writer—John-Roger needs to filter his consciousness through that of another in order to make palatable his presentation of self.

> *The measure of a man's real character is what he would do if he knew he never would be found out.*
>
> THOMAS BABINGTON MACAULAY
> (1800–1859)

have unofficially diagnosed him as sociopathic. This means he has absolutely no qualms about hurting others in order to get his way. If you're in his way, he'll run you down without a second thought. He does so without the slightest degree of guilt or remorse—and that's if you're an innocent bystander. Imagine how much more destructive he can be when he thinks you are guilty of slighting him *intentionally,* when he *intends* to punish (destroy) you for it, when he takes *pride* in the amount of destruction he has done.

The man becomes, quite simply, out of control.

If you think I've been harsh in my evaluation, please return and reread these opening comments after finishing the chapter. I think you'll find that I've been almost charitable. In the chapter "A Bird of Pray" I'll explore the torment experienced by those who believe in him. In "Against the Law or Above the Law?" I'll describe some of John-Roger's more blatant criminal activities. In this chapter, I want to consider a single aspect of John-Roger's overall campaign of retaliation: letter writing.

One of John-Roger's favorite methods of manipulation is planting poison seeds and watching them grow. He'll plant seeds of fear in people about goals they wish to achieve that, ultimately, will not serve John-Roger; he'll plant seeds of doubt in relationships that may challenge his "right" to be the most important person in anyone's life ("Do you think your husband might be stepping out on you?"); he'll plant a seed of unworthiness in just about everyone he can to strengthen the dependence of his followers. Within the Movement, he doesn't need to write anything down: all he has to do is start a rumor.

Rumors run rampant in the Movement—which is precisely what John-Roger intends. His definition of a secret is—and I'm not kidding—"A secret is something it's okay to tell other people, as long as *they* promise to keep it a secret." Is it any wonder, then, that a "secret" can be told to anyone at all, yet no one feels he or she has betrayed any trust. On the other hand, agreements made with John-Roger are *sacred:* if you tell them to another living soul, you have committed a "spiritual crime." Although it's never made clear precisely what happens to spiritual criminals—being spirited away by spiritual police is just the beginning, one supposes—the outlook is grim.

> MEPHISTOPHELES:
> *At the right time*
> *a word is thrust in there.*
> *With words we fitly can*
> *our foes assail . . . .*
>
> GOETHE
> *FAUST*

When people leave the Movement, however, and are no longer subjected to John-Roger's innuendoes and rumors, a bigger, blacker, multi-megaton poison seed is required.

John-Roger takes to his computer.

All of the letters in this chapter have been traced directly to John-Roger. His computer printer in the mid-1980s had a strange defect—a line to the left of the capital A. This printer and the computer it was attached to were kept in a locked room at John-Roger's home in Mandeville Canyon. The only people who had access to the room were John-Roger and Michael Feder. That Michael Feder joined in the composition of these letters, then, is a possibility.

In addition, many of the letters were addressed by hand, and multiple handwriting experts have identified the handwriting as John-Roger's. The reason the letters were hand-addressed is that John-Roger could never figure out how to print envelopes on his computer. Although he could ask one of his staff members for help on official letters, John-Roger kept his letter-writing campaign secret from all but possibly Michael Feder. Asking for help addressing an envelope to someone who is on John-Roger's list of enemies would, of course, appear suspicious. At times John-Roger would try to disguise his handwriting, or write with his left hand. John-Roger was apparently unaware such attempts do not prevent handwriting experts from making accurate identifications.

Some of the letters had a post office box as a return address. The post office box was rented by John-Roger, the application was signed "John-Roger Hinkins." Not only was this post office box the return address for some of John-Roger's hate mail, it also served as a place for him to receive mail-order gay pornography without alerting his office staff to his sexual tastes.

Then there is the style of the letters. The basic writing style is consistent: bad writing has a stamp all its own. Even when he *intentionally* writes badly (imitating an uneducated person or much younger person, for example), it's badly done.

He has certain illiterate quirks: he tends to separate words that should be one ("girl friend," "some one," "law suit"). Similarly, he doesn't seem to know the rules of hyphenation ("POCKET SIZED MINISTERIAL CARD"). He likes to add "and" before "etc."—which is redundant, because *etc.* means "and so forth." He makes a lot of spelling errors. The underlining and capitalization are all his. The letters are printed here mistakes and all. I've not included [*sic*] after each error. I tried it, and there were so many [*sic*]s I got dizzy.

The letters tend to contain combinations of information that could only be known by John-Roger. There is a psychological similarity to the letters—they all make the same assumptions, share the same prejudices. (Note not only his obsession with homosexual sex, but his automatic assumption that it is always wrong, always bad, always evil—a belief John-Roger clearly holds about his own homosexuality.)

Finally, John-Roger can't seem to resist making some sort of didactic dirty shot that comes straight from his heart. Whether pretending to be a thirteen-year-old girl or a drag queen from Orange County, he always seems to include the telltale "word from our sponsor."

In most cases, I'm not going to print entire letters because they ramble on and on *and on*. I do have a responsibility not to bore you *too* much. Moreover, I can only stand putting so much of his sewage into a book. I believe it was New York mayor Jimmy Walker who said, "A reformer is a man who rides through a sewer in a glass-bottomed boat." I have no intention of taking you on such a journey: I think hovering in a helicopter over the septic tank for a few minutes will be sufficient. And I'm certainly not printing even excerpts of all the appalling John-Roger letters available—we'll save that gargantuan task for the editor of the multivolume *Preceptor Papers*.

I'm going to begin with what I consider the most shocking of these letters. It wins this dubious honor— over many worthy contenders—primarily because of its recipient: a thirteen-year-old girl. I put it up front because I think that some people, after getting the gist of the man's psychosis, will skip to the next chapter. I can't say I would

> The demagogue is usually sly, a detractor of others, a professor of humility and disinterestedness, who acts in corners and avoids open and manly expositions of his course, appeals to passions and prejudices rather than to reason, and is in all respects, a man of intrigue and deception, of sly cunning and management.
>
> JAMES FENIMORE COOPER

blame anyone who did. I avoided reading these letters for years. (I only read them about a month ago.) If I had had the courage to read them earlier, it would have made all the difference in the world (in my world, at least). So, if you only want a sampling of the man's dementia, I present first the best of the worst.

In 1984, a couple who had been long-time devotees of John-Roger heard the rumors (as had everyone else in MSIA) concerning John-Roger's coercive sexual manipulation. Unlike most people in MSIA, they had the courage to investigate. They discovered disreputable dealings that went far beyond the sexual allegations. It was a difficult decision, but they found they had no choice but to leave MSIA and John-Roger.

Both were influential in an eastern seaboard city where MSIA had one of its largest populations. Although they did not bad-mouth John-Roger, the mere fact that they left MSIA spoke volumes. They were declared by John-Roger to be inflicted with the dreaded Red Monk disease (which John-Roger pilfered from the fundamentalist notion of Satan), and all ministers and initiates were instructed to have absolutely no contact with them whatsoever. In a stroke, they lost all their friends, their connection to God, and their income. (The husband was a physical therapist whose clients were primarily MSIA members.)

They received anonymous threats of violence. For months, the wife feared their home might be blown up at any moment. She was most concerned for her children. Within six months, the wife had two miscarriages. John-Roger let it be known that the miscarriages were proof positive that someone was afflicted with the Red Monk disease. If a pregnant woman even *touches* someone so inflicted, she would have a miscarriage.

The daughter had pretty much been raised in MSIA. Her

friends were mostly in MSIA.

One day she received a letter, addressed personally to her. The handwriting on the envelope has been identified by experts as that of John-Roger.

In addition, John-Roger refers to the girl by the wrong name—a name only John-Roger repeatedly and mistakenly called her. The letter began:

Dear [GIRL'S NAME],

This isn't the kind of letter that would normally be written to a descent young lady, however you have proved beyond a shadow of a doubt that you lack good judgment in the way that you tell sexual stories to young people who are around you, in school and in other social occasions. Your dirty mouth has reached all the way out here to California. I'm sure that you would not have had so much to say about so many people if you had known about the "skeletons" in your own families' closet. Many of the young people out here who were your friends do not think very highly of you and your gossipy talk.

You have made it a point to talk alot about what your father, [FATHER'S NAME] has had to say about members of M.S.I.A. and Insight. No doubt [MOTHER'S NAME] has had her say also, cause <u>she has to support her husband,</u> or he won't give her the money that she married him for.

[GIRL'S NAME], I know that your father [DOES PHYSICAL THERAPY] . . . However, what he might not have told you is that <u>he has had sex with various young men</u> that he has [WORKED WITH]. One that will tell you about it, if you ask him, is a young black man named [NAME] from Washington,D.C. Your father, [FATHER'S NAME], <u>fucked him in the ass,</u> during a [THERAPY] session though your father tried to make light of it, because [NAME] has told many people that he was gay. Now <u>others</u> are coming forward telling about your father exploiting them sexually. And this all went on while he was living with [MOTHER'S NAME]. We all doubt very much that he has told [MOTHER'S NAME] all the sordid details.

Although he has two children, you and your brother, <u>he is hiding behind the skirts of [MOTHER'S NAME].</u> In other words, he thinks that because he is married that no one would suspect him of being a HOMOSEXUAL. I'm sure that [MOTHER'S NAME] knows or at least must suspect (if she is any kind of a woman) that your father is a HOMOSEXUAL. But as long as [FATHER'S NAME] continues to make good money, [MOTHER'S NAME] won't leave him. She loves the money too much to give it up regardless of the fucking in the ass, and cocksucking that [FATHER'S NAME] does with other men.

> *You cannot have*
> *a proud and chivalrous spirit*
> *if your conduct is*
> *mean and paltry;*
> *for whatever a man's*
> *actions are,*
> *such must be his spirit.*
>
> DEMOSTHENES
> 384–322 B.C.

It does seem very funny that the same things (subjects) that you were talking about,and using to put down other people are the very same things that your HOMOSEXUAL FATHER was DOING IN SECRET. Though now the secret is out, and it got out because of your talking to your young "friends" in your area. And of course they were very upset and so they told their parents and their parents talked to other friends and then their were phone calls and then etc.,you know how this type of thing can go on and on and on.

As the letter continues (oh, yes: it does continue), John-Roger steps out of his assumed character (that of a "former girl friend" of the thirteen-year-old girl), and steps directly into a didactic tone that is pure John-Roger:

Well his attempts were to discredit M.S.I.A., Insight and its members (and you were unwittingly used by your HOMO-SEXUAL FATHER.) All he had to use was some one elses negative emotional opinionated information and now that all of that has been repudiated by the liars and gossip mongers. They did not have any facts (though they tried to make up some) to back up their so called experiences. It is now known who the liars were/are. You weren't one cause you believed your "father", but he and [MOTHER'S NAME] were some of the liars. You are just a little trouble maker and now you are making trouble for your HOMOSEXUAL FATHER.

"Negative emotional opinionated information." Now there's a classic John-Roger line—and about as far away from the writing style and vocabulary of a "girl friend" of a thirteen-year-old as possible. Now John-Roger reverts to one of his favorite tactics: "Everybody knows and thinks you're terrible because of it":

> *A man never discloses*
> *his own character*
> *so clearly as when*
> *he describes another's.*
>
> JEAN PAUL RICHTER
> (1763–1825)

The people in the Movement and Insight do not have much to say about your HOMOSEXUAL FATHER, even though the information is widly talked about in other groups, however he is ridiculed and laughed about in those other small circles, but not in a malicious manner, just because of the irony of it all . . .

We'll skip a portion of the letter here in which the sexual exploits of a couple who were good friends of the thirteen-year-old girl's mother and father—and a favorite of the girl—are explored (". . . they have engaged in sexual orgies with anyone that will do it with them"). Eventually, John-Roger returns to his main theme:

> As you can probably guess already there is much more to this than you have been told. Most of the people out here have put all the gossip behind them and are going on to other things. It's too bad that your HOMOSEXUAL FATHER still keeps the gossip going and spreads it on to you. But may be you will have enough sense to get on with your life without malicious statements about innocent people. [GIRL'S NAME] don't ruin your reputation anymore than you have already done. Maybe it is not to late for you.

John-Roger himself is the "innocent people." The gossip John-Roger refers to in the entire letter, in fact, refers to his own coercive homosexual activity. Now he explains *why* the thirteen-year-old girl's father is telling others about John-Roger's manipulative sexual practices:

> Some of the people that your father has [WORKED ON] have said that he told them about the gossip while he was [WORKING ON] them, and they thought it was being used as a come on by your HOMOSEXUAL FATHER to see if his clients wanted to have sex with him, and of course they have walked away from him saying that he is very negative in his talk and actions.
>
> [GIRL'S NAME], you don't have to believe this letter, check it out with your father and [MOTHER'S NAME] and the other people I have mentioned in this letter. I'm going to end this now. My mother wants to use the computer that I am writing this on. (she brings it home from the company she works for).

In 1984, computers were not as ubiquitous as they are today. John-Roger was writing this letter on his brand-new Lisa—the most expensive computer available. In mid-1984, however, very few of the salt-of-the-earth MSIA devotees could afford a computer of any kind; hence, the explanation—lame as it may be.

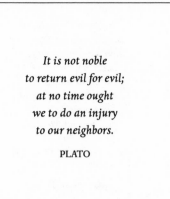

It is not noble
to return evil for evil;
at no time ought
we to do an injury
to our neighbors.

PLATO

And now John-Roger presents his coup de grace. Imagine how a thirteen-year-old girl—whose network of friends is almost exclusively within the MSIA community—would react when she read the following:

> I'm sending copies to my other friends all over the country, maybe you will be hearing from some of them also.

Not only were the adults laughing at her father; all the kids would soon be laughing at her. It's hard to be more psychologically cruel to a young girl.

And now one of my favorite parts of the letter: the signature. There is no signature. Here's the end of the letter, precisely the way John-Roger sent it—*and every word is typed:*

> Signed:
>
> A former girl friend who has been hurt by you, and your family.

Ready for more? (All the chapters can't be as much fun as reading about Arianna.) In the early 1980s, John-Roger wanted to take a handsome young man away from his wife. The husband wanted God, and was convinced John-Roger was the way. He also loved his wife. The wife wanted God, too; was devoted to John-Roger; and knew nothing about John-Roger's designs on her husband. John-Roger placed the young husband in a terrible dilemma: This was the husband's chance to break the "wheel of incarnation" forever (if he chose John-Roger) or to be eternally bound to this gross material plane, incarnation after incarnation (if he chose his wife). John-Roger even gave him $10,000 of God's money so that he might settle his marital financial obligations and feel free to leave the marriage. After a time of excruciating reflection, the young husband chose his wife.

> Character assassination is at once easier and surer than physical assault; and it involves far less risk for the assassin. It leaves him free to commit the same deed over and over again, and may, indeed, win him the honors of a hero even in the country of his victims.
>
> ALAN BARTH

John-Roger, furious, went to work. First, he began undermining the wife at work. Fortunately (for John-Roger) and unfortunately (for the wife), she worked at the national office of Insight Seminars—which meant John-Roger was, ultimately, her boss. Although her work performance at Insight remained the same, John-Roger enlisted her immediate boss, then-Insight director Russell Bishop, to turn up the heat on the hapless wife. Between John-Roger and Russell Bishop, she didn't have a chance. Unfortunately, she didn't know she didn't have a chance, so she kept struggling to live up to work expectations that shifted before she fully understood what the previous ones were.

In desperation, she wrote a letter to the man she thought was her spiritual teacher, mentor, and friend. Little did she know, he was also insanely jealous of her, and obsessed with taking his revenge. His response to her was couched in all Light and loving, but notice how he undermines her time and again, planting his poison seeds:

Dear [WIFE'S NAME],

I have heard you have recently been feeling a kind of "indifference" toward you from me and some of the Mandeville staff, that you have had a sense that things have changed since you returned from your vacation and have been wondering if there is a message I am trying to get across to you about something you are doing that you aren't seeing.

Yes, things have changed . . . it isn't really beholding to your intelligence to pretend you don't know what's going on.

In talking to Russell recently . . . Russell said to me, "You'd think [WIFE'S NAME] would be smart enough to see that something is going on." And I said, "Well, maybe she is and maybe she isn't." There are little indicators that something isn't clear with you. Russell recently found himself typing his own letters rather than bringing them to you—and you might look to see if there are other situations where you find people doing things themselves or going to other people for them—and you might ask yourself why. These can be subtle so you have to look carefully or it's easy to miss what's going on.

Also, when you were in Philadelphia for the Children's training, you didn't ask any of us if we had mail to send back to the office. You might want to look at your attitude there.

Forgetting once to ask about the mail indicates a problem in attitude? Okay. This letter also contains a typical John-Roger "screw you":

> *His mouth is*
> *full of cursing*
> *and deceit and fraud:*
> *under his tongue*
> *[is] mischief and vanity.*
>
> PSALMS 10:7

> I understand that you thought I missed some points or misunderstood some of the points you were trying to make in one of your recent letters to me. There is no need for you to write me more letters. I'd just miss those too—unless of course, I didn't misunderstand the points in the first letter and I wouldn't miss them in the next.

John-Roger, you understand, never misunderstands *anything*—he is consciously aware of all levels in all universes simultaneously. How, then, could he *possibly* misunderstand? Any *hints* that he *may* misunderstand are usually met with the sort of sarcasm above and the punishment, "There is no need for you to write me any more letters." John-Roger had made it clear time and again that writing to him was nearly essential for getting to God—it was certainly the shortcut to "clearing lifetimes of karma" with a single written request. John-Roger doesn't just *collect* sycophants: he *creates* them.

The letter ends with a kicker: After putting this innocent woman—who believes that he is her lifeline to Heaven—through Hell, he closes:

> I love you [WIFE'S NAME], as much as I ever have. And that loving will never change. God bless you, love. Take good care of yourself.
>
> In Light and Love,
>
> [signed]
>
> J-R

The wife, husband, and the husband's brother (who was a member of John-Roger's personal live-in staff) all got together, compared notes, and left the Movement. John-Roger exploded: this wife had taken not just one man but *two* men away from him! He was now in high dungeon; his only recourse was low drag. He

> Do not hold the delusion
> that your advancement
> is accomplished by
> crushing others.
>
> MARCUS TULLIUS CICERO

adopted what might have been his "bar name"* from the 1950s—Ruby of Orange County—put on his mascara, went to his Lisa, and got to work.

To understand the letter (and his writing style in general), it might help to know that John-Roger's favorite form of pornography was the gay-porn pulp novels—the really cheap paperback ones that use the words *tumescent* and *throbbing* at least once on every page. (While cleaning, a staff member found dozens of these novels hidden in John-Roger's bedroom closet. John-Roger spent so much time in the closet, he apparently wanted to take some reading material along.)

John-Roger really got *into* this letter. It was probably the longest piece of sustained writing John-Roger had done since college (or has done since). It was an epic of romance, heartache, and unrequited love worthy of Barbara Cartland.

John-Roger knew that the wife's former husband (let's call him Donald) committed suicide only days after she married her current husband (the one John-Roger was after). This was, understandably, terribly disturbing to the wife. Three years later, John-Roger pulls this tragedy out of mothballs and becomes the dead former husband's mythical male lover, Ruby of Orange County. (Donald was not gay, but he was from Orange County.)

Okay: so have we got the characters? Wife, husband, brother (of husband, former John-Roger live-in staff member), and Donald (wife's former husband, now deceased). Here we go: highlights from the gay-porn-pulp classic *Ruby of Orange County* by John-Ruby Hinkins:

> Dear [WIFE]:
>
> This is a letter that has been a long time in coming. As you read on I am sure that you will understand why. I just recently heard of the difficulty that [HUSBAND] and [BROTHER]

*John-Roger came of sexual age in the 1950s—some of it spent in San Francisco. In those pre-gaylib days, it was common in some clubs to have a "bar name"— that is, a female name that often sounded close to your male name which your friends called you while in the bar. Could Roger Hinkins have been Ruby Hinkins? It's possible.

LIFE 102: What to Do When Your Guru Sues You

said that they had with J-R, M.S.I.A., and Insight.

I was shocked and then surprised and then I sat down to figure it out. Then it came to me, that all along [HUSBAND] and [BROTHER] must have been keeping you in the dark about their sexual preferences. Although this probably didn't come as any real great surprise to you. You know [WIFE]

> *You take the lies*
> *out of him,*
> *and he'll shrink*
> *to the size of your hat;*
> *you take the malice*
> *out of him,*
> *and he'll disappear.*
>
> MARK TWAIN

there were many things that I don't know if you knew about your husband [DONALD]. I most likely would never have told you, if all these things about your present husband had not come out, [HUSBAND] confessing that he is a homosexual and his brother [BROTHER] saying that he is homosexual also. Part of me wanted to believe it cause they said it and the other part of me said "what are they up to."

[WIFE], [DONALD] and I grew up together, we looked at each other as best of buddies and needless to say we were "very close." I remember times that we would double date, and after we took the girls home he and I would go someplace together, mostly when we took turns sucking each other off it was in the car, and have sex with each other. At times, when we were in bed, I was very passive and on other occasions he was passive. Most of this took place before you were married to [DONALD], though it didn't stop after your marriage. As you know [DONALD] was very horny.

When you and [DONALD] got married I hated you so much that I could just barely stand to be in your company, even though [DONALD] wanted so much for us to be friends and had hoped that somehow we might make it a threesome, I just couldn't do it. I really wanted him all for myself. As you know he was the best sex around. I don't think that he had sex with anyother male (at that time I'd have killed him if I had found out about it), though when he was with me he often would talk about having sex with other guys, but saying that was just to make me feel jealous. He said that he was never completely sure if I loved him or not, or if I loved him as much as he loved me. (I did. I never killed myself in order to leave him).

[WIFE], very few people know this, but I was with [DONALD] two or three nights in a row before he killed himself. And I left just 2-3 minutes before he killed himself. . . . he always

> *A potent quack,*
> *long versed in human ills,*
> *Who first insults*
> *the victim whom he kills;*
> *Who murd'rous hand*
> *a drowsy Bench protect,*
> *and whose most tender mercy*
> *is neglect.*
>
> GEORGE CRABBE
> 1754–1832

came to me when he needed the loving he wanted, and I was always thore for him. He continually complained to me of your sexual difficulties, (he never complained about our sex together. he was always so warm and affectionate with me.) He told me that you liked to suck him off, but you were not as good as a man. And that sexual intercourse with you hurt you. I'm not telling you this to put you down, but just to let you know that he had told me many things. I don't think that he held back any of the secrets you two had. He would laugh about you so much of the time. "That you just couldn't take it." Then he would come to me cause I was the one who could take it, if you know what I mean.

There are times that I still miss him so much that I have often thought that I should kill myself also and just get out of this fucked up world.

[DONALD] wanted me to kill him and then kill myself, so we could be lovers forever and ever. He was so romantic. Naturally, I wouldn't do that. I wanted him alive not dead. He said that [HIS SECOND WIFE] didn't understand him and neither did you. So he would come to me and he would drink until he would fall over. I hated that part. I think that he did that so that I could really fuck him. He loved to be fucked, but only when he "acted" drunk. I think it was so he could have an excuse that he did it whon he was drunk (passed out) other wise he thought it was faggoty, you know "really queer". Him sucking me off didn't seem to bother him in the least bit. I didn't go for the just sucking him or fucking him routine. I really liked to get fucked cause I could really come that way. You understand? He often said that he wished that I had a pussy also. Not really though, he had one with you and didn't like yours. I almost went and had surgery just to please him.

At this dramatic point, John-Roger makes a cameo appearance in his own novella—to save the day, of course. (Why didn't he make his guest appearance earlier and save Donald from suicide? I guess saving Ruby from a sex-change operation that's worse than death was a more important intervention, spiritually speaking.) And now, ladies and gentlemen, John-Roger playing the dual roles of John-Roger and Ruby as we continue with John-Ruby Hinkins's masterpiece, *Ruby of Orange County*.

One of the biggest reasons that I didn't is that I went and had a talk with John-Roger when he lived over in East Los Angeles area. He told me not to have the surgery, and he gave me some of his cryptic comments that in hindsight wasn't so cryptic. I talked to J-R about [DONALD] and myself, never mentioning [DONALD'S] name and J-R said that it was not a good thing to come between a man and a woman. However, I felt that it was a woman (you, [WIFE]) that came between a "man and his man." I was not really in the movement though and you and [DONALD] seemed to be getting a lot out of it. [DONALD] had readings with J-R, and I listened to the tapes with [DONALD], he left them at my house so you wouldn't hear them. However, I've been thinking of sending them to you, I've listened to them so much that I have them memorized, [DONALD'S] voice is so sweet. [DONALD] would lie so brazenly to J-R that it was a shame, and J-R would be so straight with him. Often [DONALD] would accuse J-R to me saying that J-R didn't really understand him. One time when we were all out to dinner, both [DONALD] and I decided to proposition J-R and see if he would have sex with us individually or together, we were subtle and coy about it, so we thought. I didn't know that all along J-R knew about the two of us. When he talked on the tapes he never let on for a second.

He told us that we weren't being fair to each other, let alone to you or my girl friend, at the time. It was such a polite turn down, that we both actually felt good about it. We talked about it for days.

Let's pause here for a minute (I need to get some of the fertilizer from John-Roger's fertile mind off my shoes), and reflect on the fact that "girl friend" is the same division of the word "girl-friend" we saw in the "signature" in the letter to the thirteen-year-old girl. And now John-Roger tries for sainthood as he turns down a second sexual proposition, this time from Donald alone. (Donald was, by the way, an exceedingly handsome young man.)

[DONALD] didn't believe that J-R didn't like him, so he said

> *All cruel people describe themselves as paragons of frankness.*
>
> TENNESSEE WILLIAMS

> *Gary Cooper*
> *and Greta Garbo*
> *may be the same person.*
> *Have you ever*
> *seen them together?*
>
> ERNST LUBITSCH

that he was going to ask him alone to have sex with him alone. Well to make a long story very short. [DONALD] said that he asked and that they had sex. I was mildly amused about [DONALD'S] lies, and said nothing, and when he got no reaction out of me he said that it was a lie and not to tell J-R what he had said, because J-R would probably go straight to him and [WIFE] and raise hell with [DONALD] and throw him out of the Movement. I asked [DONALD] why he had told me he had had sex with J-R and he said to see if I was jealous or not. Well, I told him that I didn't believe it and so there was no reason to be jealous. [DONALD] got real angry with me (so what's new) that I wouldn't believe him. But most any-one can tell a lie when they hear one. At least with [DONALD] I sure could cause I had been with him so long. You know [WIFE], he said you didn't know a lie from the truth, as he could tell you just about anything and you were so taken in by it. Apparently that isn't true, cause you divorced him. I was so glad when that happened cause then I could have him, and we could get an apartment and live together, keeping up the proper appearances of course. Much like [BROTHER] does with you, only not in such a high class area.

[DONALD] was so concerned that people would find out about his sexual experiences (preference) that he said no, and that it was best for us to do it the way we were, cause that way no one would suspect. No one did. Well at least no one ever talked about it, though recently I had told a few of my very close friends about it. I thought they would keep their mouths shut, but I'm hearing from some of the girls I occa-sionally date (keeping up appearances) little statements that lead me to think that one of my friends shot off his big mouth. One girl has even refused me dates, saying why waste my or her time. She's right. I just didn't want it to get out about [DONALD], and me. Why mess up his memory with his relatives, friends and everybody who still love him. And it probably won't be long until some of your old girl friends hear of it and start talking and I hope that they don't make fun of you. Well I guess it doesn't matter cause they know that you are married to a gay man anyway. . . .

Well [WIFE], I think that I have it off my chest (consciousness), and I, for old times sake, thought you might want to know. Orange county can get really stale, so anything gets good publicity.

Oh my god, one other thing. Many of my gay and so called straight friends were talking about calling or writing to [HUSBAND] and [BROTHER] for sex dates, and as they know I know you they were asking me for the address. I never told them. But any fool can look in the phone book.

In closing this I thought I would sign it with my name that [DONALD] called me and it's the name I use in my close circle of gay friends, which I now consider you three. I do hope that you . . . are not personally hurt by the bad reputation your "husband" and brother-in-law have gotten for themselves.

Ruby of Orange County

Donald was of the generation that, if he had been gay, would never have referred to his lover by a female name. This "old queen" nonsense is simply John-Roger showing his ignorance of post-1960s gay life: he doesn't seem to get that it's okay for a *man* to love a *man* without one having to play "butch" and the other to play "fem" as had been the case in his 1950s San Francisco heyday.

John-Roger even attempted to plant a seed of suicide in the wife. He cut an article out of a newspaper that appears to be the *National Enquirer* and pasted it to a card. The headline read:

How Wives React When They Hear the News: *Your* Husband Is *Gay*

The words *your* and *gay* were underlined by hand. The first sentence of the article was also pasted on the card:

> A startling new study of wives who discover their husbands are homosexual revealed that nearly half of them eventually became suicidal.

Here, the word *eventually* was underlined by hand.

On the reverse side of the card he pasted another excerpt from

> *I'll destroy you.*
> *I am the master*
> *of disaster.*
>
> MUHAMMAD ALI

the article:

He was, is and always will be gay. Gay men often have relationships with women, marry, have children. Like straight men they want to be fathers, family men.

Next to it, in John-Roger's handwriting, is the note:

I feel so sorry for you. He is hiding behind you.

This was certainly not the first time John-Roger had attempted to destroy marriages and relationships. In 1978, John-Roger had passed the keys of the Mystical Traveler Consciousness to his lead disciple. The disciple even began giving seminars. When John-Roger discovered the young man was having a relationship with a young woman in the Movement, John-Roger openly denounced him, saying he had violated certain spiritual laws, and the higher authorities had withdrawn whatever mystical powers had been bestowed on him. For five years, the young man slowly, agonizingly worked his way back into John-Roger's good graces. Although he never got back the keys to the Traveler Consciousness, he became again a well-regarded member of John-Roger's personal staff.

Lightning struck again in the form of another woman, and this time he told John-Roger he was leaving. True-to-form, John-Roger essentially pronounced the spiritual-equivalent sentence: "You can't quit; you're fired!" The young man (and his female companion) was not only exiled, but banished, cut off from spirit—an Adam with his deceiving Eve—left alone to take their free-fall plummet into hell.

John-Roger and his trusty Lisa wrote the letter, and instructed the president of MSIA (who held the title in name only—everyone knew, and knows, who rules the roost) to sign it. The president was appalled by the letter, and refused. (It's hard to express how much courage this took on the part of the president.) Undaunted, John-Roger wrote in the president's initials himself, and sent the letter. It begins:

THIS LETTER IS TO NOTIFY YOU BOTH OF TWO THINGS THAT ARE HAPPENING AT THIS TIME.

1. YOUR MINISTERIAL CREDENTIALS ARE HEREBY REVOKED AND ARE TO BE RETURNED TO THE MINISTERIAL SERVICES IN ACTION BOARD BY RETURN MAIL ALONG WITH THE POCKET SIZED MINIS-TERIAL CARD.

> *Distrust all men*
> *in whom the impulse*
> *to punish*
> *is powerful.*
>
> FRIEDRICH NIETZSCHE

2. THAT BOTH OF YOUR RECONNECTIONS TO THE SOUND CURRENT DID NOT HOLD AND THIS IS TO NOTIFY YOU THAT YOU ARE NO LONGER INITIATES OF THE MYSTICAL TRAVELER AND OF THE SOUND CURRENT.

3. THIS LETTER IS ALSO TO SERVE NOTICE TO YOU THAT YOU HAVE BEEN DROPPED FROM THE ROLLS OF THE MOVEMENT OF SPIRITUAL INNER AWARE-NESS, INC. AND THAT YOUR NAMES HAVE BEEN DROPPED FROM THE MAILING LIST. DUE TO THE DELAY IN NOTIFYING OUR COMPUTER PEOPLE OF THIS AND THEM PURGING YOUR NAMES FROM THE MAILING LIST YOU MAY RECEIVE ONE OR TWO MORE MAILINGS, YOU MAY JUST DISREGARD THEM AS BEING AN ERROR IN MAILING.

4. EVEN THOUGH YOU ARE STILL RECEIVING DIS-COURSES THEY WILL ALSO BE DISCONTINUED AS SOON AS THIS CAN BE COMPLETED. OUR OFFICE MAY NOTIFY YOU OF THIS WHEN THEY FIND THE TIME, AS THEY HAVE OTHER ITEMS OF HIGHER PRIORITY.

5. WE WISH YOU WELL IN WHAT EVER YOU DECIDE TO EMBARK UPON, AS WE ARE SURE IT WILL NOT IN-VOLVE MOVEMENT PEOPLE OR ITS AFFILIATED ORGANIZATIONS.

Notice that wishing them well had a clear qualifier: not to involve the "MOVEMENT PEOPLE OR ITS AFFILIATED OR-GANIZATIONS." The young man was extremely popular, and the first time he had been banished, people still went to him for coun-seling, advice, and support. John-Roger certainly didn't want *that* happening again. Thus, the implied threat: if you *do* involve Move-ment people or people from MSIA's affiliated organizations, we will *not* wish you well. As the young man knew, John-Roger not wishing someone well is a deep, dark well indeed. John-Roger's plan of exile did not just rely on threats to the couple, but to everyone in MSIA (and the "affiliated organizations"):

> A belief in a
> supernatural source of evil
> is not necessary;
> men alone are
> quite capable
> of every wickedness.
>
> JOSEPH CONRAD

6. WE WILL ALSO ONCE AGAIN BE NOTIFYING THOSE PEOPLE THAT ASK THAT YOU ARE ONCE AGAIN EMBODYING THE NEGATIVE POWER IN THE FORM OF THE <u>REDMONK, AND THE CONSEQUENCES THAT GOES WITH THIS POWER.</u>

John-Roger used the term *Red Monk* (or, in this typo, he combined the words into "<u>REDMONK</u>," as though it were some sort of chipmunk) to describe a negative power that is as deceptive as it is contagious. Let's let John-Roger tell you about it in the ranting finale of this letter:

7. PLEASE UNDERSTAND THAT THIS ACTION IS NOT AGAINST YOU BUT FOR THOSE WHOM YOU WOULD ONCE AGAIN <u>CONTAMINATE</u> WITH THIS ENERGY FIELD. MOST OF THE PEOPLE IN THE MOVEMENT WHO HAVE CONTACTED US HAVE NOTICED THE PECULIAR ACTIONS AROUND YOU THAT REMINDED THEM OF THE OCCURANCES WHEN YOUR EGOS LED YOU INTO PATTERNS OF DECEIT AND HALF TRUTHS IN THE PAST. MANY OF THESE STATEMENTS HAVE BEEN BROUGHT TO OUR ATTENTION WITH GREAT DISTRESS ON THE PARTS OF THOSE WHO HAVE BEEN INVOLVED WITH YOU. I AM SURE THAT YOU BOTH FEEL THAT THIS IS NOT SO AND, NEVER THE LESS EVEN THOSE WHO HAVE TOLD YOU THAT THEY HAVE FELT BETTER AFTER HAVING SPOKEN TO EITHER ONE OR BOTH OF YOU HAVE ALSO COME TO US IN GREAT STRESS SEEKING SPIRITUAL ASSISTANCE, WHICH NATURALLY WE GAVE TO THEM AND RELIEVED THEM OF THE SYMPTOMS AND ADDING THE CAUTION THAT WHAT EVER THEY DID TO GET INTO THAT KIND OF TROUBLE THAT THEY WOULD BE WISE TO STAY CLEAR OF IT IN THE FUTURE.* ALSO MOST OF THEM (WITHOUT EXCEPTION) PEGGED THE OCCURRENCE OF THE DISTURBANCE AFTER HAVING CONTACT WITH <u>YOU</u>. THIS

---

*Let's all take a deep breath. Sometimes I think the only exercise J-R gets is writing run-on sentences.

EVEN HAPPENED WITH
PHONE CALLS.

WE HOPE THAT THIS
LETTER REACHES YOU
WITHOUT UNDUE DE-
LAY.

SINCERELY YOURS,

[initials]

THE MOVEMENT BOARD

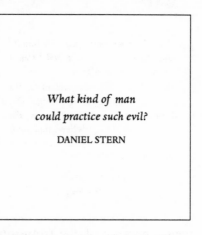

*What kind of man
could practice such evil?*

DANIEL STERN

This letter has two of my
favorite John-Roger phrases.
The first is "MOST OF THEM
(WITHOUT EXCEPTION)." Isn't that delightful? Whether illiteracy or doublespeak, it deserves recognition.

The other phrase is "THIS ACTION IS NOT AGAINST YOU."
As we have said, John-Roger guiltlessly can destroy anything or
anyone that gets in his way, without offering so much as an insin-
cere apology. He does occasionally toss an explanation over his
shoulder as he zooms off down the road of his personal desires.
That explanation: "This action is not against you, but for . . . ,"
then he gives some great mystical for-the-highest-good-of-all explanation that is really only a cover-up for the simple phrase
". . . but for *me*." I'm sure those who are run over, crumpled, and
eating his dust feel far better knowing that John-Roger didn't really
do anything *against* them.

John-Roger also uses the phrase in a seductive way. He can say
with great sincerity: "Trust me. I will never do anything *against*
you. I have never done anything against *anyone*." Once you've
trusted him, John-Roger brings in his big but: "This isn't against
you, but . . . ." At this point John-Roger feels free to commit any
destructive act against you he pleases because, after all, it is not
"against you." (As we shall see later, I got conned into signing any
number of contracts I would not normally have signed when it
was promised nothing would be done "against" me.)

This letter also shows that when one is exiled, *one is exiled:* you
are not only cut off from John-Roger; you are cut off from your
spiritual initiation, your ministry, and the entire MSIA community.
Anyone—even your closest friends or relatives in the Movement—
dares not even speak to you on the *phone* for fear of catching the
Red Monk disease. This complete exile, however, is not just a way
of punishing those who are unfaithful to John-Roger's iron whim;

> "But, dear me, that must be a fraud!" said Pierre, naively, who had listened attentively to the pilgrim.
>
> "Lord Jesus Christ!" exclaimed the pilgrim woman, crossing herself. "Oh, don't speak so, master! There was a general who did not believe, and said, 'The monks cheat,' and as soon as he'd said it he went blind."
>
> LEO TOLSTOY
> War and Peace

but, more important, a way of keeping those who had departed from giving their reasons for leaving to those still caught in John-Roger's magic web. (This set-up is what kept me from reading the letters in this chapter years ago and, undoubtedly, leaving the Movement about twenty minutes thereafter.) The foundation of John-Roger's hold on people is their ignorance of the truth—most particularly the truth about him.

When three other extremely beloved staff members left, the MSIA and Insight switchboards were overloaded with calls wondering, "What happened?" and with messages for the three departed staff. The former staff members, having lived and worked within MSIA for more than a decade, had no address books or other personal records—any time they needed to contact someone, they would use the MSIA database. Now that database was denied them. Also denied them were any messages from friends who wanted to know "what happened." Actually, what happened was darker than that.

When John-Roger heard about the calls and messages, he went to his computer and sent this memo to the staffs of *all* his organizations, this time (and it's about time) on his own stationery and over his own signature.

MEMO FROM JOHN-ROGER
THIS IS TO BE ACTED UPON IMMEDIATELY:
YOU ARE RECEIVING TWO MEMO'S THAT ARE IDENTICAL IN CONTENT. YOU CAN READ THEM BOTH. ONE IS TO BE SIGNED AND RETURNED TO ME BY THE END OF THIS WORKING DAY, AND THE OTHER ONE IS TO BE KEPT BY YOU FOR ANY FUTURE REFERENCE IF IT IS NEEDED, IT WOULD BE NICE IF YOU SIGNED BOTH OF THEM SO YOUR LOWER SELF KNOWS YOU MEAN BUSINESS. AS I WANT YOU TO KNOW AND UNDERSTAND THAT I MEAN BUSINESS.

Do you get that he means business? I think he means business. The business that he means, however, is monkey business. He is about to tell his staff that the departing staff members want no contact whatsoever with any of John-Roger's current devotees.

This statement was absolutely false.

After the memo was written, Michael Feder, on John-Roger's behalf, called and read it to the departing staff members. They told Michael in no uncertain terms that they *did* want to talk to anyone who called MSIA or Insight looking for them, and they *did not* want to be "left alone." Michael Feder said that he would relay the message to John-Roger. The memo was circulated precisely as John-Roger had originally written it, dishonesty intact.

> THERE IS A SPIRIT OF COOPERATION THAT IS EXPECTED OF YOU BY THE [DEPARTING STAFF] AND MYSELF, THE REQUESTS ARE SIMPLE AND WILL GREATLY SERVE THEM, AND WE CAN ALSO SERVE THEM IN THE GREATER WAY BY HONORING OUR REQUESTS, I AM SURE THAT YOU WILL NOT HAVE ANY DIFFICULTY IN HONORING THEM.

Note John-Roger's tendency to use a comma instead of a period, and a period instead of a comma. This is one of his literary trademarks. Most of John-Roger's remaining staff were shocked and upset by the sudden departure of the well-liked staff members. Knowing this, John-Roger takes on an uncharacteristic jaunty tone. It has the feeling of a Nixon pep-talk to his White House staff when Watergate broke. Note that there is not a word of compassion for the remaining staff members experiencing loss. It has the same depth of feeling as: "You father just died; let's go to the store and I'll buy you a new CD player!"

> WE HAVE MANY NEW AND EXCITING CHALLENGES COMING OUR WAY AND A GREAT DEAL OF FUN AND GROWTH, SO LETS ALL PARTICIPATE IN OUR LIVES AT THE 100% LEVEL NO MATTER WHAT WE ARE DOING OR WHERE WE ARE DOING IT.
>
> IN LOVE AND LIGHT AND LAUGHTER.
>
> (signed)
>
> JOHN-ROGER

Now we get to the meat of the memo:

> The truth has always
> been dangerous to the rule
> of the rogue,
> the exploiter, the robber.
> So the truth
> must be ruthlessly suppressed.
>
> EUGENE V. DEBS

THIS MEMO IS THE INFORMATION TO BE RELATED TO ANYONE WHO CALL REGARDING [DEPARTED STAFF]

1. THEIR NAME AND ADDRESS OR THEIR WHEREABOUTS ARE NOT TO BE GIVEN OUT (AS THEY ARE BEING REMOVED FROM THE MAILING LIST) AS, THIS IS THEIR REQUEST. THE PERSON ASKING IS TO BE REFERRED TO THE TELEPHONE OPERATOR. THERE ARE TO BE NO EXCEPTIONS TO THIS. AS ONCE AGAIN THIS IS THEIR REQUEST TO HAVE NO FURTHER CONTACT WITH ANYONE IN INSIGHT, MSIA, OR "ANY OTHER" OF THE ORGANIZATIONS.

2. THEY WANT TO GO TRY SOMETHING ELSE AND DO NOT WANT ANY CONTACT OR INTERFERENCE FROM ANY ONE IN THE ABOVE MENTIONED ORGANIZATIONS. THIS IS THEIR REQUEST. IT IS ASSUMED THAT IF AND WHEN THEY WANT TO CONTACT YOU THEY WILL DO SO AT THEIR OWN LEISURE. AT THIS TIME THEY DO NOT WANT PERSONAL OR PROFESSIONAL CONTACTS OF ANY KIND OR FOR WHAT EVER INNER REASONS OR GUIDANCE THAT ANYONE CAN OR WILL MANUFACTURE. THEY WILL "PHYSICALLY" INITIATE ANY AND ALL CONTACTS WITH YOU.

Note here that John-Roger directly contradicts his own teachings (yet again), and instructs people to ignore their "inner reasons or guidance."

3. THEIR STATEMENT TO ME AND THAT THEY WANT RELATED TO ANYONE WHO ASKS AS TO WHY, OR WHAT HAPPENED IS THIS: THEIR HAVE BEEN MANY TRUTHS AND UNTRUTHS, AND ILLUSIONS ABOUT THE PAST, AND THEY ARE PAST AND WE [STAFF NAMES] ARE GOING TOWARDS A DIFFERENT FUTURE. WE LOVE RESPECT AND SUPPORT ALL OF YOU IN THE WORK YOU ARE DOING IN ALL THE ORGANIZATIONS. AND WE ARE NOT DOING ANY OF THAT.

Notice that the crock is not just full, but overflowing, and *still* he ladles it on. Please remember: not *one word* about what John-Roger claims about the departed staff members is true.

4. MY [J-R'S] STATEMENT WILL BE THE SAME, ADDING THAT THE KARMA THAT THEY HAVE HAD AND ARE FINISHING UP, BY THEIR REQUEST, AND WITH MY AGREEMENT, IS NO LONGER IN-VOLVED WITH ANY OF US. THEY MUST BE BY THEMSELVES IN OR-DER TO SORT IT ALL. THIS IS ALL BEING DONE AND SUPPORTED BY ME OUT OF MY LOVE FOR THEM AND IN SUPPORTING THEIR WISHES. THE KARMA IS DIFFICULT ENOUGH WITHOUT ANYONE ELSE ADDING TO IT.

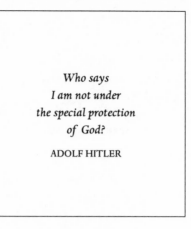

*Who says
I am not under
the special protection
of God?*

ADOLF HITLER

So now it's not just the departed staff's *preferences* that are being honored, it is *karmic law!* The man has no shame, and shows as much mercy. In order to spiritually support the departing members—who are longing for contact with their friends in the Movement—John-Roger tells his faithful, leave them alone. Ouch.

5. NOTHING IS TO BE ADDED OR SUBTRACTED FROM THEIR STATEMENTS IN #3 ABOVE, AND NUMBER 4 WILL BE MY OWN PERSONAL STATEMENT IF ANYONE ASKS ME.

IN LOVE AND LIGHT, AND THANKS,

[signature]

JOHN-ROGER.

These sudden separations prompted by John-Roger's fear of others' revealing the truth are especially painful to children. Some of the children of departing MSIA members were born and raised within the MSIA community. Most, if not all, of their friends are children within the Movement. When the parents leave, the children are cut off from access to all the other children, just like that. It's such a cruel thing for John-Roger to do.

In order to destroy relationships, another favorite John-Roger technique is planting rumors of infidelity. One of John-Roger's personal staff members was exiled simply because he wanted to *date*. He was joined in exile by a beautiful, brilliant woman who left the Movement to be with him. One day I was talking with John-Roger, and out of the blue he said: "You know they've only

> It nothing profits
> to show virtue
> in words and
> destroy truth in deeds.
>
> CYPRIAN

been married two weeks, and she's already fucked two guys behind his back." It had absolutely no connection to anything we were discussing. I shook my head: No, I didn't know that; furthermore, I didn't know *why* I should know that.

"She's a real slut," he continued, "a real whore. I guess he's so hard up, only a slut would go with him." He was, in fact, exceedingly handsome, and *any* woman in the Movement would have gone with him—and half the men; myself at the head of the line. "It won't last six months," John-Roger predicted.

That, like so many other John-Roger predictions, proved inaccurate. He made it more than five years ago, and, last time I checked the couple was still together. (Although recently, John-Roger started the rumor that they had broken up. It's important for John-Roger to create the illusion that life outside his chicken coop is dreadful.)

In fact, the doom and gloom predictions for *all* the relationships John-Roger has cursed as the couples passed out his darkened door have turned out to be wrong. Of nine couples who left the Movement "in disgrace" from 1983 to 1988, eight, as of August 1994, were still together.

John-Roger does not limit himself to letters: he seems to have a telephone fetish too. (The story of my unwanted phone contact with John-Roger will be told in the chapter, "Against the Law or Above the Law?") One couple left the Movement. He was a popular lecturer, his wife a therapist. Prior to a scheduled speaking engagement in San Francisco, the wife received a threatening phone call she believes to have been made by Michael Feder. (Michael Feder has already admitted to pouring paint thinner on cars and slashing tires for love of John-Roger. He also picked me up against my will and dropped me on my heinie—but that story later, too.) Here's a transcript of that conversation:

MAN: Is [HUSBAND'S NAME] there?

WIFE: No. He is out of town until next week.

MAN: Is this the Mrs.?

WIFE: The who?

MAN: Is this his wife?

WIFE: Yes.

MAN: Well I want you to know that your husband has been fucking my wife and I'm really upset about it. He is out there standing up in front of people telling them how to run their lives and he's pulling this kind of shit. He just better clean up his act.

> *The best liar*
> *is he who makes*
> *the smallest amount*
> *of lying go*
> *the longest way.*
>
> SAMUEL BUTLER

WIFE: Who is this?

MAN: I don't want to tell you that.

WIFE: Who is your wife?

MAN: I don't want to tell you. He's been fucking my wife and he's ruined my life. I just want you to tell him that if he comes to San Francisco where I am I will kill him.

WIFE: Who is this?

MAN: You just tell him that if he comes to San Francisco where I am I will kill him.

At this, the man hung up. A bomb threat was subsequently made to the promoter of the husband's lecture in San Francisco, and the lecture was almost canceled.

When enough became too much, several dearly departed and severely harassed former MSIA members jointly hired an attorney. The attorney wrote "Mr. John-Roger Hinkins" a letter. It cost them $800, which—primarily due to John-Roger's interference in their lives—they could ill afford. Joining them in support of the letter was another set of harassed former members who had obtained legal representation on their own.

The attorney's letter detailed the many harassments. He also told John-Roger in no uncertain terms to end the harassment ". . . an ability which we believe is entirely within your control and influence, should you choose to exercise it." Then he lays it on the line, lawyer-style:

> . . . if the above actions do not cease immediately, [HIS CLI-ENTS] will have no choice but to assume that you are actively and wrongfully undertaking their vilification. In such an event, the full force of the law will be brought to bear. Lawsuits will be filed and substantial damages sought against your

> *Fraud and falsehood only dread examination. Truth invites it.*
>
> THOMAS COOPER
> (1759–1851)

organizations, representatives, and you. Your relationship and actions towards the above parties will become public record and a jury trial will be sought to levy appropriate penalties.

The above parties would prefer that they go their way and you go your way. They have neither need nor desire to bring ridicule and investigation to your organizations and you. There is no need for the campaign that has been undertaken against them. However, if this campaign continues, there will be no alternative but to seek a public forum for the above parties' allegations. This will result in fatal damage to your organizations, and unnecessary damages to your representatives and yourself. While we urge a path of reconciliation, this path will not remain available if the campaign against the above parties continues.

You are respectfully urged to carefully consider your course of action which has the opportunity of creating either positive or negative consequences for your organizations, representatives, and yourself.

After this letter arrived, John-Roger received a good talking-to from his attorney. He seemed to listen—as much as he listens to anyone—for the frontal assaults slowed, but never ceased. This was in 1984. Ten years later, if one of these departed staff members gets a call in the middle of the night and hears nothing but the sound of a television in the background, it's just another reminder that John-Roger is keeping his promise not to forget them.

But before ordering the slowdown to the harassment, John-Roger had to have the last word.

In 1984, Dr. David Lane was working on an article concerning the various allegations against John-Roger. Although the article had not yet been published, John-Roger heard about the research, and simultaneously tried to stifle publication of the article while getting back at some of his harassed former followers for having the *audacity* to protect themselves through legal means. Naturally, he pretends to be someone else, this time a friend of "The Watchers who are everywhere." To prove that the letter *didn't* come from him (he wasn't about to endure another lecture from his attorney), John-Roger even puts himself down. The letter begins:

> SCUM BAGS:
>
> A friend from La Jolla gave me a copy of the article that David Lane is writing called the "J-R controversy". All that junk you told him just made me sick. Inference, opinion, innuendo and certainly guilty by being associated with you three.

Girls who put out are tramps. Girls who don't are ladies. This is, however, a rather archaic use of the word. Should one of you boys happen upon a girl who doesn't put out, do not jump to the conclusion that you have found a lady. What you have probably found is a lesbian.

FRAN LEBOWITZ

You [NAME #1], are the foulest. You [NAME #2], are the stupidest. And you [NAME #3], are the sickest. How do you justify living with "faggots?" Are you a LESBIAN? I'll bet that's it. Yeah, [NAME #3], you are a LESBIAN living with FAGGOTS. What do you think will happen when your daughter and her "friends" hear about that. Father a QUEER, Mother a LESBIAN, and to top it all off the Brother-in-Law a QUEER also.

All that junk you gave Lane to write down came out of your own "filthy minds, and mouths" and you know filthy mouths "must" be cleaned out don't you.

Since you were all in the same filthy organisations, that is where you learned how to be so despicable. I think we should go in an do away with those organisations also, including ALL their "so called leaders." J-R has got to go, one way or another also. If it hadn't been for Him, Lane the widower, wouldn't be writing about Swani Muktananda, or Sai Baba, or the others.

Note the line "Lane the widower . . . ." Dr. Lane's wife was alive and healthy. This comment is tantamount to a death threat against his wife. Dr. Lane certainly took it that way. Is there any other way it could be taken? Now John-Roger threatens the recipients of his letter—quite directly:

> If I were any of you I'd be very careful where I go and what I do and who I talk to, you wouldn't want anyone to get hurt now, would you? Don't you all have "innocent" friends visit you and live near you?
>
> I'd sign this but you SCUM BAGS aren't worth much more of my effort. Just a little bit more EFFORT and then it ends.

> *His letters*
> *teach the morals*
> *of a whore,*
> *and the manners of*
> *a dancing master.*
>
> DR. SAMUEL JOHNSON
> (1709–1784)

It's going to be interesting to see how this information gets back to me. In days of old the barrier of bad news to the King was done away with.

How's *that* for a Freudian slip: he obviously meant to say "In days of old the *bearer* of bad news to the King was done away with," but instead used the word *barrier*, which gives his thought an entirely different meaning. Alas, if John-Roger had only *intended* that the "barrier of bad news" to himself ("the King") were "done away with," how much different (and better) the lives of so many of us (the King included) might be. Oh, I'm dreaming again. Back to John-Roger's barrier, I mean, *letter:*

> I just got a copy of "the letter" from your lawyer to John-Roger, using the attorney to attempt to blame him and his friends for all the things that are happening to you. You must be stupid. If you think that John-Roger or anyone else in "his stinking organisations" can stop me from calling you or writing to you, then you are <u>all</u> in for one big surprise. He doesn't "control me" or <u>any part</u> of my life. <u>I doubt that he even knows who I am or who the other people are that "hate" your guts so much.</u>
>
> I also have the <u>evidence</u> that David Christopher Lane is an informant for the F.B.I. and is being financed by them to do his dirty research. It's fine with me as long as he puts you homosexuals' names in the report where it belongs.

None of the people John-Roger mentioned in the letter, incidentally, is homosexual—other than John-Roger, of course. Note how enormously well-connected the fictional author of this letter is: he has a friend in La Jolla who gives him an unpublished (and at that date, unwritten) copy of David Lane's research article; he has access to a letter to John-Roger written by the lawyer of the people being harassed; and he has an informant in the FBI. The writer is also deeply homophobic about his own homosexuality, and spends his time spewing the hatred he has for himself upon innocent others. Well, since this letter was written in 1984, and J. Edgar Hoover died in 1972, that only leaves one person who could have put it all together. Speaking of whom, let's let him have the last word in this chapter, as he winds up for his big finish:

My F.B.I. friend said that Lane had agreed not to use your names. FUCK THAT. When we print our research on you three you can fucking well bet your life on it, that your names will be prominently displayed, as well as our opinions, inuendos and inferences. Our sources will be super secret, ha, ha.

[no signature]

cc: The Watchers who are everywhere.

> *There is a lot of spiritual deceit that goes on. The word level can be very deceitful, but give people time and most of them will demonstrate by action where they are spiritually.*
>
> JOHN-ROGER

Whew! I *promise* I will not put you through anything like that again. (Now I suppose John-Roger will ask for co–author credit for *this* book, too.)

I went to Iowa and visited the baseball diamond in the cornfield where <u>Field of Dreams</u>—one of my favorite movies and the theme of the <u>DO IT!</u> workshop—was filmed. I brought back a sweatshirt for J-R. Here he humbly takes co–credit for "going the distance."

CHAPTER FOURTEEN
A Close Encounter with John-Roger

JUNE 1994. Once John-Roger's lawsuit was filed against me, I got to work. I had thirty days in which to "answer" the suit—a legal term meaning "Hire a lawyer to write an expensive paper in a language only other lawyers can understand."

Lawyers,
I suppose,
were children once.

CHARLES LAMB
1775–1834

First you have to explain your defense to *your* lawyer, who translates it into legalese, who translates it into legalese, to be deciphered by a law clerk who writes a report in plain English telling the judge what the case is about. It's such an *efficient* system.

Law is about *proof,* so I had less than a month to go through fifteen years of letters, documents, interviews with people who had left, research, and memories. "What's too painful to remember, we simply choose to forget," is right. And when you remember again, an echo of the pain reverberates.

I was appalled by what I learned about John-Roger. Reading the letters he had written to torment people made me physically ill. The people who had left were marvelous and helpful. They had absolutely nothing to gain by dragging up ten-year-old memories of devastations past, but they did. Hell, if there were an organization of people who had *left* MSIA (J-Raholics Anonymous, perhaps, or the Red Monk Society), I'd join!

With each distasteful revelation, however, I cringed: I had *personally* recommended this man and his organizations to more than

> *Remorse is the*
> *echo of a*
> *lost virtue.*
>
> EDWARD BULWER-LYTTON

2,000,000 people. At the end of each book in THE LIFE 101 SERIES, I stepped out of my co-author character and I, Peter, told people of the wonders of MSIA and Discourses and John-Roger audio and video tapes and the University of Santa Monica.

I began feeling a powerful need to tell people who might have gotten involved with John-Roger's organizations through my endorsement or my books what was going on. My goal was never (and still is not) to keep anyone from studying with John-Roger, believing he's God, or anything else. People can worship an avocado (the famed Guacamolites), and that's fine with me. I'm a firm believer in free choice.*

I want to (a) let people who may have been influenced by my former endorsement know that I no longer support John-Roger and his "spiritual teachings," and (b) caution them that the "secular" organizations founded by John-Roger might lead them unwittingly onto a spiritual path they may not be seeking.**

I was especially concerned about Insight and the University of Santa Monica, which claim to have no connection to MSIA, but in fact are primary proselytizing and indoctrination points for MSIA.

June is the month the University of Santa Monica finishes its school year, hands out its awards, and enrolls people in next year's classes. I have been told by those who run USM that a large percentage of USM students found out about USM from my books. I

---

*I'm so much in favor of free choice, I sometimes get in trouble for it. I tend to believe in more free choice than most. In fact, I believe that adults should have the freedom to do whatever they choose with their lives and property as long as they do not physically harm the person or property of nonconsenting others. My book on this is entitled *Ain't Nobody's Business If You Do: The Absurdity of Consensual Crimes in a Free Society.*

**I wrote *LIFE 102* for those two reasons, plus these: (c) to make sense in my own mind of a fifteen-year relationship that was ending, shall we say, unhappily, (d) to get it all onto paper and, thus, away from *me*, (e) to let people know "depression can make you do funny things," and (f) ideally, to make money to pay some lawyers. Also, we writers are encouraged to "write what you know," and thanks to the research I'm doing on this lawsuit, I know John-Roger far better now than when we were "friends."

felt it only fair to give these people the *other* side of the story. So, I printed up a brief letter addressed to all USM students and went to John-Roger's multipurpose building (the home of some, but not all, of his organizations) and stood on the sidewalk passing out leaflets to the USM students returning from lunch. Within fifteen minutes, John-Roger pulled up in the Lexus I had given him, complete with the

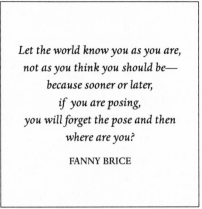

Let the world know you as you are, not as you think you should be— because sooner or later, if you are posing, you will forget the pose and then where are you?

FANNY BRICE

license plates I had chosen for him (LOVE 101). I knew he had come to see *me* because he parked on the street just in front of my car and not in his reserved off-street parking place. He was, as usual, accompanied by a handsome member of his personal staff, this one a former actor.*

John-Roger got out of his car, sauntered over to me, and said to me as casually as if we had gone to dinner together the night before, "Hello, Peter."

"Hi, J-R," I said, and handed him a leaflet. He took it, leaned on the front of my car next to me, and started to read it. The former actor took a copy, too.

While reading, John-Roger asked: "How's your health, Peter?" He said it in a sinister, almost taunting fashion, in roughly the tone that extortionists use in bad movies, when they say to the store proprietor who refuses to pay "protection" money, "Do you smell smoke in here?"

His message was clear: "I'm not protecting your health anymore, and it's going to deteriorate fast. Has the beginning of the end started yet?" He had hooked me with the health line for years. He wanted to see if the line was attached to anything worth reeling up. It wasn't.

"Good, thank you," I answered, stopping myself from adding, "And yours?" Inquiring after a hypochondriac's health is like asking a Jesus freak: "What do I have to do to be saved?" Don't ask if you don't have all afternoon.

Behind his poker face, John-Roger was not pleased. Anything short of my knocking at death's back door was displeasing. He

*I guess there *are* no "former actors," huh? Just working actors between jobs.

> I have learned silence
> from the talkative,
> toleration from the intolerant,
> and kindness from the unkind;
> yet strange,
> I am ungrateful to those teachers.
>
> KAHLIL GIBRAN

had, *after all*, kept me alive and healthy for more than five years. In the two months since he removed his protection, why didn't I shrivel up and die like Dorian Grey when his portrait in the attic caught fire? At the very least, I should be so afraid that the flames in the attic were creeping closer and closer to the portrait that I would offer the fire chief anything he wanted if he would just put out the fire.

I was not at all sorry I disappointed him.

The Santa Monica sun was bright and hot. The silence as he read I did not find in the least uncomfortable. I stood behind every word in the leaflet. I was willing to explain any portion of it to him (although there was nothing in the leaflet new to him—he had, after all, *done* everything I discussed—so I doubted that he would need any explanations).

I was happy I was so calm. I felt neither fearful, nor intimidated, nor angry, nor vindictive. I had no need to explain myself, to "make it all better," or to tell him off. I was content to lean against the front of my car in the hot sun, passing out my leaflets to the occasional student who came by. John-Roger could be there, or not. As God willed.

"This is well written," he said eventually.

"Thank you," I said, "that's my job." Pause. I guess it was my turn. "This is quite a coincidence; or were you called?" I already knew the answer, but was curious as to how straightforward he was going to be.

"I heard on the walkie-talkie you were here," and told me the name of the staff member who told him. My presence had been communicated via the long-range walkie-talkies John-Roger and his staff always carry. At that moment, his portable cellular phone (entirely separate from the walkie-talkie system) chirped.

John-Roger listened for a moment and said, "Yeah, I know. I'm talking to Peter now." Someone else was calling to tell him of my doings.

"That's quite an information-gathering system you have there," I said. I figured I owed him a compliment. He had, after all, said my letter was well written.

By this time, a dozen or so people had gathered around John-Roger in an informal group. Most gathered because John-Roger was their spiritual teacher; a few because here was John-Roger, and here was Peter McWilliams, and Peter McWilliams was passing out a letter critical of John-Roger, so what are they going to say to each other? There was some small talk and chit-chat, until one of the Insight people (who were having a seminar at the John-Roger multipurpose building that weekend) who was not a member of MSIA, asked John-Roger directly: "What's your response to this?"

> *Well, I would—*
> *if they realized that we*
> *—again if—if we led them back*
> *to that stalemate only because that*
> *our retaliatory power,*
> *our seconds, or strike at them after*
> *our first strike,*
> *would be so destructive*
> *that they couldn't afford it,*
> *that would hold them off.*
>
> RONALD REAGAN

"What part of it?" John-Roger asked.

"Why are you suing Peter McWilliams?" she asked.

"*I'm* not suing Peter McWilliams," John-Roger answered.

"Then who's suing him?" she asked.

"I think the Church is suing Peter McWilliams," he said, almost as though he had to remember it. "I'm not involved in that. I don't know much about it."

"Then why is the Church suing him?" This woman could replace Mike Wallace.

"Breach of contract, I think," he said. "Peter and I wrote these books together, and Peter signed a contract about that, and now he won't pay the money he said in the contract that he would pay the Church."

There was a slight pause in the questioning. I didn't want the next question to be from a devotee: "John-Roger, am I ready for my next initiation?" or something like that. So I chimed in:

"Are you saying we wrote these books together?"

"Sure we did, Peter," he said in the most congenial manner imaginable.

"Are you saying you actually sat down with a pen or a word processor and wrote down one word after another that actually appeared in the books?" I asked, not as congenially, I'm afraid.

"Well, a pen and a word processor are not the only way of writing," he said, avoiding the question.

"For example?" I said.

"You could dictate something," he said, "that would be writing without using a pen or a word processor."

I could see that John-Roger was playing his ever-popular semantic game.

> If I take refuge in ambiguity,
> I assure you that it's
> quite conscious.
>
> KINGMAN BREWSTER

"Do you say that you ever put one word after another in any form—pen, word processor, dictation, tape recorder, or any other way—that wound up in these books?" I asked.

"I sent you lots of written material," he said innocently, almost hurt.

"You mean transcriptions of your seminars?" I asked.

"Sure," he said, "and you sat in the back of retreats and took notes."

"Did you ever put one word after another that wound up in the finished books?" I asked.

"Oh," said John-Roger, "you mean did I *write* the books?"

"Yes," I said, ever-so-slightly beyond mild exasperation.

"Oh, no," he said, "I never wrote the books. I never said that. I just supplied the *information* for the books."

By now my adrenaline was flowing. I was not ready for a ride on his semantic-go-round. I laid it out straight: "In fifteen years of studying with you," I said, "I didn't learn a single original thing. I had heard everything else before or, I found that others had had those ideas first."

A slight shock moved through the assemblage. No one *ever* talked to John-Roger that way. My disapproval rating among the devotees rose to an all-time low. John-Roger milked it:

"Why Peter," he said, almost hurt. "I gave you *lots* of original ideas."

"Name one," I shot back. "Name one idea that is original to you."

He thought for a moment, and then two moments. John-Roger

was on the spot. For most of the assembled devotees, it was the first time they had seen John-Roger on the spot. The longer he thought, the larger the spot became. He finally spoke: "Don't hurt yourself and don't hurt others," he said triumphantly.

> The hypocrite's crime is that he bears false witness against himself. What makes it so plausible to assume that hypocrisy is the vice of vices is that integrity can indeed exist under the cover of all vices except this one.
>
> LIONEL TRILLING

It was hard to believe it took him so long to come up with such a poor example. "That's ancient," I said. "That's universal. What philosophy or religion doesn't incorporate 'Don't hurt yourself and don't hurt others'?"

"Well, anyway," he said, "you signed the contract and you're not living up to it."

When semantics run out, change subjects. All right: "Let's talk about the contract," I said. "The contract was based upon my writing books for you, and in exchange you would keep me alive and healthy. Do you have the power to keep me alive and healthy?"

"You're still alive and you're still healthy," he said, as though my mere existence was proof that he had, in fact, kept his end of the bargain. "And, Peter," he said looking kindly upon me with his best doe-eyed gaze, "I'm sure that my loving and caring contributed *something* to your health and aliveness."

"And how much were you paid for this loving? How much did you receive from me for the books *alone?*" I asked.

"I really don't know," he said, which is what he often says when the answer to the question might prove embarrassing.

"Approximately," I asked.

"Oh, maybe one hundred thousand, two hundred thousand dollars." He said it lightly, as though it were a less-than-adequate gratuity.

"Try more than five hundred fifty thousand dollars," I said.

He made a face that an ordinary man might make if you told him: "I have the power to keep people alive and healthy." The look might best be characterized as "Yeah, right." He added words to his doubting countenance: "It wasn't that much."

There seemed little point in getting into a chorus of "Yes it is," "No it isn't," "Yes it is," "No it isn't." Throughout our conversa-

> It is a sin
> to feel guilty
> about sex.
>
> ROLLO MAY

tion, as new people joined the group, John-Roger made it a point to ask them, "Do you have one of the flyers?" He would take one from me and hand it to the newcomer. It was an example of the ancient saying I just coined: "When the shit comes down, pretend you're spreading fertilizer."

About this time, some of the USM assistants came to gather the class. Ironically, one of them was a man I've always looked on with sadness. As I understand it (and I admit this was cobbled together out of several second-hand stories), in his late teens and early twenties he was gay and, like many gay people, had some difficulty adjusting to it. In a counseling, John-Roger implied that the man would be happier changing his lifestyle rather than his attitude. The young man followed J-R's advice, became an ex-gay, and got married.

He always seemed trapped in one of those MSIA relationships in which both partners are so busy "serving the Traveler" night after night, weekend after weekend, in separate-but-equal-John-Roger-founded organizations, that they never spent enough time together to leave each other.

It always seemed sad to me—but looking at him this time, my sadness turned to anger. From what I now knew about John-Roger's covert homosexual escapades over the years, I wondered how much different this young man's life might have been had John-Roger been a healthy role model on how to be gay *and* spiritual. (John-Roger once told another young man that his homosexuality was "working off bad karma from another lifetime." Jeez!) Instead, John-Roger's denial became contagious, his hypocrisy hurtful, and the young man settled for a life in which he had to deny a fundamental, intimate part of himself.

The group was about to go in for their class (although I thought there'd be a heap more learning if they had stuck around). John-Roger returned—in what he obviously hoped would be a summation—to his original theme:

"I really don't have anything to do with this lawsuit," he said, as though the mere thought of a lawsuit threw him into a mental tizzy.

"That's all the Church's business."

"Are you saying you don't want to sue me?"

"*I love* you, Peter," he said, with all the sincerity of Tammy Faye Bakker. "Why would I want to *sue* you?"

"Then will you ask the Church to drop the lawsuit?" I asked.

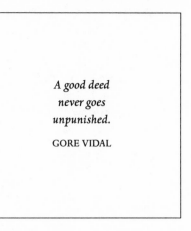

*A good deed
never goes
unpunished.*

GORE VIDAL

"The Church doesn't do what I say." It was so outrageous a lie that I sputtered and turned to the group for support.

"How many of you are members of MSIA?" I asked. Although there were at least ten people I recognized who were ministers and initiates, it was fairly clear the direction my question was heading, and no one raised a hand.

John-Roger chimed in to protect the appallingly sheep-like behavior of his devotees. "MSIA only has only three members," and he rattled off the names of the three people who share MSIA's Office of the Presidency.

He was back to Roger's First Rule of Disorder: "When trapped, and there's nowhere else to go, rely on semantic twists no matter how pathetically transparent the entire endeavor may appear." The assistants were doing what they could to hustle the innocent lambs away from the ferocious wolf, but the big bad wolf was going to give it one more try:

"Who here are initiates or ministers of MSIA?" I asked. One woman timidly raised her hand. Another either timidly raised her hand, or was brushing away a fly.

"Have you *ever* heard John-Roger ask MSIA to do something, and MSIA didn't do it?" They said nothing. What could they say? I realized it wasn't fair to embarrass the group any further. I turned back to John-Roger:

"Was there *ever* a time when you asked MSIA to stop doing something, and they continued doing it?" I asked.

"Oh, sure," he said in his best off-hand casual, "it happens all the time."

"Give me one example," I said.

> *The louder he talked*
> *of his honor,*
> *the faster we counted*
> *our spoons.*
>
> EMERSON

John-Roger paused. The sun shone down brightly. The spot grew larger. No amount of prodding from the sheepdogs was going to get these sheep to move until they heard the answer to *this* question. (I think, secretly, the sheepdogs wanted to hear the answer, too.)

"When they bought the first computer system." He had to rattle back fifteen years for that example.

"Are you saying you told MSIA *not* to buy a computer, and they bought it anyway?"

Another pause. More sun. The sheep looked like they could use a drink of water. "I told them," he said, half under his breath, "'If I were you, I wouldn't get it.'"

This was a horse that was going nowhere, so I asked what I was sure would be my final question. "Will you tell MSIA that you want them to withdraw the lawsuit?"

Some of the sheep looked heavenward. If you asked them about it today, they would probably say that they were looking up and admiring how bright the sun was. At the time, however, they looked skyward to see precisely the color of the lightning bolt that was about to strike me dead.

"Peter, you signed a *contract*," he said in a near whine, "and you're cheating the Church out of the money that rightfully belongs to it! Cheating God!"

Ah! That was the exit line the sheepdogs had been waiting for. Off to get their sheepskins went the sheep, leaving John-Roger, his former actor, and me for what I'm sure many of them thought would be a duel in the sun. In fact, we behaved more like reptiles in the sun. It was mostly silence. The audience had gone, and with them the performance. Any condemnation I might muster would only be redundant. I couldn't help but feel disappointment: I was told that he was a dirty fighter, but I didn't think he would be such a *bad* dirty fighter.

I really didn't have anything more to say to him. (I didn't have anything to say to him in the first place.) I didn't know quite what the etiquette of departure would be; he was, after all, sitting on my car.

"Well, Peter," he drawled. I knew this one. This was his "Duke" Wayne persona. Ever since he got a horse ranch and started wearing cowboy hats, the ascended consciousness of John Wayne occasionally took over John-Roger's body when the Preceptor Consciousness was out to lunch or otherwise engaged. "It's hot out here.

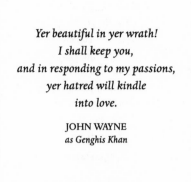

Yer beautiful in yer wrath!
I shall keep you,
and in responding to my passions,
yer hatred will kindle
into love.

JOHN WAYNE
as Genghis Khan

Do 'ya wanna go inside where it's cool and we can talk?"

"I reckon so, podner. Let's mosey on in." I suppressed my instinct, and merely said, "Okay."

We moved into the air-conditioned splendor of the lobby where we sat at right angles to each other on two couches. The former actor sat next to John-Roger. John-Roger placed his walkie-talkie on a table directly in front of me. This seemed odd: John-Roger's walkie-talkie seemed permanently attached to his hip. Maybe he was sending the signals back to base where it was all being recorded. These are the sort of thoughts that formerly naive people start to develop when their former naivete might make them homeless. So, maybe he was recording this. As Werner Erhard so aptly pointed out: "So what?" I thought I'd get down to business.

"This lawsuit is not what I want," I said, looking John-Roger directly in the eye.

"Why, Peter," he got out before averting his gaze, "why don't you just pay the Church the money you owe them, and we can all get on with our lives?"

He acted as though it were a contested parking ticket, not $407,853.52 (plus interest and his and my legal expenses).

"I don't have it, and even if I did have it, I don't owe it to you."

"Why, of course you do, Peter," John-Roger said, "you signed a contract."

"All those contracts were signed under extreme duress," I pointed out. "I was told, in essence, that if I didn't sign, I'd never find God."

"Well, you can't mess around with God, and the Church repre-

> Smitten as we are
> with the vision of
> social righteousness,
> a God indifferent to
> everything but adulation,
> and full of partiality
> for his individual favorites,
> lacks an essential element
> of largeness.
>
> WILLIAM JAMES

sents God . . ."

"I never wanted to join a church," I interrupted. John-Roger looked at me, surprised. It's probably the first time he had been interrupted since MSIA bought a computer against his wishes. "I took Insight. I was looking for personal growth and help with something I now know was my depression. Instead, I was hustled right into MSIA, which was never my intent. I wasn't looking for a guru. I had already spent seven years with a guru—a Maharishi, for heaven's sake."

John-Roger has a way of blinking which essentially means: I'm not going to deal with anything you just said, and I'm about to change the subject. He blinked that way, not once, but twice. Sure enough, the next words out of his mouth were a subject change:

"When we started writing the books together . . ."

"We never wrote any books together." I had interrupted. Twice. In a row. I was hoping his walkie-talkie was sending a message to base and was being recorded: I'd need the proof when I submitted this to Guinness's Book of Spiritual World Records. "Didn't we establish that just a few minutes ago outside?"

John-Roger blinked again. It seemed as though he was trying to get the concept of "outside" inside his head. I continued:

"I put *your* name on *my* books, published the books, did practically all the promotion myself, mortgaging my house to the hilt to do so, and the *only* reason I did this was because you promised to keep me alive and healthy after you told me I had only nine months to live!"

"But, Peter," he said, "You *are* alive." That was the second time in twenty minutes he had made that facile argument. Did he believe it, or did he have no other defense?

"Are you saying that if you hadn't kept me alive, I'd be dead now?" He shrugged, seeming to indicate, "If you're so stupid to ignore the proof of your *own life*, who am I to explain it to you?" I had accepted countless of these shrugs in the past. I wasn't about to today.

"Well?"

"When did I ever say I'd keep you alive and healthy, Peter?"

Ah, a new defense. General denial. This go 'round should be interesting: When it came to denial, John-Roger was a Four Star General.

"In 1988, you told me . . ."

"Words, words," he said in

> *There is nothing so pathetic as a forgetful liar.*
>
> F. M. KNOWLES

his best attempt to appear worldly and bemused. "I said, he said, they said, you said, who remembers any of it?"

"I do. I believed my life was in danger; I believed you could alleviate that danger; you said you would in exchange for my writing and promoting the books. I lived up to my end of the bargain, *and there is no possible way you could have lived up to yours.*"

John-Roger actually seemed to be paying attention. I quickly continued:

"That's not breach of contract: breach of contract is if you said you'd give me one of your houses in exchange for writing a book for you. If you didn't give me one of your houses but you *could* have given me one of your houses, that would be breach of contract. To say you'd keep me alive and healthy in exchange for writing books for you is *fraud*. You *never* could have delivered on your end of the bargain. You don't have the power over life and death—certainly not mine. And you got me to believe that you did. In exchange for that I gave you a rehabilitated reputation, *New York Times* bestsellers, and more than $550,000. I performed; you never could: it's fraud, pure and simple."

"Was it really that much?" he asked. Apparently he only heard the dollar figure.

"Yes," I said, "and that's just directly from the books. That doesn't include that hundreds of thousands of dollars that I 'gave to God' which *you* somehow intercepted to buy houses and horses and heaven knows what all. I figure it's more than a million dollars altogether."

John-Roger blinked. Ah: subject change.

"You signed a *contract*, Peter, with the *Church*, and you owe them the *money.*"

> *Now, he says that the Lord has talked with him, and also that angels have ministered unto him. But behold, we know that he lies unto us; and he tells us these things, and he worketh many things by his cunning arts, that he may deceive our eyes . . . to make himself a king and a ruler over us, that he may do with us according to his will and pleasure.*
>
> BOOK OF MORMON
> *I Nephi 16:38*

"Yes, and we had a verbal agreement that you repeated over the years, in front of witnesses, and put into writing. I've only gone through about ten percent of our correspondence, and I already found these two examples." I pointed to the two quotes from John-Roger's computer messages to me that I had included in my letter to USM students. The first was from a message dated March 28, 1994:

> WHEN WE WERE FIRST TALKING ABOUT WRITING THE FIRST BOOK [1988] YOU INDICATED YOUR HEALTH WAS FRAGILE AND YOU MIGHT NOT BE ALIVE TO DO ALL THAT WOULD BE REQUIRED TO PUT OUT A BOOK. I SAID AS LONG AS WE WERE WRITING BOOKS TOGETHER I WOULD HANDLE YOUR HEALTH ISSUE FOR YOU.

The other was dated January 7, 1993. I was late in paying him his pound of flesh, so he turned up the heat:

> AT THIS TIME I WANT YOU TO KNOW ONE THING. I KEPT ALL OF MY AGREEMENTS WITH YOU THAT WERE MADE VERBALLY IN YUCCA VALLEY IN THE JOSHUA TREE NATIONAL PARK [1988] REGARDING YOUR HEALTH, AND YOU AND I WRITING BOOKS TOGETHER.
>
> WHEN I STARTED TO DO THIS YOU HAD GREAT CONCERNS THAT YOUR HEALTH {YOU MIGHT DIE BEFORE WE FINISH THEM} MIGHT GET IN THE WAY. I SAID AS LONG AS WE WERE WRITING BOOKS TOGETHER I WOULD LOOK AFTER YOUR HEALTH AND THE AIDS/ARC SITUATION, AND I DID NOT LIMIT MY SUPPORT TO JUST THAT ASPECT OF YOUR HEALTH.
>
> I TOOK ON MUCH MORE. SOME OF IT DEALING WITH POLICE, ETC, LAW SUITS ETC., AND ETC.

There it was in black and white. Twice.

John-Roger read and re-read these communications with a certain sense of disbelief. (Hadn't he read the letter outside less than half an hour ago?)

His argument seemed to be: We've got your name on contracts, and all you have is your memory of words. Here, in front of him, were not one, but two smoking guns. As you may have guessed, when confronted with irrefutable evidence, John-Roger responded in the most straightforward way possible: he tried to convince me that what he had *written* was not what he meant.

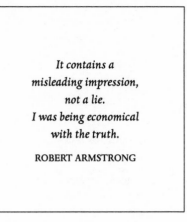

It contains a misleading impression, not a lie. I was being economical with the truth.

ROBERT ARMSTRONG

He tried one semantic trick after another, each progressively more pathetic. After the attempts became too painful to hear, I said:

"If you haven't had a good, long talk with your attorney about this, I suggest you do." John-Roger had previously indicated that he had not seen any of the letters I had sent to his attorney. "Please: read the letters I sent, and your attorneys' responses. You should go into this lawsuit with all the facts, and it doesn't sound as though you have them."

It was hard to believe that John-Roger, who approved every purchase of horsefeed for the ranch, would not have scrutinized every letter that passed between his attorney and myself.

"What do you want, Peter?" he asked.

"What I've been asking for all along: just leave me alone. You keep everything I've given you, I'll rewrite the books with only my name on them, and we'll each go our own way."

Silence.

I was not about to ask him what he wanted, that's what he had a former actor for. This guy knew a cue when he heard it.

"What do *you* want, J-R?" the actor asked.

"I want the books published just as they are, with my name on them. I want you to pay the Church all you owe it in back royalties, and continue paying us royalties on all the books that sell in the future."

I think the only thing keeping him from asking for my first-born was that he knew that I didn't have one.

"I guess we have no common ground, then," I said. "I'd rather

> Slaves and schoolboys
> often love
> their masters.
>
> GEORGE BERNARD SHAW

do something else for the next two years, but you're leaving me no choice. You want to take everything I own, so I'm going to have to defend myself with everything I've got."

"I think John-Roger's offer was fair," said the former actor, who also thought his role in a movie about cocaine smuggling should have earned him the Academy Award.

"Look," I said, never breaking eye contact with the staff member, "this man said he would keep me alive and healthy in exchange for writing books and putting his name on them. I wrote the books. I put his name on them. I gave him more than $550,000. The only problem is: *he does not have the power over life and death.* I know that's a strange concept for you to assimilate. I'm not asking you to believe that, but in order for John-Roger to prove that he could keep up his part of the bargain, he's going to have to convince a jury that he *does* have the power over life and death. If he can't, I have been defrauded, and I'm entitled to all of my money back . . ."

". . . plus damages." John-Roger said, finishing my sentence. Correctly. Was he trying to communicate to me that his dumb act about the law was just that: an act? Or was he finally just getting it himself? Or did he want to interrupt me one more time so that we'd leave the game with a tied score: two and two. I don't know.

What he said next verified for me all the sleazy stories I had heard about him.

"You know," he said with all the finesse of a loanshark moonlighting as a pimp, "what comes out in lawsuits can be pretty ugly. There's all those videotapes of you having sex, and all those photographs of you having sex. I've seen them all."

Had he really sunk this low? Perhaps he had always been that low, and I was just beginning to recognize it.

"You've *seen* videotapes of me having sex?" I asked.

"Yes," he answered.

"You have actually *seen* me, on a *video screen,* having sex?" I said, narrowing the question.

"Well," he said, "the tape was as close as this is to me." He casually reached out and touched the edge of the table.

"Did you put it in a videotape machine and watch any portion of it?" I asked.

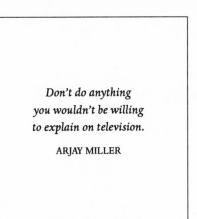

"I didn't want to dirty myself with it," he said, taking a moral high tone. A videotape of me having sex, after all, would be far too shocking for a man of John-Roger's delicate sensibilities. So much for video tapes.

"I think you're confusing me with Rob Lowe," I said. "People do it all the time. And what about the photographs?" I asked.

"Those I saw. They're of you having sex with someone."

Didn't he know *anything* about me? I'm a voyeur, not an exhibitionist.

"Who was I having sex with?" I asked.

"A girl," he said.

"A girl!? Who?" I asked.

"I can't say," he said.

"And what was I doing in these pictures?"

"You were with this girl, and she had her blouse off . . ."

Suddenly I knew *exactly* the pictures he was talking about *and* how he got them. One of his devotees (let's call her Shirley) was a friend of mine (before "it all came down") and she wanted pictures of herself. I had a studio, so I said, "Come on over." We went through the standard headshot series, and I got drunk and she got drunker, and she wanted some pictures of me, so a friend grabbed the camera. Another vodka later, she pulled off her blouse and we got some absurd pictures that could be best described as "horsing around." They were about as erotic as Benny Hill teamed up with Monty Python's Penguin Lady. (The one who had the exploding penguin on her television.)

"Look," I said, "if you release pictures of Shirley's tits, you'll lose her as fast as you lost me." Knowing well Shirley's iron-hand-in-an-iron-glove New-York ways, he had to laugh.

> I hope you have not
> been leading a double life,
> pretending to be wicked
> and being really good all the time.
> That would be hypocrisy.
>
> OSCAR WILDE

It was at this point that I felt the only sadness I felt during our conversation. We never shared much; never had any philosophical conversations; he never understood writing or publishing, so I could never share those with him; we never had a great meal together, or split a good bottle of wine; in short, there wasn't much to our social relationship. I tolerated him, because I believed he had a direct connection to God. He tolerated me, because I had a direct connection to getting books written and published. The only personal time we spent together I can look back on and say, "This was good," were the times of laughter.* But the laughter in the present moment was cut short.

"Peter," he said, "I've known you for a long time, and I know a lot about you. Why don't you just pay the Church its money and avoid a lot of embarrassment?"

I knew what he was referring to: he thought that if he revealed I'm gay, it would be devastating for me. Hardly. Anyone who looked at my book of photographs, *PORTRAITS,* and *didn't* know I was gay was blind.

But for John-Roger, being closeted is not just a lifestyle—it's an addiction. I wonder what might have happened if John-Roger had the courage to come out in 1983 when the first rumors about his homosexuality were circulating. What an inspiration his courage would have been, for both gays and straights.

In fact, in 1983, the gay world very much needed some honest, open, spiritual teachers: AIDS was forcing gays to explore issues of life, death, and eternity most people don't even think about until their old age.

In the time John-Roger was claiming his closet was not a closet, but a spiritual retreat center (1983 to 1994), Louise Hay and Marianne Williamson rose from relative obscurity to enormous popularity—catapulted to fame by a primarily gay following who saw friends dying or who may have been dying themselves, and sought

---

*Note to music director of the TV-movie of this book: "The Way We Were" would fit nicely here.

an answer to the question: "What's it all about?"

As a personal growth teacher, John-Roger could have been somebody; he could have been a contender. But fear—the very limitation he encourages others to overcome—kept him small; that made him petty, and here he was, thinking he could blackmail me into turning over

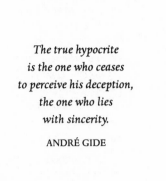

The true hypocrite is the one who ceases to perceive his deception, the one who lies with sincerity.

ANDRÉ GIDE

everything I owned to keep the world from knowing that I'm "that way." Just because John-Roger sacrificed his integrity on the altar of homophobia doesn't mean I'm going to sacrifice my *house*.

Out me if you will, John-Roger, but get out of my life!

That is not, however, what I said. I used his threat to ask a question I knew the answer to, but wanted to ask anyway just in case I ever wrote a book about all this, which, as it turns out, I am now doing, so I'm glad I asked the question:

"Are you saying you would take information you got from me in pastoral counseling, with you as my minister, and make it public information?"

"I don't recall you asking me to keep anything in confidence," he said coyly.

Was there no limit to how low he would go?

"*Everything* I told you was in confidence. According to you, one of the attributes of the Mystical Traveler is absolute confidentiality. That is what you offer to all those who come to study with you, and that was the agreement I always thought we had."

"Well, it's all in the hands of the lawyers now," he said, "they'll decide what to do with it."

It was roughly the answer I had expected, but it was good to have him say it. It was time to take my leave.

But I had to make one last attempt.

"Why are you doing this to me? You know you have no right to this money, or claim to these books. Why don't you just leave me alone and let me get on with my life?"

"I'm curious," he said. "I've never been involved in a lawsuit that went all the way to court before. I'm kinda curious to see

> *Farewell, Monsieur Traveler:*
> *look you lisp and*
> *wear strange suits,*
> *disable all the benefits*
> *of your own country,*
> *be out of love with your nativity,*
> *and almost chide God*
> *for making you that*
> *countenance you are.*
>
> SHAKESPEARE
> As You Like It

how it all works."

I stood to leave.

"Gimme a hug," John-Roger said, as he stood and grabbed me. "Whatever happens in all this," he added with a sincere look, "I'm not going to hate you."

"Well, then, I can rest in peace, now, can't I?"

He was going to drag me through at least two years of the Chinese water torture known as the American legal system ("death by deposition"), spend hundreds of thousands of dollars of MSIA's (God's) money on his own legal fees to do this (if I have one great fear in life, it is that MSIA is using the money *I* gave them to sue *me*), and for what?

To satisfy his curiosity. Whew. The more despicable this man becomes, the more pig-headedly ignorant I feel to have followed him for fifteen years. At least in all this, I have one compensation:

No matter what happens, he'll never hate me.

CHAPTER FIFTEEN
Insight from the Inside

BY MID-1979, Insight was clearly a hit—especially with John-Roger. To him, Insight was the answer to a Preceptor's prayer.

First, it made piles of money—nearly two million dollars by mid-1979. John-Roger affectionately referred to it as his "little money machine."

Second, it gave him oodles of new MSIA recruits—me being one of them.

Third, it gave those who already were in MSIA a renewed sense of commitment to the Traveler and "the Traveler's teachings."

And, finally, it nearly quadrupled the Traveler's teachings with a single stroke. When Russell Bishop stole Insight from Lifespring, he brought with him a neatly packaged set of practical tools for obtaining goals in the material world—and John-Roger gleefully fenced them.

MSIA, on the other hand, was a hodgepodge of concepts, beliefs, and techniques cobbled together from whatever spiritual, metaphysical, or philosophical teaching appealed to John-Roger— if it took his fancy, he took it. As John-Roger's interests changed, so did MSIA's theology—the dogma of one year became the dog doo of the next.

His followers didn't seem to mind, miss the past teachings, or even much notice anything had changed. The only bedrock constant in the MSIA cosmology: if you want to tell the difference between John-Roger and God, you need an electron microscope.

Since John-Roger was inconsistent in his teachings, he gathered to him followers who were inconsistent in their learning. There is little doubt that John-Roger presented practically every great truth he could pilfer—and oh, what a pilferer he was: bold or subtle, as the occasion required.

John-Roger—who thinks "Short-Attention-Span Theater" is too plodding—is always on the lookout for some diversion. While meandering around at the dawn of the New Age during the 1960s and 70s, John-Roger was bound to find something completely different at every turn. He did. He shared each new ripple of information as his latest and greatest *personal* revelation from God.

His followers, then, were trained to look for the *new* teachings. While some teachers encourage their students to spend a lifetime integrating a handful of basic truths—such as acceptance, forgiveness, and love—into their being, John-Roger offered his disciples the Great Truth *du jour.* ("Hello, my name is John-Roger. I'll be your Traveler for the evening. May I tell you about our specials?")

Insight brought with it hits of wisdom and universal profundities, which were served up in bite-sized portions of two hours each, allowing people regular trips to the bathroom so no one could complain about not being able to pee on schedule. What more could John-Roger want? Whereas before he had a bag of tricks, now he owned the magic shop.

And a Sorcerer's Apprentice came with it.

His name was Russell Bishop: short, bright, impeccably dressed, rigid—a sycophant if he thought you were better than he was; a tyrant if he thought you were not. He was as much the sycophant to John-Roger as he was the tyrant to me. Whereas John-Roger often didn't know Russell was around because Russell was behind John-Roger, trying to kiss his butt, I *always* knew of Russell's presence because he was busy kicking mine.

From the first hour of my first Insight seminar, you see, I

wanted to be a trainer. Alas, that meant being approved by Russell, but Russell only approved those he thought were better than he, and Russell was plagued by no such thoughts about me. The more eagerly I tried, the more gleefully Russell stomped me down. There was no winning with him; most of the time there wasn't even any play-

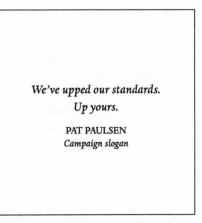

We've upped our standards. Up yours.

PAT PAULSEN
Campaign slogan

ing—even the *practice field* was off limits to all but Russell's A-list.

At some point during 1979, Insight changed the name from trainer to facilitator. Some people thought the word *trainer* was too harsh. Compared to, say, warden, drill sergeant, or slave driver, it was not harsh at all. Nonetheless, there are kinder, gentler words than *trainer*. In choosing *facilitator*, however, apparently nobody bothered to look up the word in the dictionary—someone just said it means "easy." Easy. Yeah, that's a good word. A facilitator makes things easy, like an enabler enables people to do things, and an empowerer empowers people to do things, and a dictator . . . well, let's not think too deeply here.

Not thinking too deeply was the problem at Insight. John-Roger's shallow thinking and superficial experiences (he's had *lots* of experiences, but few of them very deep) were both contagious and encouraged. When in doubt, don't think it out: ask J-R. The most popular feature in MSIA's monthly newspaper, in fact, is "Ask J-R." It's hard to control people when they take the time to think about such concepts as freedom, self, spirit, and God. Hell, they might go off and do something radical—like putting *themselves* in charge of their own lives. Dangerous thinking.

One of the few subjects John-Roger *has* thought deeply about is manipulating others. Early on he must have come to the conclusion that free wills and free minds do not freely give themselves over to the authority of another. Yes, those who think for themselves will follow *leaders*, but leading is a lot more work than simply laying down the law—and John-Roger's decision to be a law-giver rather than a leader placed a malignancy at the center of any organization he created, contaminating all who come too close to it.

Those who led Insight, then, were not called leaders; they were called facilitators, which means people who make things easy. *Facile*

> *If you were a member of*
> *Jesse James's band and people*
> *asked you what you were,*
> *you wouldn't say,*
> *"Well, I'm a desperado."*
> *You'd say something like,*
> *"I work in banks," or*
> *"I've done some railroad work."*
>
> ROY BLOUNT, JR.

also means superficial and glib.

Most of John-Roger's personal staff wanted to facilitate. They wanted to serve, but they also saw it as an opportunity to *get away from* John-Roger for a week here or there. Because they were on John-Roger's personal staff, Russell considered them better than he, so he eagerly taught them. John-Roger, on the other hand, had no such desire to facilitate—why give up being king to become minister of education? Or, an analogy both John-Roger and Russell would be more likely to agree with: why give up being God to become king?

As John-Roger's staff learned facilitation and the demand for Insight seminars* grew, J-R's staff co–facilitated seminars on their own—that is, without Russell's super-vision. At Russell's Insight seminars, I couldn't even get into the seminar room and perform the lowliest facilitator-in-training activity: sitting in the back of the room taking notes.

Yes, those of us who wanted to be facilitators were being *trained* for it. The idea of *facilitating* the process of becoming a facilitator was somehow never considered. The idea with Russell was not, "Let's put out some safety nets and see if you can fly," but, "So you think you can fly, do you? Well, prove it." With John-Roger's staff facilitating, however, anyone who demonstrated he or she *could* facilitate got to do it.

In 1979, I moved to L.A. (next door to PRANA), filed for bankruptcy (on the advice and to the enrichment of an MSIA attorney), and spent all my time pursuing my dual passions: Insight and personal computers. (More on the latter in the chapter "Computer Books: The Joy of Victory and the Agony of Defeat.") I lived in an

---

*Now that the trainers were called facilitators, someone thought it would be a good idea not to call the training a training. They had the good sense, at least, not to call it a facilitation: Insight facilitations sounded like it might be a special floral bouquet you would send to someone who discovered the meaning of the universe. It was finally decided that *seminars* was a good thing to call Insight trainings—the word had done well for John-Roger over the years, and, besides, getting the people to go from an Insight seminar to a John-Roger seminar was an easy semantic leap.

$85 a month apartment and spent $15 a week on food. (Lots of Top Ramen and eggs.) My money came from selling books I had purchased from my own bankruptcy sale (there wasn't exactly a long line to buy an inventory of poetry books), and the rest of my time was spent either reading about computers or assisting at Insight. I climbed

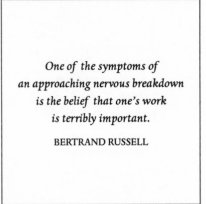

One of the symptoms of an approaching nervous breakdown is the belief that one's work is terribly important.

BERTRAND RUSSELL

the ranks from lowly assistant to lofty team captain thanks to my enthusiasm (5%), my dedication (5%), and my standing offer: I'll go anywhere anytime at my own expense to assist at an Insight seminar (90%).

In the summer of 1980, I joined thirty-nine other facilitator wannabes for the facilitator training, a.k.a. Insight IV. We spent $1,500 each to sit in John-Roger's Mandeville Canyon basement so the trainers training us to be facilitators could, as one of them demurely put it, "rip you a new asshole." What on earth *that* month had to do with learning how to facilitate, I'll never know. Eventually I began treating the entire month like the brutal initiation rights of an obscure cult (which, far more than I knew at the time, it was).

The whole place reminded me of the galley ship in *Ben Hur:* we sat in double rows facing each other, and Russell would go up and down the aisles whipping us. If he got tired of walking, we walked past him while he whipped. When he got tired of whipping altogether—which was rare: the man has the endurance of a tractor—other whipping boys were brought in.

It's amazing what you put up with when you think other people know more than you.

Occasionally, John-Roger would wander in. He was so *nice.* Like a visit from the captain of the slave ship, whenever John-Roger arrived all brutality ceased; even the brutalizers stood in awe, deferring, nay, *supplicating,* to him. He would dispense water, do a little first aid, and tell us stories about great sea adventures. After a couple of hours, he would drift back upstairs, where, we supposed, God awaited him for lunch. As he left, he would bestow a parting gift: "Give them an extra hour for lunch," "Show them a movie tonight," or "My cook baked some chocolate chip cookies

> In the mouths of many men
> soft words are like roses
> that soldiers put into the muzzles
> of their muskets on holidays.
>
> LONGFELLOW
> 1857

for you."

So there we were—paying him $1,500 each to sit in his dank, humid basement—and we were so *grateful* to him for an hour off. What seems always to be missed when one praises the benevolent monarchs—saving their subjects from the tyrannies of government and all that—is that the monarch *is* the government, and the tyrannies only take place because the monarch *permits* them. Could John-Roger have made that month a useful, productive, *facile* time? You bet your cat-o'-nine-tails. Instead, he permitted—perhaps even encouraged—the bullying, browbeating, and psychological bludgeoning Russell Bishop took such obvious pleasure in administering.

Personally, I don't think it was accidental on John-Roger's part. He knew—as long as he didn't drive people away—that the worse Russell was, the better John-Roger appeared. Pressure and release. Good cop/bad cop.

That first part—as long as he didn't drive people away— explains why Russell is sweetness and light in Insight I, but Simon Legree in Insight IV: by the time people got to Insight IV, they were not only hooked; they were crawling up the fishing line. God bless us—we of that first Insight IV were a school of tuna leaping onto the deck of a fishing boat yelling, "Put us in cans! Put us in cans!" Russell would stroll around the deck like Captain Bligh— foppish attire and all—pointing to one tuna after another, proclaiming, "You're not good enough, Charlie," and the hapless tuna would be returned to the sea. Sorry, Charlie.

That John-Roger was behind the pirate Russell as much as he was jolly-sea-captain John-Roger (I am not going to make a pun about the Jolly Roger, so you can relax) is a fairly safe bet. Once, when I stopped being the chicken of the sea and confronted Russell in front of the group on his unnecessarily abusive behavior, he explained:

> I don't make [Insight] decisions independently. Do you hear that? I know that this is Russell Bishop Human Being sitting over here. I happen to have a good buddy who's connected a little better and I sit and talk about all these things first.

The "good buddy" was *not* Mother Teresa. Little did I know that John-Roger, while playing the part of Peter Pan to Russell's Captain Hook, was in reality not just Captain Bligh, but the maniacal power behind the entire fleet: Admiral Tyrannical.

Don't try to control people.

JOHN-ROGER

For me, the reality of John-Roger would seep in much later. Now, in that summer of 1980, his carefully constructed illusion held firm. John-Roger positively glowed in my perception. He *personally* saved me from Russell time and time again. Like the bird that is saved repeatedly by the owner of a cat, I forgot that my savior was, in reality, *the owner of the cat.*

Insight IV out of the way, we were all ready to facilitate. Theoretically, we were all equally ready, but, as George Orwell pointed out, some of us were more equal than others. In Russell's eyes, I was definitely in the "others" category. Of the forty Insight IV participants, I probably ranked thirty-nine on the Bishop Scale of Facilitation Qualities.

The lowest rung on the ladder to facilitatordom was *observer*—"sitting in the back of the room and taking notes." The next step up from observer was *floater*. I have no idea where *that* name came from, but it did mean you could present certain sections of the training during the seminar on your way to becoming a *co–facilitator* and, eventually, a *lead facilitator*. Perhaps the most significant comment during the entire month of Insight IV was from the young woman who, when the term *floater* was introduced, said: "When I was a girl, floaters were what we called the turds that didn't sink."

I gave Insight my revised travel policy: I would go anywhere any time at my own expense *if* I could float in a training—I had observed my fill while team captaining. An opportunity was granted, and, on twenty-four hours' notice, I flew to Miami to float at an Insight I. Luckily, John-Roger's staff was facilitating the seminar. Whereas Russell was parsimonious in sharing the stage with others, the staff was the soul of generosity. In addition to the two staff members co–facilitating the training, there were four of us eager, recent Insight IV graduates. This was the first opportunity any of us had had to float.

We had a meeting, and the first three days of the training were divided up fairly equally among the six of us.

> A team effort is
> a lot of people
> doing what I say.
>
> MICHAEL WINNER

The three other floaters were so convinced their facilitation would be superior to mine, they were beyond smug: they were *sympathetic*. Every sentence they addressed to me began, "Don't be disappointed if . . . ." They were, after all, far more qualified that I: they were *ministers*, I was not; they were *initiates*, I was not; *and* they got higher ratings on the Bishop Scale of Facilitation Qualities.

Russell had convinced everyone that good facilitation was a direct reflection of how spiritual, loving, and enlightened you were. I believed that those attainments, while perfectly nice, did not a good facilitator make. As far as I was concerned, facilitation was a *performance* skill. A natural performer who was not particularly spiritual, loving, or enlightened would be a more successful facilitator than a spiritual, loving, enlightened person who could not perform.

Miami was the test. No one knew Miami was the test but me. I stated my facilitator-as-performer hypothesis once in Insight IV, and it caused *such* an unfavorable reaction in Russell and the entire group that I didn't even get my cookie that day. The most compassionate response anyone had to my seemingly heathen idea was: "Peter's new to the Movement. He isn't even an initiate yet."

While the three other floaters were off practicing spiritual exercises, I was practicing my presentation of Insight I. (In truth, I did do spiritual exercises, but the time spent with my eyes closed usually turned out to be mental practice sessions: I was obsessed with facilitating Insight.) The four of us each had about twenty minutes of presentation that first night "in front of the room," as they like to say at Insight. (*I* like to say "on stage.") The co–facilitators from J-R's staff would handle the rest. It was decided that I would make my presentation last; the other five more spiritual souls would "warm up" the group for me. Their idea of warming up the group was "sending the Light" to them. My idea of warming up the group was getting them to laugh.

The seminar began. Two hundred people (most of them *not* in MSIA—this was true for all Insight I seminars by the fall of 1979) sat facing the stage, er, I'm sorry, the front of the room. The facilitators were great and got things off to a good start.

THE JOKER: *"Have you any last words, Caped Crusader?"*

BATMAN: *"Just this, Joker —evil sometimes triumphs temporarily . . . but never conquers."*

BATMAN

Then the first floater got up, and promptly sank. It was painful to watch. The facilitators adeptly took over. A while later the second floater got up. The second she saw four hundred eyes focused on her, she froze. The facilitators' attempts to thaw her out proved futile, so the facilitators took over again. The third floater, perhaps the most arrogant of them all (other than myself—my arrogance is a given, like gravity), got on stage and died, simply died. As much as I disliked him personally, he went through the sort of agony you don't wish upon your worst enemy. The facilitators intervened again and made their third rescue of the evening.

By this time, there was a definite sense in the seminar room that something strange was happening. There was a lack of professionalism which threatened to undermine the group's confidence in the facilitators (as far as the participants were concerned, the floaters were facilitators, too). Confidence in the facilitators was essential to the success of the seminar.

While the participants were doing a process, the facilitators came up to me and said that unless I was *absolutely certain* I could do a *terrific* job, I should probably wait until much later in the seminar before getting up in front of the room. The decision, however, would be mine. It was a tough choice. I had experienced lecturing and performing before, but never in front of an Insight seminar—or any other seminar training, for that matter. What if Russell and all the Insight IV participants were right? What if presenting to an Insight group was based on the ability to *be* rather than the ability to *do*? If that were the case, I would do *worse* than the spiritually connected Minister-Initiate floaters who sank before me. What to do?

Not presenting my segment now would be, as the *I Ching*

> Good teaching
> is one-fourth preparation
> and three-fourths theater.
>
> GAIL GODWIN

would put it, "no blame." I could present something later in the seminar when the group is so loving that they would be amused by hand puppets *sans* hands. That would put a notch of experience in front of the room under my belt. It would be the safe and prudent way to go: reasonable, practical, reliable.

I told them I wanted to do my piece that night as scheduled.

What can I say? I was a triumph. I was clear, funny, warm, precise, connected. And I loved it. And the audience loved me. Yes, they were an *audience,* I was on the *stage,* I gave a great *performance.* As I suspected, Insight was theater, not theology.

At a meeting that evening following the seminar, the three other floaters each decided they would spend the remainder of the seminar "in the back of the room taking notes." I, however, was ready to roll: I became essentially the third facilitator. I received glowing reviews ("reports" in Insight nontheatrical terminology).

I spent the next ten months traveling around the country facilitating. The only thing missing, I was told, was that I was not sufficiently "connected to the Traveler." This, of course, could be remedied by becoming an initiate and a minister—just like all the other facilitators. I was duly initiated and, during a meal break at an Insight I in Washington, D.C., on April 24, 1981, I was duly ordained a minister in the Church of the Movement of Spiritual Inner Awareness. (People who knew me around Insight continued to tell me I was not connected enough to the Traveler, until they found out I was now an initiate and a minister, at which point they "looked deeper into it" and saw that I was, after all, connected.)

During those ten months, I paid all my expenses myself and, certainly, never charged Insight for my time.

At the end of May 1981, I returned to Insight IV—this time as an assistant. At Insight I's around the country, I was in everything but name a co–facilitator. I was regularly presenting half the seminar on an equal footing with any facilitator I worked with. Most people thought of me as a co–facilitator—except Russell. To Russell I was an uppity little bastard who dared to defy his edict that it takes at least two years to co–facilitate. I also wasn't spiritual, loving, or enlightened enough for Russell—although no one in any seminar I co–facilitated asked for any money back due to my personal endarkenment. I expected a triumphant return to Insight IV. I was a model of at least one thing Insight taught: if you want something badly

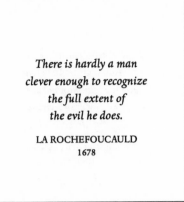

There is hardly a man clever enough to recognize the full extent of the evil he does.

LA ROCHEFOUCAULD
1678

enough, you can have it, providing you focus your full attention on it and work hard to get it. While assisting at Insight IV, I felt certain my co–facilitator status would be officially confirmed.

Russell had other ideas. After about a week, he ordered me to the front of the room, and for the next hour I was systematically, psychologically destroyed. I could do no right. If I smiled I was being glib; if I was serious, I was being negative; if I sat quietly, I was refusing to participate; if I talked, I was refusing to listen. Hadn't I come here to *serve* these forty Insight IV participants? Well, I wasn't doing it *humbly* enough. At least not humbly enough for Russell. I had to prove my humility by getting down on my hands and knees and kiss the participants' feet. Literally.

I was truly bewildered. What on earth did my humility have to do with my ability to facilitate Insight I's? I was good at facilitating Insight I's. In the past ten months I had proven that time and time again. In addition, I was one of only two people willing to be a full-time volunteer assistant for Insight IV: twelve-to-fifteen-hour days for an entire month. I didn't really expect Russell to show *gratitude*—not Russell, and certainly not to me—but I didn't expect such gratuitous attacks.

A few days later, he started again. I had a doctor's appointment in the morning, and arranged with my fellow assistant to play the morning John-Roger seminar tape, which took an hour. I told him I would arrive before the seminar was over, which I did. This was not acceptable to Russell. I was supposed to get permission from *Russell*, in writing, if I wanted to be late.

As soon as the tape was over, Russell called me to the front of the room. He began again. I have a videotape of this. When I get to the front of the room, I seem happy and relaxed. The ominous tone in Russell's voice and the extended interaction only a few

> I have always considered it as treason against the great republic of human nature, to make any man's virtue the means of deceiving him.
>
> DR. SAMUEL JOHNSON
> 1759

days before had me wondering what was going on. I grabbed my stomach momentarily and grimaced in mock fear. There were a few laughs from the group.

It was my way of acknowledging the fear but, as I thought we taught in Insight, "not let it run" me. Russell started in. He was far from amused. Here's a direct transcript of our interaction:

RUSSELL: What's this?

PETER: I wasn't expecting to be called up here and every time I've been called up here it's been [*grimace*] [*group laughter*].

RUSSELL: So, what's going on in your stomach?

PETER: In my stomach . . .

RUSSELL: That's where you grabbed.

PETER: Fear.

RUSSELL: What do you have to be fearful of?

PETER: I was a half-an-hour late today.

RUSSELL: You were a half-an-hour late today.

PETER: Yes.

RUSSELL: Anything else to be fearful of?

PETER: Not that I'm aware of. [*laughter*]

RUSSELL: You sure? [*addressing group*] Look, did you hear how this con started? Were you watching how this con started. [*group indicates "no"*] Okay, you weren't watching. [*to Peter*] So you don't want to look at that.

PETER: At *what*?

RUSSELL: The thing I call "con" that you're running, the pissed off, and whatever else you're running inside.

PETER: I would prefer a straight-out shot, Russ, rather than all the picky stuff: "What's this?" "What's the con?" What are you getting at? What do you want? What am I up here for? Would you just lay out the straight shot?

RUSSELL: Does anyone get that [*I'm*] not being straight? [*group does not agree*] I asked him what he's experiencing. He's the one who goes "uggh!" [*mimics holding stomach*]

PETER: Is there an agenda, Russ? Is there something specific I'm going to be accused of?

RUSSELL: Yeah, there is Peter.

PETER: Can I hear it, please?

RUSSELL: Yeah, you can.

PETER: Thank you.

RUSSELL: But you won't . . . How could I give you anything you could hear?

> *I don't want any yes-men around me. I want everybody to tell me the truth even if it costs them their jobs.*
>
> SAMUEL GOLDWYN

PETER: You could have given it to me straight out, rather than going through the "What's this?" "What's the con?" the whole destroy-whatever-Peter's-doing number—destroy, break down, crash in—what's the word for it that's used around here a lot? *Bust.* The whole "bust" mode of working on me I don't appreciate, and I don't want to tolerate it any more. If you have something specific to bring up, I'm happy to hear it.

RUSSELL: Okay. Do you have belongings here with you?

PETER: Yes.

RUSSELL: Why don't you just get them and leave.

PETER: All right.

RUSSELL: And I won't require your services up here any more.

I left. I was devastated. I thought I would never facilitate again. I wasn't just "busted"; I was exploded, demolished, disintegrated. My dream since 1978, the one I was so close to realizing, gone, just like that. It was a very long, dark night.

The next morning, I got a phone call: John-Roger wanted to see me immediately. I drove to his house, and after we talked for a while, he reinstated me as an assistant for the Insight IV. Pressure and release. I felt terrific—and oh, so grateful to John-Roger. It was good cop/bad cop all over again. Looking back, I am amazed how effectively the same old techniques worked on me again and again.

Whether Russell intentionally played bad cop to John-Roger's good cop, I do not know. My guess is that Russell is just a bad cop by nature, and John-Roger knows how to manipulate him into abusing others so John-Roger can appear the White Knight. After

> I would have
> made a good Pope.
>
> RICHARD M. NIXON

"saving" someone from Russell's wrath, John-Roger would have a long talk with Russell, explaining that it was Russell's *job* to "hold people to their integrity," and other euphemistic justifications for being a sadistic shit.

I, like most people, learn a great deal from role models. Ironically, several people on John-Roger's personal staff were ideal role models: they had a terrific balance of discipline and tolerance, a warmth that was perceived by all, and a single-minded dedication to serving others.

But Russell ran Insight, and J-R ran Russell. Russell made it abundantly clear: he didn't want me around. Period. John-Roger told me he thought I facilitated just fine, and didn't see any reason why I shouldn't be a *lead* (not just co–) facilitator. John-Roger's caveat: Russell *did* run Insight, and his position had to be respected. John-Roger's challenge: if I *really* wanted to be a great facilitator, I would learn to facilitate Russell into letting me facilitate. It sounded like the plot for a New Age opera.

I never did win Russell over, yet John-Roger saw in me, I think, a useful piece of talent. So, whenever Russell made my seas too choppy, threatening to capsize my boat, lo, from afar and on high, John-Roger would wave his hand, and there would be a smoothing of the waters and a calming of the wind.

Over the next year I became co–facilitator (officially) and then lead facilitator. I hated the politics of Insight, but I loved facilitating. And I loved it when people who took my Insight I's eventually got on Discourses.

That was the phrase: "on Discourses." Looking back, the drug terminology was unintentional, but very accurate. We were all addicted, and believed our addiction was not only good, but essential. Yes, the tools taught at Insight were valuable for getting through this life, but the techniques taught by MSIA were invaluable for the next. If someone around Insight were to ask how a certain seminar participant was doing and the answer came back, "Wonderful: they're on Discourses," there would be great rejoicing.

The progression at Insight was clear: at the end of Insight I, the goal was to enroll people in Insight II and into volunteering for Insight. (Insight II was more important than volunteering, because it was easier to get people to volunteer after Insight II—they were by then, after all, "under our spell.") Almost half of the people who took Insight I went on to take Insight II.

> Evil is something
> you recognise immediately
> you see it:
> it works through charm.
>
> BRIAN MASTERS

At the end of Insight II, people were to be enrolled in Insight III and for volunteering for Insight. (Again, of the two, an Insight III enrollment was more important.) Eighty percent of the people who took Insight II took Insight III.

At the end of Insight III (which was held in retreat): Discourses. Later, people would be given a choice of one of MSIA's PAT (PRANA Awareness Training) trainings. (I know that makes it "PRANA Awareness Training trainings," but that's what they're called: PAT trainings.) PAT trainings were also held in retreat. A person left PAT trainings either a committed devotee, or ran away from the whole Insight/MSIA axis forever. For the vast majority, it was the former.

The great hole through which new MSIA members fell was the transition from the first year of Discourses to the second. The drop-out rate was astronomical. Most people stopped reading them during the first year. This great weakness in an otherwise well-oiled people-processing machine was addressed repeatedly— and always unsuccessfully. Several new experiments were underway in the mid-1980s, but 1988 came along, and with it the *Los Angeles Times* article. The Insight/MSIA emphasis went from getting people over the first-year Discourse hump to damage control.

I liked doing Insight I's best: they had the most material to present, and I enjoyed presenting material. I also thought I was good at it, and I served Insight best by doing what I did best. I eventually learned to facilitate Insight II's and Insight III's, but my heart remained with Insight I's. Although we did little direct promoting of Discourses in Insight I, I knew full well I was leading unwitting participants on the first step of a three- or four-step journey that would, for many of them, lead to MSIA.

On the "products table"
we sold a few of John-Roger's
generic books and a growing
number of seminar tapes
John-Roger recorded at Insight graduations. (Graduations took place at the end of
Insight I's and II's.) "Civilian" (non-Insight graduate)
friends were invited. John-
Roger knew his audience. On
the Insight seminar tapes, he
didn't talk much of the Mystical Traveler, but talked a great deal
about "practical spirituality." The tape included the sort of practical self-help techniques gleaned from Insight or whatever personal-growth book John-Roger was reading at the time. These
techniques were what people graduating from an Insight I wanted
to hear. These were to make it sound as though the tapes were
merely an extension of Insight.

Propaganda is a soft weapon:
hold it in your
hands too long,
and it will move about like a snake,
and strike the other way.

JEAN ANOUILH

In fact, the tapes laid out a great deal of MSIA cosmology
within, around, under, and between the generic self-help tips. The
only message directly missing: J-R has a closer link to God than
anyone else.

But the Insight tapes served their purpose: to get people used
to listening to John-Roger on seminar tapes. Going, then, from an
Insight seminar tape to an MSIA seminar tape was a very short
hop. The MSIA seminar tapes contained all the homilies, self-help
tips, anecdotal miracles, and childhood memories that the Insight
seminar tapes had, but they also included that one essential element: J-R is closer to God than anyone else.

There is *no doubt* that the primary purpose of Insight was to
get people on Discourses. With only two or three exceptions I can
think of, everyone in every leadership position in every city in
which Insight had an office was an initiate, a minister, or studying
to be an initiate and a minister. It was each leader's purpose to
"bring people to the Traveler." The Insight I–Insight II–Insight III–
Discourses progression was a frighteningly effective way to do it.

In Insight I, we were under strict instructions to mention J-R as
the founder of Insight, quote him from time to time as though we
were quoting John Denver or Shakespeare, and express our personal admiration of him as an *educator.* We were *not* to mention
how much he and God had in common (or, more accurately, how

little difference there was between them). It was fine to refer to John-Roger as teacher, innovator, creator, and, especially, friend. It was *not* okay to refer to him as the Traveler, the Preceptor, the One who picked up where Jesus left off, guru, or cult leader. It was okay to be his student, but not his disciple; his admirer, but not his devotee. If a partici-

> *You are surrounded on every side by lies which would deceive even the elect, if the elect were not generally so uncommonly wide awake; the self of which you are conscious, your reasoning and reflecting self, will believe these lies and bid you act in accordance with them.*
>
> SAMUEL BUTLER
> *Way of All Flesh*

pant came up to a facilitator and asked the right questions ("How do I find God?" or "What makes you so spiritual?" for example), it might be okay to suggest—very delicately—that the person get on Discourses. Other than that, we were to push John-Roger's more generic books and Insight seminar tapes to the hilt.

By the end of Insight II, it was fine for the facilitator to spiritually come out a little more, and even approach certain selected participants individually and quietly, personally recommend Discourses. The products sold at Insight II included some of John-Roger's more spiritual books, plus some MSIA seminar tapes.

At the end of Insight III, it was flatly stated that if you wanted "more of this energy," sign up for Discourses (or, later, take a PAT training). This was an easy sell: after a week in retreat doing one "jack 'em up" process* after another, everyone was feeling groovy, and who didn't want to keep feeling groovy from now on? Also, Discourses were only a hundred dollars for the first year, and people were used to paying a lot more for Insight: Insight II was around $700 and Insight III around $600. Those who *didn't* sign up for Discourses were individually approached by facilitators to find out what was "in their way to taking their next step."

I was proud to put people on the conveyor belt—smiling and misleading all the time—that I knew would lead them to MSIA. They just didn't *understand*, you see. Later, when they understood, they would make a "better choice." I actually believed this. I feel dreadful about every person I intentionally misled, and if any of you are reading this now, I'm sorry.

---

*Jack 'em up processes make people feel good about themselves for a short time, but have no lasting effect.

Note left by burglar of David Lane's apartment, written on box containing copies of Dr. Lane's research study, "The J-R Controversy: A Critical Study of John-Roger Hinkins and M.S.I.A." Handwriting was identified by experts as John-Roger's.

CHAPTER SIXTEEN

Against the Law or Above the Law?

Much as he is
opposed to lawbreaking,
he is not bigoted about it.

DAMON RUNYON

A S I'M SURE you noticed by the end of "The Most Disgusting Chapter in This Book," John-Roger had made the transition from the immoral to the illegal. In this chapter, I lay before you, ladies and gentlemen of the jury, the criminal activities of John-Roger.

John-Roger has said repeatedly that "the Traveler is above the laws of man" and "must only answer to the laws of Spirit." It may surprise you to learn how far above the laws of man John-Roger thinks he is.

Let's start small: violations of zoning restrictions.

Mandeville Canyon is a quiet, almost sleepy, residential community. Houses are, for the most part, well-spaced, and the only thing more important than tranquility is green and flowering things. Into this traditional place of peace, John-Roger came. He brought with him his rapidly expanding church, and all the administrative support that went with it. Even the First Amendment protections guaranteeing freedom of religion do not give a church freedom to operate in a residential area that's not zoned for churches.

Cars went to and from John-Roger's Mandeville Canyon home in an endless stream. The neighbors complained directly to John-Roger. Nothing changed. One of the neighbors was particularly troublesome (that is, he was demanding that a residential property be used only for residential purposes). When he died of a heart attack, John-Roger calmly received the news with the comment: "I had to remove him. He never should have struck against me." One of his staff, overhearing this comment, couldn't help but wonder: why couldn't he just remove the man to New York—or Hawaii? Wasn't killing him a little *too* severe? To John-Roger, however, it seemed a perfectly reasonable, rational, and just punishment for one who had the audacity to challenge his authority.

> *It's right because*
> *I say it's right.*
> *It's good because*
> *I say it's good.*
> *It's legit because*
> *I say it's legit.*
>
> AL CAPONE

Finally, the Department of Building and Safety sent an inspector. John-Roger and crew failed the inspection. Miserably. No improvement was made. John-Roger, through his attorney, wrote to Senior Inspector J. Anderson, claiming that, yes, he had a lot of friends but, hey, that's not against the law. He also claimed to have a number of "hobbies" such as editing audio tapes, publishing Discourses, and filling mail-order requests from his friends who wanted to enjoy the fruits of his hobbies.

The commercial activity at John-Roger's Mandeville Canyon property has never ceased. It continues today, twenty-one years later, more flagrantly than ever. The entire lower level of the house is now an audio and video editing center, featuring state-of-the-art equipment worth hundreds of thousands of dollars and five full-time employees. Some hobby. (This video and audio tape production facility is known as NOW Productions.)

To show how totally unconcerned MSIA is with violating zoning regulations, consider this excerpt from the July 1994 issue of *Architectural Digest*, in which the Mandeville Canyon home of MSIA second-in-command John Donnelley-Morton and his wife, Laura, was profiled:

> "We look at the house as a kind of sanctuary, but it's also a work space—we often have lots of people here," says Morton. Both are ministers in the Movement of Spiritual Inner Awareness.

And later:

> The cherry cabinets conceal the sort of technology one needs to run a worldwide ministry these days—when they're

not on the road, the cou-
ple work out of the house.

The Donnelley-Mortons
seem *proud* of the fact that
they're breaking the law: they
are, after all, doing so in God's
name.

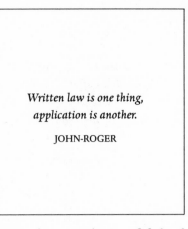

*Written law is one thing,
application is another.*

JOHN-ROGER

Like the tax laws (please
see the chapter, "God's
Money—Tax Free"), successfully sidestepping the immigration regulations is treated
at MSIA more like an everyday victory than a violation of federal
law. This is little wonder, considering that the presidency of MSIA
is made up of three men, two of whom are foreign-born and,
according to my research, entered this country with the help of
John-Roger under less than legitimate methods.

One was a plain vanilla accountant in Britain—and accountants
don't get any plainer or vanillaer than the British of the species. In
order for immigration to approve his application, he had to demonstrate that he would be providing a service or skill that could
not be done by an American citizen. MSIA made the vanilla accountant appear to be all the Häagen-Dazs Special Edition flavors
combined in one.

The case of the Frenchman was even more extreme. He had
been involved in some sort of revolt (involving tanks, no less)
while in French military service. He was thrown in the Bastille.
John-Roger went to France, ordained him in his prison cell, and
then petitioned the French government to release early this exceptional minister with the most phenomenal record. Then John-
Roger somehow persuaded the U.S. immigration authorities to
ignore all their rules about not admitting convicted criminals into
the country (especially the revolt-involving-tanks variety), because,
after all, this minister had already done *so much good* while just
visiting the United States; imagine how much *more* good he would
do if he had the chance to stay here, oh, sixty or seventy years.
Both the French authorities and the United States Immigration
Service purchased this *merde* from John-Roger, and the rest is
Franco-American history.

On the nonperformance of ministerial duties front, we have
John-Roger: hit and run parson. The MSIA *Handbook for Ministers
of Light* is clear on the subject:

> *You must always be judicious about your activities —always. But in the Soul level there is no morality.*
>
> JOHN-ROGER

Performing Marriages: After the ceremony, sign the license certificate in the appropriate places and return it to the County Clerk. (The instructions are on the certificate.) Doing this is **your** legal responsibility, so make sure you don't procrastinate about it.

After performing one marriage ceremony, John-Roger signed the marriage certificate and handed it to the bride to file. *She never filed it!* When the time for divorce came 'round (as everybody knew it would), the bride was in a quandary: should she file the marriage license and file for divorce all in one economical trip to City Hall, or should she just tear up the marriage license? Alas, I tuned out before the next thrilling episode of *Brides 'R' Us.*

On a far more serious note, there is convincing—but not conclusive—evidence that John-Roger had sex with at least one male student while he was still a high school teacher. This would mean that the boy was (a) underage and (b) under John-Roger's supposed protection. That John-Roger frequently took one student to his house where they disappeared into John-Roger's bedroom is known. What they did there is not.

The laws of foreign countries are no more respected by John-Roger than the laws of the United States—probably less. The movement of foreign and domestic currency in quantities astronomically higher than the law allows takes place regularly. Income from the South American Insight and MSIA activities is regularly brought to the United States—in cash.

When traveling to foreign countries where the exchange rate is better on the black market, MSIA brings large amounts of American currency which is exchanged underground. In Egypt, for example, the underground exchange rate for the American dollar is several times greater than the official exchange rate. Making such exchanges is, however, outrageously illegal in Egypt and, if you're traveling as part of a group with John-Roger, you are instructed *not* to do any black market currency trading. The instruction on the trip that I took: Give your money to Michael Feder, and he'll negotiate a better exchange rate at the bank than you'll be able to get. What Michael Feder did, of course, is make his exchange on the black market, return Egyptian money to the tour participants at a rate only fractionally higher than the bank pays, and divert the profits— sometimes as high as four hundred percent—directly into John-Roger's pocket.

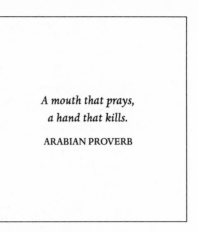

A mouth that prays, a hand that kills.

ARABIAN PROVERB

Now let's look at a crime far more insidious, far more hideous, far more vile and appalling—of course, I am referring to a crime that John-Roger committed against *me*.

In May 1994, when it was clear that John-Roger was not going to let me leave his tentacles in peace and that he was not going to accept the quiet solution of binding arbitration that I suggested, I began getting phone calls. They were all the same: no talking; just a TV in the background and breathing in the foreground. It wasn't heavy breathing as in a heavy-breathing phone call, just the breathing of somebody who breathes more loudly than most. After about thirty seconds, the caller would hang up. These calls came at all hours of the day or night, but usually started around 11:00 p.m. and continued, regularly, until 3:00 or 4:00 in the morning. Generally, the calls didn't come in often enough to warrant turning off the phone, but did come in often enough to be annoying.

It's hard to explain how annoying an annoyance call can be. There are the ones that wake you; those, of course, are annoying. Then there are those that derail a train of thought; to railroaders (writers), that can prove most irritating. There are the ones that come in while you're on another call; those are upsetting. There are the ones that come in when you're in the shower, or your hands are covered with bread dough, or you're in what Jane Fonda claims are the all-important last five minutes of aerobic glory— those are annoying. Then there are the ones that come when you really want to talk to someone, anyone (within reason), and the phone rings, and you pick up the phone and say, expectations glowing, "Hello!" and, guess who?

The calls averaged about ten a day. That's an average. Some days there were none; one evening there were more than forty between 6:00 p.m. and 8:00 p.m. (Wouldn't you know it: I was expecting an important call and couldn't turn the phone off.)

> *Leadership is not manifested by coercion, even against the resented.*
>
> MARGARET CHASE SMITH

I intuitively knew the calls were coming from John-Roger. I had to heavily discount my intuition, however, because having recently realized that I had been duped for fifteen years, my hurt and outrage concerning John-Roger was incredible. A few weeks later, when his lawsuit against me was filed, I thought, "Aha! He *is* out to get me." I still had to modify my intuition: I can't blame *every* annoyance in my life on John-Roger.

As the weeks went on and the calls developed a pattern, they also fit perfectly with John-Roger's lifestyle: he crawls into bed about 11:00 or 12:00 and channel-surfs the night away. I could just see him in his big bedroom, on his big bed, in front of his big-screen TV—a remote control in one hand, and an auto-phone dialer in the other. But I had to be careful; I had to control my imaginings—I was preparing to defend myself against a *lawsuit*, which meant I had to deal in *facts*. All I needed was to go before the judge and say: "He made all these annoying calls to me—I just *know* he did—I *feel* it in my *heart*." That is not the sort of testimony that would allow me to keep my house. I returned to fact-finding.

One day I was talking to one of the many former staff members who, after leaving J-R, was not left alone. The person was ticking off in laundry-list style all that happened to him: threatening letters, slashed tires, legal threats, annoying phone calls, nasty rumors . . . wait a minute: what's this about annoying phone calls? As it turns out, annoying phone calls are part of John-Roger's pattern of harassment. Were they hang-up calls? "No, you could hear a TV in the background." Other than the TV, was there any other noise? "There was breathing." That fit my pattern, too. Any number of dearly departed MSIAers got this treatment. Still not enough to hold up in court, but I was becoming increasingly convinced.

Then something happened that absolutely confirmed John-Roger's guilt in my mind. Several calls in a row featured a man with an obnoxious voice saying two or three vulgar words in rapid succession. I recognized it as one of those little plastic devices that,

when you push a button, proclaims the obscenity of the
moment. One of John-Roger's
current "guys," who goes by
the name of Jesus (the Spanish pronunciation, not the
biblical), had one of these devices and played with it endlessly.* After about the fourth
or fifth phone call featuring
the prerecorded dirty-word
machine, I said: "Yeah, Jesus

> You hypocrite,
> first take the plank
> out of your own eye,
> and then you will see clearly to
> remove the speck
> from your brother's eye.
>
> JESUS OF NAZARETH
> Matthew 7:4–5

played that one for me, do you have another?" The annoyance
calls continued, but never again with Jesus's favorite toy.

The police traced the calls back to the phone of a minister and
initiate who had been with John-Roger from the beginning. She
was in her early sixties, an endless giver, and adored by all—including me. When the police detective told me her name, I thought,
"She couldn't be doing it." But then, I had heard a lot of people do
a lot of things completely out of character because John-Roger
commanded it—including me.

In discussing this with one of John-Roger's former staff, he
suddenly said, "Wait a minute! She has a relay box in her house
that allows John-Roger to make calls appear that they're being
made from her number."

That was it. Further investigation showed that John-Roger had
the box placed in her house in the early 1970s when he purchased
PRANA. It seems that a call from his Mandeville Canyon home to
PRANA was a toll charge. The minister lived half-way between
Mandeville and PRANA. A call from Mandeville to the minister's
house was not a toll call, and a call from the minister's house to
PRANA was not a toll call. The switching box at the mid-point
allowed John-Roger to call the minister's house, have the box dial
PRANA, and all toll charges would be avoided.

The only tiny trouble with this system is that it's illegal. Not

---

*He and J-R thought it was *the funniest thing* to greet waitresses with a few well-
chosen pre-recorded profanities. The waitress would try to ignore the insult, and
ask if we wanted coffee. Jesus would invariably say, "Yeah. Black. Like my
women," and a new string of obscenities would echo forth. It was embarrassing
but, hey, a lot of embarrassment is a little price to pay to have dinner with God,
no? That we were never thrown out is indicative of the level of eatery John-
Roger favors.

only is it defrauding the phone company, it also evades city, state, and federal telephone taxes. It's been going on for twenty years.

> *If you screw with
> the phone company
> you end up with
> two Dixie cups and thread.*
>
> LENNY BRUCE

We must pause now and admire for a moment John-Roger: *without leaving his bed* he breaks *five** laws with a *single* phone call!

I wonder how different things might have been if John-Roger had spent as much time *loving* me as he's currently spending *hating* me; if he had personally called me with messages of love and support as often as he's dialing me now with vindictiveness and hate.

Meanwhile, the criminal investigation continues, so the police have not notified any of the culprits. The calls continue. Today (August 12, 1994) there have already been three.

The number of telephone intimidations, bomb scares, threats of violence, and death threats received by people on John-Roger's hit list are far too numerous to catalog. But the violence doesn't just stop at the threatening stage. Michael Feder, John-Roger's "bodyguard," admitted to slashing the tires and throwing paint thinner on two cars belonging to one household of "MSIA enemies." When John-Roger heard about these events, he didn't even bother to show mock disapproval. His comment: "I'm touched that someone loves me enough to do these things."**

In the two months since the lawsuit has been filed, the Prelude

---

*Annoyance calls; defrauding the phone company; failure to pay city, state, and federal taxes.

**This was a clear encouragement for other staff members to perform violent acts upon John-Roger's enemies. In an all-powerful position such as John-Roger's, one need not *command*—one need only *suggest*. King Henry II never said, "Go kill Thomas à Becket"; he merely commented one night while drinking with some of his lords: "Will no one rid me of this troublesome cleric?" In equating violence to his enemies with love for him, John-Roger was not just condoning, but encouraging violent activity. Fortunately, the other staff members hearing this had sufficient morality not to act upon it. All except Michael Feder have subsequently left John-Roger and have endured their own post-partum attacks. The physical attack I received from Michael Feder, John-Roger's second-in-command John Donnelley-Morton, and Russell Bishop (he just keeps *turning up* in this story, doesn't he?) is detailed in the chapter, "An Even Closer Encounter with John Donnelley-Morton."

Press offices have been broken into twice. On the first occasion, as noted earlier, nothing was stolen but a portion of the first draft of this book. On the second, only a signed copy of a book by John Grisham, which was carefully wrapped and placed in a drawer of the same desk where the manuscript portion was found. The warnings were clear: (1) we

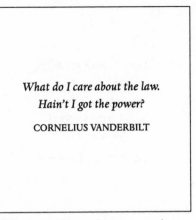

What do I care about the law. Hain't I got the power?

CORNELIUS VANDERBILT

know how to get in and out of here without being caught or setting off the alarm, and (2) whoever you are who is working at this desk on this trashy book, you've now been punished.

There's no hard evidence linking John-Roger to these break-ins, but here's a story of a break-in in which John-Roger, *personally*, is placed at the scene of the crime *and* shown to possess documents stolen in that crime.

In 1983, several of the people who left MSIA (one John-Roger's personal secretary, another a member of John-Roger's live-in personal staff) were tired of the intimidation, threats, and harassment, and also felt that the hidden story about John-Roger's evil empire needed to be told. They contacted Professor David Lane, Ph.D., who had written a book, *The Making of a Spiritual Movement,* which conclusively proved that the teachings of Eckankar came from the Radhasoami tradition of India. The book rocked the Eckankar organization to its very foundation. (Or, if you prefer, rocked the Eckankar foundation to its very organization.) Dr. Lane had also met with John-Roger on several occasions, and they were on friendly terms. To the former staff members, Dr. Lane seemed to be the ideal choice to investigate and report on what had been carefully hidden within John-Roger's organizations: he was an academician with a commitment to truth and a knowledge of spiritual practices (he himself follows a spiritual path) that would allow him to distinguish between legitimate spiritual teaching and the illegitimate—sometimes outrageous—justifications in the name of God given by John-Roger.* Dr. Lane's casual but cordial relationship with John-Roger would eliminate any basis for

---

*Traditional investigative reporters tend to think it's *all* weird and sometimes conclude—mistakenly—"Anyone who gets involved in all this nonsense deserves whatever he gets."

the charge that Dr. Lane had intentionally set out to do a hatchet job.

> I hate to advocate drugs, alcohol, violence, or insanity to anyone, but they've always worked for me.
>
> HUNTER S. THOMPSON

After doing some preliminary research, Dr. Lane found that, although he was certainly shocked by what he discovered, he was somehow not inclined to complete the project. Dr. Lane was on the verge of abandoning his article when John-Roger—who shoots himself in the foot so often he should wear stainless steel socks—began harassing Dr. Lane.

Wrong move. Dr. Lane, as he had proved when he took on the entire Eckankar organization (far larger than MSIA) did not succumb to intimidation. The fact that John-Roger was so eager to keep Dr. Lane from exploring any further indicated that there was good exploration ahead.

In mid-1984, he published *The J-R Controversy: A Critical Analysis of John-Roger Hinkins and M.S.I.A.* This article, published in Dr. Lane's research series "Understanding Cults and Spiritual Movements," was a breakthrough work on exposing the dark side of John-Roger's farce. The article revealed and documented for the first time John-Roger's plagiarism, intimidation, violence, and sexual exploits. John-Roger's response? A general denial of the facts, and a general attack on Dr. Lane.

On October 5, 1984, having driven to Del Mar, California, in John-Roger's baby-blue Lincoln Continental, John-Roger and Michael Feder broke into Dr. Lane's apartment in Del Mar, California. John-Roger is placed at the scene of the crime because of two words he wrote on a box containing copies of *The J-R Controversy.* The words were: "NO MORE." Handwriting experts have verified that this was written in John-Roger's hand, and it fits John-Roger's pattern of not being able to resist having the last word or to add a didactic comment to every situation. By writing "NO MORE" on a box containing *The J-R Controversy,* he did both.

Michael Feder was placed in the apartment because the bed was turned completely over, a physical feat John-Roger would be incapable of doing alone. Only John-Roger and Michael Feder made the trip (they told the other staff members they were going to San Diego). It is possible that John-Roger left Michael Feder behind and picked up another henchman in Del Mar, but considering Michael Feder's ongoing shady doings with John-Roger, Feder is the most likely suspect.

> My adversaries . . .
> applied the one means
> that wins the easiest victory
> over reason:
> terror and force.
>
> ADOLF HITLER
> 1933

In addition to the bed's being turned over, the entire apartment was ransacked. To make absolutely certain that Dr. Lane would not think common, garden-variety thieves had broken in, the television, stereo, and other valuables were not taken.

What *was* taken was Dr. Lane's years of research on spiritual groups and cults—the files on MSIA and Eckankar in particular. Also taken were two personal diaries written by Dr. Lane's wife, Jacquie; the list of subscribers for Dr. Lane's research series "Understanding Cults and Spiritual Movements," Dr. Lane's briefcase containing uncorrected term papers ("to the chagrin of my college students," notes Dr. Lane), and a card file containing a lifetime of Dr. Lane's collected recipes. The latter was "a heavy blow for me," remembers Dr. Lane, "the robbers probably thought it contained secret, inside information and thus was done in code."

It was not immediately clear who took the materials—it could have been someone from MSIA, or it could have been someone from Eckankar, from one of the other cults Dr. Lane was researching, or someone who gets off on reading the diaries of college professors' wives. The police, with so many possible culprits, were unable to act. Over the next year (which we shall explore next), as the information implicating John-Roger gradually appeared, the handwriting analysis of "NO MORE" confirmed John-Roger's physical participation in the robbery.

With the robbery, John-Roger's work was far from done. He began writing letters to Dr. Lane's spiritual teacher in India, referring to stolen documents and intimate entries in Dr. Lane's wife's diary. These were sent under an assumed name, but all came from the same printer connected to John-Roger's Lisa computer locked in a room at Mandeville Canyon to which only John-Roger and Michael Feder had the key. John-Roger must have supposed that Dr. Lane's spiritual teacher was the same sort of vindictive,

> *Our sense of power is more vivid when we break a man's spirit than when we win his heart.*
>
> ERIC HOFFER

rumor-mongering, petty person as John-Roger. (Tattletale letters—many anonymous—are rampant in MSIA. And John-Roger *loves them*. The rules of evidence don't apply around John-Roger: however information is obtained is fair game.)

Fortunately, Dr. Lane's spiritual teacher was genuinely spiritual: his only response was to forward the letters that John-Roger had penned over any number of names along with a note saying simply, "I see no reason to do anything about these." Dr. Lane's spiritual teacher did not even give John-Roger's nonsense the dignity of a response.

And a response was possible: John-Roger gave his post office box just in case Dr. Lane's spiritual teacher had a little dirt to share about some of John-Roger's disciples. The international spiritual kaffeeklatsch envisioned by John-Roger never materialized.

Using the same post office box, John-Roger began an organization entitled (get this) Coalition for Civil and Spiritual Rights. That John-Roger would start a campaign for civil rights is so heavy with irony that I can't even get it off the ground with a good metaphor. The only civil rights John-Roger cares about—like all the great autocratic rulers before him—are his own. And spiritual rights? Well, John-Roger likes to use the word *spiritual,* and he always needs to be right, but that's about the closest connection I can make to the term "spiritual rights" and John-Roger Hinkins.

The Coalition for Civil and Spiritual Rights was, of course, an organization with a good-sounding name that allowed John-Roger to pretend Dr. Lane was attacking John-Roger's religious freedom. Never mind that he wanted the freedom to pass himself off as the one and only person on earth directly connected to God, as well as the civil rights to manipulate others unscrupulously, without being subject to criticism or external control.

John-Roger, of course, did not step forth to defend himself: he created a triumvirate of characters (Michael Hunt, Kip Ferguson—a character he no doubt stole from one of his gay pulp porn novels—and the distinguished Peter Davidson, Ph.D.). These three have defended John-Roger's position with all the sophistication and élan of Ruby of Orange County. Fortunately (again), the Coalition for Civil and Spiritual Rights—which John-Roger no doubt envisioned as his own personal Moral Majority—never got off the ground. (Too heavy with irony, as you will recall.)

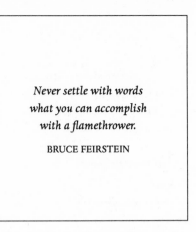

Never settle with words what you can accomplish with a flamethrower.

BRUCE FEIRSTEIN

John-Roger also sent a 28-page, single-spaced letter (probably written by Michael Feder with John-Roger's comments) to Dr. Lane's professors (he was working on his doctorate), employers, and members of the spiritual and psychological intellectual community.

By November of 1985, John-Roger had had just about as much fun with Dr. Lane as he (John-Roger) could tolerate. He packed up a good cross-section of the purloined Dr. Lane research materials, threw in Dr. Lane's wife's diaries for good measure, and sent the whole thing anonymously to Eckankar headquarters. Since all the materials sent either directly related to Dr. Lane's Eckankar research, Dr. Lane's informants, or possibly embarrassing information about Dr. Lane (his recipe for Del Mar Lentil Loaf is positively scandalous), John-Roger assumed the Eckankar people, who had previously been reported on by Dr. Lane, would take over where John-Roger left off. More torment for Dr. Lane. Good.

But there was something even better: if the Eckankar organization began using information from the robbery in its own smear campaign, the robbery would then be traced to Eckankar and not to John-Roger. It seemed a brilliant move: kill two birds plus crush every egg in the nest with one exceedingly large stone. Brilliant, brilliant! Destroy his competition (Eckankar) and his critic (Dr. Lane) with one well-placed box of papers.

Alas, John-Roger's Wile E. Coyote complex once again raised its weary head. Just as M. Coyote shoves a stick of dynamite down Roadrunner's throat, only to find it explodes in his own butt, John-Roger's best-planted bombs often wind up exploding in his own face.*

In this case, the Eckankar people opened the box, and sent it

---

*In his own strange, convoluted, entirely unintentional way, John-Roger proves that there *is* a God.

> November 17, 1984
>
> Dear David,
>
> I miss our friendship. I was sorry to hear that your place was burglarized. I assure you that I do not know anything about the occurrence. Please, may we reside in the friendship of our spiritual brotherhood?
>
> Sincerely,
>
> John-Roger Hinkins

directly to their lawyers; the lawyers immediately placed the entire box in another box and sent it to David Lane.

By this point, David Lane was entirely certain that John-Roger was not only the thief, but also the mastermind and head writer (why didn't John-Roger spend all that writing time working on a book—such as *Petulance 101?*) behind the smear campaign. Also in the box of materials returned by John-Roger (by way of Eckankar), was, as Dr. Lane puts it, "the cherry on the sundae." In the margins of Dr. Lane's wife's diary were handwritten comments. Handwriting experts verified that this was the handwriting of . . .

Beep beep.

CHAPTER SEVENTEEN

Computer Books: The Joy of Victory and the Agony of Defeat

Experience is a good teacher, but her fees are very high.

W. R. INGE

IN 1982, I published a book on the transformational pleasures of using a computer to process words. It was called, not surprisingly, *The Word Processing Book* and carried the subtitle *A Short Course in Computer Literacy*. I type very poorly and spell even worse, so naturally I fell in love with this machine that never made me retype a word and corrected my spelling. The gift that Insight had been to John-Roger, word processing was to me.

The Word Processing Book was the first explanation in plain English of these new-fangled computer things. It even made a few halting attempts at humor. I published the book myself (again, no other publisher wanted it), and as the book became more and more successful, I got busier and busier. Although I continued to facilitate Insight seminars, I had less and less time to do them. Eventually, I had no time to facilitate Insight at all. I grew busier still. (People sometimes wonder what success feels like: it feels like *exhaustion.*) I didn't have time to attend the obligatory monthly MSIA ministers' meetings, nor did I have time to do the *highly* recommended two hours of spiritual exercises (meditation) each day.

I decided to turn in my ministerial credential and "give back" my initiatory tone (mantra). I did this not because I was disillusioned with the path, but because I *respected* it. I didn't want to be among the hypocritical initiates and ministers I met who never did

> *When you're ordained
> the energy that is placed
> with you is positive energy.
> The only way you can misuse it
> is to not use it;
> then it starts backing up inside of you.
> It's like the sewer starts to plug up
> and pretty soon it erupts.
> So we tell people to get out there
> and minister, or give up
> your ministerial credentials
> so we can drain the sewer.*
>
> JOHN-ROGER

s.e's or ministered to anything but their own caprices. (Later I realized that publishing the computer books *was* a ministry—a much-needed one at that time.) I wrote J-R a polite letter turning in my ministerial credential and my initiatory tone. I received a polite letter back from John-Roger saying, essentially, best of luck. I was now free to pursue my computer book publishing without any of the spiritual energies "backing up on me," which J-R repeatedly warned would take place for those who were not using their "ministerial energies in an ongoing, dynamic way." Yes, I felt guilty but I also kept my ministerial "sewer" from erupting!

I look back and wonder: why did John-Roger let me go so easily? The answer, I'm afraid, is far from flattering to me: I was, at that moment, of absolutely no use to him. By 1983, Insight was awash with facilitators; there was a glut of them. I was no longer needed to facilitate.

Further, John-Roger might have even seen that I would be more useful to him in the future if I pursued the profession in which I had had my past successes: writing and publishing. (Although this supposition is possible, I think it's unlikely: it gives John-Roger entirely too much credit for long-term planning, an activity that is not one of his strong suits.)

I published more computer books, they were more successful, and I kept plowing the money back into the company with the idea that "one fine day" I would sell the company and make a lot of money. In 1985 I sold the company for a million dollars. However (there's that *damn* "however"), the company buying my company was bought by a larger company that already *had* a line of computer books, so they didn't need mine. In true big-business style, they decided it was cheaper in the long run to let me sue than to settle. They were right.

To pursue my suit, I went to a Movement lawyer I liked. After about a year, he turned it over to a Movement lawyer I *didn't* like. This new lawyer kept taking my money for four-and-one-half years until we were five months from trial. At that point, he dropped the case. This forced me to quickly hire other attorneys

who told me that it couldn't
possibly cost more than $65,000
to take the case through trial.
Their final bill was $295,000.
The jury awarded me $250,000.
The entire lesson in L.A. law
cost me only $45,000. The total
wealth generated by my years
of computer book success:
zero.

Naturally, I was depressed
by this, but we have gone

> *I remember when*
> *our whole island was shaken*
> *with an earthquake some years ago,*
> *there was an impudent mountebank*
> *who sold pills which*
> *(as he told the country people)*
> *were very good*
> *against an earthquake.*
>
> JOSEPH ADDISON
> 1773

ahead in time to about 1990. In 1985, when the corporate rape
first took place, I was depressed, too. I took solace in being of
service to others, and the best way I knew how, I thought, was
facilitating Insight. I had a lunch with J-R, and was reinstated as a
facilitator.

While I was away from Insight and MSIA on my three-year
computer-book sojourn (1982–1985), the second wave of John-
Roger scandals hit Hinkins Island.

The first wave was in 1978, just before I joined Club MSIA. The
man to whom John-Roger had "passed the keys of the Mystical
Traveler Consciousness" messed around with a woman (horrors!)
and was publicly stripped of his spiritual title—kind of like having
to give back the key to the executive washroom. This young man
was much beloved within the Movement, and the islanders could
not understand *why* or *how* such a drop from grace could happen.
The ex-Traveler, however, remained in MSIA and remained true,
not revealing until his departure in 1985 it was John-Roger's sexual
jealousy and not a Spiritual mandate that caused him to be de-
keyed. The storm passed. A few sandcastles had washed out to sea.

The second wave was of tidal proportions. In the fall of 1983,
three beloved staff members *left* MSIA. Not only did they leave,
they started telling stories about John-Roger's nasty personality
and coercive sexual tactics. Up until that time it was believed (because John-Roger told everyone to believe it) that he and his personal staff refrained from all sexual activity. Instead, John-Roger
was characterized by the departing staff as more cell bait than
celibate. In 1984, Dr. David Lane published his independent research study, "The John-Roger Controversy," which concluded:

> The only cure available for J-R, it seems, is to concede to the
> fact that he is more a charlatan than a saint.

> So now the frauds reckoned they was out of danger . . . First they done a lecture on temperance; but they didn't make enough for them both to get drunk on. Then they started a dancing school; but the first prance they made, the general public jumped in and pranced them out of town. They tackled missionarying, and mesmerizing, and doctoring, and telling fortunes, and a little of everything.
>
> MARK TWAIN
> *Huckleberry Finn*

This John-Roger was and is congenitally unable to do. By the time I returned, in 1985, the second storm had died down, but quite a number of grass shacks had been flattened.

The next wave, which was a veritable *tsunami*, hit in 1988 with the revelations of yet another dearly beloved (by MSIAers), dearly departed (from J-R) staff member. In addition, in early 1988, John-Roger's spiritual heir-apparent and the president of MSIA left, as did MSIA's chief administrator. The last two left very quietly, but the fact of their departure thundered through the Movement. In mid-1988 the two-part *Los Angeles Times* article hit, followed a month later by *People*—which added vandalism to the public charges made against John-Roger. Those who wanted to look further could read Dr. Lane's book, *The Criminal Activities of John-Roger Hinkins,* and add breaking and entering to the list while condominiums were swept out to sea.

But Hinkins Island survived even this—thanks, in large part, to the bestselling books some blind devotee jerk wrote and put John-Roger's name on. For this, of course, I am *grievously** sorry. (More apologies later.)

All things, however, must eventually turn toward the true white Light, and in 1994, scandal number four broke—this book, I am proud to say. Just call me the White Tornado.

But back to 1985.

By this time, Insight was probably the only corporation in the United States with a CEO named Candy. She used to be Russell Bishop's executive secretary, but she literally memo'd her way into running the entire organization. She would write Russell a memo about some administrative matter Russell thought was beneath his dignity; Candy would suggest a way of handling the administrative matter, then ask Russell to check one of three boxes: *yes, no,*

---

*My Catholic upbringing comes in handy at times like this: I can beat my breast and say "Through my fault! Through my fault! Through my most grievous fault!" It's nice to have guilt so *ritualized:* you can set aside guilt sessions every morning and evening, suffer appropriately—nay, *grievously*—and then enjoy the rest of the day.

or *other.* Invariably, he checked *yes.* At the bottom of each memo was the kicker: "Do I have your authorization to handle similar future decisions without consulting you? *Yes, no, other."* Russell usually checked *yes.* After a few years, Russell had—administrative point by administrative point—signed over the operation of the entire Insight empire to his secretary.

> *There is a cowardly propensity*
> *in the human heart that delights*
> *in oppressing somebody else,*
> *and in the gratification of this*
> *base desire*
> *we always select a victim*
> *that can be outraged with safety.*
>
> JAMES T. RAPIER
> 1873

It was a plan worthy of John-Roger, and he supported her in her quiet coup. She became CEO; Russell was demoted to director of trainings. It was a brilliantly underhanded move—but then, Candy had a good teacher: she had known John-Roger since he taught her ninth grade English class. She has not left his tutelage since.

I began facilitating Insight I's, but did not ask for the reinstatement of my ministerial credential. I wanted to make sure I had an "ongoing ministry" so that the energies wouldn't "back up on me." (I had no idea what that meant; I still have no idea what it means; but it sure doesn't *sound* very good.) When Candy found out I had not reinstated my ministry, my doing so was not a matter of a suggestion or persuasion: it was a direct order. (I remember it well: it was given at the Stage Deli in New York.) The message was clear: get reinstated as a minister, or forget about facilitating Insight. It was so uncharacteristic of Candy—whose style was to write persuasive memos—I was startled. There was no *yes, no, maybe* choice. My two choices were *yes* and *or else!* I told her I'd take care of it at once.

In 1985, Insight's connection to MSIA was undeniable and undenied. Under the jolly umbrella of the John-Roger Foundation, Insight and MSIA were, according to an MSIA publication, "kissing cousins." The process of taking hapless participants from Insight I to Insight II to Insight III to MSIA had become a science.

Of course, people were still not told when they enrolled for Insight I that their destiny was a spiritual path that worships this John-Roger character as God. The deceit was intentional.

Once again, I joined in the deception, and with a passion I had not felt since I'd gotten my first word processor four years before.

CHAPTER EIGHTEEN
J-R, M.D.

> *The Mystical Traveler*
> *Consciousness*
> *is a pure force of Light*
> *working here on the planet.*
> *It is a tremendous force of Light,*
> *and through this force*
> *nothing is impossible.*
> *Everything is possible.*
>
> JOHN-ROGER

JOHN-ROGER presents himself as a healer. John-Roger's devotees think of John-Roger as a healer. I'm not talking about a healing of the mind or the emotions and certainly not of the spirit—I'm speaking of *physical* healing: getting rid of anything from cold sores to cancers.

John-Roger even justifies his own perpetually poor health by claiming it's a self-sacrifice on his part for the greater good of his devotees: when John-Roger removes a physical illness from one of his initiates, he must "process it" through his own physical body. If they have a headache, he must have a headache; if they have high blood pressure, he must get high blood pressure; if they have a zit, he must get a zit. The only difference is that John-Roger, unlike his initiate, is not linked to the "karma" of the illness and is able to "clear it" relatively quickly. A cold or a flu he can clear in minute. Cancer may take ten minutes. A shotgun to the head might give him a migraine for an hour. The reason John-Roger is continuously in such poor health is because he "clears" physical illness from so many people: a hangnail here, a hernia there—it all adds up.

John-Roger even justifies his weight, saying it's important "extra protection" be put around his "lower chakra centers" to help him in "transmuting negative energy" taken from his followers. John-Roger, then, is not an overweight hypochondriac: he's a self-sacrificing spiritual healer who—if it weren't for all the physical maladies he voluntarily takes upon himself from his devotees—would still have the body and health of a sixteen-year-old track star.

Alas, there are these *laws* which call what John-Roger does "practicing medicine without a license." He continues to do so—he's just become coy about it. When asked for a physical healing, instead of saying what he once said, "I've healed you," he now says the less incriminating, "I did what I know how to do." All of his followers know the latter still means the former. Considering his link to God, when John-Roger does "what [he] knows how to do," that makes for quite a doing.

The ways in which people ask John-Roger for healings are either by letter or in person. The letter need not be sent but merely written. According to John-Roger, if you write a letter and burn it, he "gets it" as clearly as if you had mailed it.* Asking in person is far more difficult: J-R avoids talking to people before and after any of his public appearances, and unless you're part of the inner circle, getting him on the phone is about as easy as getting Clinton on the phone.

John-Roger's grand in-person healings usually happen during week-long retreats. Here, everyone gets away from it all—including those anti-quack laws. John-Roger, M.D., hangs out his shingle; the healing season is in session.

These healings happen during sharings, in which individuals—selected by John-Roger—stand before a microphone in front of the entire group and get to ask one question of John-Roger. Roughly a fourth of these questions have to do with relationships, a fourth with careers, a fourth with clarifications of the teaching, and a fourth with physical problems. No matter what the question is, J-R can wander into any of the other categories—and he will, he will.**

*That, essentially, is true: John-Roger never sees the majority of his mail. Secretaries write pat responses; pat the writer on the head, and recommend he or she take a PAT training.

**I once stood up and asked a question about Jesus, and ended up getting a forty-five-minute lecture about the evils of masturbation.

John-Roger diagnoses people by "reading their aura." He claims that since childhood he could see these multicolored fields of energy surrounding people. As time went on, he could discern the meaning of different colors. If someone asks about a physical illness, John-Roger thinks nothing of saying "it's in your aura." When some-

> *Because the Mystical Traveler Consciousness directs and works with MSIA, there are some rather unique spiritual actions which may take place with MSIA students.*
>
> JOHN-ROGER

thing is "in your aura," it means the illness or event is coming soon to a physical body near you: yours. John-Roger then clears the aura and a world of potential physical agony, and maybe even death, is removed from the person just like that.

John-Roger also can read a person's "karmic record." The karmic record is sort of a cosmic credit card statement—it tells what you'll have to pay for, why you're paying for it, and when you have to pay it. So, as John-Roger explains, if you shot someone in the head during a past lifetime, perhaps you will develop a brain tumor at the same place in your head during this lifetime. Usually, in order to "balance the karma," you must accept a brain tumor with equanimity, even gratitude. But not with Dr. John-Roger around! He can "lift and transmute" karma for you so that the murders you committed in other lifetimes become but the murmurs of this one.

As the *Handbook for Ministers of Light* puts it:

> Because the Mystical Traveler Consciousness directs and works with MSIA, there are some rather unique spiritual actions which may take place with the MSIA students. The Mystical Traveler Consciousness has the ability to "read" karmic records (the records of a person's past actions and any "debits" or "credits" resulting from those actions): then, if asked, that Consciousness has the ability to . . . release them.

These two types of healing John-Roger can do without moving from his chair. When things get *really* heavy duty, John-Roger gets "hands on." If, from his seat, he asks the question: "Is it okay to touch you?" everyone knows that a hands-on healing is imminent. John-Roger touches here, runs his hands along there, says the pain in the upper right shoulder is really coming from the kidney re-

> License my roving hands,
> and let them go
> Before, behind, between,
> above, below.
>
> JOHN DONNE

flexing off the pancreas which is actually a congenital defect of the left knee caused by your mother eating a cherry popsicle during her third month of carrying you. Just as soon as he's explained it and touched you all over the place, he announces: "We've cleared all that now." Thank *heavens!*

John-Roger explains that just *being around* his physical body and the "radiant Light energy" that emanates from it can and does cause healings galore. If you're not attractive, gifted, or rich enough to be around John-Roger's physical body, never fear: meditation tapes are here. John-Roger has a myriad of meditation tapes—and dozens of seminar tapes—promising physical health. The most notorious is known as Psychic Reintegration. In this tape, John-Roger systematically goes through all the muscle groups in the body, one by one, and encourages the listener to tense, *tense, TENSE* those muscles, h-o-o-o-o-o-o-o-l-d that tension, and then "with an explosion of the breath" release it. John-Roger leads the listeners to believe that their physical health and spiritual freedom lies in their ability to tense those muscles *hard.* Participants have dislocated joints, pulled tendons, and cracked ribs during this meditation.

On the whole, J-R's clearing auras, lifting karma, and laying on of hands in the name of health is relatively harmless. If the people *believe* John-Roger can heal, the placebo effect dictates a certain number will be healed. The difficulty arises at two points: 1) the people who have gotten the John-Roger healing might not get treatment from a qualified health-care professional, and 2) once J-R gets his hands on power—watch out!

The belief that John-Roger heals makes a visit to a health-care professional not only a waste of time and money, but an apparent admission one lacks faith. Combined with John-Roger's obvious distaste for Western medicine (except insofar as his prescription recreational drugs are concerned), that means his followers often get much sicker before they get better—*if* they get better.

I experienced this firsthand.

In 1986, while traveling in Africa with John-Roger, I picked up an intestinal parasite. By the end of the trip I was a mess: exhausted, irritable—all I wanted to do was sleep. Whenever I bowed out of a planned activity to take a nap, John-Roger would tell me I should "take a look at" my "lack of participation." The entire last week in Africa was torture: the more I wanted to sleep, the more John-Roger heaped on obligatory activities. "Confront this thing!" he would tell me. "Move through it!"

Be careful about reading health books. You may die of a misprint.

MARK TWAIN

When I got home to the States, sleeping as much as I wanted didn't seem to improve matters. John-Roger suggested I see a healer—a self-taught nutritionist. (I think that's what she was.) John-Roger said she would take care of my problem. To get diagnosed, there was no need to visit her—just send a drop of my blood on a kleenex, and she would take it from there.

By this time, my non-Movement friends had already diagnosed me: "You were in Africa; you've got parasites. Go to the doctor and get some . . ." and they would rattle off the name of an antiparasitic prescription medication. I told them yes, yes, thank you, thank you, I had it all under control.

John-Roger's nutritionist recommended a concoction made out of defatted almond flour, fig powder, and other yummies I could only imagine the intestinal parasites taking with them on a picnic to my liver. No, no, I was told by J-R's nutritionist: these would eliminate any bad fellas in my intestines *naturally*. She also had me taking a regular dose of herbal laxatives. Now, instead of running to the toilet every hour, I ran every fifteen minutes.

I got worse.

Not only was this illness physically painful, it was also psychologically excruciating. Lack of energy and diarrhea were, in 1986, two of the primary symptoms of AIDS. The doctors I went to said no, I don't think so, but they never could be sure—in 1986 they knew very little about AIDS. I was told to come back in a month or so if things didn't get better. (I must admit my faith in these negative diagnoses was severely undermined when one of the doctors I was going to died of AIDS himself.) Although the diagnoses continued to be "it's not AIDS" throughout the entire nine months, it was never ruled out as a possibility. My fear then that I might be dying was very real.

After about three months, I got a medical test for intestinal parasites. I tested negative. Hmmm. Back to nature. This woman had had me on almond flour, fig powder, and laxatives for nine months. I took another parasite test. Still negative. I said to the doctor: "Pretend the test was positive. Give me something for this." Fortunately for me, he did. I took the antiparasitic medication that afternoon, and the next morning I felt immensely better. Within three days, I was back to my old self—which is no great shakes, but I no longer felt like death on amphetamines.

As it turned out, the concoction J-R's healer gave me was powerful enough to *suppress* the parasites so they wouldn't show up on a test, but not powerful enough to kill them and cure me.

During the trip itself, in fact, had John-Roger not repeatedly said he was "spiritually handling" my illness (and physically, too, apparently: he once gave me an unidentified pill which he said would "handle it" for me), I would have sought proper medical treatment at the first symptom. I knew I was ill by the time we got to Johannesburg, South Africa. Johannesburg physicians probably know more about diagnosing and treating intestinal parasites than doctors in the States. Instead, thanks to John-Roger, I suffered both physically and psychologically for nine months.

When I told J-R about my rapid healing thanks to Western medicine (not as a complaint—*never* as a complaint) he told me it was just "a coincidence" that I started getting better within twenty-four hours of taking the prescription. "The natural way was working, and you would have gotten better at exactly the same time because what cured you was the natural medication. The prescription drug just polluted your system, now I've got to work on taking all the toxicity of it out of your system." More work for J-R: what a turd I was.

I was lucky: I only *thought* I was going to die. Some people following John-Roger's direction are considerably less fortunate—they actually do. One woman had a small growth in her breast. Her doctor recommended that it be surgically removed. It was detected early, so there was an excellent chance for full recovery. She shared this with John-Roger, and he said: "I wouldn't let them cut into *me.*"

> *Heal the sick, raise the dead, cleanse those who have leprosy, drive out demons.*
> *Freely you have received, freely give.*
>
> JESUS OF NAZARETH
> Matthew 10:8

He reviewed her karma, checked out her aura, and probably had someone sacrifice a chicken. He just "couldn't see" why she needed an operation. Although he never clearly told her, "don't do it," all John-Roger needs to say to a devotee is: "If it were me, I wouldn't . . ." and whatever it is *won't* be done.

The woman went from healer to healer to healer (all J-R recommended) who put her on treatment after treatment after treatment. She got progressively worse. By the time she returned to the fold of Western medicine, it was too late. They did exploratory surgery, but found there was nothing to be done. She died within days of entering the hospital.

John-Roger's compassionate response when he heard about her death: "I told her not to let them cut into her."

Power corrupts; and John-Roger corrupts power absolutely. I've already told you my story of being spiritually diagnosed by him as having two life-threatening illnesses and being given a maximum of nine months to live. (Generous of him, wasn't it?) He then traded this bogus diagnosis for money and a rehabilitated reputation. I got "healed" of AIDS and tuberculosis, neither of which I had; John-Roger got cash and bestselling books, neither of which he had done anything to deserve.

Another young man was nineteen when he joined John-Roger's staff. Although he had experimented with various recreational chemicals, he was far from an addict. Nevertheless, John-Roger "looked down his timeline" and told the young man that he was destined to die of a drug overdose in a very short time. John-Roger would, however, "hold this karma from him" as long as he was on staff. From that point on, the young man felt he had to do everything John-Roger said *or else.*

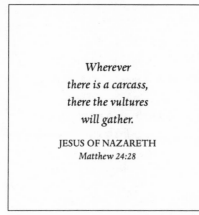

John-Roger pulls this bogus lifesaving scam (diagnose death; deliver life) sometimes for money, sometimes for obedience, sometimes for sex, sometimes for power, and sometimes for, well, "We'll see"—after all, you can never have too many people in your debt. Like the undertaker for whom Don Corleone does a favor at the beginning of *The Godfather*, Don Corleone tells him that he may call upon him in the future and ask a favor. With favors so easy to collect (a little "read the aura"; a little "hold back the karma"), why shouldn't collecting favors become a hobby, like collecting butterflies.

As John-Roger explains on one of his healing meditation tapes: "it may take a while to manifest, but know that *you've received that healing!*" Whenever one heals (as we all tend to do), it's thanks to John-Roger. If you ask someone who had a grand public healing from John-Roger, "Did the healing work?" The answer is, "Oh, yes."

John-Roger will often ask someone, "How are you feeling?" It's not that he really *cares,* it's that he wants to put himself one step higher on their pedestal. If the person says, "Fine, never better," John-Roger will say, "I guess that healing we did a while ago worked." At which point the "patient" is reminded, and makes a connection between John-Roger's mumbo jumbo and the natural healing of his or her own body. If the person answers, "I've had [PICK AN AILMENT] for about three weeks now," it's a chance for John-Roger to do another healing.

If someone gets worse after a John-Roger healing, that's not really getting worse: that's a "detoxification," "clearing," "balancing," or "the spiritual energies pushing the toxins and negative energies out." John-Roger's healings—whether public or personal—also add to the myth that John-Roger is the Master of Time and Space. An ordinary illness like flu John-Roger turns into a battle between Light and Dark. As the flu runs its normal, miserable course, John-Roger has the sufferer believing an epic battle for his or her immortal soul is taking place—the battleground being his or her own body.

John-Roger will convince one that the Dark forces have done a magnificent job of amassing their wicked battalions to drag one forever after down, down, down. Luke Sky-Roger will do what he can to rally the forces of Light, but they're awfully busy, this being the vacation season and all, so the battle will be close. As one gets sicker and sicker (as tends to happen with flu), one believes the Dark side is winning. Af-

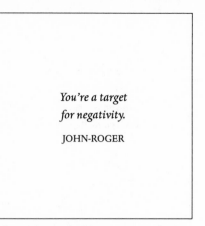

You're a target for negativity.

JOHN-ROGER

ter a number of days (as one tends to do with flu), one gets better and better. Now one feels the forces of Light are winning. When one is all better, the victory is complete. Hurray forces of Light! Hurray John-Roger! (Notice the fundamental technique here of pressure and release?)

Some illnesses have causes that go beyond metaphysical, pass quickly through the esoteric, winding up firmly entrenched in science fiction. These problems are not just confined to past life-times on this earthly plane, oh no—any lifetime in any universe, thought-field, or plane of existence is up for grabs. The more fantastic, the better.

Once, when you were a novice studying for the priesthood in a brotherhood that worshiped the third moon of the planet Sonas-tica (the only one of Sonastica's moons that radiated Light from within), you were assigned to clean out a corner of the temple, but because you didn't do a good job, the local health inspectors levied a fine against the priesthood, which they could not pay, and the temple was turned into time-share condominiums. Now the high priests of that brotherhood have gathered to take their re-venge on you, and that's why you have a pain in your right hand, which is the hand you should have used to better clean your sec-tion of the temple.

Naturally, this sort of invention soon reaches the upper limits of John-Roger's creativity, so he employs several health practitio-ners cum science fiction writers to ghost write for him. Two seem to be his favorites. Whenever John-Roger is stumped (that is, whenever his imagination bumps its head against the very low ceiling of his creativity), he will refer the "patient" to either of these more creative quacks. There you'll pay approximately $75 for a scenario that, when you tell it to John-Roger, he will nod

> *Orthodox medicine has not found an answer to your complaint. However, luckily for you, I happen to be a quack.*
>
> RICHTER

knowingly, add a slight twist the creative-quacks were not able to see due to their lower level of consciousness, and there you have it.

Have what? Nothing in particular—the illness takes whatever course the illness takes, but, boy, were you lucky John-Roger spiritually intervened because just think how much *worse* it might have been had he not.

Along these lines, John-Roger also takes credit for curing illnesses or injuries you've already had (or might have had). I once heard a person tell John-Roger an anecdote about an accident that had an amusing twist. Rather than laugh, John-Roger got very serious and said, "It's a good thing I was there. I had to push you back into the body." When John-Roger has to "push you back into the body," that means you died—"left the body"—and John-Roger grabbed your retreating soul and returned it to the body. The person was most grateful John-Roger was "there."

All this only works if one is concerned about living. John-Roger claims his teachings are to "get off the planet." Anyone who takes his teachings literally, then, is not quite as impressed by his claims to snatch your life from the jaws of death and return it to you like a mislaid pocket comb. Once when he used the I-had-to-push-your-soul-back-into-the-body line on me, I said "I don't know whether to say 'thank you' or 'screw you,'" meaning, hey, I *am* a soul initiate, therefore when I leave I leave for good, so why shouldn't I have left then?

John-Roger told me that, oh, no, I wouldn't have *left* then—the "window into spirit" was not open. Had John-Roger not intervened, I would have just hung around in a coma for, oh, twenty or thirty years in which my body would be in excruciating pain. I wouldn't be able to move, talk, or communicate, although I'd be aware of everything going on around me. So, once you've worked your butt off to fulfill all his requirements guaranteeing you freedom from hell after this life, he invents scenarios in which he saves you from a living hell right here on earth.

When John-Roger's healings fail and he can't explain them

away, he blames the "patient." Did you do *everything* John-Roger told you to do? To the letter? Precisely? Every time? If the answer is no to any of these questions, you, the patient, screwed it up. "If you don't care about your own health, why should I?" he says, dismissing the patient as too lazy to follow John-Roger's healing advice.

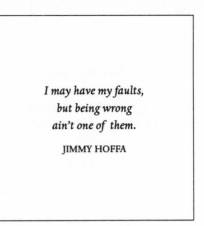

I may have my faults, but being wrong ain't one of them.

JIMMY HOFFA

In fact, if you don't precisely follow his advice (including the advice given by any healer recommended by John-Roger), John-Roger sees that as a form of *ingratitude*—"Why should I spend anymore time taking care of you when you won't take the time to take care of yourself?"

Even when one *does* do everything, John-Roger will still create an out. One particularly sad example was a young man—a minister and long-time initiate of John-Roger's—who developed lung cancer. He was married to another of John-Roger's ministers and long-time initiates. As soon as the young man was diagnosed with lung cancer, both he and his wife stopped all other activities and spent their time and resources on the young man's healing.

A plea for John-Roger's help was their first step. John-Roger promised to help (I saw him do two hands-on healings on the man, each of which took a good forty-five minutes). John-Roger recommended a series of healers who kept the couple running to and fro, racking up exorbitant medical bills (health insurance seldom covers the sort of healers John-Roger sends people to), and performing uncomfortable—sometimes painful—radical treatments. John-Roger endorsed these radical treatments because, after all, if something *radical* were not done, the young man could die.

In addition, the wife arranged for John-Roger's ministers to come to the house in one-hour visits, twelve hours each day. While there, the ministers did the official healing technique John-Roger teaches his ministers. It's not called a healing technique, of course (those pesky healing-without-a-license charges, you know), but all the ministers know it's a healing technique. The technique is known as "prayer communications."

Despite all this, the young man died well within the average

> Serious misfortunes originating in misrepresentation frequently flow and spread before they can be dissipated by truth.
>
> GEORGE WASHINGTON

range of people who have his type of lung cancer and get no treatment whatsoever.

And what did John-Roger say about his failure to heal—or even prolong the life of—the young man? He told the widow the reason the young man died was because he had abandoned his dream of a musical career. It "broke his heart," and he died.

It's hard to explain what a cruel and vicious thing this was to tell the widow—especially since John-Roger was obviously saying it to justify his own inability to heal. The young man had given up pursuing his own musical career so he could manage his *wife's* artistic pursuits. (His management, by the way, proved extremely successful for them both.) The information from John-Roger as to the cause of her husband's death plunged the widow from grief into despair: if not for *her* and *her* artistic career, her husband would *still* be alive. *She*, then, was responsible for her husband's death.

Even if John-Roger's information as to the cause of the young man's illness *was* accurate, why did he wait until the very end to mention it? Why didn't he say it before the illness developed (a mere nod in a given direction from John-Roger would certainly have had the young man and his wife leaping to obey), or, why didn't John-Roger mention it *immediately* after the young man's diagnosis? Then the young man could have spent his time and money pursuing *music*, not alternative *medicine*. At the very least, why couldn't John-Roger have just trotted out his standard excuse ("Spiritually, it was his time"), and let it go at that?

Does John-Roger practice medicine without a license? Yes. Is the way John-Roger uses his non-existent powers to heal immoral? Absolutely. Is it illegal? You bet. Does John-Roger *know* that what he is doing is illegal? Of course. He even cautions his own ministers not to do it. Take a look at what it says in the MSIA *Handbook for Ministers of Light:*

> Section 2141 of the **California Business and Professions Code** specifically makes it a crime to practice medicine without a license.

Practicing medicine includes **diagnosing,** and diagnosing can include almost any statement purporting to explain a person's disease or dysfunction. (For example: "I think you have a headache because you have been eating too much sugar.") When you are trying to define what is wrong with a person's body, you are diagnosing. Further, the giving of any drugs, herbs, or

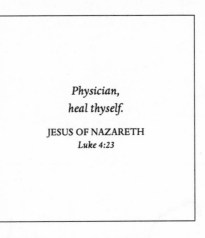

Physician,
heal thyself.

JESUS OF NAZARETH
Luke 4:23

medicines or other remedies (e.g. Bach Flower Remedies) or giving of advice to take such remedies, is specifically against the law, unless you have the proper medical license to do so.

How did John-Roger get away with hurting so many people for so many years under the guise of "healing" them? You've got me.

To quote Roseanne Roseannadanna: "It's enough to make you *sick!"*

John Morton's Valentine's Day greeting to Victor Toso, postmarked February 10, 1989, eight months after Morton received "the keys to the Mystical Traveler Consciousness."

CHAPTER NINETEEN

An Even Closer Encounter
with John Donnelley-Morton

> *The spirit of religious totalitarianism*
> *is abroad in the world;*
> *it is in the very air we breathe*
> *today in this land.*
> *Everywhere are those*
> *who claim to have a corner*
> *on righteousness,*
> *on direct access to God . . . .*
> *The bigots of the world*
> *are having a heyday.*
>
> SONIA JOHNSON

1994. The day before Independence Day. The Annual Conference of MSIA Initiates and Ministers at the Universal Sheraton Hotel, Universal City (i.e., The Valley), California. For fifteen years, the best anecdote I had to tell about the Universal Sheraton was someone else's. Today, thanks to MSIA—and especially thanks to John Donnelley-Morton, the New Mystical Traveler—I finally have a better anecdote of my own.

But first, Telly Savalas's anecdote.

Back in the 1960s when *Kojak* was the hottest TV show filming on the Universal lot, the Universal brass approached Telly Savalas yet again to beg, plead, cajole, or do whatever was necessary to get him to continue his role. His contract had expired. They had already offered him more money than had been offered to anyone in the history of television, but Telly wasn't happy with television: he wanted to return to films, such as his classic performance as Pontius Pilate in *The Greatest Story Ever Told.**

But the yes-men had approached Savalas one more time, will-

---

*This was the film in which Shelley Winters played Veronica, Ed Wynn played one of the blind who could now see, Sal Mineo played one of the lame who could now walk, Sidney Poitier helped Jesus carry his cross, and John Wayne, as usual, had the last word as the centurion under the cross, speaking his one-and-only line in his patented John-Wayne accent, "This, truly, was the son of God."

*Who loves
'ya, baby?*

LT. THEO KOJAK

ing to say yes to practically any demand. "Just tell us what you want, Telly," they pleaded, "anything; anything at all."

Savalas, who was shooting on a street set, looked across the vast expanse of hilltop acreage owned by Universal. He saw the metal framework of a building rising in the distance.

"What's that?" he asked pointing in the direction of the growing skyscraper.

"We're going to have our own hotel on the Universal lot: the Universal Sheraton," one of the executives said proudly.

"All right," said Savalas, casually turning from them, "I'll take the top floor of that building."

There were murmurs among the yes-men: this guy is crazy, but the sort of craziness tens of millions tuned in every week to watch. Savalas moved off in the direction of his next shot, and, almost as an afterthought, turned and said, "And I want the bar, too."

So, for the fifteen years I had been attending MSIA and Insight events regularly at the Universal Sheraton, I would see Telly Savalas or his mother or one of his other relatives, all of whom were comfortably ensconced in their own private suites at the top of the Universal Sheraton. Savalas liked to hang out at Telly's Bar, signing autographs, and passing out TootsieRoll Pops—which seemed to multiply in his pocket.

When I returned to the Universal Sheraton July 3, 1994, I knew that Savalas had died just a few weeks before. For me, the Universal Sheraton would never be the same. I also knew that my relationship with the members of MSIA would never be the same, either: I was about to pass out 22-page leaflets, loaded with what MSIA hates the most—the truth. (How's *that* for a pious statement?)

Just as I was concerned about the people who were attending USM from my recommendation in the books, so, too, I wanted anyone who joined MSIA directly (or got programmed into it through Insight, as I had) to know my current perception of the truth. From then on, of course, it was their decision: as I said in my leaflet, addressed to all MSIA ministers and initiates, "It's fine with me if you study with John-Roger, John Morton, MSIA, or the Pillsbury Doughboy, for that matter. I just want you to have the facts as I now know them, and as you are certainly welcome to investigate for yourself."

> *Power, like the diamond,*
> *dazzles the beholder,*
> *and also the wearer;*
> *it dignifies meanness;*
> *it magnifies littleness;*
> *to what is contemptible,*
> *it gives authority;*
> *to what is low, exaltation.*
>
> CHARLES CALEB COLTON
> 1780–1832

So I put together a packet of information: a four-page letter from me, a two-page reprint of the *Los Angeles Times* article telling about the lawsuit, a fourteen-page press release that was going out to the media, a one-page article from the *Santa Barbara News-Press* telling about John-Roger's million-dollar suit against the woman who didn't want one hundred MSIA cars per weekend traveling across her road and her property, and the 1988 article from *People* magazine in which some of the more violent aspects of John-Roger and MSIA are discussed.

Knowing that about a thousand people would be there, I printed a thousand of these pamphlets (the author of *The Bridges of Madison County* would call it a *book*), had them neatly stapled, and hired three people to help me distribute them.

We arrived during the leisurely time between the Ministers' Meeting, which took place from noon until 2:00, and the Initiates' Meeting, which was scheduled from 4:00 until 6:00. Naturally, the ministers would attend both meetings, as almost all ministers are initiates, but not all initiates are ministers. (Of the one thousand, the ratio is about eight hundred ministers to two hundred initiates.) As the ministers would be attending both meetings, an outdoor luncheon was served on the lawn just outside the Grand Ballroom, where the meetings were held. There they were, hundreds and hundreds of ministers sitting at circular tables of ten, finishing dessert.

I arrived slightly after three, so the initiates who were not ministers had not yet arrived. I grabbed large stacks of pamphlets and began handing them, ten at a time, saying, "Hi, please pass these around" to anyone at the table who would take them. There were a few pleasantries and special bits of eye contact with people whom I knew and loved but hadn't seen since I was given my official Red Monk status by John-Roger. Mostly I avoided eye contact, though: I didn't want anyone to feel "infected."

> *You never need think*
> *you can turn over any old falsehood*
> *without a terrible squirming*
> *and scattering*
> *of the horrid little population*
> *that dwells under it.*
>
> OLIVER WENDELL HOLMES, SR.
> 1858

I also knew that there'd be trouble, and I wanted to get as many pamphlets to as many people as I could before the storm troopers arrived.

It's amazing how quickly word spreads in MSIA. By the time I had delivered pamphlets to four tables, the Hundredth-Monkey Syndrome took over: Someone had already sized up my pamphlet as being "not spiritual" and spread the word not to accept it from me.

I went from table to table anyway, where I got looks that would freeze lava (except from the people who gave me looks that would ignite titanium). No one would touch my flyers. I neatly put them next to the arrangement of flowers in the center of each table, and moved on.

One woman said in overly emotional tones, "We love you, Peter! We love you!" I tried handing her a flyer. She refused to take it but continued professing not only her love, but the love of the entire table. (Or was it the entire ministerial body? Or was it all MSIA members? Or was it the entire human race?)

"If you love me, you'll read what I have to say. I wrote it because I loved you—and I love truth." (Now, was that statement more pious than the previous pious statement?) She still didn't take it, continued professing, and I moved on.

There were, however, few statements of love. For the most part, there was hatred in the eyes of these high-level initiates and ministers, and I mean *hatred*. Those who didn't openly express their hatred (not at all a spiritual thing to do, or so they believed) reverted to one of John-Roger's great unwritten teachings: *It's okay to deceive people you don't like.* Some people were perfectly capable of looking me straight in the eye, smiling, and lying. I would go to a clearly "virgin" table and someone would smile and say, "Oh, I already have one. Thank you." Or, "I've already read it."

"It's twenty-two pages long," I said, "How could you have read it already?"

"I'm a fast reader!" she said with a perkiness that didn't have a hint of sarcasm. In one of the great traditions of MSIA, she had suppressed her anger so thoroughly and so quickly that lying to me was simply *the thing to do*—there was no need for her to "get out of balance" about it. These are people who are trained to "be loving" no matter *what* they do, including deceit. Even when caught in such obvious deception, there was no sense of embarrassment. It was all part of a day's "defending the faith."

> The trouble with Eichmann
> was precisely that so many
> were like him,
> and that the many
> were neither perverted nor sadistic,
> that they were, and still are,
> terribly and terrifyingly normal.
>
> HANNAH ARENDT

I was fascinated to watch that behavior from the outside—I had been *inside* (in fact, inside *all* of their modes of behavior at one time or another) up until just two months before. These people were really *hooked*. And I, once again, had been astonishingly naive: I really expected my 22-page collection of prose and reprints to somehow *move* those in the Movement of Spiritual Inner Awareness. That was about as dumb as thinking I could walk into a gathering of junkies, pass out a 22-page report (complete with diagrams) on why heroin can be bad for you, and expect them never to touch the stuff again. Right.

On this day before Independence Day I suddenly felt so *free*. This was not my "family," as I had been carefully programmed to consider them; these were a bunch of brainwashed people blindly devoted to someone who's been saying he's God for the past thirty years and somehow hasn't gotten locked up.

It wouldn't just be *easy* to leave these people—it would be a pleasure (although I would be happy to welcome any of them who wanted to kick their addiction).

And through the sea of tables (shall I use the analogy of Moses parting the Red Sea or Jesus walking on the water?) came John Donnelley-Morton. John Donnelley-Morton was the last remaining member of "the guys." Of the six, handsome male staff members who lived in John-Roger's house and took turns "watching the body," by mid-1988, only John Morton remained.

John Morton was a strikingly handsome California youth who was used to getting by on his looks. His greatest achievement in life, it seems, was becoming a forest ranger. Fortunately, good looks were all it took to get on J-R's staff. John-Roger snatched young John out of an Insight II and immediately moved him into the house in Mandeville Canyon. (There's a wife somewhere in

John Morton's past, but the time-lines are not clear, and whether he left his wife for John-Roger, as some Movement rumors claim, I do not know.)

> It was a blonde,
> a blonde to make a bishop
> kick a hole
> in a stained glass window.
>
> RAYMOND CHANDLER

"John was hopeless," observed one of J-R's former staff. "He didn't seem to be able to get anything right. I guess today you'd say he was sort of the Dan Quayle of staff." I noticed this when we facilitated Insight trainings together in the mid-1980s. Although he would make one mistake after another, I would defer to him because, after all, he was a member of John-Roger's personal staff, and most people looked at John-Roger's personal staff with a combination of reverence, envy, and lust. (John scored especially high marks in the latter.) Whenever he would completely screw up the presentation of a certain process, I would casually make myself available in case he wanted to learn another way of doing it—like the way we were *supposed* to be doing it, for example. He never did. He would survey the chaos he had wrought (when a process is not set up correctly, endless hands of confused participants shoot in the air, and the assistants have to go from person to person and explain the proper way to do things), "I guess Spirit wanted it done another way tonight."*

By mid-1988, every heir-apparent to John-Roger's throne had abdicated—none pleasantly. John Morton was all that was left.

By mid-1988, the Mystical Traveler Consciousness was a hot potato. A scandalous (i.e., truthful) two-part article about John-Roger and the Mystical Traveler Consciousness was going to run "any day now" in the Los Angeles Times. Threats of legal action had held up the publication of the article for many months, but all facts and quotes in the article were checked, double-checked, and checked again until the Los Angeles Times' lawyers were confident that even if John-Roger filed a libel or slander lawsuit, he would

---

*The man responsible for his proper training and certification was Russell Bishop. Russell, as we have explored, is the Leonardo da Vinci of sycophants. He wouldn't *dream* of criticizing one of John-Roger's personal staff—unless John-Roger happened to be criticizing him at the time as well. So "Johnny" always got glowing reports, Russell got his requisite brownie points, and so what if the quality of Insight trainings suffered?

not be successful. John-Roger needed a quick and easy way out. "Passing the keys" of the Mystical Traveler Consciousness to John Morton was his only option.

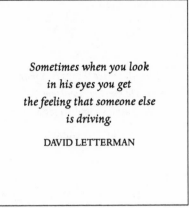

Sometimes when you look in his eyes you get the feeling that someone else is driving.

DAVID LETTERMAN

John-Roger confided to me that he was passing the keys to John Morton a few weeks before the surprise event. I have no idea how many people he confided in and swore them to strictest secrecy. I have a feeling it was quite a few. It was a way John-Roger had of making you feel a part of his Inner Circle, but one never knew how large that Inner Circle might be.

And so at the Annual Conference in 1988, John-Roger passed the keys of the Mystical Traveler Consciousness to John Morton. And there stood John, holding the bag.

The *L.A. Times* article broke on August 14, 1988. Passing the keys to John Morton only a month before gave John-Roger one of his favorite defenses: evasive semantics. By passing "the keys" to John Morton, John-Roger could answer, "No," to straightforward but perhaps embarrassing questions such as, "Are you the Mystical Traveler?" The people in MSIA knew that John-Roger had passed the keys of the Traveler to John Morton. To those who did not read about this historic passage of Travelerness on the front page of the *New York Times* or watch it as the lead story on all three network evening news shows, it seemed as though John-Roger was denying he was *ever* the Traveler. It also allowed John-Roger to brush aside any questions of MSIA's past shady dealings with the comment, "John Morton is in charge of MSIA; talk to him."

Meanwhile around MSIA, the joke was: "John-Roger passed John Morton the keys; do you think he'll pass him a personality, too?"

John Morton proved so inept at running MSIA that John-Roger had to rise from the dead yet again (almost literally) and declare that although John had the *keys* to the Mystical Traveler Consciousness, he had not yet been passed the *rod* and the *staff*. It was never made clear what the rod and the staff of the Mystical Traveler Consciousness were, but I have a feeling the rod controlled the money and the staff gave the orders. After a few bumpy

> *I require three things in a man.*
> *He must be handsome,*
> *ruthless, and stupid.*
>
> DOROTHY PARKER

months, J-R was back in charge. Everyone breathed a sigh of relief, including, I'm sure, John Morton.

On the spiritual leadership front, John Morton proved even worse. John-Roger repeatedly beseeched his followers, "If you love me, love John." We tried, we tried. It was an effort. John-Roger beseeched again. We tried again. A greater effort.

In the first place, while sexy, John Morton has the charisma of Rob Lowe.* This is the primary problem of a personality cult and why so few of them survive beyond the demise of the founder. If the founder is not replaced by someone more dynamic and adorable (which, in John-Roger's case, would not have been difficult), the followers find another cult with another personality, or gather in little groups and wax nostalgic: "Remember when our dear founder . . . ."

John-Roger seemed incapable of allowing anyone more insightful, entertaining, perceptive, humorous, or dynamic to become his successor—he drove qualified applicant after qualified applicant out the door. The only thing John Morton was better at than John-Roger was better looking. John-Roger's inability to allow a superior replacement has already sowed the seed for MSIA's eventual downfall. After a few lackluster John Morton seminars, the general consensus around MSIA was: "When John-Roger goes, I'm going, too."

In addition, John-Roger's support of John Morton was less than consistent. Although J-R initially said, "I stand firmly behind John, or in front of him, or wherever he wants me to stand," John-Roger always made sure that no matter *where* he stood, he always stood taller that John. This meant a barrage of ongoing belittlements, and an occasional cutting John off at the knees.

An example of the latter came at a major MSIA retreat about six months after John had been passed the keys. Prior to this, John Morton repeatedly used a theme he introduced of "the harvest." The celebration of John-Roger's twenty-fifth anniversary as the

---

*Casting director of the TV-movie version of this book, take note.

Traveler—planned by John Morton—had a harvest theme; John Morton spent a tidy sum of Church money on a house in Santa Barbara (three quarters of a million dollars *before* the pool and decking and hot tub that became a waterfall just like an Esther Williams movie) as part of his "harvest";* and heaven knows how many seminars John Morton had filled with harvest examples.

> At the Harvest Festival in church
> the area behind the pulpit
> was piled high with tins of fruit
> for the old-age pensioners.
> We had collected the tinned fruit
> from door to door.
> Most of it came
> from old-age pensioners.
>
> CLIVE JONES

At this retreat, someone asked John-Roger to expand upon John Morton's harvest theme. "Well, since you asked me while I'm in this consciousness," he said, carefully sidestepping all responsibility for the devastation he was about to wreak while still appearing to be so true to the Spirit that he would betray his own hand-picked disciple, "it's all a lot of hogwash." He went on to explain in great detail how, essentially, John Morton didn't know what he was talking about, and the whole harvest theme was not just a waste of everyone's time, it was *misleading*.

I was sitting next to John Morton at the staff table. I didn't dare look directly at him—too many people in the group had turned their heads to do so—but I could see his hands turn whiter and whiter out of the corner of my eye. John-Roger had essentially invalidated the first six months of John Morton's teachings. (But J-R kept the house.)

About the only thing John Morton did right in his first six years as Mystical Traveler was marry rich and have a daughter—who became the apple of John-Roger's eye (if you don't mind another harvest analogy). This marrying an heiress to the R. R. Donnelley printing fortune was strongly contested by John-Roger. (That, I think, is one of the grander understatements in this book.) When it all worked out to J-R's benefit, however, J-R claimed to be secretly behind the marriage all the time.

But now it was the day before Independence Day, 1994—six Annual Conferences after John Morton received the keys to the Mystical Traveler Consciousness, and four Conferences after I was

---

*After twenty-five years of fleecing, one gets to harvest, too. Not a bad deal this Mystical Traveler business. I guess it's just a matter of spreading around enough fertilizer.

> *The smylere with the knyf*
> *under the cloke.*
>
> *[The smiler with the knife*
> *under the cloak.]*
>
> CHAUCER
> 1387

named Minister of the Year. Chairs and tables parted* as John Donnelley-Morton approached me.

"Peter, can I help?" he asked, smiling his Mona Lisa smile that he must think makes him look devil-may-care and mysterious, but, in fact, only makes him look as though he has a touch of palsy.

Oh dear, I thought. John-Roger regaled John Morton with stories of *his* openness and benevolence in helping me pass out flyers on the sidewalk outside the University of Santa Monica. (The four letters he handed out, in John-Roger's retelling, no doubt became three solid hours of leafleting.) Well, here was John saying: "Me too! I want to appear open and benevolent, just like John-Roger!"

"Sure, John," I said, "that table over there," naming the name of an Insight facilitator who had fathered a child with one of his seminar participants in London, and after the first thousand dollars refused to pay any child support and who was now among the more vocal don't-read-anything-Peter-is-handing-out-or-your-monk-will-turn-red Movement loyalists, "they wouldn't take any." I handed John Morton approximately ten pamphlets, and continued on to other tables. About ten minutes later, I noticed that John Morton had a stack of about a hundred pamphlets in his hand. He had been *collecting* them! (Why did I add that exclamation point? Is anyone *surprised* that he was collecting them?) I walked past him.

"People just keep *handing* them to me," he said. It was sort of a spontaneous MSIA version of ritual book-burning: give Peter's pamphlet to the Traveler, and your Red Monk will turn purple again. (Purple is the very best of colors, according to John-Roger.) "I just wanted to help you pass them out," he said, not at all convincingly.

"If you really want to help," I said, "give me permission to put one on each chair in the meeting room. That way those who want them can take them; those who don't can leave them. Can I do that?" I asked.

---

*I prefer the Moses analogy.

"Sure," said John Morton cavalierly, "you can do that."

"And can I tell them inside that you said it was okay?" I asked, anticipating the bureaucratic hurdles I knew we'd encounter.

"Of course you can," he said, "didn't I tell you you could do it?"

"Thank you," I said, gathered my helpers, and went into the lecture hall.

> *I happened to catch my reflection the other day when I was polishing my trophies, and, gee it's easy to see why women are nuts about me.*
>
> TOM RYAN

There, about a thousand seats had been set up. It was dark and cool. Twenty or so assistants sat around a long table having lunch. I pointed my helpers to three different parts of the room, and took one for myself.

One of the MSIA assistants—a New Yorker whom I've known forever—got up from the table and asked one of my helpers if he had permission to be there.

"John Morton said it was okay for us to put these here," I yelled to her across the empty ballroom.

"I love you, Peter, but I have to check this out," she said.

"*Of course* you do!" I said. "He's just outside, wearing a pale green suit."

She left the room, and several of the assistants got up and hovered in that silent but ominous way MSIA assistants hover. My helpers and I continued our work under close surveillance.

A few minutes later the assistant from New York returned and declared that, yes, she had talked to John Morton and, yes, it was okay if we put pamphlets on the seats. The assistants abandoned silent, ominous hovering, and returned to noisy, omnivorous eating.

The assistant from New York approached me. "Peter, you know I trust you, but wouldn't you have checked, too, if you were in my situation?" she asked.

"You mean if you were handing out flyers and said it was okay?" I asked.

"Yes," she said.

"No, I wouldn't have checked. I would have trusted you. Not

> The peculiar office of a demagogue is to advance his own interests, by affecting a deep devotion to the interests of the people. Sometimes the object is to indulge malignancy, unprincipled and selfish men submitting but to two governing motives, that of doing good to themselves, and that of doing harm to others.
>
> JAMES FENIMORE COOPER

that either one of us is above lying, as we both know, but I would trust you not to make up such a *stupid* and *useless* lie. You and I both know that before the doors open, John Morton will check out the room, and if he or J-R hasn't approved handouts on the seats, they'll be removed before a single participant gets in."

She could see the logic in my argument, and I could also see hers: that a good intelligence network *tells* John-Roger and John Morton things long before they *discover* them. As it turned out, within a few minutes I would be extremely grateful that she had asked and made her general announcement of John Morton's permission to the assistants in the room.

As we continued, John-Roger's official videographer began following me around with a camcorder. ("Was it one of the camcorders I donated to the Movement?" I wondered.) Knowing he wouldn't have the initiative to do this on his own, I suspected John-Roger was involved. I had little doubt that he had given the order, "Get Peter on video!" from his command center nearby. I figured that, since John-Roger had been spreading rumors that I was "on hard drugs and deranged," he probably wanted to get some video of me.

Little did I know that John-Roger was arranging for his own Fourth of July fireworks, and he wanted to be able to see—though not directly take part in—the explosions.

When my helpers and I were about three quarters of the way through covering the chairs, someone from hotel security came up to me and politely said, "This group doesn't want you in here, and it wants you to leave." I looked around. There seemed to be a disproportionate number of assistants hovering in the dark spaces all around me.

"I received permission to put these here by the second most powerful person in this organization. Only one person is higher, and only he can supersede the orders of the man I got permission from." My grammar sucked, but I think I got my point across. A voice from the darkness got his point across, too: the word *was*

coming from higher up; John-
Roger was rescinding John
Morton's orders once again.

I continued to protest, saying that one of the assistants
checked with John Morton,
and he verified that I *could* put
the flyers on the chairs. The
assistants remembered this order, verified by one of their
own, and became—for a brief
moment—tentative. They

Pure truth, like pure gold,
has been found unfit for circulation,
because men have discovered
that it is far more convenient
to adulterate the truth
than to refine themselves.

CHARLES CALEB COLTON
1825

hovered around the edges of the room like the old ladies in black
in *Zorba the Greek* who would pilfer all the possessions of a dying
woman. Each time the woman on her deathbed closed her eyes,
one of the old crones would reach out and grab a scarf, another a
handkerchief, another a figurine. When the dying woman opened
her eyes, the crones would disappear. That was the sense I had
looking around the immense ballroom. The vultures were ready,
but Vultures' Honor proclaimed no feasting until the official demise of the prey. I still had a thin thread of bureaucratic life:
permission from someone higher up whose permission occasionally counts.

Through the doors, however, walked my lime-green-suited
death blow: John Donnelley-Morton.

"John, will you please tell them that you gave me permission to
put these flyers on the chairs?" I asked.

"That was then, and this is now, and you can't do it any more."

Whoosh. I looked around. Not a single flyer was left on a
single chair. It was a miracle. It was like the multiplication of the
loaves and fishes, but in reverse: I'm sure it will go down in MSIA
history as the Subtraction of the Red Monk's Flyers.

"John, you said I could, you said I could . . ." I protested.

"I said that then, and now I say you can't, and I want you to
leave this room."

His tone had that Old Testament quality to it: I was right to
choose the Moses analogy, but somehow with John, he never approached Charlton Heston's majestic tones.

John just sounded *pissed*.

Was he angry because John-Roger had made him look like a

> Deceitfulness, and arrogance,
> and pride,
> Quickness to anger,
> harsh and evil speech,
> And ignorance,
> to its own darkness blind—
> These be the signs,
> My Prince!
>
> BHAGAVAD GITA

fool again in front of the people that he, John Morton, was supposed to be Mystically Traveling for? I looked carefully at John. He surveyed the pristine, once-again empty chairs, and he saw that it was good. He was now about four feet from me, and he looked me straight in the eye: "I said you could put them on the chairs, you put them on the chairs, we have taken them off the chairs, and now you are to leave this room."

He was pissed at *me*.

Suddenly the reason why he was so visibly shaken (the anger I had previously seen from John was primarily pouting, although I've heard-tell of some physically violent outbursts whilst in the loving bosom of his family) flashed across my mind—or at least my *speculation* as to why he was so mad.

WE NOW FADE INTO PETER'S SPECULATION*

I could see John-Roger (who probably got a copy of my flyer within minutes of my arrival—one of his personal secretaries was at my shoulder picking up "her" copy almost immediately) reading the portion of the press release in which one of John-Roger's former staff members walks into John-Roger's bedroom and discovers John-Roger and John Donnelley-Morton having sex. (John Donnelley-Morton was performing oral intercourse on John-Roger, for those, like myself, who like every sordid detail.)**

The item about the staff member walking in and discovering John-Roger having sex with another male member of the staff had first been reported in the 1988 *Los Angeles Times* articles. The departed staff member, however, had withheld Morton's name, thinking that Morton would "wake up" as so many other staff members had. In this way, should Morton leave and, say, marry the heiress to a printing fortune, the family he was marrying into would be spared undue embarrassment.

But now, six years later, the former staff member is convinced that Morton has had plenty of time to come to his senses, and

---

*Screenwriters of the TV-movie version of this book, take note.

**Censors of the network that shows the TV-movie of this book, take note.

apparently has no intention of doing so.

I could hear John-Roger sarcastically reading John Donnelley-Morton this section of the press release, and saying: "Oh, great: you give Peter McWilliams permission to spread this to initiates and ministers. How's Laura [Morton's wife] going to feel? How's Claire [his daughter] going to feel when she's old enough to read this?" Are you going to put this in her baby scrapbook, next to the towel from the White House?* Good work, John. Good work.

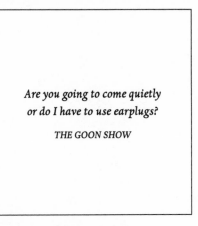

Are you going to come quietly or do I have to use earplugs?

THE GOON SHOW

[The camera dares not pan to John's face, but in the corner of the screen we see one of his hands getting whiter and whiter.]

END OF PETER'S SPECULATION.

Well, whether that was the reason, or whether he just hadn't had his major poop of the day, John Donnelley-Morton was *mad* at *me*. Actually, for a moment it was rather refreshing. John Donnelley-Morton gets mad *so* often and covers it *so* poorly, that a clear expression of anger in his face and voice was a relief.

But it soon became very, very frightening.

He began moving steadily toward me. "Do what you want, Peter!" he yelled. "Go ahead, Peter! Do what you want! Do what you want! Go ahead!" He continued moving toward me.

John is slightly taller than I, younger, and in far better physical condition (he is a self-confessed "jock").

He held his arms out wide, to either side at shoulder level. He began pushing me backwards with his chest.

*From John Morton's computer-diary, The White House, Washington, D.C., 3/2/94: "ONE OTHER MEMORABLE COINCIDENCE WAS CLAIRE CHOSE THE WAITING ROOM NEAR THE OVAL OFFICE TO HAVE HER MAJOR POOP OF THE DAY. WITH THE SECURITY, LAURA HAD LEFT HER BAG WITH DIAPERS BEHIND IN THE FIRST WAITING ROOM WE WENT TO. ONE OF THE SECRETARIES CAUGHT "WIND" OF THIS AND OFFERED TO ASSIST. SHE BROUGHT BACK A SLIGHTLY USED HAND TOWEL AND WHISPERED TO LAURA THAT IT CAME FROM THE PRESIDENT'S PRIVATE WASHROOM AND NOT TO TELL WITH A LITTLE SNICKER. SO LAURA'S NOT TELLING BUT I AM AND WE HAVE QUITE A MEMENTO FOR CLAIRE'S SCRAPBOOK"

> *There are more pleasant things to do than beat up people.*
>
> MUHAMMAD ALI

The intuitive action in such a situation is to push the other person away: it's frightening to be pushed backwards from a point slightly above your chest when you have no idea what's behind you, although you know a tangle of chairs is *somewhere* behind you—not very far behind at all. I also instinctively knew that if I did push him—or raise my arms from my sides in any way—he was going to deck me. Two dozen more-than-willing witnesses would happily testify that, "Peter hit John first," or "Peter was about to hit John, and John had to defend himself."

His pushing with his chest and his yelling—directly in my face—continued. Relentlessly. "Do what you want, Peter! Do what you want!"

For a very long moment I felt sure that I was either going to be pushed at the chest until I toppled backwards into a mangle of chairs (keeping my arms at my sides only added to my imbalance), or that I would lift an arm to balance myself or catch myself from falling against a chair, at which point he would slug me. I had no idea how many assistants might join in—to protect John, of course.

I find physical violence horrifying. My father, when he drank too much, was either a happy drunk, a melancholy drunk, or a violent drunk. When he was in the latter state, it was only my agility and his extreme inebriation which kept me from getting hit more often than I did. The bathroom was my sanctuary. I knew if I could get in the bathroom and lock the door, I would be okay. I would wait until he fell asleep, or until my mother was able to calm him down. As we only had one bathroom, necessity more than anything else often dictated my freedom.

Thank God these childhood scenes didn't happen very often, but they happened often enough to leave an indelible emotional impression.

"Leave me alone," I kept saying, in what must have been a scared child's voice. While I don't shy away from an argument, I'm an instant coward when it comes to a fight. I somehow managed to see a row of chairs out of the corner of my eye (most of this activity took place in the center aisle). I quickly side-stepped into the aisle. Somehow (I can't remember how) I put a row of chairs between us.

> *"Son, when a man knows something deep down in his heart . . . when he really knows . . . he doesn't have to argue about it, doesn't have to prove it. Just knowin'—that's enough."*
>
> BEN CARTWRIGHT
> *Bonanza*

The entire incident was still being videotaped. But, as Marshall McLuhan pointed out, the presence of a television camera changes the event it is recording.* Was this some performance for the camera? Was he doing this to appear a *machismo*-powered hero to John-Roger? His wife? His daughter? Was this a tape his daughter could play at show-and-tell in those exclusive schools she'd be attending just in case those J-R–Daddy rumors ever got mentioned?

Personally, I think a video record was made just in case I *did* push him or hit him as he attacked me. Then he'd have *proof* I started it.

Whoever or whatever he was doing it for, his attack certainly had a devastating effect on me: I was petrified. I could see that some assistants were now behind me. My helpers had been hustled out of the room (and, as I was later to discover, out of the building). I felt my escape routes being closed off. Was some sort of ritualized beating about to take place? Running no longer seemed an option. My only safety lay in facing him—not physically, but with whatever inner energy I was able to muster.

The moment I made that decision, the strangest thing happened: he began *debating me.* Now that he had proven he was my better at brute force (I would have happily given him the title without his terrorizing attack), was he attempting to prove his intellectual superiority, too? He wasn't only going to justify revoking his permission for me to put the flyers on the chairs; but also defend the right of a church to sue one of its former members who wishes to be left alone, his covering up John-Roger's sexual exploitations, and their mutual ongoing game of spiritual deceit.

As John Morton is a student of the John-Roger School of De-

---

*It might not have been Marshall McLuhan, but every comment about media, its causes, and its effects, seems to be attributed to Marshall McLuhan.

bate, there's no need to waste your time reviewing how he argued the major points: semantic shiftiness, spiritual hierarchical jumping, sudden changes of subject, and, when all else failed, threats about revealing aspects of my sex life that were *so* shocking even I would be filled with horror and disgust.

> *I should warn you*
> *that underneath these clothes*
> *I'm wearing boxer shorts*
> *and I know how to use them.*
>
> ROBERT ORBEN

It was not exactly what you'd call a song from the loving heart.

I actually got him to admit that John-Roger does *not* have the power over life and death. This is like getting a cardinal to admit that the Pope is not infallible. Donnelley-Morton absolutely refused, however, to let me finish the next logical question: "If he has no power over life and death, how can he trade my health and life . . ." was about as far as he let me go. I even pointed out that he was intentionally interrupting me on the most embarrassing question I could ask. When it seemed as though I was about to say the entire question, the *cameraman* piped in.

My favorite exchange, however, was about sex. I asked him if he had ever had sex with John-Roger. He said he wasn't going to discuss it. I told him now would be a perfect opportunity to put the entire issue at rest: yes or no. He was surrounded by his loyal assistants. "If you say no, they'll believe you." He said he wasn't going to discuss it.

"Then you are practically admitting that you have."

"I don't admit or deny anything."

The poop on the White House towel must have been contagious.

Eventually, John looked about as demoralized from our verbal interaction as I looked terrified by our physical one. In a grand gesture worthy of his mentor, I was dismissed. I was also threatened. If I did not leave at once, the police would arrest me.

The police would not arrest me, I told him, they would escort me off the property.

John made it a dare, and though I like to *think* I'm above it, I am still a sucker for a dare. Besides, there's a certain moral point here: he had offered his help, promised to let me do something, and then reneged on the promise when it was too late to do it the way I had planned (passing out the pamphlets to the new initiates who were not yet ministers as they arrived). I told him if he wanted me gone, he could keep his original agreement with me. It would take all of five minutes for the assistants to put the flyers back on the chairs, and then I would be happy to leave. John Morton walked away, I had a seat, and *SHAZAM!* there was Michael Feder, John-Roger's hit man.

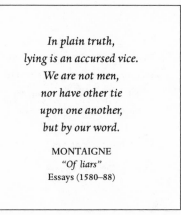

*In plain truth,
lying is an accursed vice.
We are not men,
nor have other tie
upon one another,
but by our word.*

MONTAIGNE
"Of liars"
Essays (1580–88)

The Michael Feder stories are some of MSIA's best. For example: One evening when John-Roger was lying in bed in his underwear "being attacked by the negative forces," John-Roger told Feder that he had to get completely undressed and lie down next to him so that Feder's body could "recharge" John-Roger's "electrolytes." Feder did this without hesitation. The image of Michael Feder, naked, lying next to John-Roger's body in order to balance his electrolytes is both ridiculous and repulsive. I would have brought J-R a glass of Gatorade. In our mutual days in the Movement, Feder was proudly known as the spiritual hit man, the MSIA Mafia enforcer, and Don Michael Feder. There he was now, sitting opposite me. "Be careful about Michael," I was warned the night before. "He's dangerous." While the video camera continued to roll, Michael was the soul of friendliness. He acted as though charm and congeniality—and not his reputation—were his only weapons.

As I listened to him talk, I thought of the woman who had brought him into the Movement. She had recently become MSIA's first official suicide. I attributed it directly to the fact that people in MSIA don't get proper treatment for depression. I wondered if he cared that the man whose shenanigans he defended with threats and violence had kept Feder's former girlfriend in a web of unkept promises rather than recommending she seek proper treatment for her depressive illness.

But my reverie was interrupted when the video camera was turned off and Michael's true intention became known. "You are trespassing, and I am now placing you under citizen's arrest."

"Great," I said, indicating John Morton who had recently returned, "and I place *him* under citizen's arrest for assault."

"Now just get up. We're going to walk out of here," he said, standing over me. "I'm going to hold you in the kitchen until the police arrive."

"I'm not going anywhere with you," I said. "I'm staying right here until the police arrive. There is no emergency, I'm not causing any trouble, and the police will get my full cooperation."

"You're going now," said Feder, "or I'm going to carry you."

"You are not to *touch* me," I said.

With that, he put one arm under my shoulders and another under my knees, and lifted me out of my chair. Now Feder is a tall, strong, big man. He might have pulled this thing off, oh, ten years ago, when I was leaner and he was stronger. He then might have been able to whisk me away like Rhett carrying Scarlett up the red velvet staircase.

Instead, he picked me up out of the chair, moved me a few feet from it, and dropped me. I landed—hard—on my tailbone and right hip. Without so much as an "Are you all right?" he grabbed both my wrists and began dragging me across the carpeted ballroom floor. Russell Bishop just *had* to get a piece of *this*. He grappled and scratched and tore at my legs to get a hold of them. Feder kept dragging; Russell kept grappling. *Finally*, Russell got both my legs in his hands at once (I was not putting up any struggle at all—I was just in pain), and helped carry me away. Oh! Would J-R be proud of him for *this!*

Russell Bishop. The man who stole Lifespring and called it Insight which got me into this wicked cult in the first place.

I looked up at him.

"Thanks, Russell," I said. He refused to look me in the eye. "You dragged me into this mess fifteen years ago, and now you're carrying me out."

⚖ ⚖ ⚖

At the meeting that fol-
lowed, I am told, John Morton
implied that I didn't want to
pass out flyers, but wanted to
take over the meeting. "I
would not let him disturb our
peace," he said, conferring
upon himself the new MSIA
title: Defender of the Peace.

> *By God, thou hast deceiv'd me . . .*
> *I did not think thee*
> *lord of such a spirit.*
> *Before, I lov'd thee*
> *as a brother, John.*
>
> SHAKESPEARE

He used his forest ranger background as his credentials to make
his "citizen's arrest" of me. (It's a good thing I wasn't playing with
matches.)

He told the group that he spread his arms wide, like the cruci-
fied Christ, and invited me to hit him all I liked. He did not mention that he used his chest to push me backwards, nor did he imply
that there was a threatening tone to his voice. He presented *his*
attack as though I were an evil person who was coming after
MSIA, and he was willing to sacrifice even his body in order to
"keep the peace."

I was told he started crying at my charge of sexual allegations
(which are not *my* charges, but the charges of a former staff member
who was an eyewitness to the event). He explained that his love for
J-R could not be understood by mortal men—particularly such *evil*
mortal men as I—at which point, crying uncontrollably, he knelt
down to kiss J-R's feet.

The room went nuts. "We love you, J-R!" "We love you,
Johnny!" they yelled. All the crying, weeping, shrieking attendees
of this conference—many of whom had flown thousands of miles
to be with J-R—were metaphorically kissing John-Roger's feet as
John Donnelley-Morton was doing so in fact. There could be no
clearer evidence that this was a cult that worshiped John-Roger—
personally.

It also shows the sort of power John-Roger has over people,
and how easily that power can be abused.

It was, in a sense, John Morton's Checkers speech. Richard
Nixon was always considered a bland also-ran riding on Dwight D.
Eisenhower's coattails. He was. When he was accused of accept-
ing inappropriate political contributions, however, he got on tele-

vision and told the country that he never profited from politics, that his wife was proud to wear a "Republican cloth coat," but, truth be told, while in office he *did* accept a valuable gift. It was a little puppy named Checkers, which his daughter immediately fell in love with. He kept the dog so as not to break his little daughter's heart, and if that made him a bad man, then he was a bad man.

> *I like men to behave like men—strong and childish.*
>
> FRANCOISE SAGAN

Overnight, Nixon had become, well, an overnight sensation. Some loved him and adored him; some found him maudlin and accused him of using sentimentality to cover up the real charges of political corruption. (Which, historians have shown, were true.)

In giving his maudlin, overly sentimental speech, John paved the way for followers to follow him. Personally. It also polarized opinion about John. People now loved him (the vast majority) or couldn't stand him (the small minority). A handful of people fled the meeting terrorized by what they saw. (One person told me it looked like a Jimmy Swaggart fund-raising event with J-R filling in for Jesus. Precisely.)

The group was told, once again, that the powers of negativity were about to attack the Movement, and those who were true to God and Spirit would stand firm. Those who were weak in Spirit, would fall away. All that was to follow was just another test given by a loving God to see who was going to choose Spirit and who was going to choose Mammon. (Those who believe what they read in books, newspapers, and see on TV are, of course, the Mammonites—since they love this physical world so much, they are condemned to return here over and over. Those who trust John-Roger will not believe what they see and hear against John-Roger "in the material world." These are God's Chosen, and they're ready to travel in the High Spiritual Realms.)*

*I wonder how John Donnelley-Morton will explain it when his followers watch the videotape of what *actually* happened, along with his account of what happened moments later. The true believers, of course, won't watch those tapes. They will be told that the tapes themselves have been infected by the Red Monk and Ignorance will prevail. But whom am I kidding? Learning from Nixon's downfall as well as his ascent, I have no doubt that Donnelley-Morton burned the tape with me on it long ago. (Not surprisingly, MSIA claims the tape has vanished—poof!)

John Morton then, of course, went into fund-raising. He said that, during the conference, $88,000 had been raised, and MSIA's goal was $100,000. The first thirteen people who raised their hand to give a thousand dollars would receive the donation envelope from him *personally*. Hands shot up all over the room. John began handing out donation envelopes. People were paying $1,000 for the honor of putting it into an envelope touched by John-Morton.

> *Then the Lord said to me,*
> *"The prophets are prophesying lies*
> *in my name.*
> *I have not sent them or appointed*
> *them or spoken to them.*
> *They are prophesying*
> *to you false visions,*
> *divinations, idolatries and*
> *the delusions of their own minds.*
>
> JEREMIAH 14:14

Perhaps John is finally getting the rod and the staff portion of the Mystical Traveler Consciousness.

Assistants passed out contribution envelopes to everyone, and people were encouraged to give whatever they could, "even if it was a penny."

Meanwhile, I was having a late lunch with my helpers at the Universal Hilton, a hotel a short distance from the Universal Sheraton (from which MSIA made certain that I was banned). A very dear woman came up and said, "Are you Peter McWilliams?" I said, "Yes." "I just want you to know I love the books you wrote with John-Roger, and those are the reasons I got involved with MSIA."

"Did you see the flyer I was handing out," I asked.

"Where were you handing it out?" she asked.

"In front of the initiates meeting at the Universal Sheraton," I answered.

"Oh, I've only been on Discourses for six months, so I can't go into the meetings. I came here with a friend who is an initiate who started MSIA because of John-Roger's books, too."

"Let me get you a flyer," I said.

On the way to my car I told her that I had written the books, that I no longer supported John-Roger's work, and that John-Roger was suing me for everything I owned. This seemed to confuse her more than disturb her: She thought that John-Roger had written the books, and, therefore, wanted to follow whatever path *he* was teaching. I told her I had written the books, but I had no particular

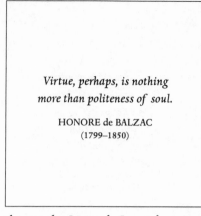

path for her to follow, other than to listen to her inner voice, and that only *she* could divine truth from falsehood. *That* was the true meaning of *divinity.* That's why I went to Insight back in 1978—when I was attending a different personal growth workshop or lecture every weekend—because I wanted more information from which I could divine the truth. Instead, I got lost in a fifteen-year detour known as John-Roger and MSIA.

She seemed to understand perfectly. I gave her several copies of the pamphlet and a copy of *How to Heal Depression,* and we went back to the lobby where she and a friend of hers wanted to have a photograph taken with me (this celebrity stuff *is* seductive), which I was only too happy to do. We wished each other well, and were on our way.

This was the type of person I came to reach. Those hard-core MSIA people are going to be hard-core MSIA people *forever.* That's fine with me. I shudder when I think that people read *my* books—which are about listening to the inner voice for truth—and then follow *him,* which is about believing everything he says, doing everything he says, and paying him for the privilege.

Major poop.

CHAPTER TWENTY

J-R, *Olé!* or
Don't Cry For Me Johnny-Roger

> I don't meet competition.
> I crush it.
>
> CHARLES REVSON

JOHN-ROGER not only steals the teachings of other spiritual and personal growth teachers—he steals their students as well. In this chapter, allow me to give you one of the more blatant examples of John-Roger's student theft.

In the late 1970s, a physician from Chile had enormous success with the personal-growth workshops he created and led. More than 80,000 people had taken his seminars in Chile, Colombia, and Argentina. He was well-respected in those countries not just by the graduates of his workshops, but by the media and government officials as well. This was no small task, because what his workshops taught was individual freedom, and the leaders of some of the countries wanted anything *but* personal freedom for their people. Nevertheless, the doctor was able to pull it off, and his reputation was impeccable.

Impressed by the near-saintliness he perceived in John-Roger's personal staff, the doctor became a member of MSIA. At first, John-Roger attempted to get control of the physician's family fortune—which was considerable. The physician demurred. Then John-Roger invited himself to South America so that he might give some "spiritual direction" to the physician's many followers.

The physician was honored to have his spiritual teacher speak to his students, but he was concerned that, should Insight seminars be taught in South America, it might appear to his students as an extension of the physician's workshops. John-Roger agreed time and again that the purpose of his visit was *not* to introduce Insight to South America, but to perform some "necessary spiritual work" and "undo with Light the darkness of dictators." John-Roger promised that, should Insight ever come to South America, the physician would—if he chose—be in charge of the entire operation. John-Roger stated, however, that there were no plans to bring Insight to South America: it was having enough trouble meeting the demand in *North* America.

With this understanding, the physician welcomed John-Roger with his characteristic warmth, generosity, and hospitality. The physician set up lectures throughout South America. He introduced John-Roger to his students as his spiritual teacher with obvious love and affection. He would then translate John-Roger's seminar, sentence by sentence, assuming the humble role of an interpreter. He also recommended MSIA and Discourses to his students.

Because the physician was so popular, the turnout to meet his spiritual teacher was enormous. If the physician was so wonderful, they thought, how much more wonderful must his spiritual teacher be? In the midst of this unprecedented generosity on the physician's part, he noticed in John-Roger not just a lack of gratitude, but *meanness.*

For example, the physician rented a small stadium in one city, and more than five thousand of his students came. Five thousand people is roughly five times more people than had ever appeared for *any* John-Roger speaking engagement. Rather than be delighted and excited by the *enormity* of it all, John-Roger, the moment he got off stage, severely berated the physician for not having introduced him as *Doctor* John-Roger."*

---

*John-Roger had no right to call himself doctor in 1980—and even the honorary degree he was given by his own university was still a while off. (Please see the chapter, "Guru U" for more on his *still*-unaccredited honorary degree mill.) Perhaps John-Roger borrowed a page from Garrison Keillor's relative, Senator Keil-

Throughout the South American trip, John-Roger shamelessly exploited the fact that he was introduced as "Dr. John-Roger" by a *genuine* physician. He would diagnose illnesses—especially among the elderly—and prescribe cures that always seemed to benefit John-Roger. He would diagnose illnesses people didn't have, and then spiritually

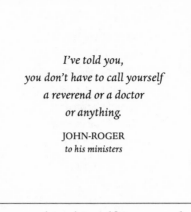

I've told you,
you don't have to call yourself
a reverend or a doctor
or anything.

JOHN-ROGER
to his ministers

"cure" them of the mythical disease, making himself appear to be a miracle worker. (Sound familiar?) He would then recommend an aura balance (performed by his staff for a fee) to "seal" the healing, recommend Discourses, or simply suggest that the newly healed individual make a "love offering" to MSIA. The fact that an authentic physician was translating John-Roger's words while the "healing" was in progress made it all the more believable.

The doctor was understandably concerned: was it an enormous blessing that his students were receiving so many healings from a man with such incredible powers, or was John-Roger taking advantage of the physician's good name and reputation to make John-Roger look good? As one carefully programmed by Insight and MSIA, the physician concluded that the latter could not possibly be the case; therefore, the former must be true.

When the physician mentioned his concerns to John-Roger, John-Roger simply explained the Traveler's presence in South America, an enormous amount of "negativity" was being "released." The physician—as John-Roger's host in the countries—was being attacked by the negative power. Causing doubt of John-Roger, of course, is one of the negative power's favorite tactics. If the physician would only stay true to his commitment to Spirit, he would come out of this stronger and more spiritually evolved than if he had never been "tested." It was typical John-Roger defensive logic: the more the negative forces attack you, the more it proves you are a student of the Traveler, because the dark forces *only* hit at the Light, so the more they hit against you in the form of doubt, the more it proves your discipleship to John-Roger is a

lor. Garrison remembered that Senator Keillor was *always* called Senator Keillor and when Garrison finally inquired as to when Senator Keillor was a senator, he was told that "Senator" was Senator Keillor's first name.

"Light action."

The physician, it seems, must have been involved in a tremendous "Light action," for his faith in John-Roger was challenged time and time again.

> *For such men are false apostles, deceitful workmen, masquerading as apostles of Christ. And no wonder, for Satan himself masquerades as an angel of light.*
>
> II CORINTHIANS 11:13–14

The doctor introduced John-Roger to the head of Chilean television. After a few minutes of playing interpreter as the two exchanged pleasantries, the physician had to excuse himself for a moment. Later, John-Roger told the physician that the head of Chilean television wanted John-Roger to move to Chile and become the host of the popular morning talk show. As John-Roger spoke no Spanish and the head of Chilean television spoke no English, the physician wondered how this remarkably unlikely offer had been communicated. He let it pass, and the subject was never brought up again by either John-Roger or the Chilean television chief.

The dark forces certainly tested the physician when John-Roger called him on the phone and said that he had "just channeled through Spirit" the following affirmations. John-Roger wanted the physician to translate them into Spanish for the seminar that evening. The physician dutifully copied down the affirmations in English, and told John-Roger he would get right on it. That evening during the seminar, John-Roger spoke the affirmations again, claiming he had recently received them from Spirit, and the physician read his translation of them. The next day, the physician received a book in the mail from a friend in the United States. The note accompanying the book said that the friend had sent a copy of the book to John-Roger, too, and the friend thought the physician might enjoy reading it. In the book were the same affirmations, word-for-word, in precisely the same order that John-Roger had "channeled through Spirit" the day before.

In March 1981, the dark forces made an extraordinary test of the physician's faith. He was dining with John-Roger and five of John-Roger's staff members in a small coastal town in Colombia. At the conclusion of the dinner, the proprietor of the restaurant brought a special gift: seven glasses of the locally produced liqueur. John-Roger proclaimed that no one at the table should drink, as they had so much spiritual work to do the next day, but that it would be rude to send the drinks back. He said he would drink them all, because he could "transmute" the alcohol as it "passed his lips." That way, no one would have the "unstabilizing influence" of alcohol, and the proprietor would not be offended. John-Roger downed all seven drinks as though they *were* water.

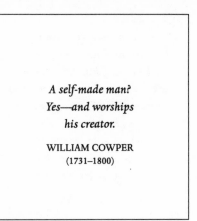

A self-made man? Yes—and worships his creator.

WILLIAM COWPER
(1731–1800)

Soon, however, as they took a walk along the beach, John-Roger's behavior became much more, shall we say, flamboyant. His behavior was not that of someone who had just drunk seven small glasses of Evian.

John-Roger bragged about how far he had come in only a decade—from high school English teacher to the absolute ruler of a half-dozen nonprofit organizations that affected the lives of tens of thousands. He talked of how the major institutions had failed humanity, and how those institutions had to be replaced by better systems—specifically, John-Roger's systems. But first, the old institutions must come down.

"We will destroy the church, the state, and the university," proclaimed John-Roger.

"You mean we will send our Love and Light into those institutions," the physician clarified, "and *transform* the church, the state, and the university."

"No," said John-Roger firmly, "we will *destroy* them."

Within a few months, the physician saw the techniques by which John-Roger destroyed. John-Roger began sending some of his people to meet directly with the leaders the physician had introduced him to. The physician was neither invited to nor notified of these meetings. Others of the physician's leaders were invited to meetings in the United States. He heard that John-Roger was using these meetings to discredit him and set up John-Roger's own independent network in South America.

Then, an even more telling blow: Insight was introduced in South America. The physician was hardly "in charge"; in fact, some of his most powerful and loyal students were enrolling his other students in Insight seminars. They answered only to Insight International, Santa Monica, California.

> *I have my self-respect*
> *as much as you,*
> *a lord and gentleman: with me*
> *your violence will be to no purpose,*
> *your wealth will have no weight,*
> *your words will have*
> *no power to deceive me,*
> *nor your sighs or tears*
> *to soften me.*
>
> CERVANTES

Insight was billed as *superior* to the seminars the doctor offered—Insight, after all, was founded by the *spiritual teacher* of the physician.

In the spring of 1982, John-Roger personally contacted the physician, cloaked him with yards of praise, and invited him to Los Angeles to receive the special MSIA award for all the incredible spiritual work he was doing in South America. The flattery worked. The one thousand cheering people at the MSIA/Insight Annual Conference—combined with John-Roger's ongoing praise—brought the physician back to the fold. Little did he know, he was not just being enfolded—he was about to be crumpled.

As it turned out, John-Roger only gave the physician an MSIA award because there were a few key areas in South America in which John-Roger needed connections. The physician had those connections, and John-Roger spiritually flattered the physician until he turned over to his reinstated spiritual teacher whatever the teacher wanted.

In 1983, John-Roger began another tour of South America. This time he openly denounced the workshops given by the physician, and recommended that everyone take Insight and subscribe to MSIA Discourses instead.

Furious and deeply hurt, the physician confronted John-Roger in his suite at the Bogota Hilton. The physician told John-Roger he was shocked by the depth of his betrayal—how could anyone promising Love and Light be so dishonest and deceptive?

John-Roger calmly explained that the physician's opinion was no longer important—not to John-Roger, not to John-Roger's staff, and not to the physician's former students. John-Roger explained how he had systematically taken over the physician's entire network, key person after key person. Now they all answered to John-Roger due to his higher spiritual connections (which the physician told the students John-Roger had), and no longer to the physician, who merely had temporal medical authority. Insight would be taught in place of the physician's workshops, and soon not just the leaders, but all of the physician's students would be worshiping

John-Roger as God.

"But I introduced you to these people as my spiritual teacher," the physician attested, too numb to take in all that John-Roger had just told him, "How could you betray me?"

John-Roger shrugged and made a face that seemed to communicate: "Well, ain't that just too damn bad?" John-Roger gestured toward the expansive view of Bogota from his twenty-second-story suite. "You might as well just jump out the window now," he said coolly.

> Believe it, my lord,
> in mine own direct knowledge,
> without any malice,
> but to speak of him as my kinsman,
> he's a most notable coward,
> an infinite and endless liar,
> an hourly promise-breaker,
> the owner of no one good quality
> worthy your lord's entertainment.
>
> SHAKESPEARE

The physician left, and it was a while before the full impact of the shock hit him: John-Roger had performed a *coup d'etat* and a *coup de grace* in the same stroke.

One departed staff member regrets ever having taken John-Roger to see *Evita* in the first place.

Get out your crayons to get the full effect of this photo. For some reason, the eyes, inside the nostril, and the exposed portion of the teeth in this black & white photo turned bright orange-red. Hmmmm . . .

CHAPTER TWENTY-ONE
God's Money—Tax-Free

> Howard Hughes was able to afford
> the luxury of madness,
> like a man who not only thinks
> he is Napoleon but hires
> an army to prove it.
>
> TED MORGAN

AUGUST 1994. As of this writing, John-Roger has available for his pleasure:

- Four houses (a mansion on West Adams Boulevard once owned by Busby Berkeley, a three-bedroom house on the largest piece of undeveloped land overlooking Lake Arrowhead, a secluded 6,000-square-foot house on six acres in fashionable Mandeville Canyon, and a four-bedroom designer home in the hills north of Santa Barbara with sweeping vistas of national parklands); several dozen vehicles; an office building in Santa Monica, taking up more than half a block of prime Wilshire Boulevard frontage twenty-one blocks from the beach

- A 140-acre horse ranch—complete with forty-or-so horses—nestled (if 140 acres can ever nestle) in the Santa Barbara mountains where the likes of Jane Fonda and Ronald Reagan have had ranches (Owning ranches the size of the Ponderosa obviously transcends political differences.)

- A professional television production center, with a video crew that follows him around the world to record his every public utterance

> Clergyman, *n.* *A man who*
> *undertakes the management*
> *of our spiritual affairs*
> *as a method of bettering*
> *his temporal ones.*
>
> AMBROSE BIERCE

- A full-time staff that ranges from thirty to fifty people whose sole function is to cater to John-Roger's every whim

- His own personal travel agency, and the freedom to take off at a moment's notice for any point in the world to do "the Traveler's work." (The Bahamas, as we all know, has need of a spiritual awakening, as has Cancun and, on many occasions, Hawaii.)

Not bad for a man who, decades ago, took a vow of poverty.

His secret? Put everything you own in the name of the Church of the Movement of Spiritual Inner Awareness, the Institute for Individual and World Peace, or any of the other nonprofit, tax-exempt organizations you control—*and keep that control.*

John-Roger's use of God's money reminds me of two old stories.

Story one concerns three clergymen who were discussing how they divided the weekly collection. The first said he draws a line on the ground, stands on the line, throws the money in the air, what lands on the right side is God's and what lands on the left side is his. The second clergyman said he draws a circle on the ground, stands in the circle, throws the money in the air, what lands in the circle is God's and what lands outside the circle is his. The third clergyman said he had an easier system: he throws the money in the air, what God wants He takes . . . .

Story two is of a man who arrives at a hotel and is told there are absolutely no rooms available. "If the president of the United States came," the man asks, "would there be a room for him?" "Of course there would," the desk clerk replies. "Well, he's not coming," the man says. "Give me his room."

Essentially, John-Roger collects money for God, and if God ever shows up and asks for it, John-Roger will give it to Him (or whatever's left of it). Until then, John-Roger feels perfectly free to spend God's money on anything his little aorta desires—being God's closest living relative and all.

Oh, yes: did I mention he gets all this tax free? Well, *of course*, he should get it tax free: it's not fair to tax holy men for the costs of going about doing God's business. Yes, executives often use corporate condos, cars, and staff for personal use, but at least the *corporation* is paying corporate income tax. All of John-Roger's organizations

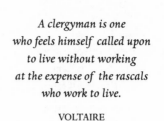

A clergyman is one
who feels himself called upon
to live without working
at the expense of the rascals
who work to live.

VOLTAIRE

have a 501(c)3 tax-exempt status—among the most exempt of all IRS tax-exempt categories. Even the *president* doesn't have that status.

John-Roger has not even filed a personal income tax return since 1971.

But don't worry—the government hasn't suffered: all the taxes that John-Roger and his cohorts have not paid since 1971 were made up for by increased tax rates to people like you and me.

Although John-Roger demands impeccable honesty from anyone who gets close to his—excuse me, the *Church's*—money, and although he insists that goods or services from outside vendors live up to every last comma of the contract, John-Roger runs the financial side of his various organizations in the management style that is commonly called "fast and loose."

Take the travel agency, for example. While Esprit Travel is, technically, open to the public, its real function is to get *for John-Roger* the many discounts, perks, VIP treatments, and outright gifts travel agencies generally receive. John-Roger, John Morton—and just about any Movement staff person who's willing to pay for the printing, has business cards with the Esprit logo and the title "travel agent" emblazoned under their names. (John-Roger, ever on the lookout for a little one-upsmanship, claims to be not just a travel *agent*, but the *owner* of a travel agency.)

In fact, it's all a sham. While not technically illegal, it is nonetheless thoroughly dishonest. The reason airlines, resorts, hotels, car rental companies, and the rest give legitimate travel agents the very best at the lowest conceivable rates (sometimes free) is because these companies want the travel agents to go back and book their customers. While Esprit Travel occasionally organizes *highly*

> When morality
> comes up against profit,
> it is seldom
> that profit loses.
>
> SHIRLEY CHISHOLM

profitable "travel with the Traveler" tours, the most seductive and expensive sales perks available are completely wasted on him because John-Roger *is not a travel agent.*

Before doing one of our *Larry King Live* appearances together, I checked into the hotel at which John-Roger was staying. I had stayed at the hotel before, but this time I was whisked to the concierge level where, lo and behold, there was an actual concierge. I didn't even have to check in. The hotel didn't ask for an imprint of my credit card. I was shown around the concierge floor lounge: a sort of large colonial-American-meets-classic-French-mahogany-tastefully-overstuffed-expensive-floral-designs room with free eats and drinks around the clock.

The eats were real classy eats, too: like those little sandwiches that don't have any crusts and are *so* refined you're not suppose to eat them with your fingers, and mounds of fresh fruit—specifically everything that was out of season and had to be flown in at great expense—and chunks of real Roquefort cheese the size of the slabs of mozzarella on the tables at Mama Leone's, everything seemed to be covered in caviar, and there were big bowls of mixed nuts everywhere *with no peanuts.*

In addition to all this, I got a room. I was personally escorted to my room (nay, suite) by an assistant manager—a woman of such charm, sophistication, and refinement, I was quite convinced Washington had not seen the likes of her since Jacqueline Kennedy left town.

She opened the door and, miracle of miracles, my luggage was already there. This place wasn't a suite; it was an *apartment.* On the antique tables that overpopulated the living room were gifts—gifts from the hotel: a bouquet of flowers here, a basket of fruit there, a bottle of wine right over here. ("Would Larry King be *really* mad at me if I didn't show up?" I wondered.) The bathroom had more white marble than Cecil B. deMille's mausoleum and was larger than the entire room I had last time I stayed at this hotel.

What did I do, I wondered, to deserve all this? Although I'd been a guest on Larry King's radio show before, this was the first time I was a guest on his *television* show. Maybe they were hoping I might casually mention to Larry on the air that I was staying at this fabulous hotel. (Hell, for this kind of treatment, I'd plug a Motel 6.)

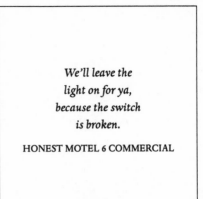

We'll leave the light on for ya, because the switch is broken.

HONEST MOTEL 6 COMMERCIAL

A plate of warm chocolate chip cookies; the valet arriving to personally make sure that every place on my clothes that should have creases had creases, and nowhere else; and a bottle of champagne later, the answer was revealed: when John-Roger checked in, he told them that I was a travel agent working for his company.

Well, if this was the style to which I planned to become accustomed, I would have to get a lot richer a lot faster—or fork over fifteen dollars to have Esprit business cards printed:

Peter McWilliams

TRAVEL AGENT

CO-OWNER*

Somehow, although the opportunity was there, I could never bring myself to become another bogus Esprit Travel agent. The people were trying *so hard* to get some of that Beverly Hills, 90210 travel money booked into their hotel. I have no problem with people being nice while trying to get out of me what I potentially can give, but when there's absolutely no chance that I can give it to them, I draw the line. (Usually.)

Once John-Roger told me, casually, in front of several other people, he was insured by two insurance companies, each of them covering only eighty percent of incurred medical costs. He told me he submitted duplicate receipts for the same medical proce-

*If I can make him a co-author, he can make me a co-owner.

> *Money is the*
> *fruit of evil*
> *as often as*
> *the root of it.*
>
> HENRY FIELDING

dure to both companies, so he ends up *making* money every time he gets sick. (Perhaps this accounts for his chronic ill health.) I thought, he might have been testing me, to see if I would jump in and ask for more details, revealing myself to be a fundamentally dishonest person. Or maybe the test was to see whether or not I would challenge him on a shabby—and probably illegal—activity. Gee: the lady or the tiger? I did neither. Looking back, however, I see his comment for what it was: a run-of-the-mill John-Roger business tip.

A perfect example of John-Roger's complete disrespect for the law ("Laws are either seasonal or legislative," he is fond of saying, as though that *explains* something) are his actions on the piece of property John Donnelley-Morton named Windermere. The property was owned by a widow. John-Roger and Michael Feder "negotiated" with her over a protracted period of time (pressure-release; pressure-release). They basically preyed upon the woman's loneliness until she sold John-Roger the property for approximately half its appraised value. The purpose of buying the property was (a) because John-Roger wanted to ride horses; (b) although retreats were very profitable for MSIA, John-Roger still resented paying other organizations for the use of their facilities, so Windermere was to become the permanent retreat ground for MSIA; and (c) John-Roger wanted to ride horses.

The property sits on a mountainside in an ecologically fragile area, bordered primarily by state forests. The handful of neighbors live in modest houses. Everyone living on the mountainside is well aware of the privilege—but also the responsibility—of living in such an environmentally delicate location.

Well, along comes John-Roger in his new cowboy look, with a rip-roarin' Wild West attitude about "his" land and an environmental awareness that was forged in the desolate coal mining country of Utah. Here he was, itchin' to build himself a retreat center, and what does he find? *God-damn zoning laws!* He was incensed, righteously indignant, and infinitely superior—an attitude that *no one* does better than John-Roger (now that Clifton Webb is dead).

The property had an agricultural zoning so that it might be

used, as many people in the Santa Monica mountains do, to raise horses (which, in limited quantities, help rather than hurt the ecosystem). The property already had a perfectly fine ranch-style house, and water enough for the house and the horses. If John-Roger had only practiced what he claims to be the first law of Spirit—acceptance—

> *I never could believe*
> *that Providence had sent a few men*
> *into the world, ready booted*
> *and spurred to ride,*
> *and millions ready saddled*
> *and bridled to be ridden.*
>
> RICHARD RUMBOLD

and used the property in a way that would be "for the highest good of all concerned," he could have used Windermere to keep and ride his horses, with a few fund-raising picnics each year (so the MSIA contributors—who are paying for it all—might get *some* tangible benefits for donating so much money). But, no: John "Duke" Roger had a hankerin' to build—*and build he would!*

The first problem—and a very serious problem in the semi-arid climate of the Santa Barbara mountains—was water. There was simply not enough water on the property to support the hundreds of people who would be staying there during retreats. So, John-Roger bought a well-drilling machine. They poked a hole in the ground and—don't that beat all?—*water.* General jubilation throughout MSIA. Yes, this truly was a miracle of biblical proportions—at least within the proportions of John-Roger's mind:

> The Lord answered Moses, "Walk on ahead of the people. Take with you some of the elders of Israel and take in your hand the staff with which you struck the Nile, and go. I will stand there before you by the rock at Horeb. Strike the rock, and water will come out of it for the people to drink." (Exodus 17:5–6)

And, of course:

> Jesus answered, "Everyone who drinks this water will be thirsty again, but whoever drinks the water I give him will never thirst. Indeed, the water I give him will become in him a spring of water welling up to eternal life. (John 4:13–15)

John-Roger ignored the eternal water, but became obsessed with the temporal water. The well-drilling machine became a razor in a monkey's paw: hole after hole was poked into the mountainside. Water, water everywhere.

"You see?" John Donnelley-Morton observed proudly, "when I

> They would deceive God
> and those who do believe;
> but they deceive only themselves
> and they do not perceive.
> In their hearts is a sickness,
> and God has made them
> still more sick,
> and for them is grievous woe
> because they lied.
>
> KORAN

first saw this land, there was no water here. Then I named it Windermere—which means the place where waters gather—and suddenly we have more water than we know what to do with. I named it what it was not, and it became that."

Alas, John-Roger was not happy that John Morton claimed the Miracle of the Wells for himself. John-Roger, however, knew that he would eventually receive full credit. (John-Roger had an unerring way of arranging that.)

Meanwhile, while John-Roger was filling ornamental ponds at Windermere with all that "excess" water, the water table for the entire mountainside was dropping fast. Nearby property owners found that wells they had successfully used for thirty years had to be drilled deeper. Others were getting mud in their drinking water.

The neighbors complained to John-Roger. To no avail. The neighbors then complained to the authorities, including the fire marshal, claiming—quite accurately—that a significantly lowered water table might prove disastrous in attempts to fight the brush fires that were an ever-present danger of the area.

John-Roger, with characteristic generosity, said the neighbors were welcome to pump water out of his pond, should the need arise. There was, after all, *lots* of water on Windermere.

The neighbors drilled their wells deeper and uneasily watched to see what was coming next from Wild Bill J-R. They didn't have long to wait. Even with all that water, those dang-blasted varmints who issued the building permits *still* wouldn't let John-Roger build his city in the desert.

Six-gun Roger went lookin' for a loophole.*

---

*John-Roger is one of the best loophole finders around. If he can't find 'em, then he goes to his full-time, on-staff lawyer, she pulls out her magnifying glass, and takes a look. If she can't find 'em, he goes to one of those highfalutin Century City lawyers. They have an electron microscope. They'll find a loophole even if they have to find it in the molecular structure of the paper the law is written on. But these Century City fellers are awful high priced, so he don't go there too often.

John-Roger found his loop-hole. It turns out that, since the property was zoned for agricultural use, John-Roger could put up a *barn*. So he went out an' bought the biggest, ugliest, prefab, metal, pseudo–Quonset hut barn money could buy. They had a barn-raising party (lots of free labor), a real celebration—at which John-Roger, following Biblical precedent, took credit for the water:

*The fawning, sneaking,
and flattering hypocrite,
that will do or be anything,
for his own advantage.*

EDWARD STILLINGFLEET

> On the last and greatest day of the Feast, Jesus stood and said in a loud voice, "If anyone is thirsty, let him come to me and drink. Whoever believes in me, as the Scripture has said, streams of living water will flow from within him. (John 7:37–38)

So, the barn went up—the most gawd-awful eyesore on that beautiful mountainside—and as soon as the inspectors had approved it for livestock, it was clandestinely carpeted, air-conditioned, wired for sound and video, and furnished with a hundred chairs.

It wasn't exactly John-Roger's dream retreat center—in fact it was *nobody's* dream retreat center except, possibly, Mr. Ed's—but a hundred people could sit in air-conditioned comfort and sleep on the carpeted floor. For those who wanted a bit more privacy at night, it turned out that the horse stalls could sleep two very comfortably. And although Windermere lacked the creature comforts of "other people's" retreat grounds—like a kitchen or flush toilets—people came to the retreats anyway and paid the same amount of money (about $750 a week) as they did in one of those citified-retreat-grounds retreats.

In 1993, however, there were dark clouds looming over Windermere—and not the sort of clouds that might bring enough rain to get the water table back up to where it belonged.

A task force reported the preliminary results of its five-year, multimillion-dollar study of future land use for Santa Barbara County. The report was exhaustive. Over the five years, environmentalists (on one side) and developers (on the other) had battled it out, square foot by square foot, over what would be preserved as the seashore-wetland-plain-mountain-and-wildlife habitat unique

> *If you just pay attention
> to the physical things of your life,
> you tend to get caught up in them.
> And most people who get caught
> in the physical things
> just aren't very happy.
> They have a lot of turmoil.*
>
> JOHN-ROGER

to Santa Barbara County, on one hand, and how much development would be permitted, on the other.

The plan, approved at last by both sides, was given to the five-member Santa Barbara City Council for ratification. The City Council made it clear: it would listen to all complaints (which came from roughly every landowner in Santa Barbara County), but it was highly unlikely that they were going to step in and mess with a plan put together over five years by ecologists, developers, geologists, city planners, and land-use professionals.

To which John-Roger replied, "They'll make a change for *me!*"

How could they thwart his plans for all those tract homes he could sell to the faithful who wanted to live on the "Traveler's land?" There was the plan for the elementary school, and the health-care center where the health-care professionals of the Movement could ply their trade (and use that enormous healing crystal John-Roger claims to be in a natural formation underground at Windermere), and the retail shops, and the restaurants, and a big neon sign at the top of the mountain proclaiming that the City on the Hill—John-RogerVille—has finally been built.

Well, upgrading agricultural zoning into spiritual-city zoning wasn't exactly what the land planning commission's task force had in mind. Windermere wouldn't be upzoned at all. In fact, Windermere was *downzoned* to "mountain wilderness." That meant no John-RogerVille, no retreat center—and they might even have to take down the barn.

John-Roger, refusing to accept the inevitable (that he owned one of the most pristine and beautiful horse ranches on either side of the Mississippi), went to work. A Santa Barbara lawyer was hired, one who understood the plight of the developer (which is the side on which John-Roger firmly fell) having his constitutional rights as a landowner taken from him by a bunch of dewy-eyed Monarch-butterfly lovers. John-Roger also hired a Santa Barbara PR firm to convince the Santa Barbara populace (and the five members of the Santa Barbara City Council) that John-Roger was not a wicked cult leader like David Koresh. Oh, no. John-Roger was a warm, happy, smiling cult leader—like Reverend Moon.

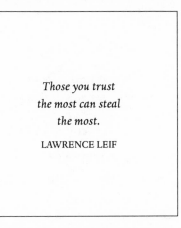

Those you trust the most can steal the most.

LAWRENCE LEIF

I got lassoed into the hey-Santa-Barbara-this-John-Roger-fellow's-a-real-nice-guy campaign. A plan was devised (not by me) to have the Santa Barbara Mental Health Association sponsor a lecture, the subject being "one of J-R's books." All costs of promoting and staging the event would be paid by the Institute for Individual and World Peace (one of John-Roger's less cult-sounding nonprofit, tax-exempt organizations), and *all* the proceeds would go to the Santa Barbara Mental Health Association.

I was given the honor of delivering the lecture because, frankly, John-Roger simply cannot give a speech to the general public. The only lectures he does are seminars, and these are almost always "closed seminars," which means someone must attend three John-Roger audio or video tape seminars (and prove it) before being allowed in. The rationale for this in official MSIA literature is so that one can familiarize oneself with the "vocabulary" specific to MSIA so that John-Roger doesn't have to define terms each time he gives a seminar. In fact, John-Roger is only comfortable enough to do an adequate job of lecturing when surrounded exclusively by people who already think he's terrific. In a standard, open-to-the-public lecture arena, John-Roger is useless, pathetic, embarrassing—like watching the worst moments of *The Gong Show.*

So, I gave the lecture to a sold-out audience, gave each of them a free copy of one of "J-R's books" (provided by me), signed autographs, and schmoozed for about 360 years after the lecture. (Meanwhile, John-Roger didn't even take the twenty-minute trip from his Santa Barbara house to the lecture hall to wish me good luck. Considering his feelings toward the Santa Barbara City Council, the land planning commission, the Santa Barbara building permit people, and the damned, soft-headed, liberal citizens of Santa Barbara, who won't let a man do on his own property what God says should be done, John-Roger might have benefited from the subject of the talk: *You Can't Afford the Luxury of a Negative*

Thought.)

> *All ambitions are lawful*
> *except those which climb upward*
> *on the miseries*
> *or credulities of mankind.*
>
> JOSEPH CONRAD

The lecture raised $6,000 for the Santa Barbara Mental Health Association—its largest single fund-raising event of the year—but John-Roger's shady reputation caught up with him again, and the organization politely but firmly refused any further contact with, or implied endorsement of, John-Roger.

Barbecues were scheduled at Windermere for the adjoining property owners so that everybody might get all neighbor-like and *together* petition the commission to let a few . . . dozen . . . modest-size buildings . . . and two or three real big ones . . . to be built in their secluded, quiet, rustic neighborhood.

Arianna Huffington did what she could do from behind the scenes. Michael Huffington, hot on the trail of the Republican nomination for the one California seat open in the U.S. Senate (a nomination which he won, by the way, after spending more than $8 million of his own money—pocket change), was not about to put his political parts on the line for John-Roger. Michael Huffington would *not* go down in California political history as the man who pulled strings to make John-RogerVille a reality. Besides, why doesn't John-Roger just go out and buy a mansion that's already built, behind high walls, the way Michael did, and *then* turn the damned thing into a retreat center and stop making so much fuss?

Arianna did what she could—a dinner here, a referral there, a well-placed phone call from time to time—but, ultimately, her husband's political future meant more to her than John-RogerVille, and she excused herself to spend more and more time on her husband's campaign.*

Finally, a desperate eleventh-hour plea was sent out to the

---

*As usual with Arianna, it was a smart move. She realized that her husband's political future was about as fragile as the ecosystem of the Santa Barbara mountains. If Michael had lost this primary, *he* could well have been put on the endangered (political) species list. He might then fall into the Tom Hayden Syndrome, (developed by Tom while he was married to Jane Fonda), which was described by Gore Vidal as "spending larger and larger amounts of money running for smaller and smaller office."

Southern California faithful: if at all possible, go to every Santa Barbara City Council meeting you can, sit in the audience, and quietly "hold the Light." (Translation: use whatever voodoo powers you can to change at least three of the council members' minds.)

> *A man of a right spirit is not a man of narrow and private views, but is greatly interested and concerned for the good of the community to which he belongs, and particularly of the city or village in which he resides.*
>
> JONATHAN EDWARDS

So we dropped everything we were doing (yes, I was part of that great northern migration from Los Angeles to Santa Barbara in the morning and back again in the evening, certain to be referred to in the illuminated manuscripts of MSIA, as the Great Pilgrimage to the Council of the Infidels). We sat for *hours* on uncomfortable wooden seats. There we were: John-Roger, John Donnelley-Morton, the Presidency, and every staff person from any J-R organization who was not doing something essential—like keeping the horses from unauthorized mating. We filled the City Council room, and we did it for days. Occasionally we got to raise our hands, and on one particularly exciting occasion, we even got to *stand*, in support of *Windermere!*

It didn't work. Nothing worked. John-Roger had pulled out every stop, spared no expense, called in every favor, and marshaled every material resource within his power in a concentrated, long-term, relentless pursuit of a single goal: to get three of the five Santa Barbara City Council members to let him build his goddamn retreat center.

It failed.

Miserably. Embarrassingly. Completely.

Did John-Roger give up then? Are you kidding? He hired more attorneys and is suing *everybody*.

In the halls of justice in John-Roger's mind, I can see the inmates of his maximum-security prison: the five members of the Santa Barbara City Council, those turds at the building permit office, every environmentalist in Santa Barbara County, all the intolerant neighbors, and me. (After this book, I will have a special place of honor in the dungeon.)

⚖️ ⚖️ ⚖️

John-Roger thinks he's privileged—more privileged than anyone else on earth. Consequently, he's *entitled* to what he wants when he wants it, and the ends always justify the means.

"Would you lie for Jesus? Would you cheat for Jesus? Would you steal for Jesus?" John-Roger might ask. If someone were willing to do it for Jesus, then John-Roger expected the same—if not more.

But whatever illicit methods John-Roger might use to avoid *spending* money, they do not compare with the evil inherent in John-Roger's methods of *getting* money.

At the basis of it is John-Roger's fundamental deception: "I am God, God wants some money, hand it over."

A primary teaching of MSIA is *tithing*—giving ten percent of everything you receive to MSIA. "Pay God first," John-Roger admonishes. John-Roger borrowed tithing from the Mormon church, but claims the idea was given to him directly by Melchizedek, a priest who mysteriously appears in the Bible, and everyone starts forking over ten percent to him. Suddenly, any looting, pillaging, or plundering the great and powerful wanted to do was God-ordained—providing Melchizedek was given ten percent of the booty. Here we have Melchizedek's first biblical appearance:

> After Abram [Abraham] returned from defeating Kedorlaomer and the kings allied with him, the king of Sodom came out to meet him in the Valley of Shaveh (that is, the King's Valley).
>
> Then Melchizedek king of Salem brought out bread and wine. He was priest of God Most High, and he blessed Abram saying,
>
> "Blessed be Abram by God Most High, Creator of heaven and earth.
>
> And blessed be God Most High, who delivered your enemies into your hand."*

---

*Sounds *exactly* like John-Roger when he's trying to get money from a powerful person.

Then Abram gave him a tenth of everything. (Genesis 14:17–20)

Or, consider this New Testament offering:

> We have this hope as an anchor for the soul, firm and secure. It enters the inner sanctuary behind the curtain, where Jesus, who went before us, has entered on our behalf. He has become a high priest forever, in the order of Melchizedek.
>
> First, his name means "king of righteousness"; then also, "king of Salem" means "king of peace." Without father or mother, without genealogy, without beginning of days or end of life, like the Son of God he remains a priest forever.
>
> Just think how great he was: Even the patriarch Abraham gave him a tenth of the plunder! Now the law requires the descendants of Levi who become priests to collect a tenth from the people—that is, their brothers—even though their brothers are descended from Abraham. (Hebrews 6:19–20, 7:2–5)

> *What John-Roger and MSIA happen to need to spread the teaching is money. It's the present day spiritual medium of exchange . . . John-Roger and his staff do have to live— and if they are to perform their services, they need money to do so.*
>
> MSIA

Is it any wonder John-Roger claims to be the current earthly leader of the Melchizedek priesthood?

As soon as tithing revenues for MSIA topped $2,000,000 per year, it became one of the more sacred "Teachings of the Traveler." Giving your money to J-R *is* giving your money to God, whether one is seeding or tithing.

According to Movement rhetoric, tithing is giving of the harvest, but *seeding* is planting the crops. And what does one seed with? Prayer? Affirmation? Devotion? Don't be silly: around J-R you seed with *money*.

Whereas tithing is fairly precise, seeding is something of a wild card. A person can seed for anything he or she wants—including intangibles such as health, personal knowledge of God, a hot new relationship—but everything you want must be reduced to a *monetary value*. Comments such as "priceless," or "beyond value," "a hell of a lot more than I've got," are unacceptable. One must come up with a *dollar amount* for everything one is seeding for.

Then (and here's where the wild card comes in) you give MSIA from *one to one hundred percent* of the monetary amount you have placed on the items you desire—the more you want it, the more *you* pay. By giving in double- or even triple-digit percentages, you are not only increasing your chances of getting what you want; you also are letting God know (wink, wink) that you want it sent Federal Express. (And overnight delivery costs more than two-day.)

So, if your father is diagnosed with a life-threatening illness, and his life is worth $50,000 to you; if you want him to get better right away, you will donate $50,000 to MSIA. You *could* donate one percent—a mere $500—but then the chances for a *complete recovery* would be dicey, and it might take so long for the cure to get to him that by the time it does, he'd already be dead.

When asking for material things—like money—it's suggested you start from where you are and build up. For example, if you want a million dollars, but only have $100 for a seeding, seed for $1,000 with the $100 (a ten-percent seed). When the $1,000 comes in, use the full amount to re-seed for $10,000. When the $10,000 comes in, use the full amount to re-seed (or, in MSIA terminology, "Let it ride!") for $100,000. When the $100,000 comes in, well, you get the idea. You'll have a million dollars in no time—*as long as you don't break the cycle.* When you get your million dollars, you, of course, tithe on the full amount, plus you can offer a double-tithe to show God you're really, *really* thankful, and you can throw in an additional ten percent for "first fruits" (don't ask), and, with what you have left, just how much is the health and safety of your family worth to you? Yes, it's seeding time again.

In addition to all this seeding and tithing there are, naturally, *donations.* Everything done around John-Roger is paid for with "suggested donations." If you don't make the suggested donation, you're not going to get whatever J-R is dishing out, but the fees are called donations nonetheless. This is another one of those tax loopholes: the person buying the book, tape, retreat, and so on, gets to "donate" the full amount to a nonprofit, tax-exempt organization. If material things around John-Roger had a *price*—like everything at K-Mart, for example—then people purchasing the products could not deduct their "donation" from their income tax because they received some *value* for the money they spent. Calling everything a donation makes it just that much easier for devotees to keep as much money as they can from the tax man so that it can go to its rightful owner, God.

> The money asked
> for anything in MSIA
> is a suggested donation,
> not a charge.
> An individual is free to give
> only if he chooses.
>
> MSIA

Then there are fund-raisers. Everything John-Roger attends personally is a fund-raiser. It's called a fund-raiser because at fund-raisers you can charge exorbitant amounts of money for the same old stuff that used to cost far less. A plain, vanilla, John-Roger live seminar, for example, usually costs about $10. Call it a fund-raiser, however, and you're charged $100. Dinner at John-Roger's house is worth about $3.95, tip included. Call it a fund-raiser, and it's $5,000 a plate. (Nice plates, though: rented.)

And then there are retreats. Among the most popular are the Peace Awareness Trainings, or PATs. Here people pay $750 for a dorm room, mediocre food, and the right to sit opposite someone, bolt upright in a straight chair, arms and legs uncrossed, knees touching, maintaining eye contact, and being asked over and over: "Who are you?" The only thing more fun than answering the question, "Who are you?" is asking it—which you have the privilege of doing precisely half the time. After a week of this self-inflicted torture (pressure) *anything* in the "outer world" is utterly magnificent (release).

But they line up for the PAT trainings. There are three of them: PAT I, PAT II, and PAT III, one indistinguishable from another. And then there's PAT IV, which is a month long, and has a suggested donation of $10,000, which includes an excursion to visit every single tomb in Egypt, including ones that have been empty for 3,000 years and ones that were just filled last week. I am not kidding. PAT IV includes a guided tour of Cairo's astonishing "City of the Dead," which is acre upon acre of little houses in which the dead "live" and are visited by friends and family. The visitors bring wine, food, and make a night of it. Most nights, the City of the Dead is the liveliest place in Cairo.

And then there are all those dusty tombs that seem to be in the desert somewhere. (Anything in Egypt more than a mile from the Nile is "in the desert somewhere.") You travel all morning, in

> *Religion, like water, may be free,*
> *but when they pipe it to you,*
> *you've got to help*
> *pay for the piping.*
> *And the piper!*
>
> ABIGAIL VAN BUREN

120-degree heat, in vehicles that look like the studio-tour trams at Universal City, pulled by a tractor which moves at about two miles an hour, to arrive by noon, only to disturb some sleeping bats. But if the tomb is dull and reeks of bat guano, take heart: you can always look forward to the afternoon trip back across the desert. After a dozen or so of these desert "temples," my PAT IV group began singing to the tune of "Guantanamera," "One tomb too many/Oh, we've seen one tomb too many/One tomb too many/Oh, we've seen one tomb too many."

While in Israel and Egypt, of course, there's plenty of time for individual sightseeing, shopping, and interacting with the indigenous peoples. NOT! Every bloody minute you're not visiting the Pharaonic-Bat Hilton is spent doing, yes, *PAT Processes!* Sitting in a kibbutz or on a Nile River cruise boat, bolt upright, hands and legs uncrossed, knees touching, eye contact, asking or being asked, "Who are you?" for hours on end.

Meanwhile, back home, the fund-raising continues. There are the Special Fund-Raising Programs. These are little ditties thought up by individuals, who, as volunteers, manage the entire program and turn over every penny to John-Roger. There's the Adopt-a-Horse Program, in which you become responsible for the financial upkeep of a horse—or as large a part of a horse as you can afford. You might even get to ride your adopted steed—the horse's health and schedule permitting. Then there was the twenty-five-dollar jigsaw puzzle of one of the ponds at Windermere. That was a big hit. And then there are any number of one-person entertainments or musicales in which the sincere amateur artisans of the Movement try to sell what they haven't been able to give away in years. And let's not forget the Easter offering, the Christmas offering, John-Roger's birthday galas, banquets celebrating the day John-Roger inherited the Mystical Traveler Consciousness, pleading letters,* and per-

---

*My favorite was the one written after Windermere donations slowed down. It stated in heavy, guilt-producing prose that Windermere (a horse ranch, for heaven's sake) was John-Roger's *personal ministry*, and how often do we get to help John-Roger *directly* with his *personal ministry*? Not often, I suppose, because the donations came pouring in again.

sonal gifts ("You know what J-R would really like . . . ?").

Did I mention auctions? Well, there are auctions. These usually happen at the end of week-long retreats and are personally led by either John-Roger, or, more often, John Donnelley-Morton (but while John-Roger is in the room to keep the bidding frenzy going). After a week of

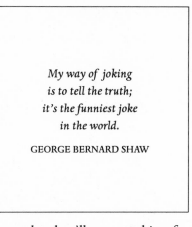

My way of joking is to tell the truth; it's the funniest joke in the world.

GEORGE BERNARD SHAW

sense deprivation, people are so punchy they'll pay anything for anything. Snickers bars go for thousands of dollars (no kidding). Anything "specially blessed by John-Roger" fetches considerably more than the same item unblessed. Before the barn was built, the whole thing was auctioned off, piece by piece—you could buy a horse stall, or the concrete foundation, or a light switch. I paid $5,200 for an "automatic fly elimination system," whatever the hell that was.*

Whatever isn't good enough for auctions ends up in yard sales. Yard sales consist of any junk anyone in the Movement wants to donate (for a tax deduction, of course) plus whatever gifts John-Roger has been given that he didn't like and couldn't get a refund on. I once gave John-Roger a signed, numbered, original silk-screen print of Robert Indiana's famous LOVE poster. (The one in which the L and the O are stacked on top of the V and the E, and the O is tipping over, being so intoxicated by love.) When I gave it to John-Roger, I explained to him the silk-screen's popularity (they even made a postage stamp out of it), and its rarity in the art world. It was worth several thousand dollars. I'm told it sold at a yard sale for $5.

⚖ ⚖ ⚖

In the past twenty-four years, John-Roger's organizations have done *nothing* for the poor, homeless, needy, sick, the environment, or the world at large. The Heartfelt Foundation, dedicated to the selfless service of those less fortunate, is a joke. It's essentially one

---

*I gave him the money for this several years ago. It has not been purchased, much less installed. I wonder where my $5,200 went.

person's service project (God bless him), and the bulk of its activity is delivering to a soup kitchen in South Central Los Angeles the canned food and used clothing MSIA ministers in Los Angeles happen to bring to their monthly meeting. This Heartfelt service doesn't cost John-Roger—or any of his organizations—a dime.

Not only do John-Roger's organizations completely ignore the needs of the world outside them; they do a miserable job of taking care of their own. In 1993, one woman—a devoted member of the Movement for twenty years, minister, initiate, who spent infinite amounts of time volunteering at John-Roger's various organizations—was about to become homeless, literally homeless. Do you think MSIA let her have a room at PRANA, "the home of the Traveler?" Nah. Would they loan her some money, pay for psychological counseling, job training, or even give her some food? Nope. I took it upon myself to do something about it and ask people in the Movement to help her. From the twenty-five ministers attending the "free" Abundance, Prosperity, and Riches Seminar (which was only free because the entire four-week course was an unabashed recruitment for the seeding and tithing programs), she collected a total of $20 (all of which came from the same person). She then overcame her pride and embarrassment and made an astonishingly touching plea to the attendees at the monthly L.A. ministers' meeting. Only two people came up afterward to offer her any tangible support. (Although lots of people told her they were "holding the Light" for her.) My letter to John-Roger didn't help, either.

After years of giving, giving, giving to John-Roger's various organizations, this was the first time I had *asked* for anything, and I wasn't asking for myself, but for "a fellow minister and initiate" who was in genuine need. I was shocked, hurt, and infuriated by the appalling lack of response.

Looking back, though, I see that these people were not being petty or selfish—they had simply been bled dry. They had given as much as they could, and still their spiritual teacher—their direct link to God—kept asking for more, more, more. There was simply no room to even *hear* the plea from "one of their own." (Ironically, one of the reasons this woman was in such a financial mess was because she responded *too* generously to John-Roger's endless pleas for cash.)*

The same people who can
deny others everything
are famous for refusing themselves
nothing.

LEIGH HUNT
1784–1859

Whereas a portion of the tithings of the Mormon church go into a special account set aside to help the faithful in times of financial need, no such system exists in MSIA.

Anytime any "ordinary" devotee wants to do anything within any of the organizations, it either (a) costs something or (b) is "free," but the devotee is hit up for a donation. Even at ministers' meetings—which are run completely by volunteers—a donation is *still* requested.

⚖ ⚖ ⚖

Although John-Roger does not share *his* wealth, he shares a wealth of information with his ministers (almost everyone in MSIA is a minister) about how to keep more of the money they make. Like all good gurus, he does this by giving a powerful mystical command, such as "Presto chango!" or "Open sesame!"

John-Roger's wealth-building mantra: "Deduct it!"

As one of John-Roger's ministers, you have a God-given *right* to deduct from your income tax almost *anything* you spend money on—provided it's a "ministerial expense." What is a ministerial expense? Well, as a good minister, you minister wherever you go and while doing whatever you do, right? So, good ministers can deduct all that. As John-Roger explains in the MSIA *Handbook for Ministers of Light:*

> Why ordain you? Because it's legal. Legal protection to do certain works in the world according to law. And not only that, you have the Supreme Court and the United States Constitution on your side.

*This story has a happy ending: I got her to a psychiatrist, who got her on antidepressants, which helped her to do what she wanted to do for a long time: move to Phoenix. Last I heard, she was doing fine.

John-Roger knows well how to hide behind the constitutional guarantee of religious freedom. (I would say it's one of the few things of which he is truly an expert.) The IRS, he knows, will audit an *individual* or a *company* at the drop of an anonymous tip (which he has been known to drop against his enemies)— but a *minister* or a *church?* Far less likely.

> *Consequences,*
> *shmonsequences,*
> *as long as I'm rich.*
>
> DAFFY DUCK

The MSIA *Handbook for Ministers of Light* lists ten "possible items you might deduct." They are aren't so much "items" as they are *areas*—vast, all-inclusive expanses of loopholes stretching toward the horizon in all directions as far as the MSIA tax-attorneys can see. Loosely interpreted (which is the only kind of interpretation John-Roger teaches), it makes nearly *everything* a minister does deductible.

Take "automobile mileage to and from ministerial meetings, appointments, and functions." If you drive your car to the movies and, say, "plant a Light column" while waiting in line to buy popcorn, that would be a "ministerial appointment," wouldn't it? How many other places can you drive to "hold the Light" or do "prayer blessings"? Ski slopes could certainly use some Light. So could beaches and national parks and doughnut shops (although the police have the latter pretty well covered). In short: with a little creative imagination, you can deduct all car expenses.

You can deduct the "cost of periodicals, books or reference materials" as well as "office supplies, equipment, postage, secretarial expenses, etc." With your ordination comes a tax-free office, library, and reading room. Not bad.

Any classes you take—and your expenses to, at, and from them—are deductible: "All registration fees and costs at conventions, conferences, etc. . . . and the cost of educational classes to further your ministry." Well, what *doesn't* "further your ministry"? Horseback riding classes, for example, are essential: the head of your church may ask you to go riding some day, and it would be a ministerial *faux pas* to say, "J-R, I don't know how."

"Telephone expenses for professional calls . . ." As a professional, aren't *all* calls professional calls? *Certainly* keeping up with the MSIA rumor mill is essential to an effective MSIA ministry; that's at least eighty percent of a MSIA minister's phone bill right there.

You'd be surprised how much it costs to look this cheap.

DOLLY PARTON

". . . professional clothing (such as robes), and their cleaning and laundering." Robes. That's a laugh. The only robes MSIA ministers wear are bathrobes. The proper attire to do ministerial work is (you're ahead of me) *whatever you're wearing.* Therefore, all your clothes and cleaning thereof are deductible.

"The cost of entertainment of church groups and official visitors, including meals in your home." Translation: tax-free food, drink, and other *accoutrements* to merriment.

(I have this gnawing fear that I am making the MSIA ministry sound *absolutely irresistible.*)

"A portion of any real property you own if you irrevocably deed that portion to a tax-exempt religious organization." Give your house to MSIA and it becomes "church property." This means you pay no property taxes while you live there (ministers, of course, get to live on church property), and God gets it when you go. This also avoids inheritance tax. Such a deal.

"Gifts given by you as a minister to your parishioners." Certainly anyone worth getting a gift from you is a part of your parish.

And let's not forget: "The cost of having professional tax advice." Making all these deductions, sooner or later you may need a good deal of that.

All of this, of course, is not really a serious problem. I'm sorry I spent so much time on it. Even if we added in all the money and property John-Roger doesn't pay taxes on, it doesn't cost the rest of us more than, oh, a few cents each per year—less than a penny deducted by the IRS from each paycheck. This seems fair to me, considering all the good John-Roger and his ministers are out there doing for us all. (They *are* out there doing good, aren't they?)

⚖ ⚖ ⚖

> *Bulls can make money
> and bears can make money,
> but hogs just get
> slaughtered.*
>
> WALL STREET ADAGE

So, if the money and resources in the various organizations don't serve the world *outside* those organizations, and if those organizations don't serve the members *within* those organizations (unless they pay for each "service"), what do they spend all the money on?

John-Roger.

Everything in, on, around, and connected to these organizations is a personal project of John-Roger's. He's invested "God's money" in one cockamamie invention after another, lost it on gambling, and on playing the stock market (a variation of gambling, of course).

The inventions and companies in which "God" lost money (along with lots of "God's children," who invested at their spiritual teacher's recommendation) include a gas station, a "New Atlantis" community in the Bahamas, molded concrete buildings, Ever-Sol Domes (cheap housing made out of styrofoam), and fireproofing paint. John-Roger once gave his nephew $10,000 of God's money to help him start a business. He sends money to one of his sisters.

John-Roger also used God's money to buy a fortune in Krugerrands; he stashed it under his bed. Gold immediately plummeted to half what he paid for it, and it hasn't gone up since. (Oh well, all those Krugerrands radiate "golden healing energy" to "the Traveler's body." How nice.) He bought silver stocks. They dropped by more than fifty percent.

Take gambling. John-Roger is a fan of blackjack, but he loses so regularly that it's painfully clear his all-knowing spiritual powers do not extend to what's-the-next-card-gonna-be? John-Roger's own personal blackjack system involves all of his cohorts taking over an entire blackjack table. One intentionally "sacrifices himself" so that the others may win. For a while, John-Roger practiced this scheme endlessly and, when it was ready for the big test, he moved it to a casino, where it never quite worked as well as it did in the hotel room. A bit more of God's money was rendered unto Caesar's.

For a while in the late 1980s, the stock market fascinated him. He would use God's money to buy five thousand, ten thousand, twenty thousand shares of the most unstable stocks, based on obscure tips from unreliable sources. Often he just "played his hunch." He carried a laptop computer, which picked up the latest stock exchange prices. He opened it anywhere he was (airports, cabs, the back of training rooms, anywhere) and would buy and sell based on his own

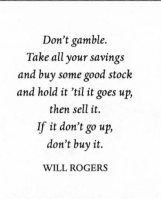

Don't gamble.
Take all your savings
and buy some good stock
and hold it 'til it goes up,
then sell it.
If it don't go up,
don't buy it.

WILL ROGERS

immutable investment strategy—which changed every hour. This nonsense cost "God" more than $1,500,000. He lost $688,000 in one month alone.

He spent more than $100,000 on a sauna and hot tub at his Mandeville house so that "initiates can come and relax." Shortly after it was built, he declared that people might get AIDS from it* and limited its use to himself and personally invited guests. (Some say it was just an expensive seduction tool.)

The list of John-Roger's personal extravagances is endless. I've already detailed some of his obsession with Windermere. That one continues. Now he's gotten litigious, and seems to be taking great fascination in suing people.

In short, the money John-Roger extorts from people in their genuine and sincere desire to know God is all funneled into various nonprofit, tax-exempt organizations, where John-Roger does what he jolly well wants to with it. He's like a spoiled child, and each of the organizations is a different playroom.

It's a travesty.

It's probably illegal, certainly immoral, unimaginatively manipulative, often fraudulent (all those bought-and-paid-for but entirely unkept spiritual promises), and a sacrilege. In collecting money in God's name and spending it on himself, John-Roger mocks God, and he mocks all those who sincerely seek a relationship with God in this lifetime.

---

*That depends on what they *do* in it, I suppose.

*To have $10,000 donated to their favorite charity, recipients of the John-Roger Founda-
tion Integrity Award had to pose for PR shots with the namesake. Here, Mother Teresa
qualifies for sainthood by enduring a photo session with John-Roger. The photo was
taken in a studio. The poor of Calcutta were added later.*

CHAPTER TWENTY-TWO

Integri-tee-hee-hee

> The nice thing about
> being a celebrity is that,
> if you bore people,
> they think it's their fault.
>
> HENRY KISSINGER

WHILE I was computer-book-publishing away (1982–1985), John-Roger had his heyday. Insight was booming, new initiates gathered like flies on cow pies, the money was rolling in, and there was hope, lots of hope, stretching as far as the heated imaginations of John-Roger's favorite sycophants could possibly imagine.

An umbrella organization was established to house all of John-Roger's nonprofit organizations. It was called—surprise, surprise—the John-Roger Foundation. An office building in Santa Monica was purchased as headquarters for various John-Roger Foundation organizations. This building was called, alternately, the Insight Building or the John-Roger Foundation Building (depending on who needed impressing about what when).

And then came that eruption of megalomania, thievery, and utter *lack* of integrity known as the Integrity Awards.

For years, Buckminster Fuller had planned to establish an International Integrity Day, on which integrity in all forms—personal, political, architectural, scientific, spiritual—could be celebrated. It was a dream he worked on long and hard, and he planned to leave it as a significant portion of his legacy.

As the *Encyclopædia Britannica* (no futurist-friendly *Whole Earth Catalog*, to be sure) evaluated Fuller's life:

> *We should stop kidding ourselves.*
> *We should let go of things*
> *that aren't true.*
> *It's always better*
> *with the truth.*
>
> R. BUCKMINSTER FULLER

Assessment. Fuller—architect, engineer, inventor, philosopher, author, cartographer, geomatrician, futurist, teacher, and poet—established a reputation as one of the most original thinkers of the second half of the 20th century. He was perhaps the first to attempt to develop, on a global basis, comprehensive, long-range technological and economic plans designed "to make man a success in Universe."

He conceived of man as a passenger in a cosmic spaceship—a passenger whose only wealth consists in energy and information. . . .

Integrity—appreciating what is whole, making whole what is not—was central to Buckminster Fuller's eighty-eight years of life.

Just as Fuller had gained enough momentum and it seemed as though his Integrity Day would become a reality at last, John-Roger stole it. He just plain, flat-out, stole it. John-Roger announced an Integrity Day, sponsored by the John Roger Foundation and the Integrity Institute (yet another new John-Roger nonprofit organization), and backed by the kind of organization, money, and publicity Buckminster Fuller simply did not have. In addition, John-Roger announced the Integrity Award—a pyramid-shaped,* crystal paperweight affair, which was all very attractive, *but* the real draw (bait) was the donation of $10,000 to the recipient's charity of choice.

What a scheme. What famous person could resist having $10,000 donated to his or her favorite charity in exchange for saying a few words of thanks—and, of course, getting photographed with John-Roger. To the namesake of the John-Roger Foundation, the latter was more important than the former. The photographs were used for the John-Roger-greatness-by-association campaign. The goal was to place J-R in the reflected glory of as many—and as many different—important personages as possible.

---

*The Integrity Award, in fact, looks *suspiciously* like a tetrahedron, which is the basic unit of Fuller's "Energetic-Synergetic geometry." Fuller's geodesic dome, for example, makes generous use of tetrahedrons. The Integrity Award, then, is a thievery of Fuller's integrity ideas *and* the symbol of his geometric discoveries.

The high point (low point) was John-Roger's appearance with Archbishop (then-Bishop) Desmond Tutu. Because the John-Roger Foundation had arranged for Archbishop Tutu's visit, when the *Today* show wanted to interview Archbishop Tutu, John-Roger was included (by John-Roger) as part of the deal. The televised results

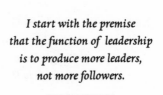

I start with the premise that the function of leadership is to produce more leaders, not more followers.

RALPH NADER

were beyond embarrassing. Even John-Roger's loyalists could only explain, "He must not have been feeling well."

The John-Roger Foundation set the official date for Integrity Day: September 24. That this just happened to be John-Roger's birthday is, of course, a coincidence.

Buckminster Fuller, when asked about John-Roger by a caller on Larry King's radio show, responded: "John-Roger is a spiritual guru who lacks integrity." The remark infuriated John-Roger. When Fuller died a short while later, John-Roger announced that Fuller died because "He crossed me: he struck against the Light." Little did John-Roger know, that one vicious comment caused four of his closest staff members to independently reevaluate John-Roger, their relationship with John-Roger, and John-Roger's claims to spiritual superiority. But, the unpleasant effects of these reflections and subsequent defections were still in the future. For now, it was Integrity Day!

Over the next few years, the people with genuine integrity who fell for John-Roger's self-aggrandizement scheme were Lech Walesa, Ralph Nader, film director Oliver Stone, Stevie Wonder, Dr. Helen Caldicott, Dr. Jonas Salk, and Mother Teresa.

John-Roger offered Buckminster Fuller a posthumous Integrity Award, but the Fuller family firmly refused. A member of one of John-Roger's organizations nonetheless pretended to accept the award "on Bucky's behalf." The $10,000 was never sent.

The black-tie Integrity Day Awards galas attracted the one thing John-Roger seemed to love most in this world: celebrities. Any number came to pay homage to a man with so much integrity he gave out Integrity Awards. John-Roger was in his element. A full moon among the stars. Once John-Roger was asked to se-

> *You'll hear the trumpet sound,*
> *To wake the nations underground,*
> *Look in my God's right hand,*
> *When the stars begin to fall.*
>
> MY LORD, WHAT A MORNING

lect, from all the famous people in the world, the one he would like to have join him at his table for the next gala. He chose Rob Lowe. (Rob Lowe later said he was completely unimpressed with the man.)

Celebrities also added credence to a strange habit of John-Roger's: inventing outrageous stories to impress people who don't much need impressing. Certain members of his staff first noticed this propensity when J-R visited his family in Utah. He would brag about the stars he met, the cars he owned, the money he made. The staff members knew a good deal of what he said was not true. John-Roger had a way of weaving truth with fiction, however, so that it *almost* seemed to fit.

John-Roger once told me he was personally responsible for Tom Cruise's film career. According to John-Roger, Cruise was top contender for *Top Gun*, but *Legend* (which John-Roger *warned* Tom not to do) bombed so thoroughly at the box office, the producers of *Top Gun* were seriously considering another up-and-coming actor. John-Roger told me he had to personally call the producers of *Top Gun*. Based on John-Roger's endorsement, they cast Tom Cruise and the rest is cinema history. Further investigation has shown that not only did John-Roger *not* influence the casting of Tom Cruise, the producers of *Top Gun* never met John-Roger, nor did they even know who John-Roger was.

Similarly, John-Roger told me he was extremely close ("good personal friends") with the heads of all the major Hollywood studios. More John-Roger Fantasyland Dumbo droppings.

Over the next few years as accusation after accusation broke, the celebrities fled.

I was told by more than one staff member that of all the things John-Roger lost due to the scandals—followers, staff, people he called friends—what John-Roger missed most were the stars.

CHAPTER TWENTY-THREE

A Bird of Pray

> The impulse to cruelty
> is, in many people,
> almost as violent
> as the impulse to sexual love
> —almost as violent
> and much more mischievous.
>
> ALDOUS HUXLEY

AS NOTED, John-Roger can be both cruel and criminal to those who leave him or those who speak against him. This can be explained—certainly not condoned but explained—as some sort of empire preservation. John-Roger's clear message to detractors: "You mess with me and I'll mess with you back so hard that you'll be happy to leave me alone." It's a policy that has worked remarkably well. Most of those who publicly criticized John-Roger in the past will not do so now. They're afraid of John-Roger and what he might do. One must give John-Roger high marks for successful intimidation.

What is inexplicable, however, is the way he treats his own followers, those who love him, those who see him as their direct link to God. Why would he treat the people who adore him so shabbily? Why would he take people who trust him to be the "Wayshower back into the heart of God," and betray their trust? Why would he take his best and his brightest and treat them like the worst and the darkest?

For normal people, there are no explanations—except to say John-Roger is not a normal person. As explored in the chapter, "a.k.a. Roger Delano Hinkins," the man is a psychotic (specifically, a sociopath) who has a Narcissistic Personality Disorder. Understanding that makes John-Roger's bizarre behavior more understandable.

> I sit on a man's back,
> choking him and making
> him carry me,
> and yet assure myself
> and others that I am
> very sorry for him
> and wish to ease his lot
> by all possible means
> —except by getting
> off his back.
>
> LEO TOLSTOY

Perhaps it's best explained by one of John-Roger's favorite stories—"The Frog and Scorpion." A frog and scorpion both want to cross a wide river, but the scorpion can't swim and the frog swims too low in the water to see the bank of the river on the other side. "Give me a ride on your back," the scorpion told the frog, "and I'll be high out of the water and be able to direct you."

"Oh, no," said the frog, "as soon as we get to the middle of the river, you will sting me and I will die."

"Nonsense," said the scorpion, "if I sting you and you die, then I will drown, too. I wouldn't do anything foolish like that to endanger myself." So the frog let the scorpion get on its back and, when they were in the middle of the river, the scorpion stung the frog and he began to die.

"Why did you sting me?" asks the frog, "now we are both going to die."

"I don't know," said the scorpion, "I guess it's just my nature."

Hurting others just seems to be John-Roger's nature. That it's also hurt John-Roger along the way is undeniable. He once had a marvelous staff of bright, charismatic, loving people. Now he has—well, not that. That John-Roger has gotten away with his meanness even among the caliber of people with whom he still gets away with it deserves a few words of explanation.

John-Roger, you see, is perfect. He is consciously aware of all levels of creation simultaneously and the pipeline for the most massive (the only, in fact) stream of "the divine ocean of love and mercy" on earth. He never judges anyone about anything. He accepts everything that happens as a manifestation of the divine will. He has no personal needs, and lives his life in an ongoing state of perpetual bliss. *As an act of loving service,* however, he will behave in an un-God-like (I almost said *un-Godly,* but I'm afraid that would too accurately communicate the message) way to either (a) teach his disciples a lesson or (b) deliver to them some necessary karma. (If the karma were delivered another way, the recipient would be far worse off than if it is delivered by the loving hands of the Traveler.)

Does John-Roger *like* leaving bliss-land and entering the world of harshness, sternness, and temper tantrums? Of course not. He does it because he loves his disciples *so much.* The more manure he delivers to your door, the more he loves you. If you're working closely with John-Roger, the day you can step outside your door without first shoveling for twenty minutes is a dark day indeed. You could well wonder: "Doesn't the Traveler love me anymore?"

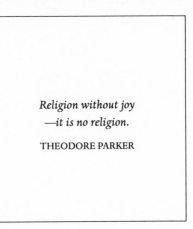

Religion without joy —it is no religion.

THEODORE PARKER

I call this the Poseidon method of human relations—it's upside down and all wet. John-Roger has carte blanche to be his demanding, spoiled, petty, arrogant, vindictive, narcissistic-complex, psychopathic-sociopathic self and everyone suffering around him says, "Isn't it wonderful how much J-R loves me!"

The necessary element to believing all this bilge is the fundamental belief that J-R is more in touch with God than anyone else. John-Roger becomes the spiritual nine-hundred-pound gorilla. Living as he has for more than thirty years without any checks on his personal behavior (except an occasional critical newspaper or magazine article), he has grown into an undisciplined, amorphic mass.*

It's like the story of the woman who checked into an exclusive hotel and asked four bellmen to go to the car and carry her twenty-one-year-old son up to his room. The desk clerk discreetly asked if the son had had an accident. "My son walks perfectly well," the woman said, "but God willing, he'll never have to." There's nothing that has challenged John-Roger to grow, improve, or even clean up his act in more than three decades. It is doubtful anything ever will.

*Just as I wrote those words, the phone rang with another of John-Roger's annoyance calls. I said, "Well, if it isn't the undisciplined, amorphic mass himself!" To get a rough idea of John-Roger today, imagine the *Star Wars* character Jabba the Hut, although the most accurate character is probably from the movie *Dune,* whose name I do not know but it's the one Sting works for. Earlier today, on my answering machine, John-Roger forgot to hang up quickly enough and I could hear his unmistakable voice talking to his secretary, who was telling him that she had gotten a copy of a Scientology handbook. Whatever he wants with *that* I do not know. The mind boggles.

> What's the eleventh commandment for wayward evangelists?
> —Thou shalt not use thy rod on thy staff.
>
> CAROLYN WELLS

We've already seen how John-Roger sexually exploited the young men on his personal staff, but that's just one example of his abuse of them.

For the most part, John-Roger refused to let them visit any family or friends not directly related to John-Roger or something John-Roger wanted. They could have no social life apart from John-Roger. The idea of a *relationship*—as in something that might lead to *sex*—well, getting permission from Smokey the Bear to start forest fires would be easier.

"I'm all you need," John-Roger would tell them. "The Traveler takes the place of all other relationships in your life." To the degree a staff member was unaware of this self-evident truth meant he had a "block" or "resistance" which "needed working on." Until he had successfully worked on it, there was no time for calling relatives or visiting friends. Once it had been successfully worked on, the staff member wouldn't *want* to call relatives or visit friends. But one of the many Traveler Catch-22s.

Although one staff member's family lived not far from Los Angeles, thanks to Roger's Rules of Order, he was able to see them only once or twice a year. In fourteen years working with John-Roger, he had not spent a single Christmas with his family. The occasion of his grandmother's eighty-fifth birthday was an event the staff member did not want to miss. Months before, he got permission from J-R to attend. Each week, he would remind John-Roger that on this certain evening he would be going. For two weeks prior to the birthday, he reminded John-Roger daily.

When he was dressed and ready to leave, he went to say goodbye to John-Roger, who asked, "Where are you going?" John-Roger denied ever having given permission, or ever having been told that the staff member would be attending his grandmother's birthday.

John-Roger told him that something "very important" would be happening that evening and that if the staff member left, he "would be left out of it." The staff member said he was going anyway, at which point John-Roger told him, "By the time you get back, all the locks on the house will be changed, and everything you brought with you [when he joined staff fourteen years before] will be on the front porch."

Somehow the staff member found the courage to go to his grandmother's anyway, and within minutes of getting in the car (he was picked up by other family members), John-Roger started paging him. First they were regular pages, then emergency pages. The staff member went to a pay phone and called John-Roger. More threats, more intimidations. Although the staff member got to go visit his grandmother on her eighty-fifth birthday, John-Roger made certain he didn't enjoy one moment of it.

The benevolent despot
who sees himself
as a shepherd of the people
still demands from others
the submissiveness of sheep.

ERIC HOFFER

The horrors of being banished from staff was many-leveled. First, they would lose their connection to the Sound Current, ministerial credentials, their opportunity to study Discourses, their spiritual path, and any chance of enlightenment during this epoch. Second, they would lose all contact with MSIA members—the only people the staff knew. Third, John-Roger usually held some life and death "I'll keep you alive and healthy as long as you . . ." promise over each staff member. Finally, as though the foregoing were not enough, John-Roger added a special curse to those who were privy to his rod and staff but now "turned from the Light."

John-Roger told them that it "would be better not to have been born" than to commit to serve the Traveler and then break that commitment. If one is fired, then *obviously* that commitment was broken—the Traveler does not fire indiscriminately. If you get fired, it's *because you've been a very naughty boy*. God—not John-Roger—will show you that it's not nice to be naughty to Travelers. In fact, your suffering is used by God as a cosmic example to all other presumptuous staff members throughout the universe.

Whenever the story of a particularly unfortunate person was in the news, John-Roger would say, "They turned from the Light thirty lifetimes ago, and they're still paying for it." Any success you might have is but part of the punishment. "At the moment of your greatest feat, of your greatest triumph," John-Roger would warn, "I'll be there to pull the rug right out from under you."

> Kings are justly called gods,
> for that they
> exercise a manner
> or resemblance of Divine power
> upon earth.
> For if you will consider
> the attributes of God,
> you shall see how they agree
> in the person of a king.
>
> JAMES I
> 1609

The Lord God is a vengeful God indeed.

The staff was in a constant state of sleep deprivation. While John-Roger was awake, the only place to be was by his side. When John-Roger was asleep (on his "night-travels"), the staff had work to do. John-Roger would be up until three or four in the morning and then sleep until noon or beyond. The staff was expected to be up first thing in the morning to attend to MSIA and household business. A good night's sleep was four uninterrupted hours. The one who had to "watch the body" to make sure no demons possessed John-Roger while he was off saving other portions of the universe sometimes didn't get any sleep at all.

The lack of sleep was not only the result of John-Roger's innate selfishness and inconsideration of the needs of those around him, it was also one of the more reliable control techniques available: when the thing you want most is sleep, it's hard to want anything else—like friends, family, fooling around, or freedom. It also gave John-Roger one more I-am-necessary-to-your-life chip— I've seen him time and time again say to a staff member, "You look tired. Let me give you some energy." At which point, he would touch them until they felt more alert. Being "on the spot" to feel the divine gift from J-R ("feel anything yet?" he'd ask every few seconds) would tend to wake one up, hence the transmission of energy "worked."

Rather than creating paragons of virtue, John-Roger did what he could to break down the character of the young men. John-Roger had a very simple standard of morality: whatever got John-Roger what he wanted was right; whatever got in the way of getting John-Roger what he wanted was wrong. Expediency, not integrity, was the order of the day. John-Roger's early staff members continuously struggled with this. It wasn't until Michael Feder came along that Machiavelli found his prince.

In time, John-Roger's spiritual teaching about honesty changed.

At first, his teaching was that "dishonesty forfeits divine aid."

Further, all ill-gotten gains "must be repaid to the last farthing."

Of the latter, John-Roger wasn't kidding. Two sixteen-year-old boys—the sons of initiates and ministers—stole some money from an unlocked cash box at PRANA that residents and visitors used to make change when paying for food. (The dining hall at PRANA is sort of a New Age 7–Eleven.) The police were called, and the boys spent one week in the juvenile detention center. One of them was scheduled to fly back to his mother's house on the east coast the next day, but that didn't matter: in the detention center he remained. John-Roger decided to press charges. There was a trial, and they both got criminal records. The amount they stole? Two dollars.

> *The tyrant, who in order to hold his power, suppresses every superiority, does away with good men, forbids education and light, controls every movement of the citizens and, keeping them under a perpetual servitude, wants them to grow accustomed to baseness and cowardice.*
>
> ARISTOTLE

The absolute rules of honesty, naturally, did not apply to the Traveler ("above the laws of man" and all that). Once John-Roger was telling a member of his staff how to buy something in a way that would, essentially, cheat the merchant. In all innocence, the staff member said, "Won't that forfeit divine aid?" John-Roger snapped back, "Maybe I don't want divine aid."

As more and more of John-Roger's undeniable untruths surfaced—even within the intellectually cloistered halls of MSIA—John-Roger changed his teaching on honesty altogether.

Now it was not what you told *others* that indicated honesty, but what you told *yourself.* As long as you tell *yourself* the truth, you can tell anyone anything you want. So, if John-Roger is caught in one lie after another, it doesn't matter: he always told *himself* the truth; consequently, his integrity was intact, his pipeline to divine aid unimpeded.

Perhaps instead of calling his work the teachings of the Mystical Traveler, John-Roger should just call it the teachings of the Sociopathic Traveler. That would at least be, well, *honest.* (And he'd probably get a whole new following, too.)

When John-Roger pinched Integrity Day, the members of his personal staff were appalled. To each of them, Buckminster Fuller was something of a hero. John Denver's song, "What One Man

> When your opponent's
> sittin' there holdin'
> all the aces,
> there's only one
> thing to do:
> kick over the table.
>
> DEAN MARTIN

Can Do," written in honor of Fuller, was played at the end of Insight Seminars to underline the importance of individual achievement. Now John-Roger was planning to announce an Integrity Day of his own. One of the staff members had the nerve to protest. John-Roger sent him to staff Siberia.

As he had done many times before, and would do many times again with whichever staff member offended him, he placed the protesting staff member in intellectual isolation and an emotional deep-freeze. No one on the staff was permitted to communicate with the errant staff member in any way. Whatever work he had was taken over by others. This was not only a punishment (the staff members, for the most part, loved their work, which often involved projects they personally started), but to show the staff member that he was, after all, dispensable. Whenever they ate, John-Roger arranged for there to be only enough place settings and chairs at the table for his loyal staff members. This meant the wayward staff member had to eat alone. Once when the in-dog-housed staff member had the affrontery to sit at the table with the rest of them, John-Roger said, "This must be the Last Supper. Judas is at the table."

The staff member who had shown the most integrity about Integrity Day was shown what happens when someone displays integrity around John-Roger.

To illustrate how little John-Roger cares about the well-being of his followers and of his personal staff in particular, one need look no further than the Days of the Death Threats. In 1982, John-Roger claimed he received death threats. No one ever saw any written death threats. John-Roger didn't record any telephonic death threats (although John-Roger had machinery that recorded almost every telephone conversation he had—seldom with the other party's permission), the police were never called, the source of the death threats was never clearly identified, no reason was given why they should be taken seriously even if they were happening, yet John-Roger demanded action. Michael Feder, who was on staff by this time, and who had attended the Clint Eastwood School of Defending Your Friends, was assigned to head up the defense team.

The entire staff took what one of them called "an intensive course in maiming and gouging." Instruction was given on assassins, how they work, and what to watch out for. They studied everything about assassins the Secret Service wasn't keeping secret. They practiced walking in formation around John-Roger.

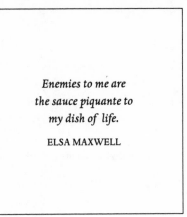

Enemies to me are the sauce piquante to my dish of life.

ELSA MAXWELL

And John-Roger got a bullet-proof vest.

Oh, what a day it was. Yes, John-Roger finally succumbed to the urging, pleading, and entreaties of those who loved him. Why, if only Gandhi had listened to his followers and worn a bullet-proof vest, think how much better off the world might be. Or if Joan of Arc listened to her soldiers and wore the flame-retardant leotards. And one hesitates to even consider how different things might be had Jesus worn the nail-proof booties and mittens Peter's mother-in-law knitted for him. So by popular demand, John-Roger deigned to wear a bullet-proof vest. (Besides when the bullet-proof vest was cinched up tight, it acted like a corset. John-Roger liked that.)

At seminars, John-Roger milked the imaginary death-threats for all they were worth. He told his devotees that by coming there that night he was risking his life. But so what? When it was a choice between life and being with those he loved, what other choice could he make? In Spirit, the Traveler lays down his life for his disciples all the time, why should he not do it physically as well? If people *only knew* what dangers John-Roger continuously faced for the love of his followers . . . and on and on.

It was a great fund-raising tool. Donations went up. So did J-R's popularity. If it were today, MSIA would probably make and sell "I'D TAKE A BULLET FOR J-R" T-shirts. Sure it traumatized any number of his followers—but what the hell? If it showed them how much they *loved* and *needed* John-Roger, it was worth it.

And so what if the staff was working longer and harder than ever not only watching the body but keeping it free from lead poisoning? It was their job, after all, to *get in the way* of the assassin's bullet. All this *without bullet-proof jackets*. Yes, John-Roger had a bullet-proof jacket, but nobody else did. Don't want any bullets ricocheting off some staff member's bullet-proof vest and hitting the Traveler, now do we? (Hell, I still would have shoved a couple of cookie sheets under my shirt.)

It's not necessary to defend John-Roger —the Mystical Traveler doesn't need this.

MSIA
Handbook for Ministers of Light

Why (other than the obvious money and adoration) did John-Roger stage such a disturbing sham? Some have speculated that it was to solidify his domination over Michael Feder. Threats of *real* danger brought out the protective instincts in Feder. Also, John-Roger could—in perfect safety—demonstrate how *brave* he was when faced with *real life peril*. Feder liked that.

Then, after a few months, as quickly as it had come, the danger passed. (Someone must have sent John-Roger some un-death threats.) The bullet-proof vest was hung next to Ruby of Orange County's slippers, and another chapter in the life of John-Roger Hinkins, showman, drew to a close.

Whenever John-Roger wanted just a *little* attention, he would fake a "psychic attack." Here, the forces of Evil were attacking Goodness personified (John-Roger), and the fate of the Light side of the farce hung in the balance. John-Roger would stand and shake, sit and shake, lie on the ground and shake, or lie in bed and shake. He would yell, give orders and contradict the orders ("Don't listen to that voice, I am the Traveler!" "No, I am the Traveler, that voice is the Impostor!") Patty Duke in *The Miracle Worker* and Linda Blair in *The Exorcist* seemed to be his role models.

It probably goes without saying that anything John-Roger wanted during or immediately after a psychic attack, he got. That, of course, *had absolutely nothing whatsoever to do* with him having them. He was just defending us all from Darth Vader.* One of his general staff (that is, non-live-in-attractive-male staff) had her doubts about the authenticity of John-Roger's attacks when, while helping him from his car in mid-attack, she inadvertently scratched his face with her fingernail. The next morning, John-Roger was proudly showing one and all the wound made by one of the "psychic spears." It was where she had scratched him.

---

*Now if I could just find someone to defend *me* from Darth Feder.

Whereas it may be said John-Roger's personal staff suffered from having too much contact with John-Roger, those on his general staff thought they suffered by not having enough. (Little did they know.) These people, who worked night and day for little or no pay, John-Roger essentially ignored. As often as not, he communicated with

*Strife is better
than loneliness.*

IRISH SAYING

them through a member of his personal staff. He preferred memos—and later computer messages—over any form of direct personal contact. The only official social contact with his staff was the annual Christmas party, which he ducked out of at the earliest possible moment. When a member of his general staff displeased him, he didn't even bother to get upset: workers at this level were to John-Roger interchangeable parts. In the hierarchy of the John-Roger Playhouse, his personal staff were members of the cast who *could* be replaced without much difficulty (although it might inconvenience John-Roger, and heaven knows there's no point in doing *that*); his general staff—which included everyone who worked for any of his nonprofit organizations—were like stagehands: replaceable without John-Roger's hardly noticing; and his devotees were like the audience: as long as they bought a ticket, one was pretty much like the next.

One of his most loyal, loving, devoted, and productive general staff members had the gall to fall in love with another minister and initiate. As soon as it began happening, she wrote John-Roger. At first, John-Roger was quiet, but when she announced her engagement, holy hell broke lose. The woman was fired. She and her fiance were exiled. John-Roger told her that not only had she betrayed the Light, the Traveler, and the Preceptor, she had also betrayed him *personally.**

John-Roger tortured her for eight solid months. The more tearful her pleas, the more terrible his replies. The more heart-

---

*She had been in love with John-Roger while he was still Roger Hinkins—they were high school teachers together—an affection which he certainly exploited, but never returned. After almost twenty years of unrequited love, she had the audacity to fall for someone else. Can you imagine? No wonder John-Roger felt personally betrayed.

> An important personal
> quality for a teacher
> is that he care
> about humanity.
> If he doesn't,
> he is taking
> his pay illegally.
>
> EDWARD C. HELWICK

wrenching her letters, the more wicked his responses.

Any time John-Roger wasn't the center of a person's life, he didn't like it. If he could do something about it, he did. Two years after starting Insight, Russell Bishop developed a very close friendship with a person he had met at an Insight I seminar he had given on the east coast. In this man, Russell felt that he had met the "spiritual brother" he had been looking for all of his life. (John-Roger was, of course, the uncontested spiritual father.) As Insight was in need of facilitators and administrators, and as this man had more credentials and success than almost anyone Russell had ever met, Russell (after checking with J-R, naturally) offered the man a job at Insight's headquarters in Los Angeles. The man accepted, sold his house on the east coast and all its contents.

A few days before the man and his wife were planning to leave for L.A., Russell called and said the job offer had been withdrawn. The man asked why. Russell, in a rare moment of candor, told him the truth.

John-Roger had told Russell that he was getting "too close" to the man. Although Russell's relationship with him was not sexual (nor was Russell's relationship with John-Roger sexual, by all indications), it was still becoming a "barrier" to the relationship between Russell and John-Roger. John-Roger told Russell that in order to grow spiritually, he must focus his love and devotion in only one direction. (I don't think I need to point out where John-Roger recommended that love and devotion be directed.) John-Roger recommended breaking off the relationship with the man for Russell's own spiritual good.

No mention was ever made of reimbursing the man for his many losses caused by accepting a firm job offer that was withdrawn.*

---

*During this man's job interview with John-Roger, the man expressed his concern that he had never worked *for* anyone else before, but had only been self-employed. John-Roger asked, "Who have you *really* worked for?" When sincerely asked this direct question, the man responded: "Well, I like to think that I've always been doing God's work." "Well, then," John-Roger said without a

To be an MSIA minister doesn't garner any special treatment from John-Roger—the truth, in fact, is quite the reverse. Next to his personal staff and general staff, the ministers are supposed to be the most understanding of John-Roger's quirks, accepting of his moodiness, and welcoming of his abuse. Meanwhile, it is also a minister's

> There is a great deal
> of hard lying in the world;
> especially among people
> whose characters
> are above suspicion.
>
> BENJAMIN JOWETT

duty to keep this "quirkiness" from the general public, and continue presenting John-Roger as a kind, compassionate, ordinary human being who just *happens* to be the most important spiritual personage on the planet in twenty-five-thousand years.

One minister was particularly popular, and his classes through the PRANA Theological Seminary (PTS) were always full. Rather than praising this minister and citing him as an example for other ministers who wanted to serve the ministerial body, John-Roger revoked the minister's credentials. There was no warning, no reason, simply a letter saying that it was "no longer clear" for him to be a minister in MSIA.

This caused a scandal. The MSIA party line, of course, was that the minister was entirely to blame. *Obviously* if he protested John-Roger's spiritual transmission of divine information, he wasn't fit to be a minister. When John-Roger told him he wasn't fit to be a minister, he questioned the validity of John-Roger's transmission of spiritual energy. By his questioning John-Roger's validity, he proved John-Roger's point. Yet another Traveler Catch-22.

Those not yet ministers or even initiates of MSIA probably have the best relationship with John-Roger—that's because they don't have much relationship with him at all. All they ever see is a heavily edited, carefully constructed facade—a God facade.* Onto this image the unblemished (by his actual presence) novitiates can project any divine image they choose. Quite often, they choose some truly divine images, indeed. They even discuss spiritual occurrences that involve John-Roger. What they don't realize, of course, is that it is *their* divine projections and *their* spiritual experi-

hint of irony, "you've been working for me all along."

*Those who work at maintaining this facade are known as the God Facaders.

ences. John-Roger was no more a part of them than a private detective who imagines Sherlock Holmes whispering direction to him or a homemaker hearing Betty Crocker provide cooking tips.

> Those who set
> in motion the forces
> of evil cannot always
> control them afterwards.
>
> CHARLES WADDELL CHESTNUTT
> 1901

Betty Crocker, Sherlock Holmes, John-Roger—all mythical characters that, like Scarlett O'Hara, Holden Caulfield, or Santa Claus, some people think are real-er than reality itself. (Remember when our former vice president criticized Murphy Brown—a mythical character—for having a mythical child without first getting married to a mythical husband?)

But myth has power, and John-Roger, in perpetrating certain portions of his myth, harms people. To pretend he's straight when he's gay, that he's celibate when he's boinking guys left and right, to say recreational drugs are inherently evil while he pops Percodan between Popsicles, sells tapes on the importance of weight loss while he grows large enough to qualify for his own zip code, that others should be disciplined while he's hedonistic, productive while he's indolent, loving while he's cruel, and, especially, that he has a greater connection to God than the rest of us, is hypocrisy—and it hurts. It encourages people to make choices based not on themselves, but on what John-Roger *claims* to be. What he claims to be, however, is false, so people base their choices on a falsehood. Can you imagine a crueler, more damaging hoax?

The entire notion that the Great John-Rogero knows all, sees all, and hears all takes a great deal of effort behind the scenes to maintain—even as poorly as he maintains it. John-Roger is not very intuitive. He *does* have an amazing ability to know when someone is in pain or in trouble. Beyond that, he couldn't get a job working for Dionne Warwick on the Psychic Friends Network. Instead of this ability—or taking time to develop the skill, which is learnable—John-Roger has created an intricate information-gathering network. He seems to prefer sleuthing to soothsaying.

His richest sources of material are probably his followers themselves. They are encouraged to write letters. They are encouraged to reveal intimate details—both about themselves and about others. In many cases, a quick perusal of the correspondence from a devotee would tell you all you needed to know. (And perhaps more than you cared to know about their friends and family.)

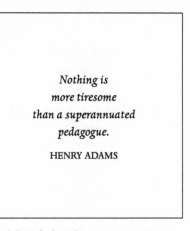

Nothing is more tiresome than a superannuated pedagogue.

HENRY ADAMS

Then there's the Movement rumor mill, in which John-Roger takes special delight. If you're curious about how much a devoted follower makes, check his or her tithing and multiply times ten. Mental, physical, or emotional health? If the devotee is going to one of the Movement health-care providers (and what good devotee doesn't?) a casual inquiry from John-Roger will get him more "confidential" health information than an FDA probe.

Aura balances are a great way to get information. Aura balances are roughly MSIA's equivalent of confession. Lying on your back with your eyes closed, you are to "forgive yourself" for any "judgments" you may be "holding against yourself."

Yes, it must be done out loud; and if the person performing the aura balance doesn't get enough information (especially if it sounds juicy) they will ask questions. All in the name of being able to forgive yourself more completely, of course. Tasty bits of forgiveness are relayed directly to John-Roger (without the newly forgiven knowing about it).

On some occasions, aura balances are used on specific people to get specific information. In one case, John-Roger wanted to know who was saying some particularly nasty (that is, accurate) things about him. The rumors flew, but he knew not their source. Various people who seemed to be close to the source of the rumors were told they had been "attacked" by the negative power and needed an immediate aura balance in order to clear it. One of the standard aura-balance question, "Have you ever heard anything that has disturbed or upset you?" was asked again and again until the information about John-Roger surfaced. Then they were asked who they heard it from. If they were reluctant to say, they were told that their aura could not be balanced until they "gave the name up to Christ." "Just say the name, and give it to Christ," they were encouraged. Thus, John-Roger uncovered the culprit.

Then there's plain old-fashioned bugging. John-Roger had the

> FAUST: *Spying is*
> *your delight,*
> *is that not so?*
>
> MEPHISTOPHELES: *Omniscient*
> *am I not,*
> *yet many things I know.*
>
> GOETHE
> *FAUST*

entire Insight/John-Roger Foundation building—including offices where private counseling took place—wired with hidden microphones. In his executive office in the building, John-Roger could switch the microphones on or off in any room, recording whatever segments of conversation he wanted. In the main seminar room, he had a camera—not hidden, but not announced to the seminar participant. It looked as though it might have been a security camera.

Also unknown to seminar participants was that every word in every Insight training was recorded and the tapes saved. So, if John-Roger wanted to find out, say, what your big secret was during your Insight II, that wasn't hard.

John-Roger has an obsession for recording everything. For a while, all staff in all organizations were ordered to record all telephone conversations. The person on the other end was seldom notified. This was illegal. John-Roger knew it, but, hey, what else is new? Anyone who had an "interesting" conversation would write John-Roger a memo summarizing the conversation. John-Roger would decide whether or not he wanted to listen to the tape.

In each city where John-Roger has a following, there is an MSIA representative. These people report back to the international MSIA headquarters about the devotees in their area. Unofficially, however, one of the MSIA presidency—with John-Roger's full permission and approval—set up an underground network of what he called "moles." The moles were people well-connected within the local MSIA communities, but were not the official MSIA representative. Without the knowledge of the local representative, the moles would report back some of the juicier bits of information that the official area MSIA representative might have missed—*including* information about the area representative. Some of the larger cities even had moles looking in on the moles. Each mole had a code name (God knoweth why), and could leave messages of any length in a special voice mail, where they could surreptitiously receive messages, too.

As more and more people became involved in John-Roger's information-gathering network, it certainly must have dawned on at least one of them: If this guy is so damned omniscient, what does he need all this for? Alas, questions such as that seldom get thought much less asked around MSIA. People were happy to be doing what they could "for the Traveler."

John-Roger, of course, uses all this information in whatever manipulative way he thinks best (for him). The only problem is that he can't take pride in his spy network. He is like the man who made money by pretending to see auras and then, one day, he suddenly *could* see auras. Who was he going to tell? Everyone already believed he did. Who can John-Roger brag to about his espionage ring? He is already *supposed* to be omniscient. Ah, the tangled webs we weave . . . .

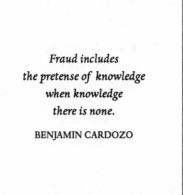

Fraud includes the pretense of knowledge when knowledge there is none.

BENJAMIN CARDOZO

Throughout the years, people have presented thousands of ideas to John-Roger about how to make the teachings more available to the poor, the underprivileged, the needy. John-Roger has resisted every attempt. He just doesn't *want* a lot of poor, needy, disadvantaged people cluttering up his movement. He wants important people, rich people, influential people. He wants his mailbox cluttered with checks and healthy bank balances.

For several years, I would say to him that I would like to record the Discourses for the blind. I recorded the first Discourse so he could hear what it might sound like. I got together with another minister who had a similar desire, and we were planning to record them together.

John-Roger would either not reply to my request to record, or, if asked in person, would put it off with a comment such as: "The time isn't right" or "It's not spiritually clear." After more than a decade, I finally cornered him: "Why not?"

"Blind people are blind because they refuse to see," stated John-Roger matter-of-factly. "They refuse to see spiritually, too. Putting the Discourses on tape for them would just be a waste of time."

I had an instinctive desire to take his head off. But then I stopped myself: I might come back next time with a hangnail as punishment. I justified his response, chalked it up to my personal

> Power intoxicates men.
> It is never
> voluntarily surrendered.
> It must be taken
> from them.
>
> JAMES F. BYRNES

ignorance, put it in the ever-growing category of things about Spirit I did not understand, and forgot about it.

John-Roger's cruelty even extends to his pets.

He uses a cattle prod on his dogs, sometimes for training, and sometimes just to see them jump. Or he'll wave it near them because just the sight of it frightens them so.

He gives the dogs inconsistent training, then expects them to "behave." If they climb on a chair one day, he will pet them and tell them he loves them; if they climb on the same chair the next day, he will hit them (or cattle prod them) and say, "You *know* you're not supposed to be on the furniture!" He blames any irregularities in the dogs' behavior not on the poor training he's given them, but on the dogs' own mean-spiritedness. Somehow, he believes the dogs *know* better—they're just acting this way to piss him off.

One day, John-Roger purchased a new toy: a can of Mace. He was sitting in bed reading the instruction book that came with it, and wondered aloud how well it worked and how far it sprayed. Across the room, he saw his pet cat, Cheerio. Without a second thought, he aimed the can of Mace at Cheerio and pushed the button. He scored a direct hit: a stream of Mace directly into the cat's eyes. As the cat screeched and ran blindly from the room, John-Roger gleefully congratulated himself on his marksmanship. After spending the better part of an hour rinsing out the cat's eyes, one staff member risked eternal perdition by telling John-Roger in no uncertain terms that that was not to happen again. Period.

John-Roger's physical cruelty was not limited to his pets. Once I was traveling with John-Roger and his staff on Insight business. A van was rented for the sound equipment, and a luxury automobile for John-Roger. About ten minutes outside the airport, Victor, who was driving the van, let the driver of John-Roger's car know via walkie-talkie that he would need to get some gas. John-Roger replied by telling Victor to get off the freeway and pull over immediately. Victor did as he was told. John-Roger got out of his car, strode to the van, and just as Victor was opening the door to get out, John-Roger hit him across the face. Hard. I was shocked. Victor was obviously both physically hurt, and mortified.

"What if I had been riding in this van and you had run out of gas?!" John-Roger yelled. "Your job is to protect the body of the Traveler! And you're doing a lousy job of it. A fucking lousy job!" With that, John-Roger strode back to his car, got in, and drove off.

*Never frighten
a little man.
He'll kill you.*

ROBERT HEINLEIN

John-Roger had not been riding in the van, Victor did not run out of gas, and even if he *had*, help would have been only a phone call away. John-Roger had *imagined* one unlikely disastrous event after another and took it out on Victor's face. John-Roger reminded me of King Louis XIV who said indignantly when his coach arrived precisely on time, "You *almost* made me wait!"

Those of us in the van rode toward the nearest gas station in embarrassed silence. After a few minutes I said, "It's a good thing you didn't have a flat tire." Luckily, everybody laughed (humor around a demagogue is dangerous), and we all had a delightful ride to the hotel without the "direct physical protection of the Mystical Traveler." (Oh, if we had only kept driving!)

When we got to the hotel about half an hour later, I noticed Victor's face was bright red where John-Roger had slapped him. I didn't say anymore about it, and chalked it up to some master/disciple thing that I probably should not get mixed up in. (Frankly, I regret not yelling, "Stop that! He hasn't done anything!" when John-Roger first slapped him.)

Later that day, John-Roger came up to me and explained that a slap from the Traveler "felt like a warm shower." He then told me how closely he was working with Victor (if I only knew *how* close), and how much he loved Victor.

He hardly showed such love for Victor a few years later when Victor got word that his father was dying. Victor's father, a Lutheran minister, was crushed when Victor did not enter the Lutheran seminary as planned but, instead, at the last minute, went off to follow John-Roger. Victor's father always saw clearly what was going on: a son he adored had gotten brainwashed by a charis-

> *The man who*
> *is worthy of being*
> *"a leader of men"*
> *will never complain*
> *about the stupidity*
> *of his helpers,*
> *the ingratitude of mankind*
> *nor the inappreciation*
> *of the public.*
>
> WM. J. H. BOETCKER

matic cult leader. The more the father told his son the truth, the more his son withdrew—typical cult-like behavior. For a number of years, there was no communication at all between Victor and his father.

In the last few years of his father's life, however, father and son reestablished their family ties, and their differences were not often discussed.

Thanks to the popularity of Insight in the early 1980s, members of John-Roger's personal staff had a degree of freedom they had not known before. There were dozens of trainings happening simultaneously in cities all over the country each week. John-Roger could not go to all of them, and his staff was needed to facilitate them. Staff members, then, could take a vacation from John-Roger as Insight Facilitator, not as infidel. Victor facilitated as many Insight seminars as he could in his hometown of Minneapolis, which gave him a chance to be with his family.

When word came from his mother that his father was dying, Victor wanted to take the next plane home. John-Roger said no. After several days of Victor's pleading and John-Roger's refusing, Victor left anyway.

Unfortunately, by the time he got home, his father had already slipped into a coma and died shortly thereafter. John-Roger robbed Victor of the chance of saying goodbye to his father. In addition, because of his insubordination, Victor was fired. Victor did not go running back begging forgiveness. John-Roger expected Victor to come running back, begging forgiveness. This firing would also reestablish the sexual relationship between them which Victor had cut off some time before. It did not happen.

Eventually, John-Roger said it was "spiritually clear" for Victor to return to staff. He did not. John-Roger offered Victor his Soul Tone. Victor was not interested. In fact, Victor found John-Roger's offering a spiritual initiation as a carrot to return to staff one more reason why he should not.

This was 1985. I was just coming back in from my computer book sojourn; Victor was just going out. We talked on the phone several times after his departure. He was confused and obviously hurt about leaving staff, but didn't want to talk much about it. Two years later, he decided it was important to tell people the truth about John-Roger. By that time, I was firmly in again, and Victor became just one more of the lunatic heretics crying in the desert.

> I believe that unarmed truth and unconditional love will have the final word in reality. This is why right, temporarily defeated, is stronger than evil triumphant.
>
> MARTIN LUTHER KING, JR.

Besides, he had the Red Monk disease, and I had no intention of getting it.

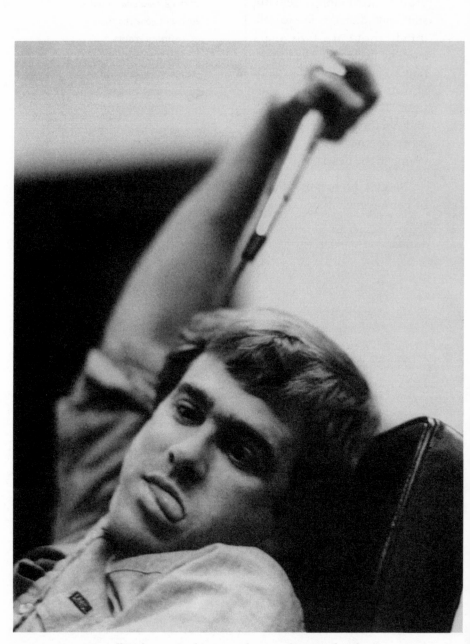

Russell Bishop—give him enough microphone cord and . . . .

CHAPTER TWENTY-FOUR
Guru U.

A poor surgeon hurts
one person at a time.
A poor teacher hurts
[multitudes].

ERNEST BOYER

JOHN-ROGER has always had an obsession with educational degrees and titles. He doesn't want to take the time to *earn* them, you understand, but he does want to *have* them. Mostly, he wants to flash them around.

According to the *Los Angeles Times*, he did earn a bachelor's degree in psychology from the University of Utah. He graduated in 1958. That was the end of his formal education.

Nevertheless, he sent $25 to the Universal Life Church, and received his mail-order ministerial credential. It is said that he mailed $50 to another credential mill, and received his doctorate of divinity. Hence, the *Dr.* John-Roger Hinkins—which alternated with *Sri* John-Roger—from the late 1960s and early 1970s. It's anybody's guess where *Sri* (an Indian term meaning *holy*), came from; perhaps Eckankar, perhaps a book he read on Sai Baba, perhaps from a late night showing of *Gunga Din*.

But John-Roger was not content merely to *obtain* dubious degrees; he wanted to hand 'em out, too. First, his PRANA Theological Seminary (PTS) offered a Ph.D. program. People spent two years in the program, only to find out that, after all, they didn't *really* expect to get a *real* Ph.D. from a *real* institution, did they? Talk about "Piled Higher and Deeper."

One of the problems with the PTS Ph.D. program was that it was run by people who were not themselves Ph.D.s. Solution:

import some Ph.D.s. John-Roger did just that. From the magnificent deserts of New Mexico, Drs. Ron and Mary Hulnick came.

> *The lust for power*
> *is not rooted in strength*
> *but in weakness.*
>
> ERICH FROMM

I had met Ron and Mary while they were still in New Mexico in 1979. They heard that I wrote books, they wanted to write books, so they invited me to dinner so they could talk about writing books.* The Hulnicks had a big black pet—sort of a cross between a German shepherd, a black panther, and Jeffrey Dahmer. During dinner, the beast came up and bit me. I mean *really bit* me.

Blood is dripping from my hand onto the glass-topped table. I am in pain. I have just been bitten by an animal of unknown origin, species, and cosmic influence. The Hulnicks cannot stop laughing.

I show them: look, I am *really* bleeding. They laugh even harder. I say, I think I better get to a hospital. They think this is hilarious. They do absolutely nothing for me. They begin petting the beast and feeding it food from the table. I thought: "Perhaps I am in a Stephen King novel—*PhiDo:* The Flesh-Eating Mystery Animal of Higher Education."

The dog started looking at me as though I were a Gainesburger. I knew what a can of Alpo felt like. I tried not to look afraid—which no doubt is what those white mice try to do when they're placed in a cage of boa constrictors.

I wrapped the napkin tightly around my hand, made some quick excuses, and got the hell out of there. As I drove away, I could hear Ron, Mary, and the beast laughing across the desert night.

The next time I saw the Hulnicks was in Los Angeles about two years later. We said hello. I asked, "How is the dog?" They said, "It died." I said, "Good." That effectively ended any hope for even a moderately cordial relationship between myself and Drs.

---

*Which is precisely what they did for the next twelve years—talk about writing books. Eventually, they wrote one. It was a book about financial freedom. Their *personal* plan for how to obtain financial freedom? Write a book on financial freedom.

Ron and Mary Hulnick.

In 1981, Koh-E-Nor University (John-Roger, founder and chancellor; Drs. Ron and Mary Hulnick, president and dean) was established. Koh-E-Nor means "mountain of light" or "mountain of wisdom" or "when you pile it this high and this deep, you get a mountain."

> *Hypocrisy is the most difficult*
> *and nerve-racking vice*
> *that any man can pursue;*
> *it needs an unceasing vigilance*
> *and a rare detachment of spirit.*
> *It cannot, like adultery or gluttony,*
> *be practised at spare moments;*
> *it is a whole-time job.*
>
> W. SOMERSET MAUGHAM

The *instant* they were established, they started handing out honorary Ph.D.s. John-Roger got the first. He got an honorary doctorate in, I forgot, but you can be sure that it was in anything he wanted. Russell Bishop got one. All the guys on staff got one. When John Morton got one, some people got suspicious about the university's academic standards: when accepting his honorary Ph.D. in (I think) nuclear physics, all John Morton could do was admire the woodgrain. ("They did a really good job finishing this. Not too shiny.")*

Suddenly, *everybody* at Insight had a Ph.D. The typesetters for the Insight brochures ran out of the letters P, h, and D. Facilitators actually started calling each other "doctor"—and they weren't kidding! Not surprisingly, Russell was the worst. If you didn't call him "Dr. Bishop," he didn't answer. As far as Dr. Bishop was concerned, from now on "Russell" was what leaves did in the wind.

Koh-E-Nor University opened its doors promising B.A.s, M.A.s, and Ph.D.s to one and all. "By the time you're done with the courses, we'll have full accreditation, and accreditation will be retroactive," it promised. But some things never change: as of August 1994, thirteen years later, J-R's University *still* isn't accredited, and Ron and Mary *still* don't like me.**

In 1988, all the John-Roger organizations began a process John-Roger called "genetic cleansing." It was yet another prophylactic measure to protect "his babies" from the forthcoming *Los Angeles Times* article. All the organizations were told to change their

---

*Okay, I admit it: I made up the part from "nuclear physics" onward.

**When Ron Hulnick first saw me pamphleting USM, he called me over in what seemed to be a conciliatory tone, and his first words were, "If you set foot on our property, we're calling the police and having you arrested." This man needs to take a summer semester at Henry Kissinger University.

> Y'are much deceiv'd.
> In nothing am I chang'd
> But in my garments.
>
> WILLIAM SHAKESPEARE

names. This way, if the *L.A. Times* reported that one of the organizations had done something wrong, it wouldn't exist anymore. Only MSIA and Insight survived the purge: they had name-recognition and therefore there was money in them there names. Every other organization changed. The John-Roger Foundation and Integrity Institute became the Institute for Individual and World Peace; PRANA Theological Seminary became Peace Theological Seminary; Atman Travel became Esprit Travel; ACE became Educare; and Koh-E-Nor University became the University of Santa Monica.

It was purely a *random coincidence* that one of the more respected community colleges in the state of California is called Santa Monica College. Could some people possibly think that Santa Monica College *grew up* and became a university? No. Nobody could make *that* kind of mistake. *And if they did,* they would get a far better education at the University of Santa Monica than they would at Santa Monica College. In connection with this name change, the Baraka Center for Holistic Health and Research became the University of Santa Monica Center for Health.

The University of Santa Monica has classes one weekend a month. A school year is nine weekends over a nine-month period. There is no *hope* that they will *ever* get full accreditation. Still, the promises continue.

Even the use of the word *university* to describe an institution that offers only two or three classes per semester is beyond me. Here's how the *New American Heritage Dictionary* defines *university:*

> An institution for higher learning with teaching and research facilities comprising a graduate school and professional schools that award master's degrees and doctorates and an undergraduate division that awards bachelor's degrees.

The only degrees USM students get are the ones they came in with, and—other than answering the burning question: "How many years can we get away with charging money for degrees the students never get?"—I don't know what the University of Santa Monica's "research facilities" either research or facilitate.

In 1994, USM made a splashy announcement when they were finally accredited by the Pacific Association of Schools and Colleges (PASC). Other institutes of higher learning accredited by PASC include acupuncture schools, massage schools, herbal schools, and other New Age learning centers.

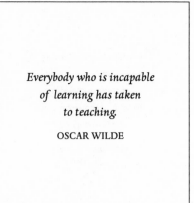

Everybody who is incapable of learning has taken to teaching.

OSCAR WILDE

Now, if the Pacific Association of Schools and Colleges can only get accredited by the U. S. Department of Education, USM can hand out *genuine* Ph.D.s! USM announced that PASC's accreditation is imminent! How exciting! John-Roger agrees to do a fundraising seminar! Seventy-five dollars per person! All money going to PASC's Accreditation Fund! It looks as though one of John-Roger's institutions will actually keep its word (thirteen years later, but, hey, what the heck?)!

Knowing that John-Roger's organizations don't always tell the full story of what's going on, I wrote to the U.S. Department of Education inquiring about the University of Santa Monica and the Pacific Association of Schools and Colleges. In a letter to me, Carl S. Person, chief of the Accrediting Agency of the Evaluation Branch of the Department of Education, wrote on July 25, 1994:

> The University of Santa Monica had contacted the Pacific Association of Schools and Colleges (PASC) concerning possible accreditation. At that time, PASC had been petitioning the Secretary of Education for listing as a nationally recognized accrediting agency. Since the regulations for recognizing accrediting agencies have recently changed, PASC withdrew its petition before any final decision was made.

The organization that accredited USM, then, doesn't even have an application *on file* to receive accreditation from the U.S. Department of Education. Meanwhile, on August 19, 1994, John-Roger still did a fundraising seminar. *Nowhere* in the advertisements promoting this fundraising event does it say that PASC is about as close to being accredited as, oh, my publishing company, Prelude Press. In fact, I might raise funds to help Prelude Press become accredited. Any donations you care to make would be gleefully accepted. (All $10,000 donors get honorary Ph.D.s *just as soon* as the accreditation process is successful!)

> Hyprocrisy can afford to be
> magnificent in its promises;
> for never intending
> to go beyond promises,
> it costs nothing.
>
> EDMUND BURKE
> (1729–1797)

That John-Roger would continue with a fundraiser for what appears to be a lost cause is nothing new. He has raised money for one project after another, and when the project failed to materialize, there wasn't a *hint* of refunding any money. There was never even a letter saying where the money would go instead.

⚖ ⚖ ⚖

I spent a school year at USM once. For nine excruciatingly dull weekends, I suffered through the boredom of the program the Hulnicks had created, and, for a change of pace, the boredom of the Hulnicks themselves. Dear God, it was painful.

Somewhere early on in the nine-month process, I came to believe that I was sexually addicted. With the full support and encouragement of the University of Santa Monica staff, volunteers, and students, I spent the next *eight months* without having so much as an orgasm. Through total abstinence, Ron and Mary said, my addictive patterns concerning sex were supposed to "come up." I think I am going to leave this paragraph now, because with that last sentence I am no longer safe here.

Sometime around month eight, I saw an ad for a lecture by Dr. Albert Ellis. (The lecture was not connected to USM.) I was thrilled. I, along with about eight hundred other Los Angelenos, filled a ballroom one Friday evening. Dr. Ellis spoke for awhile, which was a treat, and then he offered to demonstrate how swift and effective his technique of Rational-Emotive Therapy can be. He invited anyone courageous enough to sit in the chair next to him, explain his or her biggest problem, and Dr. Ellis would use Rational-Emotive Therapy to solve it.

He was spectacular. He knocked off problems left and right. You name it; he fixed it—and they seemed to me good fixes, too. In fifteen to twenty minutes each, the people were on their way with a new view of life.

When it was my turn, I sat down and told Dr. Ellis—and the

assembled masses—that I was sexually addicted.

"How do you *know* that you are sexually addicted?" Dr. Ellis asked.

"Well, in the eight months since I've had an orgasm, what's come up is . . .," I began.

"You haven't had an orgasm in *eight months?*" You could see Dr. Ellis was a be-

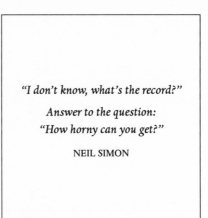

"I don't know, what's the record?"

Answer to the question:
"How horny can you get?"

NEIL SIMON

liever in Rémy de Gourmont's philosophy: "Of all sexual aberrations, perhaps the most peculiar is chastity."

"Yes," I said sheepishly. "Maybe it was only seven months and three weeks."

"You're not sexually addicted!" proclaimed Dr. Ellis. "If you had a sexual addiction you couldn't *possibly* go eight months without an orgasm. The fact that you went eight months without an orgasm proves conclusively that you're *not* sexually addicted."

Wow. I had spent eight months at USM looking for the *causes* of my sexual addiction, but no one thought to ask whether or not I was sexually addicted in the first place. In the pseudo-mezzo-spiritual atmosphere of USM, *any* sexual attraction seemed marginally perverse. Around USM, even sex within marriage seemed somehow, well, *distracting.* Ron and Mary did not exactly celebrate the joys of the physical union in either discussion or demeanor: it was somehow difficult to imagine that they ever actually "did it." It was like trying to imagine your parents doing it when you first found out *all* parents did it.

Thanks to USM's psychological (pathological?) hang-up concerning sex, I spent eight months looking for the cause of a problem I didn't have. Dr. Ellis was right; his logic impeccable. Once again—as in 1965—I was saved by the good doctor.

All of John-Roger's organizations have one of two functions: getting devotees for John-Roger or getting money *from* the devotees. USM does both. Based on the theory that if you hang around McDonald's long enough sooner or later you're going to have some fast food, if you hang around USM long enough, sooner or later you're going to join MSIA. Every staff person and most volunteers at USM are MSIA ministers and initiates. Ron Hulnick refers to USM within MSIA circles as "the Traveler's School."

☍ ☍ ☍

Meanwhile, John-Roger is busy recruiting at the *other* end of the educational spectrum—preschool, elementary school, junior high, and high school. Yes, former English teacher John-Roger wants to get back into the high schools—not personally this time, but through representatives.

In the pre-1988 glory days, some of his ministers were involved in a program called ACE. When the *L.A. Times* outed ACE, it was banned from public schools far and wide. John-Roger's solution, as usual: "change the name and do the same." The name is now Educare—a rather clever (I must admit) variation on the Latin word for education: *educare*. The Latin word means "to draw forth from within" the student. John-Roger's form of education, as it is with Insight, is to *put* something within—namely the idea that John-Roger has a superior spiritual connection to any of the rest of us.

For young people, John-Roger has *Soul Flight*. According to MSIA literature: "These monthly Discourses for children present the Traveler's teachings in a format that is fun, amusing, and always supportive of their growth." Growth towards *what?* Believing that the Traveler is responsible for everything good in their lives, and that John-Roger is the Traveler. What else does MSIA teach?

Everyone on Educare's staff and "executive committee" is both an initiate and a minister of MSIA. To avoid any seeming connection with John-Roger at all, Educare is currently run out of the home of its director. Like the people who run the University of Santa Monica or the people who run Insight, it is a firm belief of the director of Educare that the highest form of achievement is spiritual achievement, therefore, the highest form of learning is spiritual learning, and I don't need to tell you who they consider the highest spiritual teacher "on the planet."

The director of Educare? Insight's former CEO, Candy Semigran.

And guess who's writing to Educare with his bright ideas: yes, Russell Bishop. In an August 2, 1994, letter to his former Insight employee/boss, "Dr." Bishop wrote:

> By leveraging the costs, you would be able to get the work to perhaps thousands of schools, could gain the attention of various nationally focused organizations and funding sources, etc.
>
> Would you be open to relooking at the way teen and youth Insight programs are offered, in a way that would allow Insight to offer them again?
>
> Much love and light to you,
>
> RB

> *We ought to see far enough into a hypocrite to see even his sincerity.*
>
> G. K. CHESTERTON

And who do you think was sent a copy? Why, "JOHN-ROGER AT MSIA," of course.

Isn't learning fun?

"The Guys," 1979. John-Roger, far left; John Donnelley-Morton, far right.

CHAPTER TWENTY-FIVE
Spiritual Shell Game

A plagiarist is a man who succeeds in being an imitation.

ELBERT HUBBARD

IT IS ONE of my bedrock convictions that people should be free to believe whatever they choose to believe—no matter how absurd.

It is not my intention, then—in this chapter or in this book—to pick apart the teachings of John-Roger.

While I certainly do challenge the foundation of his teachings—that he's more closely connected to God than any human being in the last twenty-five thousand years—in this book, the details of his theology have pretty much gone unchallenged.

As far as I'm concerned, they can remain unchallenged.

My criticisms surrounding John-Roger's teachings are (a) how he got them, and, to a far greater degree, (b) how he uses them to abuse others.

John-Roger is not just guilty of plagiarizing everything he teaches—he is *ostentatiously* guilty of it. As previously noted, John-Roger takes the work of other spiritual teachers as though he were at an all-you-can-eat smorgasbord.

This started in the mid-1960s with Paul Twitchell's teachings of Eckankar, and hasn't stopped since. Take, for example, Paul Twitchell's first five realms of consciousness, and the sounds one should be able to hear during meditation when on that level:

> Plagiarism is stealing a ride on someone else's train of thought.
>
> RUSSELL E. CURRAN

Paul Twitchell's Cosmology

1. Physical (Thunder)
2. Astral (Roar of the Sea)
3. Causal (Tinkle of Bells)
4. Mental (Running Water)
5. Soul (Single Note of Flute)

John-Roger's Cosmology

1. Physical (Thunder)
2. Astral (Roaring Surf)
3. Causal (Tinkle of Bells)
4. Mental (Running Water)
5. Soul (Sound of Flute)

According to Dr. David Lane, while Paul Twitchell copied much of the Radhasoami tradition as he put together Eckankar, when it came to the realms and the sounds of the realms, Twitchell added "creative implantations which were uniquely his own."

John-Roger lifted them from Twitchell—unique creative implantations and all.

As the old saying goes, stealing from one source is plagiarism; stealing from many sources is research. If John-Roger had just called it *research* and given even occasional credit where credit was due, one could accuse him of being unoriginal, but not a thief.

Instead, John-Roger took the opposite tack: he claimed everything was transmitted to him—personally and exclusively—from sources on high.

During a workshop in 1981, John-Roger appeared to be suddenly "in tune" with some cosmic force. He instructed his followers to "write this down."

They all dutifully opened their time management books which all his followers carried back then (John-Roger's own leather-bound time management book lay open on his lap), and everyone sat breathlessly alert, writing instruments poised, ready for the first inspired word.

John-Roger began dictating his divine transmission. As he spoke, he looked up. He seemed to be reading golden tablets in the air. He looked down while shading his eyes with his hand, as though listening deeply to the sounds of creation.

Dictation done, John-Roger returned to "normal," and most felt honored to be part of such a magical, mystical moment.

Years later, someone noticed just a *few* similarities between John-Roger's dictation and Florence Scovel Shinn's 1925 book, *The Game of Life and How to Play It.* It will take a keen eye, but see if you can spot the similarities:

> *Sir, the pretending to extraordinary revelations and gifts of the Holy Ghost is a horrid thing, a very horrid thing.*
>
> BISHOP BUTLER
> 1692–1752

Ms. Shinn's book (1925)	John-Roger's Divine Dictation
God is my unfailing supply, and large sums of money come to me quickly, under grace, in perfect ways.	God is my unfailing supply, and large sums of money come to me quickly, under grace, in perfect ways.
Every plan my father in heaven has not planned, shall be dissolved and dissipated, and the Divine Idea now comes to pass.	Every plan my father in Heaven has not planned, shall be dissolved and dissipated. The Divine Idea now comes to pass.
Only that which is true of God is true of me, for I and the Father are ONE.	Only that which is true of God is true of me, for I and the Father am one.
As I am one with God, I am one with my good, for God is both the Giver and the Gift. I cannot separate the Giver from the gift.	As I am one with God, I am one with my good, for God is both the Giver and the Gift. I cannot separate the Giver from the Gift.
Divine love now dissolves and dissipates every wrong condition in my mind, body and affairs. Divine Love is the most powerful chemical in the universe, and dissolves everything which is not of itself!	Divine love now dissolves and dissipates every wrong condition in my mind, my body and affairs. Divine Love is the most powerful chemical in the universe, and dissolves everything which is not of itself.
Divine Love floods my consciousness with health, and every cell in my body is filled with light.	Divine love floods my consciousness with health and every cell in my body is filled with Light.
My eyes are God's eyes, I see with the eyes of spirit. I see clearly the open way; there are no obstacles on my pathway. I see clearly the perfect plan.	My eyes are God's eyes. I see with the eyes of Spirit. I see clearly the open way. There are no obstacles on my pathway. I see clearly the perfect plan.

Because John-Roger steals piecemeal and indiscriminately, his teachings are riddled with contradictions. I'm sure someone will some day receive a Ph.D. by writing a dissertation entitled "Portrait of a Spiritual Schizophrenic: A Study of the Teachings of John-Roger and the Contradictions Therein, Volume I."

> No man was ever great by imitation.
>
> DR. SAMUEL JOHNSON
> 1759

I will not bore you with such an exhaustive survey, but here's an example that goes far beyond contradiction before landing firmly in Camp Gross Deception.

When one begins studying with John-Roger, all is sweetness and light; the promises flow. Page two of the first Soul Awareness Discourse informs the new student:

> You can bring your life patterns and expressions into greater balance, experience more joy and happiness than ever before, balance and release past actions . . . all within the protection of divine grace. As you look to the Traveler as your spiritual teacher, the Traveler assumes responsibility for your spiritual growth and extends guidance and protection to you.

By the time one gets to the third Discourse, John-Roger is already reiterating what he said in the first three:

> When we get to the Soul realm, we are home. This is the Soul's home base, the Soul's home. It is so magnificent that if you were to bring back any memory of it now, you might attempt suicide on the spot in an attempt to get there again.

The first Discourse promises:

> . . . the Traveler can show you the way . . . the Traveler consciousness is able to work even more closely with you to establish you in Soul consciousness . . .

The first lines of the book sent to those who are ready for their first official MSIA initiation are:

> Initiates of the Sound Current are those specifically being taken home to God. As long as you follow these teachings and hold love in your heart, the Mystical Traveler is committed to working with you.

You receive this book, this commitment, and the first "physical" (in person by one of John-Roger's staff) initiation after two years of studying with John-Roger.

Then follow years of study, tithing, retreats, spiritual exercises, donations, Discourse readings, Innerphasings, aura balances, polarity balances, seedings, and asking John-Roger if one is "ready for my next initiation yet."

One proceeds within MSIA from initiation to initiation—from permission to permission—until one receives the much-sought-after-and-highly-praised Soul initiation. All this spiritual striving and approval-seeking usually takes a decade or more.

> For neither man nor
> angel can discern
> Hypocrisy, the only evil that walks
> Invisible, except to God alone.
>
> MILTON
> *Paradise Lost*

When you *finally* get your Soul initiation, however, John-Roger pulls a fast one—in fact, he pulls the rug right out from under you. Here are excerpts from a form letter I received from John-Roger after getting my Soul initiation:

> Being initiated to the Soul level and being established in the Soul level are two different things. A person is established in the Soul level when they have had at least one initiation above the Soul level.

According to John-Roger, he is not responsible for *establishing* one in the Soul realm, just *initiating* one into the Soul realm:

> As I have said from the beginning, my agreement with initiates is to work with them to the Soul level. After they receive Soul-level initiation, my promise is done.

His promise in Discourse #1 was "to establish you in Soul consciousness" not just to initiate one and take off—some sort of cosmic hit-and-run. After years of study, then, you'll find yourself scrambling to get J-R's "agreement" to "work together above the Soul level." Continuing from his letter:

> Any agreement we make to work together above the Soul level will be made in Spirit. . . . If you have an experience in s.e.'s, dreams, etc. that we have made this agreement . . . you can check it out by writing to me, and I will verify any agreements made.

So, the agreement is made in Spirit, which only J-R can "verify." In addition, getting "at least one initiation above Soul level" in order to be "established in the Soul level" is for J-R alone to verify.

Beyond Soul, there are no more physical initiations; that is, you don't sit down with someone who touches your head and gives you a few more "names of God." Initiations above Soul happen in s.e.'s or dreams, but you can ask J-R to verify that they really happened. Again, from his form letter:

> We in the spirit game
> have a saying:
> *What you don't know can*
> *hurt you a whole lot.*
>
> DR. CLOVE
> *The Odd Couple*

> If you think you have had an initiation into one of the 27 levels above Soul, you can write me for verification. . . . (Please note that if you have had an initiation above the Soul level, this does not necessarily mean that you and I have agreed to work together above the Soul level.)

Noted. But why isn't all this said up front in the very first Discourse? Indeed, the first Discourse mentions nothing about "27 levels above Soul." It states:

> We all come from the supreme realm of Light, the Soul realm, and we all seek to return to that supreme realm . . .

How can there be any realms above the "supreme" realm? By definition, there can't.

In fact, it's all a con. The reason for redefining terms after a decade or more of study is twofold.

First, by the time they reach the Soul initiation, John-Roger's students do not experience the bliss-city states of consciousness that John-Roger promises. As Discourse #1 gushes:

> You can consciously travel in the Soul realm while living in this world. You exist on all levels of consciousness *right now.* All you have to do is expand your awareness to encompass all levels . . . there are ways to move into [the supreme state of consciousness], to know what it is, and to arrive in this lifetime.

In my fifteen years of studying with John-Roger, I have not met *one* person within MSIA who has even *remotely* achieved this goal. Only John-Roger claims to have achieved it—and as is obvious from his behavior, he has, in fact, achieved nothing of the kind. It is necessary, then, for John-Roger to invent a new paradigm, a new way of looking at life. The goal is no longer "conscious Soul travel." Life is no longer aimed at the bliss of "the Soul realm while living in this world," but (again from his letter to Soul initiates):

> If you think it was a challenge to get your Soul initiation, it's an even greater challenge to maintain it . . . After they receive Soul-level initiation, my promise is done, and they are responsible for working off any karma in the lower levels that they have not yet cleared.

> *The demagogue is one who preaches doctrines he knows to be untrue to men he knows to be idiots.*
>
> H. L. MENCKEN

Life, then, goes from becoming a "challenge" to "an even greater challenge." Oh, joy.

Second, this system of getting John-Roger's agreement to work above Soul and getting his acknowledgment of whether or not one has been initiated into any of the twenty-seven levels above Soul, keeps John-Roger firmly in the driver's seat.

After years of scrambling for John-Roger's permission in order to progress spiritually, one might think that getting John-Roger's approval for the Soul initiation—the last initiation given physically—would be the last approval one would have to get. Think again.

By contrast, it's interesting to see the way the "five names of God" are given by traditional Masters of the Sound Current. (John-Roger claims to teach the Sound Current.) Traditionally— and even today—the true masters of this path give initiates all five names of God at once. The initiates then chant the five names of God as they continue in their spiritual studies. When the student is ready, the appropriate name of God opens the door to the new level of awareness. The names of God, then, are used for obtaining awareness, and the time line on which that awareness is obtained is between the initiate and God.

John-Roger, on the other hand, breaks the five names of God into four initiations. One must have written permission from John-Roger to receive each of the four. The soonest one can get an initiation is after two years of study in the Movement. John-Roger, then, *deprives* his students of one of the most valuable tools of the Sound Current tradition so that he can indelibly link his followers' *spiritual* growth to their *physical* relationship with John-Roger.

> The world is a kind of
> spiritual kindergarten where
> millions of bewildered infants
> are trying to spell "God"
> with the wrong blocks.
>
> EDWIN ARLINGTON ROBINSON

To make matters worse, John-Roger doesn't give the five names of God in their correct order! Somewhere along the line he mistakenly inverted the second and third names, and has never bothered to correct it. Those who believe in the Sound Current and study it with a traditional master, find this among the most absurd—and most damaging—of all John-Roger's forgeries. Saying the names of God in the wrong order, they maintain, is like trying to program your VCR in the wrong order: if you put the channel you want to record where the time should be and vice versa, you are not going to end up with the program you want. It seems the *least* John-Roger can do if he claims to teach the Sound Current is *teach the bloody Sound Current.*

Promising conscious Soul travel in this lifetime (and all the bliss that entails) and then delivering, more than a decade later, "an even greater challenge," is but one obvious example of John-Roger's spiritual bait and switch. He treats God and those who sincerely seek God as P. T. Barnum treated his customers: "There's a sucker born every minute." W. C. Fields elaborated: "Never give a sucker an even break." John-Roger takes the innocence, trust, and simplicity of seekers, and traps them on a path that does not deliver what it promises or—in far too many cases—turns seekers into cynics who flatly refuse to pursue the divine in anything.

John-Roger's motto: "There's a seeker born every minute—never give a seeker an even break."

CHAPTER TWENTY-SIX

Living on Borrowed Time—
and J-R Holds the Note

> *The wolf in sheep's clothing is a fitting emblem of the hypocrite. Every virtuous man would rather meet an open foe than a pretended friend who is a traitor at heart.*
>
> H. F. KLETZING

LATE 1988. California. I only had nine months to live. Maximum. And they were apt to be rather unpleasant months at that.

Yes, we have come full circle, but the story is not yet over.

Getting *You Can't Afford the Luxury of a Negative Thought: A Book for People with Any Life-Threatening Illness—Including Life* into bookstores was no easy matter. The buyer for one of the two major book chains thought the content was fine, but hated the cover. The buyer for the other book chain loved the cover but hated the content. I had no network or system set up to get the books into independent bookstores (bookstores not owned by book chains). Bookstore buyers in general knew of me, but mostly through my computer books. "What does a computer writer know about curing life-threatening illnesses?" I kept pointing out that I was also the co–author of *How to Survive the Loss of a Love* and *The TM Book*, which traveled along the same avenue as *You Can't Afford the Luxury of a Negative Thought*. Ironically, only eight years before, booksellers would ask: "What does a self-help author know about computers?"

In bookselling, you're only an expert in the field in which you had your last bestseller.

Through begging, cajoling, pleading, crying, and having hysterical breakdowns (the only sales techniques I know, which, come to think of it, are the only seduction techniques I know), I was

> Destiny, *n.* A tyrant's authority for crime and a fool's excuse for failure.
>
> AMBROSE BIERCE

able to get a few copies of *You Can't Afford the Luxury of a Negative Thought* out, and when they sold, a few more, and when they sold, some more, and so on. Fortunately, the books *did* sell when they got into bookstores. Working eighteen-hour days, getting orders and reorders, I gradually, gradually, gradually got the book around.

As sales increased, I began hiring people to help me. Eventually, there wasn't a square inch of my house or one spare moment of my life that wasn't spent making *You Can't Afford the Luxury of a Negative Thought* a success.

I also did whatever PR I could: newspaper and magazine interviews, TV and radio appearances, dressing up like a copy of the book and walking through shopping malls—I have no shame.

The first major show I appeared on was Larry King's radio show. The producer didn't want to book me: he didn't think the subject matter would be interesting enough to carry an entire show. (In 1989, the guest on Larry's show would fill two full hours, and Larry did the third hour alone taking calls from listeners.) The producer said, however, if I wanted to come on and talk about *computers*, that would be fine. The Larry King shows I did to promote the computer books were very popular.

I offered the producer a compromise: How about if we open the show talking about *You Can't Afford the Luxury of a Negative Thought*, and, if Larry thinks the subject is no longer interesting, or if the listeners are not responding (which the production staff can judge by the number of calls coming in), then I'd immediately switch to computer-talk for the remainder of the show. This, thank heaven, was accepted by the producer. Also, thank heaven, Larry found the discussion interesting enough and the callers plentiful enough to continue for the entire two hours. Thanks to Larry's show, the sales of *You Can't Afford the Luxury of a Negative Thought* soared.

I called *The Oprah Winfrey Show* so many times in 1989 the number was on my automatic dialer. The rejections were all very cordial, but they were rejections nonetheless. I thought that if I

sent enough copies of the
book for her entire staff, one
of them might read it and recommend it. I sent the copies.
That didn't work. Then one
day I heard Oprah was visiting
Los Angeles. The radio said
which hotel she was staying
at. I sent a case of books to
the hotel. I didn't really expect
her to get them, but what the
hell, cover all the bases, right?

> *It's funny the way
> some people's name just
> suits the business they're in.
> Like God's name is just
> perfect for God.*
>
> EDITH BUNKER
> *All in the Family*

In December of 1989, after spending a full year on the publication of *You Can't Afford the Luxury of a Negative Thought*, I received
yet another rejection letter from one of Oprah's producers. It was
sitting on the desk in front of me when the phone rang. It was
someone saying she was calling from *The Oprah Winfrey Show*.
Could I fly to Chicago the next day to appear on the show? Yeah,
right. All my friends knew how much I wanted to be on the show.
This was obviously a crank call. *But you never know.* After the producer talked for awhile, however, I knew she wasn't kidding.
Oprah! My big goal for *You Can't Afford the Luxury of a Negative
Thought* fulfilled!

The producer told me that she had a list of books Oprah had
read and enjoyed. Every so often they gather several of these
authors and do a show. I was thrilled to hear that Oprah had read and
liked the book. It frightened me to learn, however, that if I had not
been home, the producer would simply have gone down the list until
she reached enough authors to make up a show. (The producer had
asked for either John-Roger or me. I made the booking, then offered
John-Roger the spot. He told me to do it.) "You make the third,"
the producer said, "do you think we need a fourth?" Knowing how
precious time is on these shows and knowing how self-help
authors fight over that time like hungry jackals thrown a PopTart,
I quickly assured her that three would be more than enough.
(More than enough by two, as far as I was concerned.)*

*As I'm sure you've probably guessed, the vast majority of the self-help authors
who preach love, giving, generosity, and sharing on talk shows *scratch and claw
like cats in heat* for the airtime to say such benevolent things. I am certainly no
exception. I thought I did pretty well at it, too—but on *The Oprah Winfrey Show* I
was up against *a pro.* One of Oprah's guests was a psychiatrist who was *so* good
at stealing the spotlight I moved beyond outrage and actually began to *admire*
him. Oprah would ask me a direct question, I would get out the first sentence of

> The spiritual form is not to be used in this world for material gain.
>
> JOHN-ROGER

After the show, Oprah told me how she came to read *You Can't Afford the Luxury of a Negative Thought*.

While visiting someone's house, she was scanning her host's bookshelf. Oprah is a voracious reader with a genuine interest in personal growth. She saw the spine of *You Can't Afford the Luxury of a Negative Thought*, thought to herself it was an interesting title, but was distracted by a question from her host. Months later, she was walking out the door of her hotel suite in Los Angeles, and saw stenciled on the side of an unopened box *"YOU CAN'T AFFORD THE LUXURY OF A NEGATIVE THOUGHT."* This was the box of books that I had sent to the hotel. The hotel staff delivered them to the suite while Oprah was out, set them in a corner by the door, and left. Oprah opened the box, took out a copy of the book, and read it as she flew from Los Angeles to Chicago.

She liked the book very much, and excitedly showed it to her staff. Unimpressed, one of the staff members said, "Yeah, there's five cases of it over in the corner." The books I had sent for the staff had never been distributed. I was put on Oprah's "authors to have on the show sometime" list, which prompted the invitation.

Oprah's story reminded me of the delicate thread that ties together certain experiences that eventually have significant impact. Had I not heard Oprah was staying at a certain hotel in Los Angeles, had I not sent over a box of books, had the hotel not placed the box of books in her suite, had Oprah not seen the stenciling on the side of the carton, had she other more pressing work to do on the airplane, had I not been put on the list of authors to call, had I not been home when the call came, had the airport closed due to a blizzard in Chicago, I never would have been on *The Oprah Winfrey Show*, and *You Can't Afford The Luxury of a Negative Thought* might not have gotten over that magical hump

my answer, and he would put his hand on my knee in the warmest possible way and say with great enthusiasm: "Peter is so right!" and then finish answering the question himself. The variety of his techniques was amazing. I kept thinking, "I can learn something from this man." The voice of my inner press agent, however, screamed: "Learn later—talk now!"

that makes it standard back-list—a book stocked and sold year in and year out at most bookstores.

From the beginning, John-Roger and John Morton (he was not yet John Donnelley-Morton, but he *was* the Mystical Traveler) would contact me with what they thought were good ideas on the sale, distribution, and promotion of the book. They were presented—as all John-Roger/John Morton ideas are—not just as suggestions but essential instructions from on high. The trouble is, these invariably involved money, something I invariably had little of.

> *If God wants us to do a thing, he should make his wishes sufficiently clear. Sensible people will wait till he has done this before paying much attention to him.*
>
> SAMUEL BUTLER

John Morton approached me with an offer: If I would make John-Roger the senior author on the book (that is, put his name first) and agree to devote at least one page to promoting MSIA and whatever else John-Roger wanted promoted, MSIA would loan me some money. Well, I certainly wanted to take advantage of all of these divinely inspired business tips that John-Roger and John Morton had given me, and since his terms seemed not at all difficult to abide by, I accepted.*

I made only one request: that we remove the hyphen from John-Roger's name. I had two reasons for this:

First, publishing a book written by "John-Roger and Peter McWilliams" was seducing disaster. In bookstores, non-fiction books are listed alphabetically by the senior author's last name. Technically, then, a book by John-Roger should be alphabetized under J. But some stores were bound to alphabetize it under R, and still others would—not without logical cause—put the books under M thinking that "John-Roger" was the first name of my brother, as in "Erik and Lyle Menendez." This request was refused: it wasn't "spiritually clear" for John-Roger to lose his hyphen. An alphabetization nightmare has followed ever since. (In one bookstore, I saw the title listed under J, R, *and* M.)

Second, I was already tired of answering the question, "Why is

---

*Just for the record, these loans amounted to less than I had put in, and they were fully paid off—with interest—by August 1992. Also, as far as I can tell, I *lost* money on every bright idea that came from Traveler Central.

there a hyphen in John-Roger's name?" (I finally settled on the avoidance answer: "For the same reason Ann-Margret has a hyphen in her name, I guess.")

As *You Can't Afford the Luxury of a Negative Thought* became more and more successful, John-Roger started asking me, "What are we going to write next?" I presented to him the overview book of a personal growth series I had been planning for some time. The book was *LIFE 101: Everything We Wish We Had Learned About Life In School—But Didn't*. John-Roger talked it over with God and they both thought the idea was just peachy.

> *There are some men who, in a fifty-fifty proposition, insist on getting the hyphen, too.*
>
> LAWRENCE J. PETERS

This is how "we" wrote the book: I sent John-Roger a rough outline, which he returned without any changes. I then began sending him finished chapters, and what I received back from him had "OK—J-R" written in the corner of each page, and not much else. John-Roger would occasionally make a typographical correction. Sometimes, in the tradition of Dan Quayle, he would "correct" spelling or punctuation that was already correct. The only editorial changes he made were to change trade names to their generic counterparts. I remember he changed *Häagen Dazs* to *ice cream*. In context, Häagen Dazs was funny; ice cream was not. He never even read the whole book—one day I got a message on my answering machine saying it looked good, there was too much to read, good luck, and he was off to Hawaii: Aloha!

And that was the sum total of John-Roger's contribution. He never saw the quotes (which fill half the pages in the books of THE LIFE 101 SERIES) (except this one), contributed no ideas, and, except when he was directly quoted, *didn't write a single word.*

LIFE 101 came out in the spring of 1990. Thanks to the success of *You Can't Afford the Luxury of a Negative Thought*, and thanks to another appearance by me on Larry King's radio show, Tom Snyder's radio show, and some other good PR, the book became a *New York Times* hardcover bestseller.

John-Roger, however, took all the credit. He said it was because of the "energy" he was sending its way. At the time, I believed this wholeheartedly. When I heard the book was on the *New York Times* list, I called John-Roger and gave him the good news. I was so pleased to give my spiritual teacher a gift.

I also thought that a *New York Times* hardcover bestseller would get me a permanent cure for the illnesses John-Roger was "keeping from me." (He didn't offer to *cure me of them,* he merely said he would "take care of my health," which he later explained meant "holding the karma" away from me.) I had hoped a *New York Times* bestseller would not just keep the karma held from me, but get the karma gotten rid of. Alas, no.

> *Humility is not my forte,*
> *and whenever I dwell for any*
> *length on my own shortcomings,*
> *they gradually begin to seem mild,*
> *harmless, rather*
> *engaging little things,*
> *not at all like the staring defects in*
> *other people's characters.*
>
> MARGARET HALSEY

The *New York Times* bestseller *did,* however, get me the MSIA Minister of the Year Award at the 1990 Annual Conference. The plaque read:

God's Light Shines Through Your Expression,
And Those Of The World Have Celebrated You.
Now The Ministry Of This One Is Recognized
For What Has Been Done In Silence.
In The Spirit Of Loving
With Which You Have So Graciously Given Of Yourself
Let This Award Affirm For You
Spirit's Acknowledgment Of Your Good Works
As We Acclaim You
MINISTER OF THE YEAR

REV. PETER MCWILLIAMS

Each year, the MSIA conference has a theme. The 1990 theme was "The Conference of the Spiritual Warrior." Little did I know that four years later I would be warring (defensively) against the very organization which affirmed and acknowledged my "Good Works."

John-Roger wanted us to write another book "together," and MSIA wanted a new contract.

The original contract drawn up between John-Roger and myself said that we would split the *profits.* I, in my own perverse little way, wasn't aiming for profits, but for *distribution.* I thought the goal of these books was to provide the people who wanted it with valuable information, so, I figured the more books we got out

> Why *does the way of the*
> *wicked prosper?*
>
> JEREMIAH 12:1

there, the more people would be reached by them, and the more completely the goal would be fulfilled. I had this strange habit of giving books away—to charities, prisoners, and anyone who wanted them who couldn't afford them. I even sent 40,000 copies of *You Can't Afford the Luxury of a Negative Thought* and *LIFE 101* to our troops fighting in Saudi Arabia. (As I'm sure you recall, before it became Operation Desert Storm, its code name was Operation Desert Shield. I code-named sending the books Operation Book Shields.)*

John-Roger, it seems, was not as interested in the good the books might be doing as much as he was interested in the *money*. In February 1994, he told me directly that his motivation all along was money. At this point, however, he was not as forthright with me—so he had the presidency of MSIA negotiate a new contract.

Basically, they wanted a royalty for every book as it was sold whether or not Prelude Press profited. I told them that wasn't my original understanding. I had set up the company to sell lots of books (with a lower-than-usual retail price, for example). Royalties were not built into my financial structure.

The Presidency argued that, after all, *I* was getting royalties. I pointed out that I was not getting royalties, I was taking a salary *for running the company*, not for writing books. My job was publishing, promoting, and writing the books, and this took up *all* my time. John-Roger, on the other hand, was spending essentially *no* time on any aspect of the books. He made his income from other sources. I told the Presidency that if I was making my living doing something else, I wouldn't accept any more of a royalty on these books than John-Roger. When and if there were profits, we would split the profits. The Presidency didn't see the logic of my argument.

They told me they would not press me for the money, but it was important that they have a different agreement in writing because they were the "stewards of a nonprofit organization," and they didn't want to do anything to jeopardize their tax-exempt

---

*Much to his credit, John Donnelley-Morton—who by now had married Laura Donnelley—donated $5,000 of her money to this effort.

status. I didn't quite understand what having a different contract had to do with MSIA's tax-exempt status, but they told me I should sign the contract on good old-fashioned *faith*. "You are MSIA, and MSIA would never do anything to hurt you, because you would never do anything to hurt yourself." I was told that most of my problems

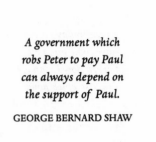

A government which robs Peter to pay Paul can always depend on the support of Paul.

GEORGE BERNARD SHAW

stemmed from the fact that I didn't have enough faith in God, and questioning MSIA (the organization most completely representing God on earth) was simply my fundamental lack of faith in God. If I had *total* faith, I would receive *total* protection. Signing the contract, then, was a leap of faith. Providing me with a contract I had doubts about was God's way of giving me an opportunity to trust him even more. And on and on.

I signed the contract.

I proposed to John-Roger a new book: *DO IT! Let's Get Off Our Buts.* The writing procedure was essentially the same, and by the summer of 1991, the paperback edition of *LIFE 101* was on the *New York Times* paperback bestseller list, and *DO IT!* was a #1 *New York Times* hardcover bestseller. (*LIFE 101* in hardcover never got higher than #3.)

You might think this was a high point in my life. It was not. They were among my darker days. And things would only get worse.

The ideas offered so freely and so frequently by John-Roger and John Morton did not just cost money, they also cost time. If I didn't have the money, I couldn't spend it. But how could I say in all good conscience that I didn't have the time? *Of course* I had the time—I just had to work harder, sleep less, and have a social life that made Francis of Assisi seem like Madonna. And this is just what I did. Each time I wanted to take part in a truly pagan activity such as, oh, watching TV, I always thought: "Is there something else John-Roger wants me to do instead?" The answer was always yes.

I felt this pressure not so much to *please* my spiritual teacher as I did from *fear* that I wasn't keeping my end of the bargain. I had agreed to write and publish the books. If I expected John-Roger to

> A great many people
> have come up to me
> and asked how I managed
> to get so much done
> and still look so dissipated.
>
> ROBERT BENCHLEY

keep *his* end of the bargain—which I believed to be a spiritual one—I'd certainly better keep mine. Publication meant doing all that I knew how to do, plus all that John-Roger and John Morton laid on top of that. There was, then, *always* something to do.

I would go to sleep and wake up with a start two hours later. "Why am I wasting my time *sleeping?*" I would ask myself and get busy working on some aspect or another of publishing. (Having the publishing company in my home made this painfully easy.) I was exhausted.

The only "vacations" I took were when I went to "hang out with John-Roger" at various retreats. Being around John-Roger's physical body was a good thing. Now that I was "special" and able to do this, I did it as often as I could. I even arranged my east coast publicity tour to correspond with John-Roger's whistle-stop seminar tour. Mostly, however, I was just one of many traveling sycophants, and I would return from these junkets not just worn down from flattering John-Roger and—even more depleting, John Morton—but also "good ideas."

I think I first realized how much I *wasn't* enjoying it when I heard *DO IT!* was number one on the *New York Times* list. I was thrilled for perhaps three seconds. This was immediately followed by the thought: "What about next week?" To keep the book at number one, I knew I had to work harder than ever.

One of the more painful aspects of John-Roger's new-found (and utterly unearned) publishing fame was that he thought it suddenly gave him PR abilities, too. Whereas before he had the wisdom of unworthiness to keep him from going on *The Oprah Winfrey Show,* now he had the benediction of bestsellerdom and he wanted to do the really big PR. This is something like having your grandfather, who can really crack 'em up over at the firehouse, wanting to perform on open mike night at the local comedy club—you know it's going to be bad, you just don't know *how* bad.

Fortunately, not many shows wanted us. Unfortunately, Larry King's did. Somehow, with our appearance promoting *DO IT!,* we sneaked by. A year later, with *WEALTH 101,* the lords of karma (or the law of averages) declared *disaster*. It began before we even went on the air.

Larry's television show is, of course, live. This means you have precisely two minutes from the time someone says "Mr. Rogers, Mr. McWilliams, please take your seats" until your face is going out to millions of homes all over the world. Ideally, you sit down, get

> *Working on television is like being shot out of a cannon. Someone lights a fuse and—BANG—there you are in someone's living room.*
>
> TALLULAH BANKHEAD

situated, do a little microschmoozing with Larry, and you're on.

On this particular night, when we were given our call to the chairs, the floor manager said, "Mr. McWilliams here, Mr. Rogers here," and indicated where to sit. John-Roger wouldn't move. He looked directly at me: "I want to sit next to Larry."

My spiritual teacher was giving me not just a request but an *order*. There must be some significant cosmic reason for his energy field being in the chair closer to Larry King's. I said to the floor manager, "Would you mind if I sat here?" indicating the chair farther away from Larry King.

"Yes," he said in that no-nonsense way of people who are responsible for the nuts and bolts of live television. With a sense of finality and a growing sense of urgency (or was it impatience?), he said again: "Mr. McWilliams here, Mr. Rogers here."

I looked at John-Roger with panic in my eyes. What else could I do? Rather than practicing what John-Roger calls "the First Law of Spirit," *acceptance*, John-Roger did not move. He simply glared at me.

"*You got to sit next to Larry last time*," he said in a slow, angry, measured tone. Oh my God. What was I supposed to do? My spiritual teacher, on one hand, versus every media instinct I had on the other. No one knew it was John-Roger who was causing the delay. I would obviously have to take the other chair *and* the blame for being a jerk.

I moved toward the chair that was forbidden unto me. By now three technicians had joined the floor manager. One could only imagine what the director was shouting at them through their headphones. I was physically stopped from taking the chair, John-Roger was forcibly escorted by two of the stage persons into his chair (the one forbidden unto me) and I just stood there.

John-Roger turned and gave me a look that would wither the heartiest variety of plastic houseplant.

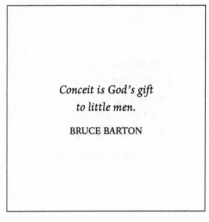

Conceit is God's gift to little men.

BRUCE BARTON

I had failed my spiritual teacher! Why didn't I fight, kick, scream, and *claw* m y way into that chair? Like Peter, who denied Jesus because he was afraid of what people might think of him, I had denied John-Roger because I was afraid of what the crew of *Larry King Live* might think of me. Oh, worthless slug was I!

John-Roger's glare continued. The shot of spiritual energy given from master to student is called *darshan*. The look John-Roger was giving me could only be called *Klingon*. But, no time to worry about the eons of infomercials I would have to watch in hell—I was hustled into my seat by the increasingly impatient floor personnel, and . . . four, three, two, one . . . "This is Larry King, live . . ." and the nightmare was off to a sinking start.

On the first Larry King show we did, the calls from John-Roger's loyal opposition were, for the most part, screened out. Screeners are there to keep the show on subject, not necessarily to censor anyone. Asking about John-Roger's past was not the subject at hand, so the calls were not put through. This time, however, the callers told the screeners false questions—on topic—and when they got on the air asked the embarrassing (truthful) question they had been waiting *years* to ask John-Roger. If several million people were listening, so much the better.

In the past, I'd always fielded these questions by either (a) making a joke about them, or (b) saying that the books are entirely *secular* by nature, and John-Roger's spiritual and religious life would be a fascinating subject to explore, but to do justice to your question, that would have to be done on another show. Next caller.

For whatever reason, John-Roger felt the need to defend *himself* on this show. I would begin with a fifteen-second Arianna answer, and John-Roger would interrupt with an answer designed to last ten minutes. John-Roger was told by the producers to be brief, and for a man who's used to spending an hour or two answering a question, a ten-minute answer *was* brief. Alas, one head talking for more than thirty seconds on television is intolerable (watch C-SPAN some time), so it's Larry's job to move it along. After waiting an exceptionally long time for John-Roger to get to the point—*any* point—in his rambling attack on those who had attacked him, Larry finally had to cut in.

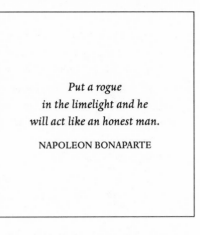

Put a rogue in the limelight and he will act like an honest man.

NAPOLEON BONAPARTE

I simply died. Here's my spiritual teacher making a horse's ass of himself in front of a worldwide audience, and I had to keep pretending that what he was saying was interesting and somehow convincing. It was not easy. I also watched our best chance for *WEALTH 101* becoming a bestseller slide right down the tubes—in this case, television tubes far and wide.

The next day, friends not in MSIA would say: "What on *earth* did you go on a show with *him* for?" I found myself defending John-Roger as Arianna Huffington had to defend him from the criticisms levied by New York's elite. "If they had only given him more time . . ." I found myself saying, and the all-purpose "he wasn't feeling well."

To this day, I have been unable to watch the tape of that show.

WEALTH 101 sold alright, but it wasn't a bestseller. I did all I knew how to do, but sometimes a book just doesn't "catch." A book, like love, has a life of its own, and although it can be nurtured, it cannot be forced. After about six months, I was ready to move on to another book, but then John-Roger called with another of his ideas that, at the time, I believed to be divinely inspired. This time he guaranteed that if I did these "simple things," *WEALTH 101* would become a hardcover *New York Times* bestseller.

I spent the next four months and close to $150,000 doing those things, did not write the new book I'd planned, and the sales of *WEALTH 101* hardly made a blip—certainly nothing that would even begin to approach *New York Times* bestsellerdom.

When it came time to pay MSIA some more money, then, I didn't have it.*

*In all, I paid MSIA more than $550,000 in royalties—which were nearly *all* the

> "It would be particularly pleasant to him to dishonor my name and ridicule me, just because I have exerted myself on his behalf, befriended him, and helped him. I know and understand what a spice that would add to the pleasure of deceiving me."
>
> LEO TOLSTOY
> *War and Peace*

The pressure on me was relentless.

It was summed up in John-Roger's three word reply to a long and honest appraisal of Prelude Press's finances and my simple *inability* to pay MSIA all it wanted when it wanted it:

!!PAY THE MONEY!!!!!!!!!!!!!!!!!!!!!!!!!!!!!!!!!!!!

John-Roger's promises to keep me alive and healthy became thinly veiled threats: if you *don't* pay, you'll get sick and die.

As John-Roger explained time and again, he can take the karma from someone and hold it, but if the person should ever leave MSIA, John-Roger lets go of the karma—it all comes crashing down on the person with one traumatic splat. (The splat is not the sound of the karma hitting the person, but the person being crushed under the weight of the karma.) Another analogy John-Roger was fond of using was that the karma was attached to the original owner by a rubber band, and the farther away they got from John-Roger (metaphorically speaking), the more taut became the rubber band. If John-Roger releases the karma, not only do they get the weight of the karma, but the slingshot action of the rubber band.

In my case, the AIDS and tuberculosis John-Roger "took from me" in 1988 which was to have killed me in 1989 would, by 1992, '93, or '94 annihilate me. Instantly. "Crispy critter," John-Roger described it. Like Dorian Grey, I would disintegrate the instant my portrait was burned. My attic was in flames. John-Roger was the fire chief. If he didn't work overtime keeping them away from the portrait, I was a goner.

Please understand that until March 1994, I sincerely *believed* this. I believed that if John-Roger removed his divine protection, I had a few weeks, at most, to live. Yes, I gave him all the time and money that I had, but now he was demanding money I *didn't* have and *didn't* know where to get. Rather than the kind, understanding,

profits on the books. I took operating capital from the company and gave it to MSIA that I should not have. I took enough to live on, and the rest went to MSIA. In addition, I had donated more than $450,000 to MSIA over the years.

forgiving Traveler portrayed in Discourses and other fictional MSIA publications, John-Roger was being demanding, ruthless, and tyrannical.

> When you want it, it's a handout; when I want it, it's seed money. When you're that way, you're naive; when I'm that way, I'm open. When you have it, it's a hang-up; when I have it, it's a priority. When you're that way, you're uptight; when I'm that way, I'm liberated. When you're that way, you're not hearing me; when I'm that way, I'm telling it like it is. When you're that way, you're being irrelevant; when I'm that way, I'm being prophetic.
>
> CARROLL SIMCOX

The funny thing was, he didn't need the money. He had lots of money. MSIA has lots of money. It owns outright every building and piece of land. (Bad money management, but a product of John-Roger's Depression-era upbringing.) I never told MSIA I *wasn't* going to pay it the money, I would just need some time.

I finally asked John-Roger to take some small degree of responsibility for giving me the poor advice concerning *WEALTH 101* and the money I would have had to pay MSIA if I hadn't followed his advice. John-Roger claimed it was all *my* responsibility—the full-page ads in the *Los Angeles Times* and the *New York Times* he suggested I place "didn't have a border around them." That was it. That was why the ads weren't successful. That's why *WEALTH 101* was not on the *New York Times* list. I failed to put a border around the ad. Did John-Roger *tell me* to put a border around the ad? Of course not. If the ad had *had* a border around it, he would have said it *shouldn't* have had a border.

I was in the same damn financial mess I had been in before—and swore I would never be in again. With the greeting card company and the computer book publishing company, I felt I had learned my lesson. I just wanted to be a *writer*. Now I had built up a publishing company—with the guarantee of John-Roger's divine protection and guidance—and I was spending lots of time running the company, and very little time creating.

Not only had John-Roger failed to keep his promise about the success of the company, his "divine guidance" was directly responsible for the financial mess I was in. If I'd started the publishing company without any guidance from him at all, everything would be going along just fine.

When MSIA realized it couldn't get blood from a turnip (but did settle for as much turnip juice as they could possibly squeeze), it wanted more and more collateral. It had me personally guarantee the outstanding royalties. John-Roger insisted I sign a UCC filing on the company's assets which meant, in the case of bankruptcy, MSIA would get paid before anyone else.

As but one example of John-Roger's use of spiritual pressure to get money out of me—and *when he wants it*—here's a copy of a computer message John-Roger sent to me. I had given MSIA a check for $112,703.73. I asked MSIA to hold the check for a few days so the check I had deposited to cover this check would clear. Here's the message one of John-Roger's bookkeepers sent to him:

> When I went to Wells Fargo at 5:00PM today, I was told I could not deposit it in MSIA's account, since the funds in the Prelude Press account (which happens to be at Wells Fargo also) were not collectible for the next 4 days. In other words, although Prelude shows enough funds, the bank has a hold order for them and won't release them until next Monday.

The communication, then, was that Prelude Press had the money in the bank, but the bank was holding it for the next four days. What is John-Roger's response? Did he thank me for the check? Did he congratulate me for gathering a nice chunk of money and giving it to him? No. Here, in its entirety, is John-Roger's response dated April 6, 1993, to the bookkeeper, with a copy—and an obvious message—sent to me:

> THIS IS NOT FAIR PLAY. WE DO WHAT THEY ASK AND THEY DO SOMETHING ELSE. TRUTH AND FAIR PLAY ARE GOOD WAYS TO ELIMINATE KARMA, THE OPPOSITE MAKES THE KARMA INTOLERABLE. I CERTAINLY FEEL SORRY FOR THE PEOPLE THAT PLAY THOSE GAMES.

Having to wait four more business days for $112,703.73 that he knew he never deserved in the first place was all it took to spark this particular John-Roger tirade. Imagine how threatening he got when he didn't get *any* money.

At another point, I shared with John-Roger my epitaph and asked him what he thought. His response, in its entirety, was:

> GREAT, ESPECIALLY IF YOU'RE GOING TO DIE SOON.

That was sent on May 13, 1993. I certainly had no *plans* to die soon—but John-Roger always liked to hold that over my head.

And while I was being threatened for my mortal life, there was also that little matter of my immortal soul. When I expressed a few doubts as to the wisdom of signing yet another contract with terms even better for MSIA than the con-

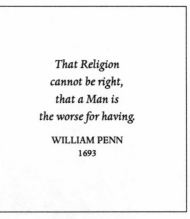

*That Religion
cannot be right,
that a Man is
the worse for having.*

WILLIAM PENN
1693

tract I was having trouble paying on now, John Donnelley-Morton ascended the pulpit (this time) and delivered the by-now familiar sermon (this one dated June 7, 1993):

> JUST LOOK AT ALL THE GOOD THAT HAS COME MY WAY. [HE MARRIED RICH.] IT IS NOT ON MY PERSONAL ACCOUNT BUT THE ACCOUNT OF MY PARTNERSHIP WITH SPIRIT THAT ALL THIS DOTH COME TO BE.

The fact that he was a hunk didn't hurt.

> HEY, HERE'S THAT SILLY SAYING COMING AROUND, "IF YOU CAN'T TRUST THEM WITH YOUR MONEY AND A SIGNED CONTRACT THEN WHY TRUST THEM WITH YOUR SOUL?" DO YOU REALLY THINK THAT MSIA IS OR WOULD BE OUT TO DO YOU HARM? YOUR TRUST WITH SPIRIT TRANSCENDS THE MATERIAL ASPECT OF MSIA. DON'T YOU GET IT? YOUR [*sic*] SAFE WITH SPIRIT.

> WHY NOT GIVE US THE VERY BEST DEAL IN TOWN. HONK YOUR HORN IF YOU LOVE JESUS AND SIGN THAT CONTRACT FROM MSIA AND TELL IT FROM THE ROOFTOPS. DO YOU SUPPOSE THAT IF YOU HAD CHOSE [*sic*] TO GIVE MSIA AN INCREDIBLY GENEROUS DEAL THAT SPIRIT JUST MIGHT HAVE CHOSEN TO GIVE YOU AN INCREDIBLY GENEROUS RETURN ON YOUR TRUST? . . .

> WHERE'S THE THRILL? IT'S NOT GONE, IT'S JUST NOT VERY THRILLING TO GO FOR A RIDE ALL STRAPPED DOWN TO THE GROUND ONCE YOU'VE SOARED IN THE AIR WHILE LEAPING TO THE FAITH OF THE GOD IN YOUR HEART.

About this time, I was in need of psychiatric help.

CHAPTER TWENTY-SEVEN

Comic Relief: A John-Roger Quiz,
Written by John-Roger

TIME FOR a little amusement—courtesy of John-Roger.

A schoolmaster should have an atmosphere of awe, and walk wonderingly, as if he was amazed at being himself.

WALTER BAGEHOT
1826–1877

What follow are John-Roger's "Twelve Signs of the Mystical Traveler." See if you can find even *one* of them that applies to John-Roger.

Ironically, or absurdly, or pathetically (take your choice), this list of criteria was created by John-Roger *when he could have created any criteria at all.*

John-Roger, having coined the term *Mystical Traveler*, can (and does) define it any way he likes. Why didn't he, then, define it according to his own personal likes and dislikes? Why not just describe the behavior he already does? Then the attributes of the Mystical Traveler Consciousness would be automatically, effortlessly his.

Instead, he lists qualifications that are, in almost every case, diametrically opposite his own behavior.

This list was not quickly come by—John-Roger gave a seminar on the subject in the early 1980s. This list was provided as course material for an official 1992 MSIA class. John-Roger, then, had more than a decade to think about this. When he revised the list, the articles in the *Los Angeles Times* and *People* were already out. Why, then, he published this list is anybody's guess.

But let's just relax and enjoy as we ponder how John-Roger

> "Sin" means ignorance
> and not knowing God
> and not knowing that the Spirit of God
> resides within us.
> When we are ignorant of
> the God inside of us,
> we live and dwell in that ignorance,
> and we can get real confused in our life—
> lying, cheating, stealing,
> hurting other people,
> being resentful and vindictive
> towards others, and so forth.
>
> JOHN-ROGER

fulfills *not one* of the Traveler qualifications.

Twelve Signs of the Mystical Traveler

by John-Roger

1. He lives like an ordinary citizen. (Ordinariness)

2. He does nothing to distinguish himself from people among whom he lives. (No separateness)

3. He has never separated his initiates or set one part of the group apart from another or allowed a caste system to evolve. He does not make choices for his followers. He encourages the experience of oneness in all ways.

4. He does not hide himself in jungles, caves or on mountains. He puts himself on the line for the salvation of the souls of people by demonstrating how the positive power can prevail in the midst of negativity.

5. He is not interested in founding religions or organizing sects or cults.

6. He does not promise worldly wealth or success.

7. He does not practice any form of occultism nor does he call forth dead spirits.

8. He is spiritually perfect and can extend spiritual perfection to his initiates by connecting them to the word of God.

9. He comes here as a giver, not a receiver. He gives the very essence of life.

10. He comes to dispel superstition.

11. He does not perform miracles for public exhibition, but he may do so for the spiritual advancement of an initiate.

12. He relies only on the word of God (as it is given inwardly), and he gives the word to his initiates.

All right, enough humor—let's get on to the chapter about my depression.

CHAPTER TWENTY-EIGHT
How I Healed My Depression

> If we live all our lives under lies,
> it becomes difficult
> to see <u>anything</u>
> if it does not have anything
> to do with these lies.
>
> LE ROI JONES

IN MID-1993 I *finally* got proper treatment for my depression. I had exhausted every avenue of help available through Insight, MSIA, and the many therapists, healers, and outright quacks John-Roger had to offer.

I was miserable. John-Roger's unrelenting pressure for money, money, money—backed by the fear that if I didn't pay him I would immediately lose my life both here and hereafter—had taken its toll. I was living on borrowed time, two years in arrears in my payments to him, and had no idea where the money to pay it off would come from. I was exhausted—spent—mentally, emotionally, and physically. I was *so* tired. I would have had to rally to become suicidal.

One of my co-authors on *How to Survive the Loss of a Love* (1976, revised 1991), Harold H. Bloomfield, M.D., had for the past year or two dropped subtle hints that *just maybe* I was depressed, and did I know how remarkably effective the new generation of antidepressants was proving to be? Like most people in serious denial, I smiled and nodded and promptly changed the subject.

But by mid-1993, I was ready to try anything—even psychiatry. I called Harold, told him I wanted to make a professional appointment, and met him at his office. We spoke for an hour. Finally, he said, "Peter, you've been suffering!"

Yeah. That's what I was doing—although I had never applied the word *suffering* to myself. His official diagnosis: depression.

Like many people, I had some serious misconceptions about depression. I didn't *like* depression. I didn't *want* depression. But then, I guess you don't get to pick your disease.

> The tricks that work on others
> count for nothing in that
> very well-lit back alley where one
> keeps assignations with oneself:
> no winning smiles will do here,
> no prettily drawn lists
> of good intentions.
>
> JOAN DIDION

To my surprise, I learned that depression was a *physical* illness, a biochemical imbalance in the brain most likely caused by certain neurotransmitters (the fluid through which the brain communicates with itself) being pumped away too soon. When there are too few of certain neurotransmitters, brain function becomes inharmonious, and the complex mental, emotional, and physical manifestations of depression result.

These manifestations can include a "down" feeling, fatigue, sleep disorders, physical aches and pains, eating irregularities, listening to Julio Iglesias, irritability, difficulty concentrating, feeling worthless, guilt, addictions (attempts to self-medicate the pain away), suicidal thoughts, and my favorite, *anhedonia*.

Anhedonia means "the inability to experience pleasure." The original title for Woody Allen's movie *Annie Hall* was *Anne Hedonia*—the perfect description of Woody Allen's character. It was also the description of my life. Although I had spikes of happiness, nothing gave me pleasure for any length of time. The concept of "just being" was entirely foreign to me. My intensive self-help seeking since 1965 had been my attempt to obtain the simple enjoyment of living that many people seemed to have naturally.

All my attempts had been unsuccessful—I had a *physical illness* that prevented even the best-built self-esteem structure from standing very long. In the book Harold and I later wrote, *How to Heal Depression*, the chapter explaining this phenomenon is entitled, "The Power of Positive Thinking Crashes and Burns in the Face of Depression." You can plant all the personal growth seeds you want, but they become like the seeds that fell on the rock in Jesus' parable:

> Some [seed] fell on rocky places, where it did not have much
> soil. It sprang up quickly, because the soil was shallow. But
> when the sun came up, the plants were scorched, and they
> withered because they had no root." (Matthew 13:5–6)

That's what depression had wrought inside me: one, vast, barren rock garden—without the garden.

I also learned that most depression is inherited. I realized that if I looked around my family tree and saw a lot of nuts, there was a very good chance I was not a passion fruit (which is *just* what I thought I was). Since depres-

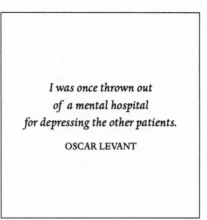

I was once thrown out of a mental hospital for depressing the other patients.

OSCAR LEVANT

sion was a genetic biological illness, like diabetes or low thyroid, it wasn't lack of character, laziness, or something I could "snap out of"—it would be like trying to snap out of a toothache. This meant the dozens of *other* causes for depression given to me by John-Roger and other Movement quacks were invalid, too.

I was ready to consider what the good Doctor Bloomfield recommended I do about my depression.

He explained several options, which included two short-term "talk" therapies (Cognitive Therapy and Interpersonal Therapy) and antidepressants—as in Prozac. I, who had been programmed by John-Roger to think drugs were the devil's own tool, thought—as many people did—that Prozac was the devil *itself.*

The Church of Scientology had done a *brilliant* job programming the media and, hence, the general public, into believing that not only was Prozac unsafe, but *astonishingly* unsafe. They accomplished this (for whatever reason) by finding a handful of people who had done some aberrant things. Scientology then presented the aberrant behavior of these people as typical side effects of Prozac. It was a thoroughly imbalanced and unscientific presentation. More than five million people take Prozac in this country every day—ten million worldwide. Millions more have used Prozac since its introduction in 1987. It is among the safest of all prescribed medications. (No one has ever died from taking Prozac—although hundreds die each year from allergic reactions to penicillin, or from internal bleeding caused by aspirin.)

Still, I didn't like the idea of taking a pill that would—as *Newsweek* pointed out on its cover—give me a different personality. I didn't necessarily like the personality I *had,* but I also didn't want to become a *Stepford* writer.

> Aristotle was famous for knowing everything. He taught that the brain exists merely to cool the blood and is not involved in the process of thinking. This is true only of certain persons.
>
> WILL CUPPY

Harold explained that antidepressant medications do not give one a new personality. There is no "high" connected to them. They're not tranquilizers, pep pills, or mood elevators. All antidepressants do is keep the brain from pumping away certain neurotransmitters too quickly. This allows the neurotransmitters to rise to appropriate levels, which lets the brain function harmoniously again.

An analogy might be that antidepressants plug a hole in a rain barrel so the rain barrel can fill. The depression lifts because the brain's *naturally produced* neurotransmitters are allowed to rise to natural levels. Antidepressant medications, then, don't add a synthetic chemical to the brain that alters the brain's function; they merely keep the brain from pumping away its own naturally produced neurotransmitters too quickly.

Further, if you take antidepressants and feel better, *it's because you are depressed*. If you take an antidepressant and are not depressed, you won't feel much of anything. In this antidepressants are like aspirin: if you have a headache and take an aspirin, your headache goes away and you feel better. If you don't have a headache and take an aspirin, you won't feel much. The good feelings touted so enthusiastically by people taking antidepressants are not *caused* by the antidepressant medication, but by the lifting of the depression—when a pain you've grown accustomed to goes away, the feeling of just plain "ordinary" can seem like euphoria.

Okay. I was ready. Lay on the Prozac.

Within a week of beginning the medication, I felt not exactly better, but as though the bottom of my emotional pit had been raised. In the past, small setbacks caused a toboggan ride all the way down to an emotional state best described as "What's the point of living?" In the choice between life and death, I would reluctantly choose life (with about the same enthusiasm as Michelangelo's Adam on the Sistine Chapel receiving the spark of life from God), and crawl back up to "normal" again.

Normal for me, however, *was* depression. As it turns out, I've had a long-term, low-grade depression since I was *three*. This de-

pressed state was my benchmark for "normal." On top of
this, I would have from time to
time, major depressive epi-
sodes—lasting from six months
to more than a year. When the
two of these played together
(that is, played havoc together
on me), I had what is known in
psychiatric circles as a *double depression* (a fate I would not wish
upon my worst Traveler).

> *There is surely a piece of
> divinity in us,
> something that was
> before the elements,
> and owes no homage unto the sun.*
>
> SIR THOMAS BROWNE
> 1642

After two weeks on Prozac, the floor of the dungeon had risen
even higher. By the third week, I felt I had—for the first time—
some level ground on which to build my life. I still was concerned
how firm it was, so I walked across it lightly, as one does across a
piece of land that was once quicksand.

That was the image I had: any good deed, any positive project,
any accomplishment, I placed on the quicksand where—like Janet
Leigh's car in *Psycho*—it would slowly, painfully, inexorably sink.

Now I inched a little farther toward the center of my land,
seeing how *firma* the *terra* really was. It was a great victory when I
could jump up and down in what was once my pool of emotional
quicksand and know it was finally safe to build there.

What I built, of course, was up to me: if I built depressing
things, it would be depressing. But now I had a chance to build
something stable, something reliable, something good.

I also began feeling *spiritual* for the first time. I felt connected
to God in a solid, unpretentious way. The discovery of this connection was no great "hooray, hooray, I found God," but a slow
clarification—like watching a Polaroid picture develop. It all
seemed so *natural*—and simple. It had nothing to do with John-
Roger's intricate cosmology I had so carefully memorized.

And—just as Jesus and so many other great teachers had said—
the kingdom of God *was* within.

I also found myself simply *enjoying* things: ordinary, everyday,
no-big-deal activities were *pleasurable*. I remember sitting in a
chair, waiting for a table at a restaurant, and I was enjoying just
sitting there. I felt so contented, all alone, sitting there, it was
almost like being in love.

> To love oneself
> is the beginning of
> a lifelong romance.
>
> OSCAR WILDE

In fact, it seemed that I *was* falling in love—with myself.

As the depression lifted, I realized I didn't need John-Roger any more.

I never had.

⚖ ⚖ ⚖

During diagnostic discussions with John-Roger and professional visits to dozens of MSIA "health-care professionals," including licensed therapists, not *one* of them mentioned that depression might be my problem.

The first year at the University of Santa Monica is, theoretically, designed to teach people how to do counseling. In that entire year, *not one word* was mentioned about clinical depression, its symptoms, and its treatments—even though clinical depression is the number one mental health problem in this country.

I looked around the Movement. All I saw were depressed people. Was I, perhaps, seeing depression in *everyone?* Had I gone from denying depression to discovering it everywhere I looked? No. People *outside* the Movement seemed to have roughly the same ratio of depression as the national average. (About one person in twenty in the United States is clinically depressed.)

Was there a connection between clinical depression and John-Roger's ability to program people? You betcha.

John-Roger had a pet phrase: "When you're at your worst, I'm at my best." The intended interpretation of this phrase was: "When you are most in need, I am there to help you the most." As memories of his past counselings with me and others came flooding back, I realized the more accurate interpretation of that statement was: "When you're at your lowest, most emotionally vulnerable point, I can get in there and program up a storm."

John-Roger was a heat-seeking missile when it came to finding emotional vulnerability in people. He could zero in on vulnerability like a barn owl swooping down on a rodent. When people were up, happy, and successful, J-R glad-handed them all the way. When they stumbled, John-Roger was there to plant a few seeds. When they tripped and fell, the next sound you'd hear was John-Roger moving in for the kill. A matador he was then, a vulture, a vampire bat.

When someone has a clinical depression—especially a *double* depression—John-Roger can program as he pleases.

If someone isn't depressed, John-Roger can temporarily make them depressed. This was the *pressure* side of the pressure/release in Insight and MSIA retreats. It was also the way John-Roger gained the upper hand with anyone with whom he was in personal contact. With a disapproving glance, an impatient shake of the head, or a well-placed criticism (usually undeserved), John-Roger drove those who loved him into the necessary depressed state for him to do "his best work." Windermere might be John-Roger's "home on the range," but the "seldom is heard a discouraging word" portion of the ballad just ain't true.

> *A thought can do us more good than a doctor or a banker or a faithful friend. It can also do us more harm than a brick.*
>
> DR. FRANK CRANE

By using variations on withdrawal of love and direct criticism—which is the same as *God's* withdrawing love and criticizing—John-Roger leads a devotee to a depressed state. When the person is sufficiently vulnerable (and John-Roger is remarkably good at knowing when), he programs in what he wants, then reinforces it with a hit of praise or affection. Like training his dogs—a cattle prod to break them down; a doggie biscuit when they learn a new trick—John-Roger also programs those around him. It's crude, but frighteningly effective.

All this rejection and criticism of course, is a lot of work for poor John-Roger. It's much easier finding people who are *already* depressed—due to a biological imbalance—and then just do the programming. Hell, with a healthy person or a depressed person receiving proper treatment you might have to wait months or even *years* for a really good low point. Depressed people? If they're not depressed when you're ready to do the programming, go out and get some lunch and by the time you get back, they'll be ready.

Does John-Roger keep his disciples *intentionally* in the dark concerning proper treatment for depression? I think so. John-Roger has done seminar after seminar on depression and *not once* has he suggested antidepressant medications as even a *possible* treatment.

In his seminar "20 Ways to Leave Your Depression," John-Roger suggests such scientifically proven cures for depression as:

> I did not sleep.
> I never do when
> I am over-happy,
> over-unhappy,
> or in bed with a strange man.
>
> EDNA O'BRIEN

"Get worry beads," "Make your mind a total blank" (good luck), the Movement favorite "Call a friend you can gossip with," John-Roger's favorite, "Find a scapegoat," "Get a gadget," "Go to an Insight training seminar workshop," and the invaluable advice, "Do something different."

Is John-Roger unaware of antidepressant medications? Like any good hypochondriac, John-Roger keeps up with the latest and greatest achievements of medical science. I asked John-Roger personally on at least three occasions whether or not I was depressed. On the first two, he looked at me and laughed as though I had just asked: "Am I an antelope?" The third time I pressed him. He said all I needed to do was read *You Can't Afford the Luxury of a Negative Thought.*

That reminded me of the man who went to see a physician and complained of being sad. The physician said, "Grimaldo the clown is playing tonight. He is the funniest man on earth. Go see him. He will cheer you up." The chronically unhappy patient said, "But doctor, I *am* Grimaldo." That's how I felt.

J-R's suggestion made me more depressed than ever. It was his way of telling me what he had told me in different ways time and time again: all I had to do was *apply* what I *knew*, and I would be just fine. My depression was my own fault—if I wasn't so damn *lazy*, I would have gotten over it long ago.

When a follower tries one of Dr. John-Roger's "treatments" for depression, it may work for a while, but eventually it fails. When it does, it is never John-Roger's *technique* that failed—it is always the improper *application* of the technique by the again- (or still-) depressed devotee. Now the follower has failure on top of depression, and he or she rallies to try another of John-Roger's techniques. The technique fails, but John-Roger tells them it wasn't his divinely inspired technique. If the devotee wants to see the cause of the failure, all he or she has to do is "look in the mirror." Another defeat.

After a while, people *simply stop trying to get out of depression.* They take on the philosophical outlook (certainly encouraged by

John-Roger) that they are "working off extra karma" this lifetime so that they don't need to "come back again." Why not work off *all* your karma in *this* lifetime while you have the Preceptor Consciousness *physically manifesting?* If you don't, you may have to come back five or ten or fifteen or four thousand more times, and although

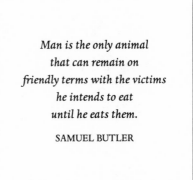

Man is the only animal that can remain on friendly terms with the victims he intends to eat until he eats them.

SAMUEL BUTLER

there will always be a Traveler, there *won't* be a Preceptor (unless one of those four thousand return trips happens in twenty-five thousand years when the Preceptor Consciousness Comet deigns to visit us earthlings physically again).

Your suffering, then, is a *blessing.* So what if this theory is a total violation of John-Roger's original promise to experience the blissful soul realm while still here on earth? Enough of his followers buy it, so don't mess with it.

Keeping his followers depressed so he can more easily manipulate them might seem merely pathetic if it wasn't so dangerous. In early 1994, MSIA had its first official suicide. Those who left MSIA and *then* committed suicide were easily explained away—they left the protection of the Traveler, so who would blame them for not wanting to live? But this 1994 suicide was from a current initiate and minister, a dedicated volunteer, and a member of John-Roger's video crew. I saw her at MSIA events often. She was clearly depressed. I have no doubt that antidepressants would have helped her immeasurably. But it's not really an option in "the Traveler's teachings." I shudder to think of how many people are suffering needlessly because of this significant omission.

In order to get John-Roger's permission to take antidepressants, I had to word my request very carefully. Rather than ask whether or not I *should* take them, I asked whether taking them would *interfere* with his *spiritually* working with me. He had to admit they would not. I snuck through on a semantic loophole.

After fifteen years of studying with him, I'm glad I learned *something* from the guy.

John-Roger's permission, however, is as flexible as the whim. As soon as I began getting better, permission was withdrawn. On

> *Pain is inevitable.*
> *Suffering is optional.*
>
> M. KATHLEEN CASEY

November 10, 1993, John-Roger sent me some fairly significant modifications to his original comment about antidepressants and his spiritual work. He wrote:

THEY DON'T INTERFERE WITH ME, THEY INTERFERE WITH THE PERSON KNOWING THEY ARE BEING WORKED WITH.

Oh. So *he'll* be working with me but *I* just won't know it. Cute.

I AGREE THAT A LIFE LONG DEPRESSION MUST BE HARD TO TAKE. . . . EACH PERSON HAS THEIR OWN KARMA [S] TO WORK OUT AND IF THEY SHORT CIRCUIT THE LEARNING THAT IS BEING BROUGHT FORWARD THEN THEY CAN SET UP TO RETURN AND LEARN IT. IT DOESN'T CARE WHAT WE SAY OR THINK OR WHAT OUR REASONS ARE.

In other words, by taking antidepressants, I was avoiding the suffering through which I would learn the lessons I was scheduled to learn this lifetime. The logic is that, if you break your leg, you should not get it set, but hobble around crippled and in pain the rest of your life because, after all, there's a karmic lesson in there somewhere. Similarly, diabetes, low thyroid, and high blood pressure should not be treated. (One shudders to think what John-Roger would be like if he stopped taking his high blood pressure medication.) (Actually, I know what he'd be like: he'd be like *dead.*)

But, at the time, my ability to draw reasonable analogies was not as clear. I was tossed back into a quandary, one that was becoming all too familiar: common sense said white, John-Roger said black, and my life became several shades of gray.

Fortunately, I was well enough that I didn't want to return to that bottomless pit of depression. No: I *could not* return. If it meant coming back for another lifetime, so be it. I had no idea *what* lessons I had left to learn from the depths of despair—that was territory I had not just mined, but over-mined.

I was ready to move on.

CHAPTER TWENTY-NINE

Counter-programming and Reprogramming

> *A good end*
> *cannot sanctify evil means,*
> *nor must we ever do evil*
> *that good may come of it.*
>
> WILLIAM PENN

THE ANSWER to freeing yourself from other people's programming is to use the same techniques they use. Counter-programming can protect you from programming while the attempt is taking place; you can use reprogramming to instill and enhance what *you* want to believe rather than what *they* want you to.

The only question is: will you be as persistent as they are? (And they *are* persistent.)

Let me say at the outset that when I use *reprogramming* I'm not talking about kidnaping people, locking them away somewhere, and brainwashing them "back to reality." This is sometimes referred to as reprogramming. It's not the type I'm discussing here. I do not approve of such actions. As painful as it is to see someone you love dancing to the tune of someone like John-Roger, the ends do *not* justify the means: that's John-Roger's game.

The reprogramming I want to describe is what you as an adult *choose* to believe, and you keep repeating it until you do. Another word for this process is *affirmation*.

Here's my technique for reprogramming:

1. Make it positive.

2. Keep it simple.

3. Keep repeating it.

4. Connect it to physically pleasurable sensations.

> *One of the best ways to safeguard yourself from being deceived is always to form the habit of looking at things for yourself, listening to things for yourself, thinking for yourself.*
>
> MALCOLM X

Let's take a look at each.

Keep it positive. If you want to program *out* something, replace it with a *positive* opposite. For example, rather than saying "I don't love John-Roger, and he certainly doesn't love me," I'm currently in the process of programming in: "I love myself." Rather than saying "John-Roger is not my connection to God," I repeat to myself: "God is within me."* Find a positive statement that—when it clicks inside you—will automatically eliminate the programming you no longer want.

Keep it simple. There is no need to write the Declaration of Independence; just a simple, direct statement—the shorter the better.

Keep repeating it. Whether you believe it or not, in good times or bad, repeat your affirmation as often as you can. You can say it out loud, or to yourself. You can be doing practically any other activity and your positive thought can be chugging away. You can say it over and over on an audio tape, put it in an auto-reverse tape player, and let it play continuously in the background. Say it to yourself over and over as you fall asleep at night. Say it to yourself as you wake up. Tell yourself that when you see certain things (a lamp, a picture, the toaster), that will be a reminder to begin repeating. The more frequently you repeat the new message, the more quickly the old, other-programming will be replaced by the new, magnificent you-programming.

Connect it to physically pleasurable sensations. Make a special point to say your affirmation whenever you do something physically enjoyable: when first getting into a hot bath, while getting a massage, while eating tasty food. If you have nothing else better to think of other than, "Oh! Oh! This feels great!" think of it when you have an orgasm. (If someone else is around, it is strongly recommended that your affirmation be *thought not spoken.*)

---

*This does not mean to imply, of course, that God is *not* within you. If pressed, I'm even willing to acknowledge that God is in John-Roger, too. (But please, don't press me.)

If you find yourself thinking some of the old programmed thoughts (and you will, you will), don't tell yourself "I *shouldn't* think that," start thinking your positive statement on top of it. The good will drive out the bad *if you are determined it will.*

> *It is easier*
> *to stay out*
> *than get out.*
>
> MARK TWAIN

Determination is not so much forcefully winning a single battle, but by repeating, repeating, repeating. After all, it is *your* mind—someone or something else grabbed squatter's rights when you weren't looking. And eviction doesn't take place by throwing the rascal out; it happens when *you* move back in.

Reprogramming takes patience and persistence. Don't expect immediate results. It took a long time to install the programming: it's going to take you a while to program in what you'd *rather* have there. Stick with it. Persevere. You can bet those who want to hold you in *their* programming will be doing just that.

Counter-programming is protection against attempted programming *while it is going on.* It's simple, and it can be fun. If you see or hear something you don't want going into your subconscious, tell yourself its positive opposite.

If the positive opposite is not readily available, take a counter-programming tip from *Wayne's World:* just add "NOT!" to the offending message. If you prefer the more mature approach, you can add "The preceding was simply not true." You can also use attempts at other-programming to remind you to repeat your own message of reprogramming.

As I said in the introduction, the price of personal freedom is external, internal, and eternal vigilance.

Self-reliance—a term John-Roger does not like to hear. (He also does not like the fact that it uses a hyphen.)

CHAPTER THIRTY
Self-Reliance

*If only we'd stop
trying to be happy
we'd have a pretty good time.*

EDITH WHARTON

THIS IS ONE of the strangest chapters I've ever written: here *I* am strongly suggesting that you rely more on *yourself.*

A part of me wants to be too clever (again!) and turn over the writing of this chapter on self-reliance to *you.* But, hey, you paid for a book, and you're entitled to get *my* chapter on self-reliance.

Frankly, I'm still working on it. I guess I should say *obviously* I'm still working on it. As of this writing (August 15, 1994), I've only spent four and a half months free of a fifteen-year mental Alcatraz.

I include the chapter on self-reliance not because I'm at all knowledgeable on the subject (I'm sure I'm the dunce of the class) but because I intuitively know that self-reliance is essential to personal freedom.

Personal freedom, to me, is to be programmed in the way that I want to be programmed and not the way that others—either well-meaning or power-grubbing—want me to be programmed.

I know I need to rely more on my own intuition, thoughts, plans, approval, encouragement—and when all those aren't enough, I have to rely simply on my ability to *survive.*

I'm going to shut up and join you in listening to what those who know far more about self-reliance than I have to say.

Society everywhere is in conspiracy against the manhood of every one of its members . . . The virtue in most requests is conformity. Self-reliance is its aversion. It loves not realities and creators, but names and customs.—*Emerson*

Don't follow any advice, no matter how good, until you feel as deeply in your spirit as you think in your mind that the counsel is wise.—*David Seabury*

To believe your own thought, to believe that what is true for you in your private heart is true for all men—that is genius.—*Emerson*

Give to every human being every right that you claim for yourself.—*Robert Ingersoll*

These dark days will be worth all they cost us if they teach us that our true destiny is not to be ministered unto but to minister to ourselves and to our fellow men.—*Franklin D. Roosevelt*

Whoso would be a man must be a nonconformist.—*Emerson*

I am inclined to think that one's education has been in vain if one fails to learn that most schoolmasters are idiots.—*Hesketh Pearson*

I myself believe that the evidence for God lies primarily in inner personal experiences.—*William James*

Never commit yourself to a cheese without having first examined it.—*T. S. Eliot*

The world is all the richer for having the devil in it, so long as we keep our foot upon his neck.—*William James*

The doctrine of hatred must be preached, as the counteraction of the doctrine of love, when that pules and whines. I shun father and mother and wife and brother when my genius calls me.—*Emerson*

Wise men don't need advice. Fools don't take it.—*Ben Franklin*

Joy in the universe, and keen curiosity about it all—that has been my religion.—*John Burroughs*

It is a tragedy when the mind, soul and heart are in slavery in a way of life which refuses to recognize that people have rights before God. It is a war which makes hate a badge of honor, slavery the keystone to prosperity. Not to resist would make one an accomplice to crime. Resistance was part of the program of Jesus. We must resist oppression and tyranny. We have to end it no matter what it costs.—*Joseph R. Sizoo, D.D.*

> *No matter what your religion, you should try to become a government program, for then you will have everlasting life.*
>
> LYNN MARTIN
> *U. S. Representative*

You're not famous until my mother has heard of you.—*Jay Leno*

It is easy in the world to live after the world's opinion; it is easy in solitude to live after our own; but the great man is he who in the midst of the crowd keeps with perfect sweetness the independence of solitude.—*Emerson*

The surest defense against Evil is extreme individualism, originality of thinking, whimsicality, even—if you will—eccentricity. That is, something that can't be feigned, faked, imitated; something even a seasoned impostor couldn't be happy with.—*Joseph Brodsky*

Do we know that truth is life and falsehood spiritual death? Do we know that beauty is joy and ugliness sin? Do we know that justice is the condition of well-being and happiness, while injustice of any kind is defeat? In a universe of uncertainties these values alone are certain. They give order and design to living.—*Sydney Bruce Snow, D. D.*

To teach one's self is to be forced to learn twice.—*Ellen Glasgow*

The mutual confidence on which all else depends can be maintained only by an open mind and a brave reliance upon free discussion.—*Learned Hand*

> *We hold these Truths*
> *to be self-evident,*
> *that all Men are created equal,*
> *that they are*
> *endowed by their Creator*
> *with certain unalienable Rights,*
> *that among these are Life, Liberty,*
> *and the Pursuit of Happiness.*
>
> THOMAS JEFFERSON
> *Declaration of Independence*
> *1776*

A foolish consistency is the hobgoblin of little minds, adored by little statesman and philosophers and divines. With consistency a great soul has simply nothing to do . . . Speak what you think today in hard words and tomorrow speak what tomorrow thinks in hard words again, though it contradict everything you said today.—*Emerson*

Don't compromise yourself. You are all you've got.—*Janis Joplin*

The ability to discriminate between that which is true and that which is false is one of the last attainments of the human mind.—*James Fenimore Cooper*

Education is the ability to listen to almost anything without losing your temper or your self-confidence.—*Robert Frost*

To be great is to be misunderstood.—*Emerson*

Only the shallow know themselves.—*Oscar Wilde*

I admire the serene assurance of those who have religious faith. It is wonderful to observe the calm confidence of a Christian with four acres.—*Mark Twain*

I like the silent church before the service begins, better than any preaching.—*Emerson*

Be courteous to all, but intimate with few, and let those few be well tried before you give them your confidence. True friendship is a plant of slow growth, and must undergo and withstand the shocks of adversity before it is entitled to the appellation.—*George Washington*

Forgive your enemies, but never forget their names.—*John F. Kennedy*

Discontent is the want of self-reliance: it is infirmity of will.—*Emerson*

I have yet to encounter that common myth of weak men, an insurmountable barrier.—*J. L. Allen*

Self-confidence is the first requisite to great undertakings.—*Dr. Samuel Johnson*

Liberty means responsibility. That is why most men dread it.—*George Bernard Shaw*

Follow your bliss.

JOSEPH CAMPBELL

In matters of principle, stand like a rock; in matters of taste, swim with the current.—*Thomas Jefferson*

I wish I was as cocksure of anything as Tom Macaulay is of everything.—*Lord Melbourne*

Nothing can bring you peace but yourself.—*Emerson*

Believe in no other God than the one who insists on justice and equality among men.—*George Sand*

I cannot give them my confidence; pardon me, gentlemen, confidence is a plant of slow growth in an aged bosom: youth is the season of credulity.—*William Pitt*

Peace is not absence of war, it is a virtue, a state of mind, a disposition for benevolence, confidence, justice.—*Spinoza*

No man is great enough or wise enough for any of us to surrender our destiny to. The only way in which anyone can lead us is to restore to us the belief in our own guidance.—*Henry Miller*

You gain strength, courage and confidence by every experience in which you really stop to look fear in the face. You are able to say to yourself, "I lived through this horror. I can take the next thing that comes along.". . . You must do the thing you think you cannot do.—*Eleanor Roosevelt*

To be poor and independent is very nearly an impossibility.—*William Cobbett*

One last thought: some questions don't have answers. Personally, I'm learning to enjoy the mystery.

CHAPTER THIRTY-ONE

What Is the Sound of One Guru Suing?

> For certain people,
> after fifty,
> litigation takes the place
> of sex.
>
> GORE VIDAL

MARCH **1994.** The Ides of March had passed. There was no doubt about it in my mind: John-Roger was not the great and powerful wizard, just a man behind the curtain. I wrote and told him so. I told him, essentially, that he played an interesting game of Guru, but the game was now over because I *declared* it to be over. (According to the Official Rules: "The game is over when the one getting gurued realizes he or she has been gurued, declares the game over, and walks away.") I told John-Roger he could keep the million dollars I "gave" him, but he wouldn't be getting any more from me. I wished him well, and said goodbye.

Now, any experienced player of Guru knows the game is now *over*. Find a new disciple. If you need a writer, try perhaps Jackie Collins—sort of a cross between Arianna and me. If you needed a publisher, wasn't one of your top ministers doing it with one of the top people at one of the top New York publishing companies? Why not, then, start at the top? What *did* John-Roger need that he couldn't get from some other player? I don't know, but that's a logical question, and asking logical questions of John-Roger is illogical.

John-Roger kicked the game into sudden death overtime.

PETER, IS ALL THIS WHAT YOU REALLY WANT? DID I PERSONALLY DO SOMETHING TO YOU? PERHAPS IT

> *The secret of life is to appreciate the pleasure of being terribly deceived.*
>
> OSCAR WILDE

WAS SOMETHING I SHOULD HAVE DONE AND DIDN'T DO? IS IT SOMETHING YET TO BE DONE? IS THE NEW DRUG YOU ARE TAKING CAUSING THESE TYPES OF REACTIONS AS SOME KIND OF SIDE EFFECT?

If he calls clear thinking, common sense, and freedom from his intimidation "some kind of side effect," then I guess it is.

I AM ASKING ALL OF THE ABOVE BECAUSE I CARE.

He cares about the money.

NOTHING YOU HAVE WRITTEN SO FAR HAS GOTTEN ME MAD, UPSET, ETC.,

How nice. I am relieved. Jubilant, in fact.

IT JUST DOESN'T SEEM LIKE YOU.

Certainly not the "you" John-Roger had carefully programmed me to be. My *me* and his *you* would never see eye to eye again.

WE HAVE BEEN FRIENDS FOR QUITE A LONG TIME, AND IT SEEMS THAT IN 2/3 WEEKS YOU ARE QUITE WILLING TO THROW IT ALL OVER FOR ? SOMETHING?

Yeah, it's called freedom, a.k.a. my life.

ARE YOU REALLY THAT ANGRY AT ME AS YOU ARE MAKING IT SEEM IN THESE MEMOS? WAS IT A MISTAKE TO UPDATE YOU ON INFORMATION THAT MIGHT HAVE CONCERNED YOU WHILE YOU WERE OUT OF TOWN? I REALLY THOUGHT YOU MIGHT WANT TO KNOW THE INFORMATION IF FOR NOTHING ELSE AS AN FYI.

Good God, he's a bad writer! No doubt the incident he was referring to was when he and several of his staff went to his favorite witchdoctor in Malibu. Dr. Witchdoctor threw some bones on the floor, bit a boa constrictor, and said their collective and individual problems were all due to my "negative energy." They were told to get a Magic Marker and black out my picture on all copies of our latest book, *We Give To Love,* and do some other ceremonial nonsense all designed to protect them from my evil rays.

Frankly, the event didn't bother me at all. It was so silly, so typical. What *did* concern me was that I, too, had gone to Dr. Witchdoctor and it reminded me of all the *time* and *money* I wasted on the entire endeavor. For John-Roger to think I would leave a spiritual path I had followed for fifteen years over something as mundane as Dr. Witchdoctor showed how little he actually knew me. "PETER, ARE YOU MORE ILL THAN YOU HAVE LET ON TO US?"

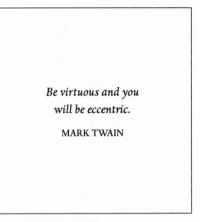

Be virtuous and you will be eccentric.

MARK TWAIN

He thought I was dying! Here the man who was supposedly guarding my health doesn't even know how well or how sick I am! It merely confirmed to me what I already knew: that his whole I'll-save-you-you-write-books-for-me arrangement was just another shell game. John-Roger then trundled out the old If-it-weren't-for-me-Peter-you-would've-been-dead-long-ago routine:

> IF YOU REMEMBER OUT IN YUCCA VALLEY WHEN WE WERE TALKING ABOUT WRITING THE FIRST BOOK YOU INDICATED THAT YOUR HEALTH WAS FRAGILE AND THAT YOU MIGHT NOT BE ALIVE TO DO ALL THAT WOULD BE REQUIRED TO PUT OUT A BOOK. I SAID THAT AS LONG AS WE WERE WRITING BOOKS TOGETHER I WOULD HANDLE YOUR HEALTH ISSUE FOR YOU. I DID KEEP MY WORD. THAT WAS THE ONLY WORD/PROMISE I MADE TO YOU, NO MORE OR NO LESS. IS SOMETHING UP WITH YOUR HEALTH, I CARE PETER, DON'T YOU GET IT?

Yeah, I get that he was worried, but I didn't get that he cared. If he cared, why didn't he pick up the phone and call me? He cared about me in the same way that a juggler who has twelve plates going simultaneously on those little sticks cares whether or not one falls off. His letter was just an attempt to keep my plate spinning.

And then, in a marked contrast to the opening, in which he asked if it was something *he* had done, he reverts to form and explains that it's all something *I* must be doing:

> PERHAPS YOU THINK I HAVE OVERSTEPPED THE NEW LINES YOU HAVE DRAWN. SO BE IT. THOSE ARE YOUR LINES, NOT MINE. I DREW NO LINES FOR OR AGAINST YOU. THERE IS JUST A PATHWAY, AS ALWAYS.

> *The Spiritual Warrior*
> *withholds the striking,*
> *knowing full well*
> *that the karma in process*
> *is going to strike them enough.*
> *And people will try to antagonize*
> *you to strike at them,*
> *to which you must say*
> *"Get behind me.*
> *If I strike, I fall."*
>
> JOHN-ROGER

The "new lines" I drew were these: the game is over, you are no longer my spiritual teacher, you flimmed-flammed a nice chunk of money and a major chunk of my life out of me, and I leave that behind as I head for the door.

I wrote John-Roger a reply, calmly but firmly and factually stating my case and again saying *hasta la vista.* Nothing more from J-R. Then, the MSIA presidency wants to know when it's going to get more money. My reply: never.

So, next, it's time for another enervating episode of *L.A. Law.* The same high-powered attorney MSIA hired in 1987 to intimidate the *Los Angeles Times* into not printing the John-Roger story was now aiming his cannon at little Prelude Press. I explained my side of things to the attorney, who I thought would counsel his client to let sleeping ex-ministers, ex-initiates, and ex-inner circle writers lie. In vain, in vain.

If there was a disagreement, I insisted that it be handled through binding arbitration. The lawyer sent me a binding arbitration agreement, but wouldn't give me basic pieces of information such as John-Roger's legal name. (I'm pretty sure it's still Roger Hinkins, although the lawyer says it's not.) I get a letter about the arbitration: *their* way or *no* way, take-it-or-leave-it. I leave it.

Then the annoying phone calls began. Then the lawsuit. Damn. This bastard was *not* going to let me go. He wanted to go from playing Guru to Big Time Mud Wrestling. Why? Why?

In a court of law, you must prove *everything.* If John-Roger made a statement, "MSIA doesn't do what I tell them." I would somehow have to *prove* that it does. If I claimed Insight was a recruiting arm of MSIA, my say-so is not proof—other people (other *knowledgeable* people) have to say so, too. That meant putting on my investigative reporter hat and getting to work.

If I was going to investigate it, I knew I had to write a book about it. The book, when finished, might be just for me and a few selected attorneys, but I knew I had to write one. It was my way of figuring things out, sorting them, putting them in order—the discipline of facts, figures, and time lines had a way of stirring my memory like nothing else. To remember it all, I knew I had to recall the important things. To remember them accurately would demand the rigors of writing it all down.

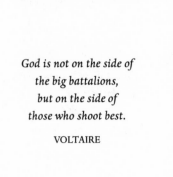

I got on the phone. My first call was to Victor Toso. He had carried the torch against John-Roger more consistently than anyone. He also had the courage to discuss—openly and frankly—John-Roger's sexual manipulation of him. Victor and I had our share of skirmishes back when I was trying to promote the *LIFE 101* books, and he was trying to promote the truth about John-Roger. He kept calling up radio stations asking embarrassing questions (read: accurate and informative questions) concerning John-Roger—it was *most* unnerving.

After the *Los Angeles Times* and *People* articles in 1988, the books in THE LIFE 101 SERIES single-handedly cleaned up John-Roger's reputation and made him look respectable again. Victor did not like that I did this. Looking back, I do not like that I did this, either. After I called him in 1994, Victor sent me a video tape he had made in 1988. On it, he tells his story with John-Roger. In the middle of watching the video, I called and apologized to Victor for all that I'd done. He told me that in his prime he'd done quite a lot, too: getting *me* into MSIA, for example—it was all part of the programming.

I began contacting other people who had left, and found intelligent, compassionate, well-adjusted people busily living their lives. They were happy to talk—although doing so sometimes brought back painful memories. Some did not want their names used. I can't blame them. Why unnecessarily subject yourself to a psychopath? I decided not to use anyone's name except Victor's and David Lane's, who were more than happy to be included. The names were not important; the information was. By guaranteeing anonymity (but willing to testify in court if need be), people spoke more freely, more frankly.

Oh, what I learned!

Now that I was open to it, all the information that was available but that I simply did not want to know surfaced. Only then I

Go not in and out of court that thy name may not sink.

THE WISDOM OF ANII
c. 900 B.C.

read letters John-Roger had written pretending to be others, I got facts about the extent and sleaziness of his sex life, I saw John-Roger lie to me and about me repeatedly, I saw John Donnelley-Morton physically attack me and endorse the battery by Michael Feder and Russell Bishop, and I heard the pain in the voices of those who left; the pain of betrayal—the fundamental, spiritual betrayal—that we all felt by going from devotees to departees.

I discovered within myself a depth of pain I did not wish to acknowledge, a sense of shame for all the people I misled onto this sociopath's path, a sense of shock that I could be so *completely* misled myself, a fear that it might happen again (although the names would be changed to protect the indolent), and an anger that someone would take such advantage of me for so long in such a despicable way.

This book is almost done (for me as well as you). I am writing this final chapter the day before it goes to the printer (August 17, 1994). In my best Southern California style, I can only say: I hope it was as good for you as it was for me. It's not likely I'll be following a guru again, but what about something else equally enchanting, equally enthralling, equally entrapping?

If I can remember what I've learned about programming, I stand a chance. That's always the trick, isn't it? Remembering what we already know.

Well, here's to remembering what we know when we need to know it. Here's to remembering what we need to know even if we never knew it before.

Here's to common sense, to reason, and to Light.

Here's to freedom.

Appendix A

A Brief History of Me

> Success didn't spoil me;
> I've always been insufferable.
>
> FRAN LEBOWITZ

THIS IS about as optional as chapters come—in fact, it's not even a chapter at all; it's an appendix. I put it in at the end because by this point some people may be curious about my personal history insofar as spirit, religion, personal growth, and book-writing is concerned.

Please keep in mind that during this time I was falling in love, getting dumped, moving from one rented domicile to another, working dull jobs, getting sick, getting better, doing all those things ordinary human beings do. I didn't include these things—and so many others—because they weren't the subject of this book. Besides, I have to keep *a few* secrets for my autobiography.

I was born August 5, 1949, and raised in Allen Park, Michigan, a middle-class suburb of Detroit. My mother, raised a Catholic, married my father who was not only twice her age, but had been divorced *three times*. According to Catholic teaching at the time (and, who knows, maybe still), in marrying a divorced man my mother was condemning her mortal soul to eternal perdition, but if she raised her children to be good Catholics, the children *might* have a chance. This allowed the infidel who married the heathen special privileges in hell—in my mother's case, this might include a cold can of Diet Squirt down there—on occasion. My mother did her best: Mass on Sundays, catechism on Tuesdays, no meat on Fridays.

> *A Sunday school is a prison*
> *in which children do penance*
> *for the evil conscience*
> *of their parents.*
>
> H. L. MENCKEN

I didn't enjoy the dogma much, but somewhere about the age of seven I remember being fascinated by the *magic* of it all. If encouraged, I probably could have gone on to become a priest. If anything, however, my mother *discouraged* me, and for this I am eternally grateful.

I think my rift with Catholicism came when, around ten, I failed to understand why my mother and father, the people I loved most in the world, were both condemned to hell. No priest or catechism teacher could properly explain it to me.

The final break came thanks to Father Maycheck. Father Maycheck was my catechism teacher for eighth grade. My mother kept saying: "Maycheck, Maycheck, that's a familiar name." One day it dawned on her: Maycheck was the priest who, while assigned to another parish, baptized me thirteen years before. Excited, I went to catechism that Tuesday and told him that he had baptized me. I thought this gave us some incredible spiritual connection. By the end of class (I must admit, I *was* a behavior problem), he had thrown me on the floor, kicked me, and announced to me, the class, and God—not in that order—that if he knew when he baptized me how I was going to turn out, he would have drowned me. So much for priestly saintliness and incredible spiritual connections.

By this time I was already lost in the spiritual act of creativity. Throughout junior high and high school, if it was creative, I was involved: acting, painting, writing, designing, singing, skipping class, you name it. (A playbill from that period has my name on it an embarrassing number of times, ending with the phrase: "Program written, designed, typed, and printed by Peter McWilliams." One neighbor claims that in this production I would pull open the curtains, come out and take a curtain call, leave the stage, close the curtains, open the curtains again, and come out and take another curtain call.)

Somewhere around 1964 or 1965, when I was about fifteen, I began reading *The Realist*. This was a publication edited by Paul Krassner from which I gleaned my first glimpses of enlightenment. It was enlightening on all levels: intellectually, spiritually, creatively, psychologically, politically, humorously. It was a ray of pure light that shone into my bleak Allen Park High School existence.

One of Krassner's most impressive articles was an interview with Albert Ellis, Ph.D. Ellis had founded what he called Rational Therapy (later Rational-Emotive Therapy) and he was so damned,

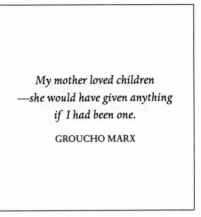

My mother loved children
—she would have given anything
if I had been one.

GROUCHO MARX

well, *rational*. It made perfect sense. It still does. "It's not what happens to you," Ellis said, "it's the decisions you make *about* what happens to you that determine how you feel." It's a teaching that goes back two millennia to Marcus Aurelius—and to Epictetus before him—but Ellis couched it in modern terms and created for its implementation a psychotherapeutic model.

In the chapter, "Guru U.," I tell how Albert Ellis entered my life again almost thirty years later—this time in person—to once again "save the day."

Nineteen sixty-seven was quite a year. I was seventeen going on eighteen, and in the span of a few months had fallen in love for the first time, wrote poetry about it, published the poetry, had my first religious experiences, and watched my musical tastes change from Broadway shows, Mantovani, and 101 Strings to Bob Dylan, Jefferson Airplane, and *Sergeant Pepper's Lonely Hearts Club Band*.*

It's hard to describe how most of us viewed LSD in 1967. Within seven years, young people would be "dropping acid," going to discos, and dancing all night to the Bee Gees. "What's the younger generation coming to?" us old-timers—then twenty-five—would lament.

In 1967 it was different. Our belief was that LSD induced religious experiences; the attitude ("set") and environment ("setting") in which we took it reflected that belief. And so, for the most part, we had religious experiences. (What we had, of course, was a clearly altered state of consciousness which we *called* a religious

*Twenty years later, when the CD of *Sergeant Pepper* finally came out, I put it on and heard it for the first time in all its digital splendor. A young man who worked for me stopped and listened intently to two or three songs. I was pleased that "my" music transcended the generations. Eventually he asked: "That's The Beatles, isn't it?" I felt very old.

experience. But then, who is to determine what is and is not a "genuine" religious experience?)

> *Think for yourself and question authority.*
>
> TIMOTHY LEARY, Ph.D.

In time, however, LSD became dull. I kept having the same trip over and over. It was as though I walked to a door, opened it, looked in, liked what I saw, but could not enter. Walking through those "doors of perception," as Aldous Huxley called them, was my goal, and I realized I needed something other than LSD to pass through.

First, I tried reading—books like *Doors of Perception*. I didn't understand much of it. The best book on the subject was Alan Watts's *The Joyous Cosmology*. Then I tried yoga, saunas, and massage. Enjoyable, but not enlightening.

In 1968, I had one of the most significant meetings of my life. I had driven to Chicago to attend a weekend meditation workshop with Alan Watts. Absolutely nothing significant happened during the workshop, but I can now look back with pride and say, "Yes, I met Alan Watts."

Alan Watts wrote beautifully and spoke eloquently. He had an upper-class British accent, an extensive education, and an obvious love of language. He knew something interesting about everything. His book, *THE BOOK: On the Taboo Against Knowing Who You Really Are*, was the first to "spill the beans" in plain English about what the East believed but the West denied. Fortunately, *THE BOOK* was not as popular as est would be, so Alan Watts didn't get into the same kind of trouble for "taboo breaking" that Werner Erhard later did.

Allow me to get ahead of my story for a moment and fast-forward to 1973: I was in Italy where I had (get this) taught Transcendental Meditation to a Jewish divinity student at a Catholic university on Halloween night in the room in which Elizabeth Barrett Browning had died. I had been traveling in Italy, which is permeated with Catholicism, and eventually I became permeated with Catholicism, too. I talked to a priest about what I had to do to return to the fold. He told me he wouldn't even *consider* readmitting me (that is, hearing my confession) until I promised (faithfully) never to do Transcendental Meditation again. This made no logical sense, as I knew Catholic priests who practiced TM, so I did not re-Catholicize myself.

> You yourself are
> the eternal energy
> which appears as this universe.
> You didn't come into
> this world.
> You came out of it,
> like a wave from the ocean.
> You are not a stranger here.
>
> ALAN WATTS

While in Europe, I heard Alan Watts had died. In an issue of *Playboy*, which I read when I returned home, was one of Alan's last articles. It was on the Bible, and to this day stands as one of the most insightful pieces I've ever read on the Good Book. (It won the *Playboy* article-of-the-year award, and certainly deserved it.) It was Alan's final message to me, one he had preached over and over: don't be bound by tradition; spirit is not found in books, not even my books—*especially* my books. Move on, move on.

[Back, now, to the chronological tale of our Candide of Consciousness.]

I "got into" (as we used to say in 1968) foreign films: Huxley, Leary, and Alpert were replaced by Bergman, Fellini, and Antonioni. The films did not bring enlightenment, but all those subtitles did increase my reading speed.

I decided to include more *people* in my quest. In early 1969, I took my first sensitivity training (a.k.a. therapy group, a.k.a. T-group). The motto of sensitivity training was: "You don't have to be sick to get better." These were groups of about ten people and a "leader" who got together one evening each week for about ten weeks. I was remarkably fortunate to have Melba Colgrove, Ph.D., as my first leader. The purpose of sensitivity training was to explore feelings: "Feelings are facts!" Melba would say again and again. It's hard to remember how stifled emotions once were in this country: to feel something—anything—was considered a sign of weakness (especially for men), hurt was considered a lack of character, tenderness was viewed as a sexual advance, anger was completely *verboten*.

So, into the sensitivity-training pool, where it was not just okay to explore feelings but encouraged, we dove in. I was fascinated. It was all so *clandestine*. Here were all these adults (at nineteen, I was by far the youngest), who seemed as impregnable as adults tend to seem to nineteen-year-olds, and they were all *breaking down. They*

> *I don't like Diane Keaton anymore. She's had way too much therapy.*
>
> PATRICIA WENTZ-DALY

revealed the sham of "adult life" that I had sensed but never dared fully to believe. Eric Berne's *Games People Play* was a popular book, and these people acknowledged one destructive game after another—the very cultural games that I, as a "young adult," was expected to master; the rules of which I *had better* obey. (My two 1968 arrests for marijuana possession were clear "had better obey" signals.) I watched these adults break down—breaking out of programming that was not of their choosing—and they seemed the better for it.

What *seemed* to be breaking down was, in fact, *setting* down: setting down burdens. Some left them sitting there; others picked them up again.*

I was hooked. I took one ten-week session after another—always with Melba. (I took a weekend intensive once, not with Melba, and saw how important proper leadership was in group work. Where Melba made *soufflés*, the guy who led the weekend intensive could only manage broken eggs.)

I began seeing Melba professionally in private psychotherapy sessions. She would charge me for a half-hour session ($35), but always gave me an hour. My individual therapy with Melba continued for the next five years; she always seemed to have a group going, and I always seemed to be a part of it.

There's a book, *Psychotherapy: The Purchase of Friendship*, whose title describes my relationship with Melba. Well, not quite: the book about Melba should be titled *Psychotherapy: The Purchase of Love*. In addition to our professional relationship, we had a deep personal connection. More than anyone else, Melba helped me become the person I wanted to be.

Also in 1969, I was initiated into Transcendental Meditation, made famous by The Beatles' association with Maharishi Mahesh Yogi. My first initiation!** My first Maharishi! (*Rishi* means teacher; *maha* means great.)

---

*Someone once said: "Enlightenment is simply the process of setting a burden down, and not picking it up again."

**The word *initiate* divides neatly into in-it-i-ate.

I chose TM by default: it was the only spiritual practice available in Detroit in 1969. People criticized Maharishi for being commercial. He would reply that *commerce* meant making something available only in one area available in others; therefore, commerce was good. I agreed then; I still do. TM was taught as a simple, twenty-minute,

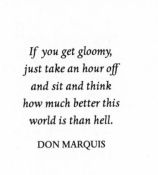

If you get gloomy,
just take an hour off
and sit and think
how much better this
world is than hell.

DON MARQUIS

twice-a-day technique that would, in eight years of regular practice, lead to Cosmic Consciousness. I practiced it for precisely eight years—without missing a single meditation—did not achieve Cosmic Consciousness, and stopped.

In that eight years, I became a TM teacher (a.k.a. Initiator), wrote a book about TM *(The TM Book: How to Enjoy the Rest of Your Life),* published the *TM Book* myself when no other publisher wanted it, watched it become a #1 *New York Times* bestseller (both in trade paperback and mass-market paperback),* and I became (along with Harold H. Bloomfield, M.D., the author of that *other* book on TM, *TM),* the media spokesperson for that brand-new ancient phenomenon: meditation.

All this full-time TM work was financed by my poetry books. Rod McKuen had become a sensation putting what were essentially unrhymed lyrics of love songs into books and calling them poetry. Rod McKuen, however, was only available in hard cover. I put *my* romantic poetry into trade paperback. Thus, by becoming the paperback Rod McKuen, I became a success. In the late 1960s and, especially, the early 1970s, my books of poetry (eventually there were fourteen) sold something like two million copies. Because no one else wanted to publish poetry, I published it myself.**

*To Maharishi's immense credit—and the credit of the entire TM organization—they never once asked for a penny of the profits from this book. They were more than happy that people were learning about TM through the book. Although my co-authors and I did donate money to the TM organization, it was entirely voluntary and, when it happened, immensely appreciated. Maharishi was, however, very helpful in negotiating deals. In general, his advice when buying was, "Offer them half!" and, when selling, "Ask for twice as much!" In a surprising number of cases, it worked.

**Doubleday did publish two of my books of verse, but they were less successful. I was hoping to jump on their bandwagon while they were hoping to jump

> *I sold my memoirs*
> *of my love life*
> *to Parker Brothers*
> *and they are*
> *going to make*
> *a game out of it.*
>
> WOODY ALLEN

I probably didn't spend as much time with poetry and publishing as I should have—I was captivated with TM and wanted everyone, everywhere to learn it. (Not just learn it, *practice* it.) TM was, after all, "the solution to all problems," and I certainly wanted to help others solve all their problems. I became one of Maharishi's elite group, the 108, who were financially self-sufficient proponents of TM willing to donate all their time doing just that.

The only thing that gave me trouble during this time was celibacy. Maharishi recommended celibacy for the 108. I would spend months and months on special 108 courses where no one had sex, but at the same time sex was the only thing anyone ever talked about. Men weren't supposed to have wet dreams: anything even approaching a wet dream was referred to as "trouble in the night." TM was becoming almost Benedictine—without the advantage of fine brandy.*

More serious trouble began after the success of *The TM Book* and the general popularity of Transcendental Meditation. I found myself lying more often than I wanted. Although TM was marketed as a "simple, scientific technique with no religious affiliations whatsoever," the more involved one became in TM (weekend retreats, month-long retreats, six-month retreats, teacher training courses, and the like) the more aware one became of Maharishi's cultural and religious biases. Some would call these Hinduism, but they are as much *Indianism* as Hinduism.

What many people don't realize is that Hinduism the culture, and the lifestyle of India are inseparable. What we would call a Hindu practice, someone from India would say, "That's just the

on mine. With each of us jumping all over each other's bandwagons, nobody bothered to promote the books.

*I stopped all drug use in 1969. I found pot made me irritable and significantly decreased my productivity. The difficulty with LSD I discussed earlier. Besides, as a TM teacher, "no drugs" was an absolute rule. Occasional caffeine was acceptable, but alcohol was frowned upon. So was eating meat and white sugar. The fine line between what was and was not a "harmful drug," was constantly explored—not as constantly explored as sex, but explored, nonetheless, in great detail.

way things are done." The concept of Hinduism is a Western attempt to extract the more spiritually directed aspects of the Indian lifestyle so that they can be understood by the Western mind. To the Indian/Hindu, there is no distinction.

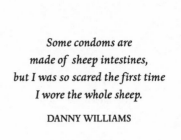

Some condoms are made of sheep intestines, but I was so scared the first time I wore the whole sheep.

DANNY WILLIAMS

Maharishi, being an Indian/Hindu, simply wanted things to be the way he thought worked best. That included vegetarianism, celibacy, and, of course, meditation, meditation, meditation.

It also included worshiping one's guru. Any praise given to a Hindu teacher is immediately passed on to his or her guru. "I alone am nothing; everything I am or have is thanks to my guru." This is designed to keep all teachers humble and grateful. If a teacher is not permitted to accept praise, how can the teacher catch "the teacher's disease" (a.k.a. megalomania)? So, the phrase often used is "jai guru dev," which means "thanks to my guru." (John Lennon used the phrase in his song, "Across the Universe.")

The devotion Maharishi had for his dearly departed guru—and our similar devotion for Maharishi—certainly gave the whole thing religious trappings. Whenever Maharishi came into a room, we would stand, press our palms together, and bow our heads in his direction while saying, "jai guru dev," meaning him. He would put his palms together, bow, and say, "jai guru dev," meaning his guru (a picture of whom was always behind him when Maharishi spoke).

As I mentioned, I stopped doing TM in 1977 when the promise of Cosmic Consciousness in eight years of regular meditation was not fulfilled. I stopped quietly: no great announcements. I had to formally disassociate myself with TM, however, when the Sidhi Program began.

The Sidhi Program promised such handy household tools as invincibility, immortality, the ability to walk thorough walls, and, of course, levitation. All this in a simple six-month course, results guaranteed or your money . . . well, let's not get too carried away just yet with those guarantees. Rumors spread of people floating around the lecture halls where Maharishi spoke. Photographs were circulated of people, legs crossed, smiling blissfully, hovering over beds. The first *Superman* movie had just come out, and the teaser billboards read: "Today, you will believe a man can fly." I'm sure some enterprising TMers wanted to take the billboard below it saying: ". . . and Maharishi can teach you how."

> No one is ever
> old enough to know better.
>
> HOLBROOK JACKSON

I remained skeptical. No: I remained a devout disbeliever. When the first people came back from the first Sidhi course, a public lecture and "demonstration" was announced. Of course, I went. The whole evening was amazingly tawdry. "Just before we demonstrate levitation, let us tell you a little bit about the Sidhi Program . . . ." And three hours of droning lecturing later we were told there would not, after all, be a demonstration of levitation: the two speaker-graduates of the Sidhi Program did not feel they could levitate "gracefully" enough, and they did not want to do anything embarrassing to diminish Maharishi's "dignity." Groan.

Personally, I'm convinced Maharishi *intentionally* put together a dog-and-pony show (with no dog, no pony, and no show) to turn off the casual meditator while drawing the devout believers closer to him. It was his way of separating the wheat from the chaff. TM had grown unmanageably large in just a few years. By 1977, something like a million people had learned TM in the United States alone. Ironically, the greater the success it had at recruiting new initiates, the more trouble the TM organization was in.

TM was sold for a one-time, up-front price that included all future support, including free "checking," a procedure that made TM easy again if it ever became difficult. With a million people flocking to TM centers for checking and other free support, the TM organization was in danger of bankruptcy. It had built something of a pyramid scheme. As the number of new people learning TM decreased, but the services to the old meditators continued, there was a serious cash crunch. How to pay the bills? My suggestion was to charge for checking, as one would for any other professional service. Maharishi, it seems, had another plan. (And, again, that this was his plan is *my* conjecture.)

If he could promise something *truly* outlandish, something no

LIFE 102: What to Do When Your Guru Sues You

rational person would be-
lieve—but Maharishi's true
believers *would* believe—he
would be like Moses on the
rock: "Let he who is on the side
of the Lord come to me." In
other words, *choose:* the golden
calf or the Ten Command-
ments; Western logic or Eastern devotion. The vast majority of meditators—appalled—
went away, never to darken

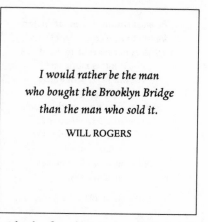

*I would rather be the man
who bought the Brooklyn Bridge
than the man who sold it.*

WILL ROGERS

TM center doors again—doors which, for the most part, closed
forever, and the TM organization went into the business of selling
Sidhi Programs to a much smaller but far more faithful group.*

My fondest remembrance of that time is not the bestseller list,
my ten minutes of fame (I still have the raincheck for the other
five), the people I reached, or even the money. It was at a month-
long retreat I took only a year or so after starting TM. I was—as I
had been with Catholicism as a young child—enchanted by the
magic.

One evening, Maharishi was lecturing to a packed house of
probably five hundred. People sat in chairs, but also gathered on
the floor around the riser on which Maharishi's chair sat. (Maharishi always lectured sitting down.) I was down front. (It's hard for
me to imagine—much less remember—but for nineteen-year-olds,
sitting on a floor for *hours* was perfectly comfortable.)

Maharishi was explaining his theory of how to get the material
things you want. Unlike the Western tradition of "go out and get
it," Maharishi held that if you *thought* about something long
enough and *desired* something strongly enough, it would automatically *come* to you. This concept, of course, rattled our culturally

---

*To this day, I have seen no reliable evidence or heard one credible story of
genuine levitation. TM Sidhi people merely seem to hop around on mattresses
with their legs crossed. They say it gives them "bliss." So what the hell: hop
yourself out. I spent the weekend with some friends who were still very much
into TM long after I left. They showed me to the bedroom I was to stay in.
There was nothing in the room but wall-to-wall mattresses. I began laughing uncontrollably. I thought they had taken every mattress in the house and laid them
on the floor of this one room for my amusement: here's where we practice our
Sidhis. In fact, it *was* the room where they practiced their Sidhis. They were ir-
reconcilably convinced that I was laughing *at* their spiritual technique. It was a
chilly weekend.

> *The most casual student of history knows that, as a matter of fact, truth does not necessarily vanquish. What is more, truth can never win unless it is promulgated. Truth does not carry within itself an antitoxin to falsehood. The cause of truth must be championed, and it must be championed dynamically.*
>
> WILLIAM F. BUCKLEY, JR.

conditioned Western minds, so Maharishi found himself explaining it over and over. (I never understood why the man didn't just say, "Go out and give it a try, damn it, and see if it works!" But Maharishi—unlike me—was infinitely patient and answered the same question to the same group again and again, each time as though it were the first.) When questioned about the mechanics of physical manifestation, Maharishi toyed with the saffron scarf he was wearing.

"I see this orange color," he said, "and I think orange, orange, orange, and I think, 'I want an orange,' 'I would like to have an orange,' 'I want an orange.'" At this moment, I realized that I had with me—an orange. Some force beyond me took it from there. I stretched out my body, offering the orange to Maharishi, and he said, without missing a beat, "I want an orange, I want an orange, *and here it comes!*" He reached down, received the orange (it looked something like Michelangelo's God giving life to Adam on the Sistine Chapel, except in reverse), and the audience went nuts. Here was an actual *demonstration* of how thoughts and desires alone could produce tangible, material results.

It also showed me, once again, how much *joy* I feel as "the messenger." (Maharishi left the orange behind, I retrieved it, peeled it, and distributed it amongst the dozen or so people who had the simultaneous desire: "I want to eat that orange." I only got a small piece of it, but I recall it as the sweetest orange I ever tasted.)

When I left TM in 1977, whatever vacuum I may have had in my personal growth or spiritual life was already filled by est. *Est* either stood for Erhard Seminar Trainings or was Latin for "the essence, the best, the most, that which is." More likely, it was both.

Est began when Werner Erhard (or was his name Rosenberg?), a student of Mind Dynamics (or was it Psycho Cybernetics?), achieved enlightenment (or was it illumination?) while driving across the Bay Bridge (or was it the Golden Gate?) and invited twenty (or was it thirty?) of his closest friends to his apartment in San Francisco (or was it his home in Marin County?) so that he might share with them the enlightenment he received. He kept everyone there until they all "got it." They all did, and est was born.

I liked est. I liked Werner. I still do. In the world of personal growth, he was a true pioneer. What later became known as the "Personal Growth Seminar" was, as far as I can tell, invented by Werner in his San Francisco (or Marin County) apartment

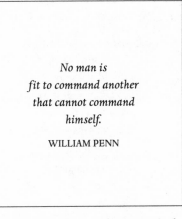

No man is fit to command another that cannot command himself.

WILLIAM PENN

(or house). He's one of the few people I've met who genuinely had charisma: something around him crackled with electricity, the sort of presence people say John Kennedy had.

Werner's greatest triumph was also his greatest mistake: he, more than anyone else before him, challenged the most fundamental taboo of the Western world. That taboo: Let's pretend that life is *very serious*—that we only have one brief chance (this lifetime) to earn our *eternal* paradise, or be *forever* damned to perdition. In other words, the Western mind, due to its programming, has enormous difficulty accepting the idea that *nothing matters.** In order for Christianity in the West to survive as the religious (as opposed to spiritual) force it has grown into, *everything* must matter; *everything must matter very, very much.* A single slip in a single moment can cast you eternally into hell. Therefore, in each moment, one must be intensely *searching* for sins *not* to commit.

This, not surprisingly, gets in the way of enjoying the moment. The moment, however, is where truth, God, enlightenment, and paradise are found—according to the Eastern philosophies.**

*This realization, by the way, was what Werner called "getting it." The "it" was that life is lived in each moment, our problems in life are caused by either regretting the past or worrying about the future, and if we would simply live in the moment, all problems would disappear. Integral to this "it" is the it-corollary: Life has no intrinsic meaning and, if it does, so what? (That's another great thing Werner did: he asked "So what?" so often that some people began to wake up and realize about their most pressing problems, "Yeah, so what?")

**Also according to the teachings of Jesus—if the New Testament is an accurate representation of Jesus' teachings. Two of Jesus' most ignored teachings by the Western Christian church are, first: ". . . the kingdom of heaven is within you" [Luke 17:21]. The next most ignored teaching: "So do not worry, saying, 'What shall we eat?' or 'What shall we drink?' or 'What shall we wear?' For the pagans run after all these things, and your heavenly Father knows that you need them. But seek first his kingdom and his righteousness, and all these things will be

> *If you knew exactly what*
> *God wanted you to do,*
> *you would be happy doing it*
> *no matter what it was.*
> *You are doing what*
> *God wants you to do.*
> *Be happy.*
>
> WERNER ERHARD

So, here's Werner Erhard challenging the most fundamental of Western taboos, and doing so *on national television*. When anyone challenges fundamental taboos on a large scale, they're sometimes made a hero, and usually destroyed, but generally not in that order. Werner Erhard has certainly been destroyed (between the IRS and vilification of the press); his potential herodom is up to history.

There's no doubt est was harsh medicine, but I was, at the time, in need of some harsh medicine. To a tough steak comes a sharp knife, as the saying goes. If that doesn't work, it's on to the meat grinder. Est was sometimes a sharp knife, and sometimes a meat grinder. That's okay with me—I prefer tender hamburger to tough steak.

Among the most important practical things I learned from est was simply *keeping agreements*. Maharishi was notoriously poor at this, and his followers were as bad. I remember keeping several people waiting for *two and one-half hours* in front of Disneyland while I la-di-dahed my way down there. There they were in the hot sun, just outside "the happiest place on earth," waiting for me. The most appalling part of it was, *I didn't give it a second thought*. Besides, to my still-juvenile mind, breaking agreements was a sign of freedom, of independence, a demonstration that "no one and nothing controls me!"*

Werner Erhard's teaching: "Your life works to the degree you keep your agreements." It was one of those arrows that Bob Dylan meant when he sang: "If the point is sharp and the arrow is swift, it can pierce through the dust no matter how thick."

given to you as well."[Matthew 6:31–33]. "Consider how the lilies grow. They do not labor or spin. Yet I tell you, not even Solomon in all his splendor was dressed like one of these. If that is how God clothes the grass of the field, which is here today, and tomorrow is thrown into the fire, how much more will he clothe you, O you of little faith! And do not set your heart on what you will eat or drink; do not worry about it." [Luke 12:27–29]. How many sermons have you heard on *those* subjects?

*I, of course, was only following the advice of my first spiritual teacher, Peter Pan, who, on TV in 1955, taught me "Never grow up!"

I also learned from Werner the importance of moving through fear and taking risks. In meditation, I had learned to move through *passive* fear—the fear of sitting alone in a room; the fear of loneliness. Through est, I learned the benefits of *active* fear: "Whatever you're afraid to do most, that's the thing to do next." There was, of course, a fundamental morality involved: don't physically harm the person or property of nonconsenting others; and logic: if something was going to be physically harmful to yourself, don't do it. If, however, something just *might* be physically harmful, make the best precautions possible, then do it. The sooner the better.

Fear is a kind of bell . . . It is the soul's signal for rallying.

HENRY WARD BEECHER

At the est Six-Day Course, for example, they had me running 1.1 miles each morning and sleeping only two hours each night. As hard as it is for me to believe (even now) I not only survived, I thrived. I graduated on July 4, 1976, and went back to New York while the city exploded with fireworks.

Est lost me when they handed out a several-page, single-spaced list of what was expected of trainers. I wanted to be a trainer, but this list did not just describe perfection—it mandated divinity. I didn't want to put undue limitations on myself, but I knew I'd never achieve *all this,* so I moved on.

Somewhere during this time (1975–1977), I took the First and Second Year Course in the Science of Mind. My cousin, Dr. Carlo DiGiovanna, was a minister of Religious Science in North Hollywood, and he sent me the weekly audio tapes of the class, including the questions and answers. I listened to the tapes, did whatever homework there was to be done, and enjoyed all I learned.

Also around this time, Melba, Harold Bloomfield, and I got together to expand a book of poetry and advice I had written in 1971, *Surviving the Loss of a Love.* The book we created was called *How to Survive the Loss of a Love,* and I published it in hardcover in 1976. I sold the rights to Bantam, and they published the mass-market paperback edition in 1977. To date, it has sold more than two million copies. In 1991, we took the rights back from Bantam, revised the book extensively, and I published a new, expanded version.

> *Your life story*
> *would not make*
> *a good book.*
> *Don't even try.*
>
> FRAN LEBOWITZ

My next "official" study was with Actualizations, which consumed much of early 1978. The name came from Abraham Maslow's concept of self-actualization. Maslow, in a pioneering effort, examined *healthy* people and saw what they *did*, rather than studying *unhealthy* people to find out what *not to do*. The founder of Actualizations was a charming Australian named Stuart Emory. I admired the work he did, I took many Actualizations courses, and sent a lot of people to it, but didn't do much volunteering. I had no illusions that I would ever be able to impress Stuart sufficiently so he would let me lead an Actualizations seminar.

Next to Alan Watts,* Stuart Emory was the most eloquent teacher I've studied with. At graduations, glasses of champagne were passed around with a strawberry in them. (Organic apple juice was available for teetotalers.) He spoke beautifully, carefully choosing his words as one who has a love of language. Unfortunately, his books never caught on. I can vaguely remember the title of only one of them, which was something like *Being In Love Is Insufficient Grounds for a Relationship*. He had style.

All of which brings us to fall 1978, my first Insight, and my first meeting with John-Roger.

---

*Audio cassette recordings of Alan Watts's lectures are available by calling 1-800-969-2887. I highly recommend them.

Index

A

Abraham 76, 298–299
ACE 340, 344
"Across the Universe" 409
Actualizations 45, 416
Adam 75–76, 166, 378, 412
Adams, Abigail 300
Adams, Henry 171, 329, 344
Addison, Joseph 235
Adler, Stella 136
Affirmation 34, 280, 385
AIDS 12–14, 24–25,
         198, 243, 245, 368
AIDS Project Los Angeles 12
*Ain't Nobody's Business If
   You Do* 182
Akhenaton 77
Alcoholics Anonymous 38
Alcott, Amos Bronson 59
ALF 93
Ali, Muhammad 166, 268
All in the Family 357
Allen, J. L. 392
Allen, Woody 5, 45, 98,
         125, 376, 408
"Amazing Grace" 101
Ambrose, St. 107
Amiel 48
Amos 77
Andrews, Lynn V. 88
Anhedonia 376
Animal Farm 59
Ann-Margret 360
Annie Hall 376
Anouilh, Jean 31, 216
Antidepressants . 377–378, 382–384
Antonioni 405
Architectural Digest 220
Arendt, Hannah 257
Aristotle 77, 321
Armstrong, Robert 195
As You Like It 200
Asimov, Isaac 17
Asquith, Margot 133
Atman Travel 340
Aura balance 86, 114,
         279, 329, 351
Aurelius, Marcus 403

B

Baba, Sai 60–61
Baby Blessing 133–134
Bacon, Francis 79
Bagehot, Walter 373
Bakker, Tammy Faye 189
Balzac, Honoré de 276
Bankhead, Tallulah 365
*Baptism Through the Holy
   Spirit* 125
Baraka Center for Holistic
   Health 340
Barnum, P. T. 354
Barrie, J. M. 20
Barth, Alan 158
Barton, Bruce 366
Batman 209
Beatles 403, 406
Becket, Thomas 226

Bedlam 89
Bee Gees 47, 403
Beecher, Henry Ward 201,
         298, 415
*Being In Love Is Insufficient
   Grounds for a Relationship* 416
Bellow, Saul 147
Ben Hur 205
Benchley, Robert 364
Beneš, Barton Lidice 53
Bergman, Ingmar 405
Berkeley, Bishop 140
Berkeley, Busby 97, 285
Berne, Eric 406
Beyond the Fringe 101
Bible 142
Bierce, Ambrose 74, 78, 286, 356
Bishop, Russell ... 19, 42–44, 52, 66,
         85, 158, 201–208, 210–214,
         226, 236–237, 258, 272,
         326, 336, 339, 345, 400
Black, Clint 37
Blair, Linda 324
Blake, William 79
Bligh, Captain 206
Bloomfield, Harold 17, 375–378,
         407, 415
Blount, Roy, Jr. 204
Boetcker, Wm. J. H. 334
Bonanza
   Ben Cartwright 269
Bonaparte, Napoleon 367
Book of Mormon
   Alma 66
   Mosiah 138
   Nephi 194
*THE BOOK: On the Taboo Against
   Knowing Who You Are* 404
Boone, Debby 51–52
Boosler, Elayne 184
Boyer, Ernest 337
Brewster, Kingman 186
Brice, Fanny 183
Brickman, Marshall 30
*The Bridges of Madison
   County* 255
Brodsky, Joseph 391
Brothers, Joyce 22
Brown, Jerry 132
Brown, Murphy 328
Browne, Thomas 379
Bruce, Lenny 226
Buckley, William F., Jr. 412
Buddha 105, 126
Bulwer-Lytton, Edward 182
Burke, Edmund 69, 342
Burroughs, John 391
Bush, George 139
Butler, Bishop 349
Butler, Rhett 272
Butler, Samuel ... 175, 217, 359, 383
Byrnes, James F. 65, 332

C

C-SPAN 367
Caesar's Palace 308
Caldicott, Helen 313
Callas, Maria 131, 144
Cambridge Union 129, 136, 144
Camille 14
Campbell, Joseph 393
Camus, Albert 108

Candide 405
Capone, Al 220
Cardozo, Benjamin 331
Cartland, Barbara 160
Casey, M. Kathleen 384
Cervantes 282
Chandler, Raymond 258
Channing, William Ellery 7
Charenton 89
Chateau Marmont Hotel 96
Chaucer 262
Chesterton, G. K. 345
Chestnutt, Charles Waddell 328
Chisholm, Shirley 288
Church of Scientology 377
Church of the Movement of
   Spiritual Inner Awareness
   See MSIA
Cicero, Marcus Tullius 78, 160
Clampett, Jed 54
Cleaver, Ward 54
Cleopatra 126
Coalition for Civil and Spiritual
   Rights 230–231
Cobbett, William 393
Cognitive Therapy 377
Colgrove, Melba .. 17, 405–406, 415
Collins, Jackie 395
Colton, Charles Caleb 61, 255,
         265
Columbus, Christopher 15
Confucius 54, 77, 105
Conrad, Joseph 168, 296
Cooper, James Fenimore 153,
         264, 392
Cooper, Thomas 176
Copernicus 78
Corleone, Don 246
Counter-programming 9,
         385–387
Cowper, William 281
Crabbe, George 162
Craig, Jenny 46
Crane, Frank 381
*The Criminal Activities of
   John-Roger Hinkins* 236
Crisp, Quentin 39
Cruise, Tom 314
Cuppy, Will 378
Curran, Russell E. 348
Cyprian 174

D

da Vinci, Leonardo 79, 258
Daffy Duck 306
Dahmer, Jeffrey 338
Dallas Cowboys Cheerleaders .. 48
Daniel 77
Davidson, Peter 230
Davis, Sammy, Jr. 93
de Gourmont, Rémy 343
Death and dying 15–16, 23, 198
Debs, Eugene V. 172
Declaration of Independence ......
         386, 392
DeGaulle, Charles 130
Dementia 14
deMille, Cecil B. 288
Demosthenes 155
Denny's 65
Denver, John 216, 321
Depression 45, 374–384

ABOUT THE AUTHOR

PETER McWILLIAMS has been writing about his passions since 1967. In that year, he became passionate about what most seventeen-year-olds are passionate about—love—and wrote *Come Love With Me & Be My Life*. This began a series of poetry books which have sold nearly four million copies.

Along with love, of course, comes loss, so Peter became passionate about emotional survival. In 1971 he wrote *Surviving the Loss of a Love*, which was expanded in 1976 and again in 1991 (with co-authors Melba Colgrove, Ph.D., and Harold Bloomfield, M.D.) into *How to Survive the Loss of a Love*. It has sold more than two million copies.

He also became interested in meditation, and a book he wrote on meditation was a *New York Times* bestseller, knocking the impregnable *Joy of Sex* off the #1 spot. As one newspaper headline proclaimed, MEDITATION MORE POPULAR THAN SEX AT THE *NEW YORK TIMES*.

His passion for computers (or more accurately, for what computers could do) led to *The Personal Computer Book*, which *TIME* proclaimed "a beacon of simplicity, sanity and humor," and the *Wall Street Journal* called "genuinely funny." (Now, really, how many people has the *Wall Street Journal* called "genuinely funny"?)

His passion for personal growth continues in the ongoing LIFE 101 Series. Thus far, the books in this series include *You Can't Afford the Luxury of a Negative Thought: A Book for People with Any Life-Threatening Illness—Including Life; LIFE 101: Everything We Wish We Had Learned About Life In School—But Didn't* (a *New York Times* bestseller in both hardcover and paperback); *DO IT! Let's Get Off Our Buts* (a #1 *New York Times* hardcover bestseller); *WEALTH 101: Wealth Is Much More Than Money*, and *We Give To Love: Giving Is Such a Selfish Thing*.

His passion for visual beauty led him to publish, in 1992, his first book of photography, *PORTRAITS*, a twenty-two-year anthology of his photographic work.

Personal freedom, individual expression, and the right to live one's own life, as long as one does not harm the person or property of another, have long been his passions. He wrote about them in *Ain't Nobody's Business If You Do: The Absurdity of Consensual Crimes in a Free Society*.

His most recent book is with Harold H. Bloomfield, M.D., entitled *How to Heal Depression*.

All of the above-mentioned books were self-published and are still in print.

Peter McWilliams has appeared on *The Oprah Winfrey Show, Larry King* (both radio and television), *Donahue, Sally Jessy Raphael*, and, a long time ago, the *Regis Philbin Show* (before Regis met Kathie Lee—probably before Kathie Lee was *born*).

Author photograph: Christopher McMullen

Other Books by Peter McWilliams

Come Love With Me & Be My Life

How to Survive the Loss of a Love

Surviving, Healing & Growing

You Can't Afford the Luxury of a Negative Thought:
A Book for People with Any Life-Threatening Illness—Including Life

Focus on the Positive

LIFE 101:
Everything We Wish We Had Learned About Life In School—But Didn't

The Portable LIFE 101

DO IT! Let's Get Off Our Buts

The Portable DO IT!

WEALTH 101:
Wealth Is Much More Than Money

We Give To Love:
Giving Is Such a Selfish Thing

PORTRAITS: A Book of Photographs

I Marry You Because . . .

Ain't Nobody's Business If You Do
The Absurdity of Consensual Crimes in a Free Society

How to Heal Depression

To order any of these books, please check your local bookstore, or call

1-800-LIFE-101
or write to
Prelude Press
8159 Santa Monica Boulevard
Los Angeles, California 90046

Please call or write for our free catalog!

NO MORE